D1570109

Republican Party Politics and the American South, 1865–1968

In *Republican Party Politics and the American South, 1865–1968*, Heersink and Jenkins examine how National Convention politics allowed the South to remain important to the Republican Party after Reconstruction, and trace how Republican organizations in the South changed from biracial coalitions to mostly all-white ones over time. Little research exists on the GOP in the South after Reconstruction and before the 1960s. *Republican Party Politics and the American South, 1865–1968* helps fill this knowledge gap. Using data on the race of Republican convention delegates from 1868 to 1952, the authors explore how the "whitening" of the Republican Party affected its vote totals in the South. Once states passed laws to disenfranchise blacks during the Jim Crow era, the Republican Party in the South performed better electorally the whiter it became. These results are important for understanding how the GOP emerged as a competitive, and ultimately dominant, electoral party in the late twentieth-century South.

BORIS HEERSINK is Assistant Professor of Political Science at Fordham University in New York. His research focuses on American political parties, and campaigns and elections.

JEFFERY A. JENKINS is Provost Professor of Public Policy, Political Science, and Law at the University of Southern California. His research focuses on federal lawmaking, separation-of-powers, political economy, and American political development.

Republican Party Politics and the American South, 1865–1968

BORIS HEERSINK
Fordham University, New York

JEFFERY A. JENKINS
University of Southern California

CAMBRIDGE
UNIVERSITY PRESS

CAMBRIDGE
UNIVERSITY PRESS

University Printing House, Cambridge CB2 8BS, United Kingdom

One Liberty Plaza, 20th Floor, New York, NY 10006, USA

477 Williamstown Road, Port Melbourne, VIC 3207, Australia

314-321, 3rd Floor, Plot 3, Splendor Forum, Jasola District Centre, New Delhi - 110025, India

79 Anson Road, #06-04/06, Singapore 079906

Cambridge University Press is part of the University of Cambridge.

It furthers the University's mission by disseminating knowledge in the pursuit of education, learning and research at the highest international levels of excellence.

www.cambridge.org
Information on this title: www.cambridge.org/9781107158436
DOI: 10.1017/9781316663950

© Boris Heersink and Jeffery A. Jenkins 2020

First published 2020

A catalogue record for this publication is available from the British Library

ISBN 978-1-107-15843-6 Hardback
ISBN 978-1-316-61092-3 Paperback

Cambridge University Press has no responsibility for the persistence or accuracy of URLs for external or third-party internet websites referred to in this publication, and does not guarantee that any content on such websites is, or will remain, accurate or appropriate.

Contents

Black and white photos appear between pages 193 and 209

Tables

Figures

Preface

This book tells the story of the Republican Party in the South from Reconstruction through the late 1960s. The history of the Grand Old Party (GOP) in the South during Reconstruction is fairly well known, as is its reemergence in the region during the Barry Goldwater and Richard Nixon presidential campaigns in 1964 and 1968. What is not well known, however, is the period in between: what did the GOP in the South look like between the end of Reconstruction and before the modern "Southern Strategy"? A common assumption is that the Republican Party in the South all but disappeared after the demise of Reconstruction and that it only reemerged when the national Democratic Party went all in on civil rights in the mid-1960s, while the national Republican Party (led by Goldwater) largely rejected civil rights.[1] Certainly, the Southern GOP achieved little electoral success in the region in this period. Yet, the Republican Party remained in existence in every state of the ex-Confederacy.

Why was this? The principal reason is that even while the South became largely a one-party, Democratic system, the eleven states of the ex-Confederacy still retained significant representation at the Republican National Convention every four years. Indeed, for much of the post-Reconstruction era, the South controlled around 25 percent of GOP convention delegates. Thus, Southern states were in a position to wield influence at the convention and have a meaningful hand in picking the Republican presidential nominee. Southern party representatives had such influence despite the fact that between 1880 and 1916 – or for ten consecutive presidential elections – Republican presidential nominees received exactly *zero* Electoral College votes from the eleven Southern states. It was this basic puzzle that got us interested in the topic

---

[1] For a summary of this conventional view, see Eric Schickler, *Racial Realignment: The Transformation of American Liberalism, 1932–1965* (Princeton, NJ: Princeton University Press, 2016), 1–3.

of GOP politics in the South during this period: why would a party continue to provide sizable convention representation – and thus, influence on crucial intra-party decisions – to a set of states that it knew were almost certain to provide no benefit on election day?

In answering this question – in the article "Southern Delegates and Republican National Convention Politics, 1880–1928,"[2] published in *Studies in American Political Development* in 2015 – we noted that Republican Party leaders struggled mightily for more than a decade to keep a Southern GOP electorally viable after Reconstruction. Only with the failed Federal Elections Bill in 1890 – which was intended to protect suffrage in the ex-Confederacy – and the emergence of state laws to disenfranchise blacks in the South in the 1890s did national Republican leaders largely give up on a serious Southern wing of the party. Thus, for a time, providing Southern states with GOP convention representation was reasonable – based on hopes of a Southern Republican comeback. Additionally, with the rise of Jim Crow, arguments were also made that eliminating Southern representation would grossly harm black Americans, as such representation was the only remaining political participation that they could enjoy.

By the 1890s, however, national Republicans began to conceive of the Southern states as a set of "rotten boroughs," in which delegates could be bought and sold prior to (and during) the convention. Candidates for the Republican nomination could promise Southern party leaders a wealth of executive patronage (which they could then distribute or sell) in exchange for their delegations' votes. While some Republicans railed against this naked vote-buying arrangement, enough national GOP politicians wanted to keep the Southern states and their considerable delegate totals in play so that they might use them to build a base of nomination support. Thus, for decades, Republican leaders – including presidents and presidential candidates – prevented any real reforms from occurring.

But in laying out these politics, we discovered that we were only scratching the surface. The Republican Party's activities in the post-Reconstruction South were not well known, and there was considerable variation in the GOP across the various states of the ex-Confederacy. Most importantly, factional battles defined the Southern Republican Party during the post-Reconstruction years, as the Black-and-Tans (black and white Republicans who represented the "party establishment") faced off against the Lily-Whites (white supremacist Republicans who sought to expel blacks from the party). These factional battles occurred in every state, with the promise of executive patronage as the prize. But little was known of them. For example, Michael K. Fauntroy argues that the Lily-White movement was "one of the darkest and under-examined eras" of

[2] Boris Heersink and Jeffery A. Jenkins, "Southern Delegates and Republican National Convention Politics, 1880-1928," *Studies in American Political Development* 29 (2015): 68–88.

Republican Party history.[3] Indeed, with the notable exception of work by Hanes Walton, Jr.,[4] almost no political science research has investigated the conflict between the Black-and-Tans and Lily-Whites. And no systematic data exists to determine which faction was winning or losing in a state at any given time. Thus, we determined that a book was necessary to fully explore these intra-GOP factional battles and data needed to be gathered to determine factional strength.

We describe our data-gathering process in Chapter 2. In short, we rely upon historical census information – and ancillary sources – to code the racial composition of a state's GOP convention delegation in every presidential election year from 1868 through 1952. We explore how different states went Lily-White at different times and incorporate these data in a statistical analysis to determine how the "whitening" of the Southern GOP by state affected the party's electoral vote totals. We find that as a state Republican Party became whiter in the post-disenfranchisement period, its vote totals increased significantly. We ascribe this whitening as a necessary condition in keeping with the Lily-White argument at the time: that in the Jim Crow South, when the electorate was almost exclusively white, the Republican Party could only hope to become electorally viable by becoming a Lily-White party. That is, Southern whites would only vote for a "respectable" party – where respectability was directly connected to its whiteness. Much more had to happen before the GOP become electorally competitive – and then dominant – in the second half of the twentieth century. But becoming a Lily-White party was a crucial first step. The remainder of the book fills out the narrative details around these quantitative findings. We describe the national politics of the GOP and the South in Chapters 3–6, and provide in-depth case studies of local GOP politics in *all* eleven Southern states in Chapters 7–9.

We owe a number of people thanks for their help and support in writing this book. In collecting the delegate data, we were assisted by several research assistants: Anthony Sparacino and Jennifer Simons at the University of Virginia, and Nico Napolio and Jordan Carr Peterson at the University of Southern California. We also received useful data from Daniel Galvin and Scott James. Along the way, we presented portions of our research at various conferences over the years: the Midwest Political Association meetings (2014, 2015, 2016, 2017), the Southern Political Science Association meetings (2016, 2017, 2018, 2019), and the American Political Science Association meetings (2016). In so doing, we received helpful feedback from a number of people including John Aldrich, Jeff Grynaviski, Kris Kanthak, Ellie Powell, Daniel Schlozman, and Ryan Williamson. Comments from Anthony Fowler, Sean Gailmard, Thomas Gray, and John Sides, while we were designing the argument and

---

[3] Michael K. Fauntroy, *Republicans and the Black Vote* (Boulder, CO: Lynne Rienner, 2007), 164.
[4] Hanes Walton, Jr., *Black Republicans: The Politics of Black and Tans* (Metuchen, NJ: The Scarecrow Press, 1975).

statistical model at the heart of Chapter 2, helped us clarify our thinking. Additionally, in January 2019, David Bateman, Eric Schickler, and Charles Stewart met with us for a day at the University of Southern California to give the full book manuscript a comprehensive review. Bateman, Schickler, and Stewart were their usual selves – tough but fair – and their comments helped us make the book considerably better. Finally, during the time in which we were writing (and revising), Robert Dreesen, our editor at Cambridge University Press, was both patient and supportive.

While this book is now done, we find ourselves still drawn to Republican Party politics in the post-Reconstruction South. A book can answer many questions, of course, but not *all* of them. Many interesting inquiries remain, and we (with the help of new co-authors) intend to pursue at least some of them in the future. So the "Southern project," as we have often referred to our joint work in the past, remains ongoing. We thank our respective families, friends, and pets for supporting us through the writing of this book, and for sticking with us through what comes next.

I

Introduction

In 2016, Donald Trump, the Republican nominee for president, won an unlikely victory.

In the weeks before the election, political commentators largely agreed that Trump's path to the presidency was extremely limited and that various contingencies would have to be met for him to emerge victorious. By the end of the campaign, a Trump presidency was considered quite unlikely and election forecasts based on statistical models gave Trump little chance of winning in his matchup with Democratic nominee Hillary Clinton – anywhere from 29 percent (FiveThirtyEight) to 15 percent (*New York Times*) to less than 1 percent (Princeton Election Consortium). Election forecasts based on betting markets yielded similar, low odds – 11 percent (PredictWise).[1]

And yet, Trump *did* win. Key to his victory was his performance in the "rust belt" states of the Midwest and Mid-Atlantic, where he won Wisconsin, Michigan, and Pennsylvania (and their 46 electoral votes), which had been considered Republican longshots. He also added Iowa and Ohio (and their 24 electoral votes), which were considered toss-ups. Why Trump won these states and ultimately emerged victorious in the election has been the subject of intense speculation, debate, and analysis since then. A host of competing (and complementary) explanations have been offered – from Trump's and Clinton's ability to connect with key voting groups, to their choice of which states to target with their resources, to news just before the election regarding an FBI investigation of Clinton's improper use of private email while serving as President Obama's secretary of state, to allegations of Russian tampering in the election.

---

[1] For these various forecasts and predictions, see Josh Katz, "Who Will Be President?" *New York Times*, November 8, 2018. www.nytimes.com/interactive/2016/upshot/presidential-polls-forecast.html (accessed June 1, 2019).

While a consensus will probably never be reached on what factors were most important in deciding the outcome of the 2016 presidential election, one crucial element of Trump's victory was his ability to rely on the South – which we define as the eleven ex-Confederate states – as the foundation in his drive to the White House. Trump carried ten of eleven Southern states (losing only Virginia), which provided him with 155 electoral votes – more than half of his entire total.[2] His performance in the South was no surprise, as the former Confederacy has been the GOP's electoral base in presidential elections for almost a half-century: since 1972, in all but one election (1976), the Republican presidential candidate has carried a majority of Southern states. And, in five elections (1972, 1984, 1988, 2000, and 2004) the GOP nominee swept the South.

Republican dominance has also been established below the presidential level in recent years: since 1994, the GOP in every Congress has claimed a majority of Southern seats in both the House and the Senate. And in recent elections (2014 and 2016), the GOP yield has exceeded 75 percent in both chambers. At the gubernatorial level, Republicans first won a majority of governorships in 1994 and the party has controlled at least six, and as many as ten, Southern governorships since then. Finally, in Southern state legislatures the Republicans began to build success during the Clinton administration – winning as much as 40 percent of state legislative seats by the late 1990s – and finally achieved a majority breakthrough in 2010 when the Democrats were "shellacked" across the board in President Obama's first midterm election.[3] Since 2010, GOP state legislative gains have continued to increase; the 2016 elections represent the zenith, with the Republicans controlling roughly two-thirds of both state House and Senate seats in the South.

All of these national and subnational data point to the same fact: the contemporary Republican Party's electoral base is in the South – a fact that would have been nearly unimaginable to political actors on either side during the decades in the nineteenth and twentieth centuries when it was the Democratic Party that dominated the South. As a result, a number of important books have been written in recent years to investigate the causes and consequences of the GOP's emergence and ascendancy in the South. Most of these accounts begin in the mid-to-late 1960s, with the rise of the Civil Rights Movement in the South, Barry Goldwater's racially conservative presidential campaign in 1964, the passage of the Civil Rights Act of 1964 and the Voting

---

[2] Trump won 304 electoral votes overall. One caveat to this – in winning Texas, Trump received only 36 of the state's 38 electoral votes, as two members of the Electoral College who were pledged to vote for him did not do so. These "faithless electors" cast their votes for John Kasich and Ron Paul instead.

[3] Peter Baker and Carl Hulse, "Deep Rifts Divide Obama and Republicans," *New York Times*, November 3, 2010. www.nytimes.com/2010/11/04/us/politics/04elect.html (accessed June 1, 2019)

Rights Act of 1965, and Richard Nixon's "Southern Strategy" (a softer version of Goldwater's racial messaging) in 1968. From there, scholars describe how conservative white Southerners first came to vote Republican – for president initially and then later for congressional and state legislative offices – and ultimately to identify as Republicans. And with that, the Solid Democratic South of the first half of the twentieth century was effectively replaced by a Solid Republican South by the early twenty-first century.

But what role did the Republican Party play in the South *before* the mid-1960s? If scholars of the contemporary era mention the GOP prior to the mid-1960s at all, it is usually in passing.[4] Some note, for example, that the Republican Party's initial presidential election gains in the South started with Dwight Eisenhower's candidacy in 1952. But aside from citing this – and Ike's subsequent gains in 1956 along with Nixon's lesser Southern success in 1960 – little is made of it. Of course, historical scholars have long studied the Republican Party's role in the South during Reconstruction, when the GOP came to power in nearly every Southern state in the late 1860s but lost control everywhere by 1877. However, the lengthy period between the end of Reconstruction and the mid-1960s is something of a black box. The general belief is that the Democrats had firm control of the South during this period – to the point where scholars routinely refer to these years as one-party Democratic rule.[5] Any number of metrics can be used to support this belief. For example, in the eighteen presidential elections from 1880 through 1948, when 198 Southern states were up for grabs, the Republicans won just six of them, or 3 percent.

Yet, despite Democratic electoral dominance in the South in this period, Republican Party organizations remained active in every Southern state – though, as we will demonstrate, not with the intent of reaching the traditional partisan goal of winning elections and pursuing policy outcomes. Our goal in this book is to tell the story of the Republican Party in the South during this ostensibly one-party Democratic era. We show that the South remained important to the national GOP throughout this period, as the ex-Confederate states continued to make up a sizable proportion of delegates to the Republican National Convention. Because of this, local GOP leaders in the South had a meaningful hand in selecting Republican presidential and vice-presidential candidates, despite their states not contributing any electoral votes in the

---

[4] See, for example, James M. Glaser, *Race, Campaign Politics, and the Realignment in the South* (New Haven, CT: Yale University Press, 1996); Earl Black and Merle Black, *The Rise of Southern Republicans* (Cambridge, MA: Harvard University Press, 2002); David Lublin, *The Republican South: Democratization and Partisan Change* (Princeton, NJ: Princeton University Press, 2004).

[5] For example, Robert Mickey states: "In the 1890s leaders of the eleven states of the old Confederacy founded stable, one-party authoritarian enclaves under the 'Democratic' banner." Robert Mickey, *Paths Out of Dixie: The Democratization of Authoritarian Enclaves in America's Deep South, 1944–1972* (Princeton, NJ: Princeton University Press, 2015), 4. On this topic, see also Devin Caughey, *The Unsolid South: Mass Politics and National Representation in a One-Party Enclave* (Princeton, NJ: Princeton University Press, 2018).

general election. This strength at the convention increased the value of Southern party organizations to national leaders, who began to use federal patronage to "buy" Southern convention votes, as well as to local state party leaders, who hoped to benefit from receiving such patronage (either by distributing it or selling it).

We show that, on the national side, this meant that Republican presidents and presidential candidates engaged in near continuous attempts at winning Southern state support at national conventions. In addition, a number of Republican presidents – including Hayes, Arthur, Harrison, Harding, Hoover, and Eisenhower – invested significantly (though, most often unsuccessfully) in rebuilding local party organizations in the South. Importantly, we show that every single Republican president between Grant and Nixon relied on some form of a Southern strategy aimed at winning (re-)nomination at the national convention and/or strengthening state party organizations in the South. This corrects a misconception in various historical accounts that Republican presidents effectively gave up on the South by the early twentieth century.

We also show that, at the state level, executive (federal) patronage and the considerable profits that could be gained from controlling it inspired frequent contestation over control of the local party organizations. That is, while many Republican state parties no longer functioned as regular political parties – often failing to even run candidates in state elections – control of the state party organizations continued to be valuable to local party elites. Initially, these contests largely involved different biracial groups surrounding (former) elected officials and federal office-holders. But over time, contests began to take on an increasingly racial hue, as Black-and-Tans (a faction of black and white Republicans) vied for control with Lily-Whites (a faction of white Republicans that sought to ban blacks from leadership positions in the party).

Importantly, this history of the Southern Republican Party is not merely a historical artifact. In an analysis looking at the racial makeup of state Republican Party organizations in the South, we find that changes in the racial makeup of local GOP leaders had an effect on the party's performance in elections. Specifically, we show that in elections prior to the introduction of disfranchisement laws banning blacks from voting, an increase in white control of the state party is associated with a decline in the party's electoral perform-ance – suggesting that the black-dominated GOP electorate in the pre-Jim Crow era punished the state party for a decline of influence. However, *after* disfran-chisement laws were introduced, an increase in white control is associated with an increase in the party's performance in presidential, gubernatorial, and congressional elections – especially in the Outer South – which indicates that the now white-dominated Southern electorate became more open to voting Republican once the local GOP party organization became "whiter."

These findings suggest that the degree to which the Republican Party in the South became a "white party" in the first half of the twentieth century can help explain the electoral performance of the Southern GOP in the modern era. That is, we argue that the whitening of the Southern Republican Party in the first half of the twentieth century was a *necessary condition* for its subsequent emergence – and eventual dominance – in the second half of the twentieth century. Other developments were also necessary, of course, like the national Democratic Party's leftward move on civil rights and the national GOP's related rightward move on civil rights (and continued economic conservatism).[6] Together, over time, these various developments became sufficient for the Republican Party's Southern success. However, the first step for the GOP to become viable electorally in the Jim Crow South was to become a Lily-White party. Everything else, we argue, followed from that.

RECONSTRUCTION AND ITS AFTERMATH

Before examining the state of the Republican Party in the South after Reconstruction, we first explore how the GOP emerged in the former Confederate states. A Southern GOP was not a foregone conclusion after the Union emerged victorious in the Civil War. In fact, creating a Southern wing of the Republican Party in the South was initially a minority view – pushed only by Radical Republicans, who sought to enfranchise the new freedmen (former slaves) and recreate society in the former Confederacy. Moderate Republicans, the dominant GOP coalition at the time, sought a more amicable restoration of the Union – and readmittance of the ex-Confederate states – and believed widespread black suffrage was too radical for the Northern public to accept. Only after President Andrew Johnson had fought the Republicans on Reconstruction, and seemed to desire a New South that placed the former white leaders in dominant positions once again with the ex-slaves clearly subservient to them, did moderate Republicans (and Northern opinion) begin to shift. By 1867, the desire to enfranchise the former slaves in the South – and use them as the foundation for a Southern wing of the GOP – was the modal Republican position. And the first Reconstruction Act, in December 1867, set the stage for the creation of Republican constitutions and governments in the Southern states.[7]

Republican successes during Reconstruction varied by state, but GOP governments came to power, at least for some period of time, in every Southern state but Virginia. During those years, black voters used their new franchise to

[6] Indeed, as we will argue, the GOP had to become the party of racial conservatism – widely understood – before the Republicans could make a significant electoral breakthrough in the Deep South.

[7] On the shift in thinking within the GOP, and the decision to build a Republican Party in the South, see Richard H. Abbott, *The Republican Party in the South, 1855–1877* (Chapel Hill: University of North Carolina Press, 1986), chapter 4. See also W. R. Brock, *An American Crisis: Congress and Reconstruction, 1865–1867* (New York: Harper & Row, 1963), 182–83; Michael Les Benedict, *A Compromise of Principle: Congressional Republicans and Reconstruction, 1863–1869* (New York: Norton, 1974), 210–13.

support the party and elect white Republican leaders, as well as some of their own. But the Democratic Party would rebound, thanks to voter restrictions on ex-Confederates being lifted, paramilitary groups (working on the part of the Democracy) roaming the South to terrorize black voters, a financial panic in 1873 followed by an economic depression, and the Northern public's growing fatigue with all matters Southern. State by state, Republican governments fell, until only Florida, Louisiana, and South Carolina were left. With the conclusion of the (disputed) presidential election of 1876–77 – and as part of a rumored deal between Republican and Democratic leaders – the GOP would no longer use the US army to oversee elections or protect civilian governments, and all three states would be quickly "redeemed" by the Democrats.[8]

But while the Republicans were vanquished throughout the South, and their Reconstruction initiative had thus come to an end, the GOP did not disappear overnight in the former Confederacy. This fact is not terribly well known outside of historically conscious scholars of party politics and the US South. Relatedly, in his classic book *The Strange Career of Jim Crow*, C. Vann Woodward makes the case that "Jim Crow" – which he defines as the racial segregation in education, public accommodations, and the labor market in the South – did not emerge immediately after the fall of Reconstruction. Rather, it took decades to occur. In telling this story, Woodward notes that the rise of disenfranchising provisions (which would rob the Republican Party of its electoral base) also took time:

The impression often left by cursory histories of the subject is that Negro disfranchisement followed quickly if not immediately upon the overthrow of Reconstruction. It is perfectly true that Negroes were often coerced, defrauded, or intimidated, but they continued to vote in large parts of the South for more than two decades after Reconstruction.[9]

Woodward also notes that blacks "continued to hold offices as well" during this time. And this was because much of the South was still contested electoral terrain for two decades after Reconstruction. The Republicans continued to compete in Southern elections, and national Republican leaders – Presidents Rutherford Hayes, Chester Arthur, and Benjamin Harrison and several key figures in Congress – actively sought to maintain a viable Southern wing of the party.[10]

---

[8] See C. Vann Woodward, *Reunion and Reaction: The Compromise of 1877 and the End of Reconstruction* (Boston: Little, Brown & Co., 1951); Keith Ian Polakoff, *The Politics of Inertia: The Election of 1876 and the End of Reconstruction* (Baton Rouge: Louisiana State University Press, 1973).

[9] C. Vann Woodward, *The Strange Career of Jim Crow* (New York: Oxford University Press, 1955), 53–54.

[10] A small literature examines the GOP's efforts regarding the South in these years. See Vincent P. De Santis, *Republicans Face the Southern Question: The New Departure Years, 1877–1897* (Baltimore: Johns Hopkins University Press, 1959); Stanley P. Hirshson, *Farewell to the Bloody*

GOP leaders mostly attempted to rebuild the party in the South by reaching out to white voters. This was the strategy employed by Hayes, Arthur, and Harrison, as they tried either to sell "Whiggish" white Southerners on economic-development policies or to enter into fusion arrangements with Independents who were revolting against the Democratic Party. These strategies produced minimal electoral successes. Rep. Henry Cabot Lodge (R-MA) and Sen. George Frisbie Hoar (R-MA) took a different tack, leading Republicans in Congress to seek a new federal elections bill (or, per Southern thinking, a "Force bill") that would have authorized the federal courts (through the appointment of federal supervisors) to ensure the fairness of Southern elections. The "Lodge Bill," as it would become known, failed narrowly in the Senate (after passing in the House), due largely to defections by western ("silver") Republicans.

Throughout this period, as Republicans battled to maintain a foothold in the South, Democrats in the former Confederacy fought back – both through rhetoric (painting the Republicans as the "black party") and through terrorism (toward blacks and their white supporters). Eventually, faced with continued attempts by national GOP leaders to reclaim ground in the South along with the rise of populism and Populist leaders' willingness to cross racial lines and work with Republicans in fusion arrangements, Southern Democratic leaders sought a more reliable way to protect themselves. They settled on a legal remedy – the adoption of a set of disenfranchising provisions (poll taxes, literacy tests, residency requirements, and felon restrictions) that would severely limit participation by blacks (and sometimes by poor whites as well) in elections.[11] While some Southern states passed some of these provisions by statute in the 1880s, the Mississippi legislature went a step further in 1890 and embedded them in a new state constitution (thus making them that much harder to change subsequently). The "Mississippi Plan" withstood a Supreme Court challenge in *Williams* v. *Mississippi* (1898) – whereby the Court ruled that the poll tax and literacy requirements were not discriminatory, as they applied to all voters – and was quickly copied by South Carolina (1895) and Louisiana (1898).[12] By

---

Shirt: Northern Republicans and the Southern Negro, 1877–1893 (Bloomington: Indiana University Press, 1962); Charles W. Calhoun, *Conceiving a New Republic: The Republican Party and the Southern Question, 1869–1900* (Lawrence: University Press of Kansas, 2006).

[11] To prevent poor whites from being disenfranchised, some states adopted the "grandfather clause," which allowed citizens to bypass the voting restrictions if their grandfathers were able to vote prior to the Civil War. In 1915, the Supreme Court ruled the grandfather clause to be unconstitutional.

[12] On *Williams v. Mississippi*, see R. Volney Riser, *Defying Disfranchisement: Black Voting Rights Activism in the Jim Crow South, 1890–1908* (Chapel Hill: University of North Carolina Press, 2010), 46–73; Lawrence Goldstone, *Inherently Unequal: The Betrayal of Equal Rights by the Supreme Court, 1865–1903* (New York: Walker and Company, 2011), 171–76.

1908, all states in the South had adopted disenfranchising provisions of some sort.[13]

As white Democrats were disenfranchising blacks in the South, and thus eliminating the GOP's electoral base in the former Confederacy, the Republicans were expanding their electoral support in every other region of the nation. Beginning in 1894–96 and solidifying with President William McKinley's reelection in 1900, the Republicans asserted their electoral dominance, and the GOP established itself as the majority party in the United States – outside of a brief period between 1912 and 1920, when a Republican Party split allowed Woodrow Wilson to claim the presidency and ushered in six years of unified Democratic rule – for the first three decades of the twentieth century. As a result, GOP leadership concerns about a Southern wing of the party ebbed considerably. Presidents Warren Harding and Herbert Hoover would make efforts to rebuild a viable Southern Republican Party, but such efforts lacked the momentum and urgency of the late nineteenth century.

REPUBLICAN SUCCESSES IN THE SOUTH, 1877–1952

What, then, are we to conclude about the Republican Party's electoral success in the South following the end of Reconstruction in 1877 and prior to Dwight D. Eisenhower's presidential run in 1952? The typical characterization of this era as "one-party Democratic rule" is not far off the mark. But the GOP did have some successes, and it is important to make note of these.

The most significant successes occurred prior to the turn of the twentieth century, when national GOP politicians were actively trying to maintain a Southern wing and the Democrats' disenfranchising-law strategy was not fully vested. The Republicans held a small number of Southern seats in the House of Representatives during this time, exceeding single digits on four occasions: 12 seats in the 47th Congress (1881–83), 14 in the 51st (1889–91), 13 in the 54th (1895–97), and 11 in the 55th (1897–99). In these Congresses, however, seventeen of those fifty GOP seats, or 34 percent, were generated not by explicit election wins but rather by contested (or disputed) election cases in the House and majority decisions to "flip" the seat (or declare the ostensible loser of the election the winner) based on evidence of fraud or other irregularities in the electoral process. Overall, between the 45th (1877–79) and 56th (1899–1901) Congresses, the Republicans controlled 102 of 1,004 House seats in the South, or 10.2 percent. And 22 of those 102 GOP seats would occur because of

---

[13] On the rise of disenfranchising laws in the South, see J. Morgan Kousser, *The Shaping of Southern Politics: Suffrage Restriction and the Establishment of the One-Party South* (New Haven, CT: Yale University Press, 1974); Michael Perman, *Struggle for Mastery: Disfranchisement in the South, 1888–1908* (Chapel Hill: University of North Carolina Press, 2001).

contested election cases.[14] Seven blacks would be among the Republican House members during this time.[15] In the Senate, Republicans elected during this era included William Pitt Kellogg from Louisiana (45th–47th Congresses); William Mahone from Virginia (47th–49th), as part of a fusion arrangement with the Readjuster Party; Harrison H. Riddleberger from Virginia (50th–52nd), as part of a fusion arrangement with the Readjuster Party; and Jeter C. Pritchard (53rd–57th) from North Carolina. These very modest congressional victories far exceeded what the GOP was able to do at the presidential level, where no Republican candidate was able to win a Southern state (or electoral vote) in the six elections between 1880 and 1900.

At the subnational level, GOP success was sporadic prior to the turn of the twentieth century. Republicans elected three governors during this period: Alvin Hawkins in 1880 (served from 1881 to 1883) in Tennessee; William E. Cameron in 1881 (served from 1882 to 1885) in Virginia, as part of a fusion arrangement with the Readjuster Party; and Daniel Lindsay Russell in 1896 in North Carolina (served from 1897 to 1901). The GOP also had some state legislative success in these three states for a period of time: in both chambers in Virginia between 1879 and 1883, in a fusion arrangement with the Readjusters; in the state House in Tennessee between 1881 and 1883, thanks to the tie-breaking vote of a Greenbacker; and in both chambers in North Carolina between 1895 and 1899, in a fusion arrangement with the Populists.

The first half of the twentieth century saw far fewer Republican electoral successes in the South. As disenfranchising laws took hold and spread in the Jim Crow South, black voting – except in some select urban areas – dried up almost completely. As a result, the GOP's nineteenth-century electoral base in the South was virtually eliminated, and the party's ability to consistently compete electorally largely vanished. Writing in 1949, V. O. Key in his book *Southern Politics in State and Nation* said this about the Republican Party:

It scarcely deserves the name of party. It wavers somewhat between an esoteric cult on the order of a lodge and a conspiracy for plunder in accord with the accepted customs of our politics. Its exact position on the cult-conspiracy scale varies from place to place and

---

[14] For information on election contests and Republican House seats in the former Confederacy, see Jeffery A. Jenkins, "Partisanship and Contested Election Cases in the House of Representatives, 1789–2002," *Studies in American Political Development* 18(1): 112–35, Table 11.

[15] The seven were John R. Lynch (47th Congress: Mississippi's 6th district), Robert Smalls (47th–49th: South Carolina's 5th and 7th districts); James E. O'Hara (48th and 49th: North Carolina's 2nd district); Henry P. Cheatham (51st and 52nd: North Carolina's 2nd district); John Mercer Langston (51st: Virginia's 4th district); Thomas E. Miller (51st: South Carolina's 7th district); George W. Murray (53rd and 54th: South Carolina's 7th and 1st districts); and George Henry White (55th and 56th: North Carolina's 2nd district). Some notes on these members: Lynch also represented Mississippi's 6th district in the 43rd and 44th Congresses; Smalls also represented South Carolina's 5th district in the 44th and 45th Congresses; Smalls represented the 5th district in the 48th Congress and the 7th district in the 49th Congress; Murray represented South Carolina's 7th district in the 53rd Congress and the 1st district in the 54th Congress.

time to time. Only in North Carolina, Virginia, and Tennessee do the Republicans approximate the reality of a political party.[16]

Between the 57th (1901–03) and 82nd (1951–53) Congresses, the Republicans controlled just 86 of 2,655 House seats in the South, or 3.2 percent.[17] And, per Key, all but six of these seats came from North Carolina, Virginia, and Tennessee.[18] For the first half of the twentieth century, the Appalachian areas of eastern Tennessee, western North Carolina, and southwestern Virginia constituted the GOP's electoral base – mountain whites who supported the Union during the Civil War and their descendants.[19]

Beyond House elections, GOP electoral success in the first half of the twentieth century is similarly bleak. During this time, *no* Southern state elected a Republican as US senator. In the four presidential elections from 1904 to 1916, no Southern state went for a GOP presidential candidate. This changed in 1920, when Warren Harding won a single Southern state: Tennessee. And in 1928, a potential breakthrough occurred, when Herbert Hoover won five Southern states: Florida, North Carolina, Tennessee, Texas, and Virginia. Hoover generated no congressional coattails, however, and much of his success was likely due to religious bigotry – as white Protestants in the South rejected Democratic presidential nominee Al Smith (NY), who was a Catholic.[20] Moreover, Hoover lost the entire South in 1932, amid Democrat Franklin Delano Roosevelt's landslide victory. And the Republicans won no Southern states in the next four presidential elections (1936–48). Below the federal level, the only GOP successes came in Tennessee, where two Republicans were elected governor: Ben W. Hooper in 1910 (reelected in 1912) and Alfred A. Taylor in 1920. The GOP did not hold majorities in any state legislative chambers in the South during this era.

SOUTHERN DELEGATES, REPUBLICAN NATIONAL CONVENTIONS, AND PATRONAGE POLITICS

Given the Republican Party's lack of electoral success in the post-Reconstruction South, especially in the first half of the twentieth century, one

[16] V. O. Key, Jr., *Southern Politics in State and Nation* (New York: Knopf, 1949), 277.

[17] Party data taken from Kenneth C. Martis, *The Historical Atlas of Political Parties in the United States Congress, 1789–1989* (New York: Macmillan, 1989).

[18] These six House seats all came from the 14th congressional district in Texas, where Republican Harry M. Wurzbach served from the 67th through 72nd Congresses. He was elected outright five times (67th–70th, 72nd) and successfully contested the election of Democrat Augustus McCloskey to the 71st Congress. Wurzbach died in office on February 10, 1930.

[19] Digging deeper, the 1st and 2nd congressional districts in eastern Tennessee have elected Republicans in every election since 1880 – from the 47th (1881–83) through the 116th (2019–21) Congresses.

[20] The one coattails exception might have been in Tennessee, where the Republicans won 5 of 10 House seats. They would win no more than 2 in the decades before or after the 1928 election.

might wonder why focusing on the GOP in the South during these years is important or relevant. In fact, while the South provided little to the Republican Party on election day during this era, the South continued to play a major role in intra-GOP politics. Specifically, the Southern states continued to send delegations to the Republican National Convention and thus had a meaningful hand in selecting Republican presidential nominees. To understand why this was so, we must first start at the beginning and examine why Southern states – *slave* states – received representation in the pre-Civil War GOP in the first place.

The Republican Party began in the early 1850s as an anti-slavery party – specifically, one opposed to the extension of slavery in the western territories – and comprised members of the old Liberty and Free Soil Parties and anti-slavery members of the collapsing Whig Party. As a result, the Republicans did not have much of a following in the slave states – the eleven Southern states that would make up the Confederacy along with the border states of Maryland, Missouri, Kentucky, and Delaware. Thus, in 1856 when the Republicans convened in their first national convention, there were no delegates from the South present. At that convention, however, the GOP delegates discussed the possibility of allowing delegations from states that were anathema to Republican principles. In 1860, the issue came to a head when delegations from the South – Texas and Virginia – were present. Pro and con arguments were made for seating the Southern delegates, but eventually the pro argument won out – in effect, Republican delegates from the North noted that they "[had] been charged for years with being a sectional party," and they wanted to eliminate that misnomer and make clear that they were open to citizens from the slave states that supported the GOP's principles.[21] Hence, from 1860 on, all states in the Union were welcome at the Republican National Convention.[22]

By 1868, all eleven ex-Confederate states were represented at the GOP national convention, and for the remainder of the nineteenth century the South comprised roughly 25 percent of the total number of convention delegates. In the first few conventions, Southern representation was not an issue. But with the Democrats regaining power throughout the South, and the entirety of the former Confederate states going Democrat in presidential elections beginning in 1880, grumblings from Northern Republicans began to be heard. A first attempt to reduce Southern representation at the Republican National Convention was offered in 1883–84 but was defeated soundly – for several reasons. First, many national GOP leaders still held out hope that a Southern wing of the party could be resuscitated. Second, many Republicans believed that Southern

---

[21] Quote was from Connecticut Delegate Chauncey Fitch Cleveland (and former governor of the state), cited in Victor Rosewater, "Republican Convention Reapportionment," *Political Science Quarterly* 28 (1913): 613.

[22] As noted, only Texas and Virginia sent delegates to the 1860 convention. Four years later, during the course of the Civil War, only Arkansas, Louisiana, and Tennessee were represented.

co-partisans – especially blacks – should not be punished (i.e., have their representation reduced) because Democrats used violence and fraud to illegally control the electoral process in the former Confederacy. Third, Republican presidents (and presidential hopefuls) had gotten used to working with Southern delegates and using them as an important foundation in building a majority for the GOP nomination.

In time, the third reason above would be the dominant one for protecting Southern representation at the GOP convention. By the late 1880s, hopes for a viable Republican South were dwindling, as efforts to prop up the party in the South failed. As a result, Southern delegations became increasingly known as "rotten boroughs,"[23] whereby individual delegates – representing a state party with no real chance for electoral success – willingly sold their convention votes to the highest bidder. Despite this normatively negative turn, presidents and presidential hopefuls saw efficiency benefits with this change and actively sought to work with individuals from the Southern state delegations who could deliver sets of votes – and possibly even the whole state delegation. To be sure, a number of Republican presidents maintained the hope that a Republican resurgence in the South remained a possibility and would invest considerable time and resources in trying to achieve this through party-building activities in the region. However, those attempts largely failed. Instead, the South's most consistent role remained in national convention politics. As a result, Southern state "bosses" emerged and maintained power by being able to consistently deliver votes at the GOP convention; in return, they received executive patronage, which they could divvy up and sell to maintain control of the party at home. Thus, from the 1890s onward, Republican state parties in the South became known as "patronage parties" or "post office parties" (as positions associated with the US Post Office, like postmasterships, constituted the bulk of executive patronage appointments).

---

[23] Note that the technical definition of the term "rotten borough" – which was introduced to refer to parliamentary boroughs in the United Kingdom in the eighteenth century that had such a small electorate that voters could not vote freely since they were dependent upon the "owner" of the borough for employment – does not entirely match the reality of the South's role in the Republican Party. However, the term was used both at the time and since then to describe the South's role in the GOP. Most notoriously, Theodore Roosevelt used it to describe the role Southern delegates played in the 1912 Republican National Convention: "In the Convention at Chicago last June the breakup of the Republican Party was forced by those rotten-borough delegates from the South ... representing nothing but their own greed for money or office" and who (in Roosevelt's perspective) "betrayed the will of the mass of the plain people of the party." Cited in Geoffrey Cowan, *Let The People Rule: Theodore Roosevelt and the Birth of the Presidential Primary* (New York: Norton, 2016), 265. Similarly, historian George B. Tindall argued that "William McKinley's campaign for president illustrated perfectly the standard uses of what had become the rotten boroughs of Republicanism in the South." George B. Tindall, "Southern Strategy: A Historical Perspective," *The North Carolina Historical Review* 48 (April 1971): 137.

The Southern Republican Party through the late 1890s was a biracial coalition. Blacks were the electoral bulwark of the party, with whites controlling most of the leadership positions – although the latter was fluid by state over time. Beginning in the mid-1880s and growing more prevalent in the late 1880s and 1890s, a rival Republican coalition – known as the Lily-Whites – began to emerge in the South. The Lily-Whites were white supremacists who believed that blacks should not hold positions of power in the party. Their argument was straightforward: with blacks in the South increasingly being disenfranchised (thanks to legislation and constitutional changes), the only way the Republican Party would have a real electoral future again would be to appeal to the remaining electorate, which was almost exclusively white. And, per Lily-White thinking, whites in the South would only vote for a "respectable" party, which meant one that was led by whites. While in the toxic context of race in Southern politics these were strategically logical arguments, it was also clear that the Lily-Whites wanted to be in control of patronage in their respective states and believed that they would have less success in achieving that by working within the established party organizations, which were controlled by the traditional biracial GOP coalition – which became known as the Black-and-Tans.

BLACK-AND-TANS AND LILY-WHITES

While occasional references are made to the Black-and-Tans and Lily-Whites in histories of the South, almost no systematic examination of their activities and relative strength during the last decades of the nineteenth century and first half of the twentieth century exists. The best analysis by far of these intra-GOP factional dynamics is provided by Hanes Walton, Jr., in his book *Black Republicans: The Politics of the Black and Tans*.[24] Walton provides a detailed analysis of Lily-White and Black-and-Tan politics, both at the national level and within the various Southern states. *Black Republicans*, however, is now dated – having been published more than forty years ago – and while it provides much useful information and data, it falls short of being complete and systematic. Thus, there is a clear need for an update on the important work that Walton began. We provide that update in this book.

The story of the Republican Party in the South from the mid-1880s through the mid-1950s revolves around clashes and competition for power between the Black-and-Tans and Lily-Whites. As the Southern wing of the GOP ceased being a viable electoral party with the advent of black disfranchisement laws, Republican factional politics heated up – as Black-and-Tan and Lily-White leaders sought to build or maintain machines to control executive patronage

---

[24] Hanes Walton, Jr., *Black Republicans: The Politics of the Black and Tans* (Metuchen, NJ: The Scarecrow Press, 1975).

and manage GOP convention delegates. Factional leaders on both sides appealed to leaders in the Republican National Committee (RNC) and the White House to back their group and ignore the entreaties of the other group. National politicians, especially presidents, made use of the rotten-borough machines in the South for their own benefit. Some presidents, like William McKinley, worked with whichever group they felt could deliver the delegate votes at the convention. Others, like Warren Harding and Herbert Hoover, sought to restructure political organizations in the South for their own benefit. Regardless, intra-GOP factional politics were active and often hard-nosed during this era, and the state of affairs (especially when presidential action was part of the story) was covered widely in Southern newspapers. In the end, the Lily-Whites' "respectability" argument would win out, as they replaced the Black-and-Tans at different points in time throughout the South.

To assess the "horserace" between Black-and-Tans and Lily-Whites in the eleven ex-Confederate states over time, we assemble an original dataset on the racial composition of Southern state delegations to the Republican National Convention between 1868 and 1952. We combine these new data with histories of Republican factional politics in each of the eleven Southern states to identify the transition from Black-and-Tan leadership to Lily-White leadership. Some transitions were extreme in terms of the exclusion of black delegates – as in North Carolina, Virginia, Alabama, and Texas – as blacks were eliminated entirely (or nearly so) and permanently from leadership positions. Some transitions were less extreme – as in Tennessee, Arkansas, and Florida – where whites came to dominate the party, but a small percentage of blacks were kept in place to maintain party harmony. And, finally, some transitions were very slow – as in South Carolina, Georgia, and Mississippi – as Black-and-Tan leaders retained control of the party deep into the first half of the twentieth century and sometimes beyond.

Finally, we incorporate the racial composition of Southern state delegations in another way – specifically, we use the percentage of white delegates in a state by election year as a proxy for the perceived "whiteness" of the Republican Party. We call this variable the "Whiteness Index" and incorporate it as the key independent variable – conditioned by the onset of Jim Crow era disenfranchisement – in a regression model to explain electoral support for the Republican Party. Just as whiteness has come to be important in modern Republican politics, especially around the rise of Donald Trump,[25] we argue that whiteness was an important factor in the slow rise of the Republican Party in the Jim Crow South during the first fifty-plus years of the twentieth century. In short, this is a way to test the Lily-Whites' "respectability" thesis: did the white

---

[25] See, for example, John Sides, Michael Tesler, and Lynn Vavreck, *Identity Crisis: The 2016 Presidential Campaign and the Battle for the Meaning of American* (Princeton, NJ: Princeton University Press, 2018); Ashley Jardina, *White Identity Politics* (Cambridge: Cambridge University Press, 2019).

electorate begin to support the Republican Party in the South once the GOP leadership took on a Lily-White cast? We find the answer to this question is yes – the "whitening" of the Republican Party in the South led to a significant increase in the GOP's vote totals, especially in the states of the Outer South. And this increase manifested not just in presidential elections but in congressional and gubernatorial elections as well. From this, we conclude that the Republican Party in the modern era developed more quickly as a viable electoral party in states where the GOP leadership went Lily-White earlier and more fully in the twentieth century.

OUTLINE OF THE BOOK

Much of this book is devoted to charting both the national and the state-level history of the Republican Party's involvement in the South in the pre-modern era. Before delving into these histories, however, we first discuss in Chapter 2 the original data that we use to measure the decline of black control in each state party organization. We collected information on the race of national convention delegates for each Southern state between 1868 and 1952. Using this data, we show that the increase or decrease of black delegates within a state's delegation to the Republican National Convention affected the party's electoral performance. Crucially, the direction of this relationship depends on whether a state had already implemented legislation barring black citizens from voting. If black representation in a delegation increased *before* disenfranchisement, the party's electoral performance improved (all else equal). If black representation increased *after* disenfranchisement, the Republican Party's electoral performance in the state declined (all else equal).

In Part I of the book, we focus on the national story by looking at how party leaders – including presidents and members of Congress – came up with "Southern strategies" aimed at entrenching a Republican Party in the South, winning control of Southern national convention delegates, or both. In Chapter 3, we examine how national GOP leaders built a Republican Party in the South during the Reconstruction era by requiring the former Confederate states to guarantee voting rights for freedmen (as a condition for being readmitted to the Union) and (generally) limit suffrage for whites who had been actively involved in the Confederacy. The result was a brief period in which the Republican Party was dominant in the South – winning unified control of government in nearly all Southern states in the late 1860s and early1870s. However, this Republican electoral success was largely based on artificial majorities: as whites were reincorporated into the voting population, Southern Democrats began to frame political battles along strict racial lines. Additionally, white paramilitary groups – such as the Red Shirts and the White League – acting on behalf of the Democratic Party terrorized black voters and Republican politicians. As a result, Democrats began to regain ground quickly and by 1877 had won back unified control of every former Confederate state.

Chapter 4 covers the Republican Party's response to the Democrats' "redeeming" of the South. We show that through the 1890s GOP presidents – Hayes, Arthur, and Harrison – actively sought to maintain a viable Southern wing of the party. They did this mainly by emphasizing economic issues rather than civil rights, in order to re-brand the party and attract white Southerners with "Whiggish" interests. Such attempts proved futile, and facing highly competitive (re-)elections those same presidents often abandoned their Southern strategies and returned to "Bloody Shirt" rhetoric to mobilize Republican voters in the North.[26] Republicans in Congress took a different tack, by seeking to protect the voting rights of blacks though a new federal elections bill. Their attempt, while valiant, came up just short. And while local GOP organizations failed to recover electorally amid these national defeats, state party leaders remained politically relevant through their role as delegates to Republican National Conventions. We show that presidents and presidential candidates in the 1880s and 1890s actively sought to bind Southern delegates to their candidacy through federal patronage or direct bribes. Indeed, we show that Harrison's re-nomination in 1892 relied on the pivotal support of Southern delegates.

In Chapter 5, we examine how Republican leaders built on this rotten-borough approach to the South during the "System of 1896." We show that national leaders – most often presidential candidates and incumbent presidents, including Theodore Roosevelt, William Howard Taft, Calvin Coolidge, and Herbert Hoover – all relied on a version of a Southern strategy to ensure their (re-)nomination at (often unpredictable) national conventions. In response, their GOP opponents began to call for a reduction in the size of Southern delegations. Thus, the South became an often controversial, and frequently crucial, element in national Republican politics. At the same time, national leaders never entirely abandoned hope for a Southern electoral resurgence. In particular, Presidents Warren G. Harding, Hoover, and (to a lesser extent) Roosevelt sought to replace some of the corrupt party organizations in the South with new organizations built around handpicked, high-quality local leaders. Those attempts largely failed but did place these presidents at the center of major clashes over control of state GOP organizations – where black Republicans and their white allies (the Black-and-Tans) faced off against whites who wanted to remove blacks entirely from positions of authority in the party organization (the Lily-Whites).

In Chapter 6, we conclude our focus on the national Republican Party's relationship to the South by examining the emergence of a comprehensive Southern strategy in the 1940s and 1950s. We discuss how national Republicans sought to take advantage of the growing regional schism in the national

---

[26] "Waving the Bloody Shirt" was a campaign strategy used by politicians in the North, to recall the passions and sacrifices of the Civil War. It was often employed by Republicans against Democrats, who they claimed were the party of rebellion.

Democratic Party by offering their party as a reasonable alternative to conservative Southern whites. And, to some extent, the GOP was successful in this regard, as it began to win Southern states in presidential elections from 1952 onwards. But the strategy also involved risk: appealing to Southern whites in practice meant, at the very least, condoning segregation. This was highly controversial within the party and unappealing to many GOP voters outside of the South. In 1968, however, Richard Nixon developed a Southern strategy that threaded the needle, by appealing to the South in a way that did not alienate voters elsewhere. Rather than support segregation, Nixon promised to slow down the civil rights process while pursuing a broader law-and-order campaign, which appealed to both Southerners and non-Southerners alike. This created a Southern-strategy blueprint that the Republican Party would follow in the 1970s and beyond.

In Part II of the book, we present case studies of the development of each state GOP organization in the South during this era. We show that in all states there was frequent – and in some cases continuous – competition over control of the state party organization. In the 1870s, this conflict largely involved which candidates were to be on the ballot representing the party. By the late nineteenth century, conflicts still occurred but party nominations become increasingly irrelevant. Indeed, in many states the Republican Party often failed to run candidates in statewide races. Control of the state party remained relevant, however, because the party organization was the institution through which national leaders delivered patronage – as well as the institution most likely to produce national convention delegations that actually got seated.

We focus on the battles for control between the Black-and-Tans and the Lily-Whites. In every Southern state, the Lily-Whites eventually won out – but *when* and in what *form* they won out varied considerably. In Chapter 7, we focus on those states – Virginia, Texas, North Carolina, and Alabama – in which the Lily-White takeover of the state party organization resulted in the (near) complete exclusion of black Republicans from positions of authority in the party. In Chapter 8, we examine those states – Arkansas, Louisiana, Florida, and Tennessee – in which the Lily-Whites gained control, but blacks continued to have a small but consistent level of representation at state and national conventions. In Chapter 9, we focus on three states – South Carolina, Georgia, and Mississippi – where the Lily-White takeover occurred much later than in the other states.

Finally, in Chapter 10 we conclude by assessing how this history should be incorporated in our understanding of the relationship between the Republican Party and the South. We also consider what it teaches us about American political history, American presidents as party leaders, and political parties as institutions.

2

The Republican Party and the South: Some Preliminaries

While much of this book is a developmental account of the Republican Party in the South from Reconstruction through the late 1960s, covering both the national and the state levels, we must set the stage in various ways before we can proceed. Specifically, we will use this chapter to do three things: (1) discuss the various data and measures – some existing and some new – that we will use throughout the book; (2) identify how apportionment of Southern delegates was determined, discuss how Southern delegation size varied over time, and explain why the South was able to maintain a significant presence at GOP conventions while not providing any electoral votes for generations; and (3) explain why focusing on factional GOP politics in the South in the late nineteenth and early twentieth centuries matters for understanding the emergence of the Republican Party as an electoral force in the South in the late twentieth century, through an innovative multivariate analysis of "whiteness politics." We discuss each of these briefly in turn.

First, we will incorporate a variety of data and measures along the way to support our qualitative accounts. To be sure, like most political science research that assesses politics from a historical perspective, our analysis of the GOP in the South during this period faces clear limitations in terms of the data – both quantitative and qualitative[1] – that are available. As Eric Schickler has argued,

---

[1] One issue in terms of the qualitative secondary sources that any study of the American South has to face is the presence of a considerable number of studies of the internal politics of Southern states that fall in the so-called "Dunning School." These studies were mostly produced by Columbia historian William Dunning and his students around the turn of the twentieth century and were deeply affected by these scholars' racist beliefs regarding the capacities of black citizens for self-governance. In some cases, these Dunning School era studies remain some of the most in-depth accounts of the politics of individual Southern states during the era of Reconstruction and beyond, despite their clear racial bias. In cases where we cite these studies, we rely solely on their historical factual accounts (that is, details on the timing of specific events), not on the authors'

scholars facing such limitations are best served by "drawing on diverse types of evidence and methodological approaches in order to gain insight into a question that is not ideally suited to isolating the causal effect of a single variable."[2] Thus, we combine qualitative historical data with quantitative data measuring both the GOP's electoral performance in the South and its internal racial dynamics, across this time period. Some of these data will be "off the shelf," such as data used to construct various national- and state-level measures of party strength across time. Some will also be original, such as our data on the race of GOP convention delegates, which we use to build a measure of the racial composition of Southern state delegations to the Republican National Convention between 1868 and 1952.

Second, we will provide a brief history of how Southern representation at the Republican National Convention was determined. We first describe how Southern representation came about, as the Republican Party was organized as an anti-slavery party (or, more precisely, as an anti-slavery-extension party) and the South was virulently pro-slavery (and would, of course, secede from the Union to preserve their "peculiar institution"). We then discuss how Southern representation, once granted, continued in force over time, even as it became clear to everyone in the GOP that the former Confederate states would provide no electoral votes in the party's drive to win the presidency. In doing so, we document how Southern representation changed over time, and how attempts to reduce the size of the South's share of convention delegates failed or (in one case) succeeded.

Third, we will argue that an examination of Republican factional politics in the South in the late nineteenth and early twentieth centuries is important beyond its historical significance. Specifically, we will show that the degree to which Lily-Whites took over state GOP organizations in the South mattered for subsequent GOP electoral support in the South. This Lily-White takeover was conditioned by the passage of disenfranchising laws (at different times) in the Southern states. Once blacks were essentially disenfranchised in a state, whites became the effective electorate. And whites would only vote Republican (per the Lily-Whites' rhetoric) if the party seemed "respectable" – where "respectable" was synonymous with "white." We find that some states went Lily-White more quickly and more completely than other states and that there was a significant electoral benefit associated with becoming a whiter party – where we measure the "whiteness" of the Republican Party by state and over time using our original dataset of the race of GOP convention delegates. This

---

theoretical assessments of the causes of any historical events they describe. For an assessment of the Dunning School, see John David Smith and J. Vincent Lowery, eds., *The Dunning School: Historians, Race, and the Meaning of Reconstruction* (Lexington: University Press of Kentucky, 2013).

[2] Eric Schickler, *Racial Realignment: The Transformation of American Liberalism, 1932–1965* (Princeton, NJ: Princeton University Press, 2016), 17.

whitening of the party was an important first step toward making the Republican Party a viable electoral choice for white Southerners and set the stage – given other necessary conditions – for the GOP to become a dominant force in Southern politics.

We begin with a discussion of measures of party strength over time. We then cover the history and political dynamics of Republican National Convention apportionment in the South. We then move on to a discussion of our racial composition measure and conclude by using a form of that measure (which we will call the "Whiteness Index") in a multivariate regression model of GOP party strength.

REPUBLICAN PARTY STRENGTH IN THE SOUTH

To measure the electoral party strength of the Republican Party in the South across time, we incorporate a variety of measures that have been used by scholars for more than forty years. The principal measures that we use were developed by Paul T. David in his book, *Party Strength in the United States, 1872–1970*.[3] In assembling his data, David stated that "the primary objective" was to create "a set of index numbers that can be used as measures over time of party strength at the polls."[4] He subsequently generated updates[5] and provided the data through 1996 electronically via the Inter-university Consortium for Political and Social Research (ICPSR).[6] We have expanded these data both backward (through 1868) and forward (through 2016) in time. David offers a variety of national- and state-level measures of party strength, including GOP presidential candidate vote percentage, GOP congressional vote percentage, percentage of House and Senate seats held by Republicans, GOP gubernatorial candidate vote percentage, and percentage of a state's upper and lower chambers held by Republicans. In addition to these institution-specific measures, David provides a variety of composite indices, which combine federal data, state data, and overlapping (federal and state) data. David's data have been used by a number of scholars over time, and we believe their variety and flexibility suit our needs well.[7]

[3] Paul T. David, *Party Strength in the United States, 1872–1970* (Charlottesville: University of Virginia Press, 1972).
[4] Ibid., 3.
[5] Paul T. David, "Party Strength in the United States: Changes in 1972," *The Journal of Politics* 36 (1974): 785–96; "Party Strength in the United States: Changes in 1974," *The Journal of Politics* 38 (1976): 416–25; "Party Strength in the United States: Changes in 1976," *The Journal of Politics* 40 (1978): 770–80.
[6] See Paul T. David and William Claggett, *Party Strength in the United States: 1872–1996* (Ann Arbor, MI: Inter-university Consortium for Political and Social Research [distributor], 2008-09-10). https://doi.org/10.3886/ICPSR06895.v1.
[7] See, for example, Jeffrey M. Stonecash, Mark D. Brewer, and Mack D. Mariani, *Diverging Parties: Social Change, Realignment, and Party Polarization* (Boulder, CO: Westview Press,

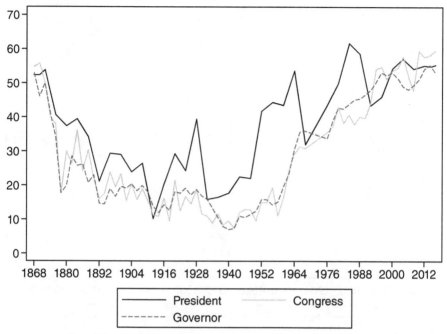

FIGURE 2.1 Republican presidential, congressional, and gubernatorial vote in the South, 1868–2016

We incorporate several of the David party-strength measures, both institution-specific measures and composite-index measures. We employ mostly institution-specific measures in this chapter (which will be the basis of the multivariate models in a later section) and focus on composite-index measures later in the book, in the case-study chapters. At times, we also use data and measures developed by Jerrold G. Rusk, from his book *A Statistical History of the American Electorate*.[8] Rusk's data come in handy specifically for analyses of South vs. non-South electoral performance.

In Figure 2.1, we present biennial measures of the share of the GOP presidential, congressional, and gubernatorial vote in the South from 1868 through 2016.[9] What we see is that after some initial success in the South, during Reconstruction, the Republican Party struggled electorally – and that GOP

2003); Seth C. McKee, *Republican Ascendancy in Southern U.S. House Election* (Boulder, CO: Westview Press, 2010); M. V. Hood III, Quentin Kidd, and Irwin L. Morris, *The Rational Southerner: Black Mobilization, Republican Growth, and the Partisan Transformation of the American South* (New York: Oxford University Press, 2012).

[8] Jerrold G. Rusk, *A Statistical History of the American Electorate* (Washington, DC: Congressional Quarterly Press, 2001).

[9] We incorporate biennial measures to create comparability between the congressional vote and the presidential and gubernatorial vote.

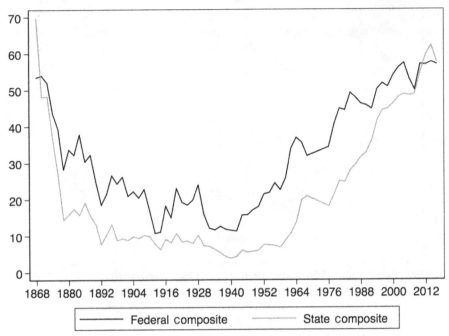

FIGURE 2.2 Republican federal and state composite indices in the South, 1868–2016

vote share across all three measures dropped quickly and precipitously. For much of the late nineteenth century, all three measures continued to decline, until a general flattening occurred. GOP congressional and gubernatorial vote share would hover between 10 and 20 percent from the 1890s through the late 1920s. Republican presidential vote share was somewhat higher during the same time frame, cycling between 20 and 30 percent with some low spikes (in 1912, thanks to the division in the party and Theodore Roosevelt's third-party run) and high spikes (in 1928, when Herbert Hoover did well in the South, carrying five states) along the way. The New Deal era (1932–1948) saw a general decrease in all measures. Starting with Dwight Eisenhower's presidential campaign in 1952, however, Republican presidential vote share increased substantially and stayed over 40 percent through the late 1970s. With Ronald Reagan's election in 1980, GOP presidential vote share has generally been above 50 percent (with the exception of the 1992 and 1996 elections). Republican congressional and gubernatorial vote share tracked presidential vote share, except those increases were about 15 percentage points lower initially. Beginning in the early 1990s, however, GOP congressional and gubernatorial vote share both grew steadily, such that by the late 1990s all three measures were largely aligned. That has been the status quo since then – with all three measures hovering above 50 percent.

In Figure 2.2, we present two composite measures: a federal index (which is a composite of GOP presidential vote, GOP House vote, and GOP Senate vote)[10] and a state index (which is a composite of GOP gubernatorial vote, the GOP percentage of seats in the state lower chamber, and the GOP percentage of seats in the state upper chamber).[11] The two measures produce U-shaped distributions, with the federal measure being slightly higher throughout most of the period – except in the last decade when the two measures overlap. More generally, while the two Republican measures were somewhat high during much of the Reconstruction era, both dropped off quickly and significantly once the Democrats regained power throughout the South. Starting in the 1890s and extending through the late 1950s, the GOP state index hovered between 5 and 10 percent. During the same period, the Republican federal index was a bit higher, fluctuating between 10 and 25 percent. Starting in the late 1950s, both measures began a steady increase, with the federal index breaking the 50 percent barrier in the mid-1990s and the state index following suit around fifteen years later.

The trends shown in these figures obviously involve many details. We will cover those details in subsequent chapters, as we discuss the political history of the Republican Party in the South – at both federal and state levels.

GOP NATIONAL CONVENTION APPORTIONMENT AND THE SOUTH

As noted in Chapter 1, all eleven ex-Confederate states were represented at the Republican National Convention starting in 1868, and for the next forty years the South would comprise roughly 25 percent of the GOP convention delegates. While Southern representation was not an issue in the first few conventions, once the Democrats regained power throughout the South, the Republicans – starting in 1880 – would not receive any electoral votes in presidential elections. Thus, beginning as early as 1883, Republicans in the North began complaining about the South's excessive level of representation at GOP national conventions. Yet, for a variety of reasons, the status quo prevailed. Complaints would continue to be raised, however, and Southern representation would be a recurring issue for the Republicans in the early decades of the twentieth century.

To understand the "problem" of Southern representation at the Republican National Convention in the post-Reconstruction era requires an understanding of how the GOP apportioned delegates. From the Republican Party's inception, representation was based on a dual "equality+size" model, where all states would be provided with a baseline delegate level that was then enhanced in

---

[10] For each state, the three institution-specific measures are averaged (and thus equally weighted). So the federal measure is (GOP presidential vote + GOP House vote + GOP Senate vote) ÷ 3.

[11] For each state, the three institution-specific measures are averaged (and thus equally weighted). So the state measure is (GOP gubernatorial vote + GOP percentage of seats in the state lower chamber + GOP percentage of seats in the state upper chamber) ÷ 3.

proportion to the number of congressional districts each state possessed.[12] In 1856, for example, the rule chosen at the first Republican convention was: each state would receive six "at large" delegates plus three for every one of its congressional districts. Incorporating such an equality+size model was pragmatic, as the Republicans in 1856 were a new party, so there was no obvious measure of party strength that could be used in the delegate allocation process.

While the decision to adopt an equality+size model was straightforward, the decision to provide representation to *every* state in the Union was not. Some states, primarily in the South, were effectively closed off to the Republican Party. That is, as opposition to slavery extension was the guiding principle of the new party – and the position that bound together disparate groups of former Free Soilers, former Liberty Party members, and anti-slavery Whigs, among others – the pro-slavery South was enemy territory, and Southerners were hostile to (and sometimes violent toward) any Republicans within their midst.[13] Thus, the question was: should a party built consciously on free-soil principles allow *slave-state* representation at its national convention? This issue was brought to the forefront in 1860, when the convention's Credentials Committee proposed a delegate list that included several slave states and territories. Amendments were quickly offered that would have recommitted (i.e., eliminated) several slave-state delegations (Texas, Maryland, Kentucky, Virginia, the Nebraska and Kansas Territories, and the District of Columbia). A spirited debate then ensued, with those seeking to exclude the slave-state delegations expressing concerns about the Republican Party's mission being undermined by their inclusion (per the belief that members from pro-slavery regions might work to destroy the party from the inside) and those seeking to seat the slave-state delegations stressing fairness and the need for the party to be truly national in scope (and not just a sectional party, as many opponents of the GOP had claimed). In the end, the pro-inclusion position won out, as the convention adopted a report advocating the seating of *all* the delegations, including the slave states and territories. The allocation changed slightly from 1856, with each state given four at-large delegates and two for every congressional district it possessed – which was equal to twice its number of votes in the Electoral College.[14]

Thus, in subsequent years, these two sets of decisions – on (1) equality+size driving a state's delegation allocation and (2) convention inclusivity, regardless of a state's receptivity to GOP tenets – would steer Republican National

---

[12] Much of the content of this section is based on Victor Rosewater, "Republican Convention Apportionment," *Political Science Quarterly* 28 (1913): 610–26.

[13] For a broader treatment of the Republican Party's formation and ideology, see Eric Foner, *Free Soil, Free Labor, and Free Men: The Ideology of the Republican Party before the Civil War* (New York: Oxford University Press, 1970).

[14] For coverage of the debate, along with key vote results, see *Proceedings of the Republican National Convention Held at Chicago, May 16, 17, and 18, 1860* (Albany: Weed, Parsons & Co., 1860), 44–70.

Convention politics down a certain path. With each new convention, and the re-adoption (tacit or otherwise) of the two aforementioned sets of decisions, precedents were set that would be hard to alter later. For example, an apportionment rule divorced from party strength and a general policy of inclusion were not problematic during the Civil War and early Reconstruction years, when the Republican Party was present and dominant in every region of the country. In this case, "real" influence in the convention was in keeping with "real" influence in presidential selection (in the Electoral College). With the declining fortunes of the GOP in the South following the end of Reconstruction, a fissure opened between the two modes of influence – Southern delegations retained their ability to affect Republican presidential nominations even as they lost *all* ability to affect outcomes on election day.

Despite the fact that the political reality changed in the post-Reconstruction years, the status quo arrangement proved impervious to change. Basic beliefs regarding fairness and inclusion continued to hold strong appeal, in part because a sizable segment of the GOP – the Stalwart wing, predominantly, which was the keeper of the Radical flame on Reconstruction policy and black civil rights – held out hope that the Democratic resurgence in the South could be reversed.[15] Southern Republicans themselves also lobbied to maintain their position in the GOP governing hierarchy. And, of course, Northern Republican politicians who benefited from a sizable and stable Southern delegation at the convention also opposed a change.

By the end of the nineteenth century, opponents of the pro-Southern status quo began to gain some traction. Arguments about a Republican resurgence below the Mason–Dixon Line had lost credibility, as GOP electoral gains in the South – which had produced some successes in the late 1870s and early 1880s, in part by fusing with various independent movements – were largely stymied by the mid-1880s. The Republicans' last statutory stand occurred in 1890, during the Harrison administration, when the party controlled both chambers of Congress and Rep. Henry Cabot Lodge (R-MA) pushed a new federal elections bill that sought to resuscitate black voting rights in the South by granting new oversight powers to the federal judiciary. The Lodge Bill passed in the House but was stopped in the Senate when "silver" Republicans in the West defected from the party position.[16] The Democrats responded to this GOP "near miss" by adopting state-level restrictions on black voting rights in the

---

[15] On the Stalwarts, see Allan Peskin, "Who Were the Stalwarts? Who Were Their Rivals? Republican Factions in the Gilded Age," *Political Science Quarterly* 99 (1984–85): 703–16.

[16] For a lengthy discussion of the politics surrounding the Lodge Bill, see Richard M. Valelly, "Partisan Entrepreneurship and Policy Windows: George Frisbie Hoar and the 1890 Federal Elections Bill," in Stephen Skowronek and Matthew Glassman, eds., *Formative Acts: American Politics in the Making* (Philadelphia: University of Pennsylvania Press, 2007), 126–52; Richard E. Welch, Jr., "The Federal Elections Bill of 1890: Postscripts and Preludes," *The Journal of American History* 52 (1965): 511–26.

South – which led to large-scale disenfranchisement – and repealing the existing Reconstruction-era Enforcement Acts at the federal level that were still on the books.[17] In addition, while the Democrats were consolidating their hold on the South, Republicans made popular vote gains in every other region of the country in the 1894–96 elections;[18] once these initial gains were seen as stable, following William McKinley's reelection in 1900, the GOP leadership was comfortable in asserting the party's national dominance. As a result, fewer and fewer Northern Republicans had any instrumental reason for working to maintain a foothold in the South and, perhaps more importantly, for honoring the decades-old status quo arrangement that disproportionately benefited the South at the Republican National Convention.[19]

As a result, motions began to be offered at the Republican National Convention to tie states' delegate allotment in part to party strength, as measured by state votes cast for the most recent Republican presidential nominee. The first motion, made in 1900, would have provided each state with four at-large delegates and one additional delegate for each 10,000 votes (or majority fraction thereof) cast for the Republican nominee at the last presidential election.[20] The 1900 motion was quickly dropped, but it surfaced again in the same form in 1908 and generated a close roll-call vote (which failed, 471–506). A similar motion was offered four years later, in 1912, which would

[17] See J. Morgan Kousser, *The Shaping of Southern Politics: Suffrage Restriction and the Establishment of the One-Party South* (New Haven, CT: Yale University Press, 1974); Michael Perman, *Struggle for Mastery: Disfranchisement in the South, 1888–1908* (Chapel Hill: University of North Carolina Press, 2001).

[18] James L. Sundquist, *Dynamics of the Party System: Alignment and Realignment of Political Parties in the United States* (Washington, DC: The Brookings Institution, 1973).

[19] Another way that the Republicans tried to maintain a foothold in the South – beyond statutory attempts like the Lodge Bill – was through contested (disputed) election cases. In the five Houses in which the GOP maintained majority control in the twenty-year period between 1881 and 1901, the Republicans "flipped" 20 seats in the former-Confederate South from Democratic to Republican, based on charges related to fraud, intimidation, election irregularities, etc. The breakdown of those 20 is as follows: 5 seats in the 47th Congress (1881–83), 5 in the 51st (1889–91), 4 in the 54th (1895–97), 3 in the 55th (1897–99), and 3 in the 56th (1899–1901). In the five succeeding Congresses, the 57th–61st (1901–11), in which they maintained majority control of the House, the Republicans flipped *no* seats in the former Confederate states. See Jeffery A. Jenkins, "Partisanship and Contested Election Cases in the House of Representatives, 1789–2002," *Studies in American Political Development* 18 (2004): 112–35; Jeffery A. Jenkins, "The First 'Southern Strategy': The Republican Party and Contested Election Cases in the Late-Nineteenth Century House," in David W. Brady and Mathew D. McCubbins, eds., *Party, Process, and Political Change in Congress*, Vol. II: *Further New Perspectives on the History of Congress* (Stanford, CA: Stanford University Press, 2007), 78–90. On the broader subject of disputed House seats and GOP strategy, see Richard M. Valelly, "National Parties and Racial Disenfranchisement," in Paul E. Peterson, ed., *Classifying by Race* (Princeton, NJ: Princeton University Press, 1995), 188–216.

[20] Note that the 1900 motion was based on a similar motion first introduced in 1884, at a time when the Republicans were not yet ready to give up on a Southern wing. Additionally, the

have provided one delegate for each congressional district within a state, along with one additional delegate for each 10,000 votes (or majority fraction thereof) cast for the Republican nominee at the last presidential election.[21] While this motion was tabled at the convention, a breakthrough finally occurred in December 1913, when the RNC agreed to adopt the 1912 proposal.[22] This rules change was subsequently ratified by Republican organizations in states that produced GOP electoral majorities in 1908, and at the 1916 Republican National Convention – and went into effect at that time.[23]

During a June 1921 meeting, the RNC agreed to another reapportionment scheme, which provided states with one delegate for each congressional district that maintained a Republican organization and had cast at least 2,500 votes for a Republican in the most recent presidential election plus one additional delegate for each district that cast at least 10,000 such votes. If implemented, this plan would have eliminated the automatic delegate that states received for each congressional district and resulted in a further reduction in Southern delegates, drawing the total down by 40 percent since 1912.[24] During an RNC meeting in December 1923, however, the 1921 reapportionment was abandoned and the system of one delegate for each congressional district was reinstated, with a new provision that provided three "bonus" at-large delegates to each state that voted Republican in the most recent presidential election.[25] The 1923 RNC plan was adopted at the 1924 convention and served as the status quo for the next several conventions.

motion was also considered at an 1899 Republican National Committee meeting. We cover both cases in detail in Chapters 4 and 5.

[21] The 1912 motion also would have provided two delegates each for Alaska, the District of Columbia, Hawaii, Puerto Rico, and the Philippines.

[22] In implementing the change, the RNC followed the advice of a Committee on Representation that it had appointed earlier that year. See "Harmony the Note of Republican Talk," *New York Times*, May 25, 1913; "Republicans Vote Delegate Reforms," *New York Times*, December 17, 1913.

[23] This account is confirmed in an examination of delegate lists included in the official proceedings of the 1916 Republican convention. See *Official Report of the Proceedings of the Sixteenth Republican National Convention, Held in Chicago, June 7, 8, 9, and 10, 1916* (New York: The Tenny Press, 1916). Hanes Walton, however, states that the cuts in Southern delegates were not agreed to until the 1916 convention and did not go into effect until 1920. Walton's account appears to be based on a misreading of W. F. Nowlin's *The Negro in American National Politics*, which states that the cuts went into effect in 1916 and were kept in place for the 1920 convention. See Hanes Walton, Jr., *Black Republicans: The Politics of the Black and Tans* (Metuchen, NJ: The Scarecrow Press, 1975), 152; W. F. Nowlin, *The Negro in American National Politics* (Boston: The Stratford Company, 1931), 72–73.

[24] "Republicans Cut Quota from South," *New York Times*, June 9, 1921.

[25] Under this plan, "voting Republican" meant casting the state's electoral votes for the Republican candidate running in the most recent presidential election. In 1944, this was extended to include electing a Republican senator in the most recent senatorial election. And in 1952, this was extended further to include electing a Republican governor in the most recent governor election.

In the 1940 convention, a delegate-apportionment change – for representation at subsequent conventions – was made that eliminated the automatic
district delegate that each state received and instead required a district to cast
1,000 votes or more for a Republican for president in the last presidential
election or for the Republican nominee for Congress in the last congressional
election to receive a delegate.[26] This change was meant to encourage Republican leaders to build up the party in the South.[27] In the 1948 convention, the
"bonus" of three at-large districts for voting Republican was raised to six for
representation at future conventions.[28] And in the 1952 convention, the
district-vote threshold was raised to 2,000 votes for representation at subsequent conventions, to further incentivize leaders to develop the party in the
South.[29] This would be the status quo through the 1968 Republican National
Convention.[30]

We will recount the political details surrounding the various reapportionment motions in subsequent chapters. For now, though, it is helpful to get a
sense of what was at stake in the reapportionment conflicts, and the extent to
which the Republican Party found itself marginalized electorally in the South.
Figure 2.3 reveals the percentage of the vote that GOP presidential candidates
received both nationally and regionally (South vs. Non-South) between
1868 and 1968, while Figure 2.4 illustrates the Southern state delegation
percentages at the Republican National Convention from 1856 through
1968. (The number of delegates by Southern state is detailed in Table A2.1 in
the Appendix to this chapter.) As Figure 2.3 indicates, GOP presidential candidates often won national victories in the late nineteenth and early twentieth
centuries, despite dramatically underperforming in the South. Indeed, for ten
straight presidential elections – 1880 through 1916 – the GOP did not win a
single state in the ex-Confederacy. Yet, for most of these years, the Southern
states constituted around 25 percent of Republican convention delegates, a
substantial total for a region that provided the party with nothing on election
day. (This percentage declined slightly until 1912, thanks mostly to the South
losing House seats in a relative sense after each congressional
reapportionment.)

[26] See *Official Report of the Proceedings of the Twenty-Third Republican National Convention, Held in Chicago, June 26, 27, and 28, 1944* (Washington, DC: Judd & Detweiler, Inc., 1944), 103–04.
[27] See "Democrats Study Delegate System," *Baltimore Sun*, July 7, 1940; "Democrats Map Delegate Bonus for Solid South," *New York Herald Tribune*, July 7, 1940.
[28] See "Raise Delegate Total for 1952," *New York Times*, June 23, 1948.
[29] David G. Farrelly, "Afterthoughts on the National Conventions," *Los Angeles Times*, August 12, 1952.
[30] See Francis R. Valeo, Richard D. Hupman, and Robert L. Tienken, *Nomination and Election of the President and Vice President of the United States Including the Manner of Selecting Delegates to the National Political Conventions* (Washington, DC: US Government Printing Office, 1968), 56–57.

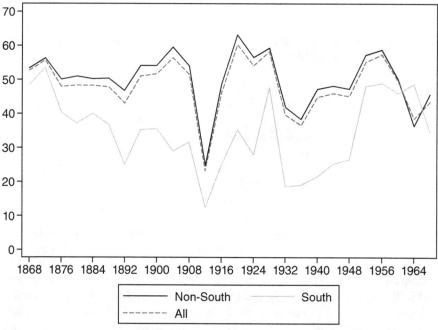

FIGURE 2.3 GOP presidential vote by region, 1868–1968

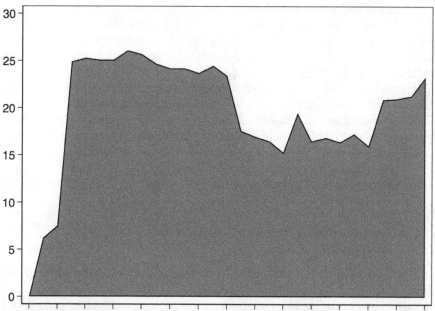

FIGURE 2.4 Southern share of delegates to Republican National Conventions, 1856–1968

Beginning in 1916, the GOP's new delegate reapportionment scheme went into effect, and the South saw its representation at the national convention drop by nearly 6 percentage points. The region lost an additional half percentage point in the two succeeding conventions (1920, 1924) and more than a percentage point in 1928 (as a result of losing the 1924 gain in Tennessee, after Warren Harding's victory there in 1920). In 1932, the South's representation increased to 19.5 percent, thanks to Herbert Hoover's 1928 victories in Florida, North Carolina, Tennessee, Texas, and Virginia. But Hoover's landslide loss to Democrat Franklin Delano Roosevelt in 1932 resulted in the South losing representation once again – an initial three percentage point drop in 1936 that roughly lingered through 1944. The South gained almost a percentage point of representation in 1948 but dropped more than a percentage point in 1952 (due mainly to the extra bonus delegates that were distributed exclusively to states in the North). Beginning in 1956, however, the South's representation began increasing, starting with a near 5 percentage point increase thanks to Dwight Eisenhower's 1952 victories in Florida, Tennessee, Texas, and Virginia. In 1956, Eisenhower added Louisiana to that group of four. In 1960, Richard Nixon carried three Southern states – Florida, Tennessee, and Virginia – but he did well in the South generally and the region's proportion of GOP convention delegates continued to rise as a result. In 1964, Barry Goldwater carried five states in the Deep South – Alabama, Georgia, Louisiana, Mississippi, and South Carolina – which meant that when Richard Nixon won the GOP presidential nomination in 1968, the South's share of Republican convention delegates was the highest it had been since 1912.

Goldwater's Southern performance also was the first time that the GOP did better – in terms of a higher percentage of the vote – in the South than the non-South. Nixon's performance in 1968 indicated a significant drop, but this was mainly due to the third-party candidacy of George Wallace, who won five Southern states. Nixon would do exceedingly well in the South in 1972, better than his performance in the non-South. And after one election (in 1976) where the GOP candidate once again did better in the non-South than the South, beginning in 1980 with Ronald Reagan's election, the Republican presidential candidate consistently (in every election) performed better in the South than the non-South. This can be seen in Figure A2.1 – in the Appendix to this chapter – which extends Figure 2.3 through 2016.

FACTIONAL GOP POLITICS: LILY-WHITES VS. BLACK-AND-TANS

As noted in Chapter 1, any hopes for a meaningful Southern wing of the Republican Party had dwindled considerably by the late 1880s. Thus, how presidents and presidential hopefuls (and their patrons and lieutenants) viewed the South changed considerably – Southern delegations would increasingly be considered "rotten boroughs," with individual delegates available to the highest bidder. Southern leaders who could deliver sets of votes – and perhaps even the entire state delegation – became state "bosses." In return for their efforts, these bosses received executive patronage, which they used to maintain control of the party back home.

Through the 1890s, the Republican Party in the South was a coalition of blacks and whites. Blacks provided most of the votes for the party, while whites held most of the leadership positions (although the white–black leadership ratio fluctuated over time, and by state). This coalition of black and white Republicans – the heirs of the Reconstruction-era GOP – became known as the Black-and-Tans. Near the end of the nineteenth century, as the ex-Confederate states began actively disenfranchising black voters, another coalition of Republicans in the South – known as the Lily-Whites – emerged to vie for leadership control with the Black-and-Tans. The Lily-Whites were white supremacists who believed that blacks should not hold positions of power in the GOP, arguing that the only way the party would become capable of winning elections in the South again would be to appeal directly to the new Jim Crow electorate – which was almost exclusively white. In essence, the Lily-Whites contended that the GOP would become "respectable" in the eyes of Southern white voters only if they showed themselves publicly to be a white party – something that could not happen if blacks held meaningful leadership positions. To be sure, the Lily-Whites had other (arguably, more important) incentives to make such a white supremacist argument: they wanted to be in control of patronage in their respective states instead of the Black-and-Tans. Yet, many Republicans (both North and South) found the argument persuasive, and it helped frame the battle between the two factions during the first half of the twentieth century.

While we cover the battles between the Lily-Whites and Black-and-Tans in detail in subsequent chapters, we also want to be able to systematically measure the variation in the factional conflict over time. To this end, we have collected data on the racial composition of delegations from the eleven ex-Confederate states to the Republican National Convention from 1868 through 1952. We argue that the conflict between the Lily-Whites and Black-and-Tans should have been fought largely with the prize of convention delegate seats in mind. Specifically, as voting restrictions took hold throughout the South and excluded nearly all blacks from voting or holding elected office, the GOP's electoral viability in the region withered away – and being a delegate to the national convention became the only remaining form of representative political office that most Southern Republicans could achieve. The racial composition of state GOP convention delegations in the South thus becomes a useful metric (and perhaps the only one) for systematically assessing Lily-White vs. Black-and-Tan control.

During this period, the names and hometowns of each delegate (both regular and alternate) seated at the Republican National Convention were published in the convention proceedings. Beyond these two basic pieces of demographic data, however, the proceedings do not provide any other information. Most importantly, they do not list the race of the individual delegates.[31] Hence, we turn to the US census, the most comprehensive dataset that *does* identify the race of nearly all US citizens.

As required in the constitution, the census has been executed every ten years since 1790.[32] The role of the census has changed over time, from focusing predominantly on providing population counts to collecting other statistics about US citizens – leading to a more expansive list of questions. However, the three-fifths compromise (reached during the constitutional convention) meant that measuring the racial makeup of the American population was (and would continue to be) an essential part of the census's mission, from the first census onward.[33] While the exact racial classifications and language used on the forms have changed over time,[34] the census is the most consistent and reliable historical source for identifying the race of individual American citizens.[35]

---

[31] The sole exception being a set of Southern state delegations (Florida, Mississippi, South Carolina, and Texas) printed in the proceedings of the 1896 convention: for these states, black delegates are identified as "colored" while white delegates receive no racial identification. See *Republican National Convention, St. Louis, June 16th to 18th, 1896* (St. Louis: I. Haas Publishing and Engraving Company, 1896), 175–210.

[32] Specifically, Article I, Paragraph 3, Section 2 of the Constitution of the United States: "The actual Enumeration shall be made within three Years after the first Meeting of the Congress of the United States, and within every subsequent Term of ten Years, in such Manner as they shall by Law direct."

[33] Margo J. Anderson, *The American Census: A Social History* (New Haven, CT: Yale University Press, 1988), 9–12.

[34] Race – together with age and sex – has been one of the few items consistently asked in every census. However, the option available to respondents has changed over time: in censuses collected between 1790 and 1840, information was collected by household and not individual – and a distinction was made between free white males, free white females, all other free persons, and slaves. After 1850 the Census Bureau began relying on a form that identified each individual person in a household, whereby each free individual was identified as being white, black, or mulatto. After the Civil War the distinction between free and slave was dropped, but the threefold definition of race remained in use. For the 1890 census, workers were given instructions as to how to further characterize black Americans (noting a distinction between black, mulatto, quadroon, and octoroon depending on the extent to which an individual was deemed to have "black blood"). The term "negro" was introduced in the 1900 census. The term "mulatto" was not included in the 1900 census but reappeared in 1910 and 1920. For the purposes of this study we identify any delegates whose census lists their race as any of the terms listed above as black. Margo J. Anderson, ed., *Encyclopedia of the U.S. Census* (Washington, DC: CQ Press, 2000), 19.

[35] As Anderson notes, the end of slavery and, thereby, the three-fifths compromise provides no reason to believe local Democratic Southern leaders would subsequently have an incentive to frustrate attempts by census workers to incorporate black Southerners; while black Southerners were banned from voting, after the Civil War they did count as full citizens, increasing the population count for the South and the number of House seats provided to Southern (solidly Democratic) states. See Anderson, *The American Census*, 72.

We have attempted to match each individual delegate listed in the convention proceedings to their original census forms. To do so, we used the online demographic aggregation search engine Ancestry.com, which allows us to search for historical records based on the (limited) information we have for each delegate: name, residence, and year in which the delegate lived in that town or city. Census records that match on name and hometown, and for which the matching census respondents were of voting age at the time of the convention, were accessed and the race listed on the census form was matched to the delegate. We tried to find other sources of information regarding the race of those delegates that we were unable to match to an original census form. Specifically, we looked for any references to the race of those particular delegates in primary or secondary historical sources.[36] As can be seen in Table 2.1 and Figure 2.5, we were able to identify the race of almost 84 percent of the 8,660 delegates included in the dataset. The extent of 'unknown' racial identification (16 percent) is not surprising given the limited biographical information in the proceedings: for example, a date (or even year) of birth for each delegate would dramatically increase the number of matching census forms, but the proceedings do not provide this information. Additionally, potential misspellings of names or hometowns in the proceedings, the census form, or both complicate the matching process further. Finally, with the exception of those elections that occurred in a year during which the census also took place, there is also a two- or four-year gap between the information provided in the proceedings and the most recent census: it is likely that some percentage of delegates may have moved inside or outside their state in that time, or may have even died.[37]

[36] These sources include any references to specific delegates in historical accounts of Republican party politics – during the Reconstruction era and beyond – that explicitly identify the race of individual delegates. Two books that were especially helpful in this regard were Eric Foner, *Freedom's Lawmakers: A Directory of Black Officeholders during Reconstruction* (Baton Rouge: Louisiana State University Press, 1996) and Hanes Walton, Jr., *Black Republicans: The Politics of the Black and Tans* (Metuchen, NJ: The Scarecrow Press, 1975). We also used lists of black delegates featured in newspaper articles or the *Negro Year Book*, a reference volume that appeared in eleven editions between 1912 and 1952. The *Negro Year Book* provided lists of black delegates by state for the 1912 through 1936 conventions in the following editions: 1912 and 1916 convention delegates (1918–19 edition, 208–10); 1920 (1921–22 edition, 183); 1924 (1925–26 edition, 245); 1928 (1931–32 edition, 92), 1932 and 1936 (1937–38 edition, 100–01). Monroe Work was the editor, and it was published by the Tuskegee Institute in Alabama.

[37] Finally, for delegates to the 1948 and 1952 conventions there is a limitation in that the US Census follows the "72 years" rule: individual census forms are not released until seventy-two years after the census was taken. As a result, the 1940 census is currently the last census that has been fully released. For the 1948 and 1952 conventions, delegate data is based on repeat delegates (that is, delegates who were also present at previous conventions) or on census data that was eight or twelve years old. As a result, coverage drops for these last conventions – from 8.9 percent and 11.2 percent of delegates for which a match could not be made in 1940 and 1944 to 12.1 percent and 21.6 percent in 1948 and 1952, respectively.

TABLE 2.1 *Racial division of Southern GOP convention delegates, 1868–1952*

Year	Total delegates	White delegates	Black delegates	Race unknown
1868	175	103	17	55
1872	319	166	101	52
1876	339	176	86	77
1880	369	179	132	58
1884	404	171	151	82
1888	428	173	145	110
1892	451	190	154	107
1896	436	197	155	84
1900	444	224	130	90
1904	517	283	130	104
1908	520	313	121	86
1912	504	330	113	61
1916	404	296	74	34
1920	384	268	69	47
1924	377	260	66	51
1928	352	243	66	43
1932	458	389	41	28
1936	330	263	37	30
1940	337	270	37	30
1944	348	275	34	39
1948	379	285	48	46
1952	385	279	23	83
Total	8,660	5,333	1,930	1,397

The number of delegates that could not be matched to a corresponding census form is also hampered by problems related to the 1890 census, which was the first to be counted and tabulated using electronic machines. As a result, no copies were made of the original census forms. A subsequent fire in 1921 in the Department of Commerce, where the 1890 census documents were stored outside of a fireproof vault, destroyed nearly all of the original forms.[38] For our purposes, this means that the data for delegates to the 1888 and 1892 conventions are particularly scarce. That is not to say that no data are available at all: delegates who were present at earlier or later conventions are frequently covered in the 1880 or 1900 censuses. Nonetheless, the percentage of delegates for whom we cannot identify race is high for these two convention years (see Figure 2.5).

While we would like to have racial categorizations for all Republican convention delegates, we have no reason to believe that the racial breakdown of the unknown category is biased in any way. Thus, we feel comfortable setting aside

[38] Robert L. Dorman, "The Creation and Destruction of the 1890 Federal Census," *The American Archivist* 71 (Fall–Winter 2008): 350–83.

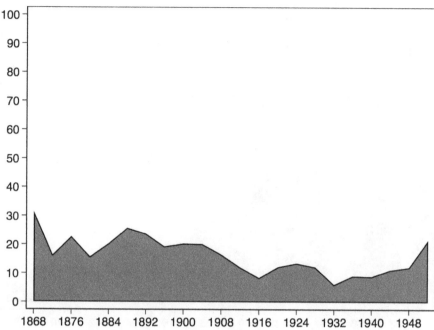

FIGURE 2.5 Percentage of Southern GOP delegates without racial identification, 1868–1952

the unknowns and focusing strictly on the delegates with known racial identities from here on out.

In Figure 2.6, we plot the percentage of Southern GOP convention delegates that were black (based on the summary statistics in Table 2.1). These data largely confirm the traditional perspective of the Lily-White takeover of the Southern Republican organizations in the late nineteenth and early twentieth centuries (and their success at slowly but surely pushing black Southerners out of the party in the decades that followed). While never constituting a majority, blacks consistently represented between 40 and 50 percent of Southern delegates at Republican National Conventions between 1880 and 1896. However, starting with the 1900 convention (the first after the realignment election of 1896), the percentage of black delegates began to drop considerably. Between 1916 and 1924, only around 20 percent of Southern GOP delegates were black. While the number increased slightly for the 1928 convention, black convention attendance suffered a lasting drop beginning with the 1932 convention. This decline can be attributed to a general development of Lily-White challenges across the South – initiated with President Herbert Hoover's blessing – which resulted in a dramatic change of fortunes for black representation.[39]

[39] See Donald J. Lisio, *Hoover, Blacks, and Lily-Whites: A Study of Southern Strategies* (Chapel Hill: University of North Carolina Press, 1985). Blacks in the North also began shifting into the

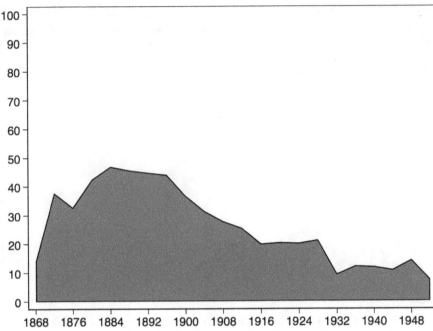

FIGURE 2.6 Percentage of Southern GOP convention delegates that were black, 1868–1952

However, as can be seen in Table 2.2 and Figure 2.7, these summary statistics disguise a set of important state-by-state distinctions: some states moved toward Lily-Whiteism considerably earlier, while others managed to avoid the Lily-White development through most of the first half of the twentieth century (or even entirely).

Four states – Tennessee, Arkansas, Louisiana, and Florida – had relatively low levels of black representation in their GOP convention delegations throughout the twentieth century. In Tennessee, black representation was always low – hitting a high point of just 38.2 percent in 1884 – but blacks still remained a (small) minority part of the state's delegations throughout this period. Arkansas maintained a sizable black representation in the late nineteenth century, peaking at 45.5 percent in 1888, but declined slowly thereafter – to the point where blacks disappeared entirely from the state delegation in 1920. Some degree of racial compromise emerged thereafter, but blacks remained a small proportion of the delegation (never rising even to 20 percent).

Democratic Party around this time. Most historians believe the 1936 election was the point at which a majority of blacks voted Democratic in presidential elections. See, for example, Nancy J. Weiss, *Farewell to the Party of Lincoln: Black Politics in the Age of FDR* (Princeton, NJ: Princeton University Press, 1983).

TABLE 2.2 *Percentage of Southern GOP national convention delegates that were black by state, 1868–1952*

	Alabama	Arkansas	Florida	Georgia	Louisiana	Mississippi	North Carolina	South Carolina	Tennessee	Texas	Virginia
1868	0.0	16.7	0.0	6.7	21.4	10.0	12.5	38.9	10.0	14.3	0.0
1872	30.0	10.0	25.0	41.9	45.5	45.5	29.6	65.4	20.0	33.3	45.9
1876	23.8	13.6	42.9	52.9	43.5	31.8	16.0	59.3	22.2	27.3	25.0
1880	48.6	35.0	46.7	63.9	56.0	34.5	42.3	56.0	26.3	22.2	37.1
1884	57.9	39.1	64.3	52.6	54.2	51.9	46.4	58.6	38.2	28.0	33.3
1888	65.8	45.5	42.9	60.5	50.0	44.4	25.9	75.0	16.1	44.1	31.7
1892	50.0	36.0	41.7	57.1	61.5	51.6	38.9	64.3	18.2	43.6	31.6
1896	51.4	23.1	53.3	62.5	61.9	64.5	40.6	69.4	7.5	38.2	25.0
1900	45.7	25.0	53.8	65.0	37.5	53.3	13.3	60.6	12.8	31.8	15.8
1904	25.6	26.9	47.1	43.2	16.3	63.2	11.6	69.0	8.3	43.9	9.5
1908	27.0	24.1	31.3	46.7	37.9	59.5	0.0	65.6	8.3	10.0	9.1
1912	14.3	20.0	28.6	48.1	24.2	55.6	0.0	78.8	5.3	18.6	2.2
1916	6.7	4.3	26.7	60.6	20.5	61.5	0.0	80.0	7.9	3.8	3.0
1920	7.4	0.0	30.0	71.4	28.6	47.8	0.0	80.0	6.5	8.7	0.0
1924	0.0	8.7	16.7	66.7	32.0	60.0	0.0	61.9	11.9	2.3	0.0
1928	0.0	16.7	5.9	69.7	16.7	60.0	0.0	63.6	12.1	0.0	0.0
1932	0.0	14.3	0.0	23.3	18.2	66.7	0.0	16.7	13.6	2.1	1.9
1936	0.0	15.0	0.0	18.5	13.0	83.3	0.0	42.1	10.3	0.0	0.0
1940	0.0	19.0	13.0	29.6	19.0	68.8	0.0	12.5	12.1	2.1	0.0
1944	0.0	10.0	13.8	56.5	13.0	72.7	0.0	0.0	9.1	1.7	0.0
1948	0.0	9.1	21.4	48.3	23.1	100.0	0.0	18.2	10.0	1.8	0.0
1952	0.0	11.1	3.2	26.7	11.1	88.9	0.0	0.0	6.3	0.0	0.0

Note: Percentages reflect known delegates only.

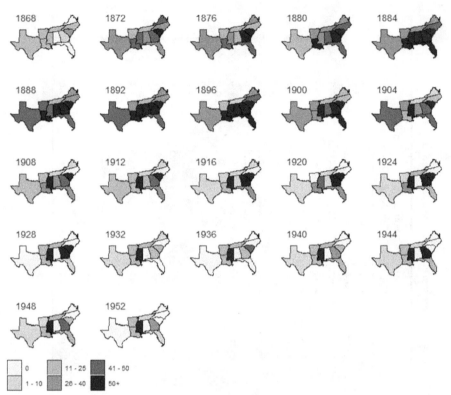

	0		11 - 25		41 - 50
	1 - 10		26 - 40		50+

FIGURE 2.7 Percentage of Southern GOP convention delegates that were black by state, 1868–1952

Similarly, Florida's delegation in the nineteenth century was generally between 40 and 50 percent black – and over 50 percent in three conventions through 1900; beginning in 1908, however, black representation started to decline. And after 1920, with the exception of 1948, the Florida delegation was never more than 20 percent black. Finally, in Louisiana, blacks dominated in the nineteenth century: between 1872 and 1896, blacks made up between 43 percent (in 1876) and 62 percent (in 1892) of the state's delegation. However, in 1900, black representation dropped to 37.5 percent. While whites were consistently the majority thereafter, some blacks remained in the Louisiana delegation in all subsequent conventions.

Unlike Arkansas, Tennessee, Louisiana, and Florida, many Southern states saw a period of significant black representation followed by major decline. For example, four states – Alabama, North Carolina, Texas, and Virginia – all at some point had GOP convention delegations with meaningful black representation, which dropped off considerably and permanently (or nearly so) in the late nineteenth and early twentieth centuries. For example, Alabama went from a high of nearly 66 percent black in 1888 to 27 percent in 1908. Black representation in subsequent conventions continued to drop until 1924, when no black delegates represented the state – which was the status quo thereafter. A similar pattern occurred in North Carolina, where as late as 1896 black representation was more than 40 percent; by 1908, it was zero, where it would remain from then on. In Texas, black representation was nearly 44 percent in 1904; it dropped markedly after that, to single digits (and sometimes zero) starting in 1916. Virginia saw considerable black representation early on (45.9 percent in 1872), but from 1880 on black representation dropped steadily; by 1904, it would hit single digits, and starting in 1920 – except for a small blip up in 1932 – it was zero thereafter.

In contrast, three states – South Carolina, Mississippi, and Georgia – mostly bucked the trend of Lily-Whiteism. In South Carolina, Lily-Whites did eventually take over the state's GOP delegation, but not until 1932. In every convention between 1872 and 1928, blacks made up at least half – and as much as 80 percent – of the state delegation. In Georgia, black influence waxed and waned over the period, with blacks constituting a majority of the state delegation from 1876 through 1900, again from 1916 through 1928, and yet again in 1944. Mississippi was even more unique; unlike any other Southern state, the Lily-Whites *never* displaced the Black-and-Tans during this period.[40] In fact, between 1892 and 1952, Mississippi's delegation was majority black with only one exception (1920, when 47.8 percent of delegates were black).

These data thus raise considerable questions. While it is true that Lily-White elements appear to take control of most state party organizations in this period, the data indicate that there was also considerable variation across states as to *when* these shifts took place. And control was not always permanent; backsliding sometimes occurred. A number of factors could have produced such state-level differentiation, including the specific timing and context of black exclusion from electoral participation, and (un)related shifts in preferences of national party leaders with regard to the different competing organizational groups. A better understanding of some of these factors, and their relation to Lily-White vs. Black-and-Tan dynamics over time, requires extensive case-study analysis of the individual states. We will do just this, by conducting a deep historical examination of the eleven ex-Confederate states in Chapters 7–9.

THE LILY-WHITE MOVEMENT AND THE DEVELOPMENT OF THE SOUTHERN GOP

Beyond categorizing the racial makeup of Southern state delegations to the Republican National Convention from 1868 to 1952, as a way of documenting

---

[40] The Black-and-Tans would finally be replaced by Lily-Whites in 1960.

how the composition of the Republican Party in the South changed over time, we believe these data provide a means to examine something bigger – namely, how the GOP began to emerge as a viable *electoral party* in the last half of the twentieth century. In this way, per the claim made by Lily-White leaders from the faction's inception, the battle between the Black-and-Tans and Lily-Whites was not just about executive patronage (and who would receive it), it was also about whether the Republican Party would develop as a viable alternative for the Southern (white) electorate after disfranchisement laws were passed.

More concretely, Lily-White leaders argued that with the emergence of voting restrictions (such as poll taxes and literacy tests) between 1888 and 1908 across the South, which successfully disenfranchised a large majority of black voters, the GOP's only recourse – if it wanted to actively contest (and win) elections in the new electoral environment – was to be an exclusively white-led party. Indeed, C. Vann Woodward argues that Lily-White leaders *favored* the adoption of voting restrictions, stating that "The Lily-white faction ... more or less openly welcomed the [disfranchisement] movement in the belief that the removal of the Negro would make the party respectable."[41] And "respectability," in this case, was synonymous with "white."[42]

Lily-White Republican leaders were not alone in their assessment that Southern whites would only support a party that was white in makeup. One particular case, in Mississippi, illustrates that at least some white Southern Democrats shared this understanding and feared that state GOP organizations under Lily-White control formed a threat to Democratic hegemony and the one-party system that emerged in the South after black disfranchisement. As Table 2.2 indicates, from the Grant era through the Coolidge era, the Black-and-Tans controlled the Mississippi GOP and consistently selected delegations to the Republican National Convention that were majority black. In the late 1920s, however, Black-and-Tan control was threatened for the first time.[43] A Lily-White faction in the state had emerged and received strong financial backing from important Mississippi businessmen. Perry Howard, who was black and the leader of the Black-and-Tans (and boss of the Mississippi GOP), was under indictment for selling federal patronage appointments

---

[41] C. Vann Woodward, *Origins of the New South, 1877–1913* (Baton Rouge: Louisiana State University Press, 1951), 324.

[42] This notion of respectability was widespread at the time. In 1928, for example, Horace A. Mann, a Tennessee politician, worked to recruit Democrats for Republican presidential nominee Herbert Hoover in the South – the so-called Hoovercrats. Mann stated the following in discussion with a Hoovercrat leader in Florida: "We are going to have a respectable party in every southern state and that means the elimination of the negro in so far as political activities and office holding is concerned." Quoted in Lisio, *Hoover, Blacks, and Lily-Whites*, 116–17.

[43] This section is based on David J. Ginzl, "Lily-Whites versus Black-and-Tans: Mississippi Republicans during the Hoover Administration," *Journal of Mississippi History* 42 (1980): 194–211; Neil R. McMillen, "Perry W. Howard, Boss of Black-and-Tan Republicanism in Mississippi, 1924–1960," *The Journal of Southern History* 48 (1982): 205–24.

(notably federal marshal positions) and faced conviction.[44] As a result, white Democratic leaders sprang into action. Colonel Frederick Sullens, editor of the *Jackson Daily News*, made clear what he believed was at stake: "A Republican party in Mississippi under the leadership of negroes offers no peril to white supremacy. A Republican party led by white men backed by almost limitless wealth and greed for power and prestige, would constitute a decided menace."[45] Key Democratic politicians in Mississippi – Governor Theodore Bilbo and US Senators Pat Harrison and Hubert Stephens – along with the Grand Dragon of the Ku Klux Klan supported Howard's acquittal. Moreover, as Neil McMillen writes, "lily-whites complained that 'influential Democrats,' in order to keep the Republican party black and perpetuate Democratic rule, raised money for Howard's defense."[46]

These Democratic efforts produced the desired result: Howard was acquitted and remained the boss of the Republican Party in Mississippi. Twelve jurors – all white and all Democrats – found for Howard, and did so, according to Sullens, based on the belief "that if a Republican party is to exist in Mississippi it is better to have it under the leadership of negroes than white men."[47] While the trial and overall federal scrutiny would cost Howard his career as a patronage broker, he would continue to guide the Mississippi GOP until 1960.[48] And the white Democrats in the state worked to ensure that this was so.

While this historical anecdote is suggestive, it raises a deeper question: was there in fact a systematic connection between the "whiteness" of the Republican Party and its electoral vote totals in the Jim Crow South? The data on the racial makeup of Southern states' GOP convention delegations offers an opportunity to examine these issues empirically. We believe that the whiteness – and hence, "respectability," in the vernacular of the time and place – of the Republican Party can be determined by examining the proportion of a state's Republican National Convention delegation that was white. We call this proportion – essentially 100 percent minus the percentages listed in Table 2.2 – the "Whiteness Index," which nicely captures the racial composition (or in this case, white composition) of a state's Republican Party by presidential election year at a time when other systematic measures simply do not exist. As Republican National Convention delegates were chosen at state conventions, which were made up of delegates chosen from county conventions, the black–white ratios should reasonably approximate the racial breakdown of the party in the

---

[44] For more on Perry Howard and the Republican Party in Mississippi, see Chapter 9.
[45] *Jackson Daily News*, March 27, 1929.   [46] McMillen, "Perry W. Howard," 218.
[47] *Jackson Daily News*, December 15, 1928.
[48] Indeed, Howard would be acquitted again in a second trial in the spring of 1929. Again, twelve white jurors found in his favor. See Ginzl, "Lily-Whites versus Black-and-Tans," 201; McMillen, "Perry W. Howard," 220.

state.[49] Thus, this Whiteness Index provides a continuous measure – from o to 100 – for all eleven Southern states in each presidential election year from 1868 to 1952.[50]

With our measure of whiteness established, we now investigate its relationship to GOP electoral support in the Jim Crow South. Specifically, we use the *Whiteness Index (WI)* as a key independent variable in the following regression equation:

$$GOPvote_{st} = \beta_0 + \beta_1 WI_{st-1} + \beta_2 Disfranchisement_{st} + \beta_3 WI_{st-1} \\ \times Disfranchisement_{st} + \alpha_s + \delta_t + \varepsilon_{st}$$

[49] To be sure, the Whiteness Index remains an indirect measure of the racial division within the broader state party at any given moment in time. However, as the histories of state party organizations in Part II show, changes in the index do correlate with specific historical events. For example, the Whiteness Index for North Carolina (see Figure 7.5) shows considerable black representation at the national convention, up through 1896. Subsequently, black representation drops dramatically until it reaches zero in 1908. This decline is in line with the history of the Republican Party in North Carolina, which represented a biracial coalition until the introduction of Jim Crow disenfranchisement laws in 1900. In 1902, Senator Jeter R. Pritchard (R-NC) began a campaign to exclude blacks entirely from the party – resulting in all- white delegations from 1908 onwards. For Arkansas, the Whiteness Index shows a peculiar development in which black representation declines to zero in 1920 but subsequently recovers to around 20 percent for most of the rest of the period (see Figure 8.2). This temporary drop coincides with the short-term takeover of the Arkansas GOP by Lily-White leader Gus Remmel in 1914. At the state convention in 1920, Remmel successfully blocked blacks from being nominated to the national convention, resulting in an all-white national delegation. However, Remmel died shortly after the 1920 elections, and Black-and-Tans leaders succeeded in regaining control of the state party and began sending black delegates to the national committee again from 1924 onwards. Finally, in Florida, a similar image of the decline and subsequent reappearance of black representation at the national convention emerges: through 1928, blacks made up at least some part of Florida's national convention delegation. In 1932 and 1936 black representation was zero, yet by 1940 black representation reappeared (see Figure 8.6). The cause of this reemergence of black delegates was the repeal of the poll tax in 1937. In subsequent years, black activists in the state began to mobilize black citizens to register to vote again and sent a rival delegation to the 1940 national convention. As part of a compromise, a small number of black delegates were seated at this and subsequent conventions.

[50] We note that our use of "whiteness" as an analytic concept to explain political behavior is not new. In contemporary American politics, as Ashley Jardina notes, "a large portion of whites actively identify with their racial group and support politics and candidates that they view as protecting whites' power and status." Ashley Jardina, *White Identity Politics* (Cambridge: Cambridge University Press, 2019), i. The 2016 presidential election has been viewed as one in which whiteness played a significant role, as Donald Trump successfully appealed to white consciousness – and threats posed to whites from non-whites – for political gain and, arguably, to achieve election. Trump, however, did not invent the use of whiteness in presidential politics. George Wallace (1968) and Pat Buchanan (1992), for example, both used whiteness to enhance their presidential bids and score some electoral successes – they just did not ride whiteness politics all the way to the White House, as Trump did. See John Sides, Michael Tesler, and Lynn Vavreck, "Donald Trump and the Rise of White Identity Politics," paper presented at the "2016 U.S. Presidential Election: Tumult at Home, Retreat Abroad?" conference, Mershon Center, Ohio State University, November 2017.

TABLE 2.3 *Disfranchisement provisions in the South, by state and year*

	Type	Years	Chief form
Alabama	1, 5, 6, 8	1901	Constitutional
Arkansas	1, 4	1891–92	Statutory
Florida	1, 3	1889	Statutory
Georgia	5, 6, 7, 8	1908	Constitutional
Louisiana	1, 2, 4, 5, 6, 8	1897–98	Constitutional
Mississippi	1, 4, 5, 7	1890	Constitutional
North Carolina	1, 2, 3, 5, 6, 8	1899–1900	Constitutional
South Carolina	1, 2, 5, 7	1894–95	Constitutional
Tennessee	1, 2, 4	1889–90	Statutory
Texas	1, 4	1902–03	Statutory
Virginia	1, 5, 6, 7	1902	Constitutional

Source: J. Morgan Kousser, *The Shaping of Southern Politics: Suffrage Restrictions and the Establishment of the One-Party South, 1880–1910* (New Haven, CT: Yale University Press, 1974). "Type" and "years" taken from page 239; "chief form" based on descriptions throughout the book. On the latter, see also Monroe N. Work, ed., *Negro Year Book: An Annual Encyclopedia of the Negro, 1931–1932* (Tuskegee, AL: Negro Year Book Publishing Co., 1931), 111–12.
Note: (1) = poll tax; (2) = registration law; (3) = multiple box law; (4) = secret ballot; (5) = literacy test; (6) = property test; (7) = understanding clause; (8) = grandfather clause

where *GOPvote* represents the dependent variable, or outcome to be explained. We will examine Republican Party vote percentage by state and year in several ways: at the presidential level, the congressional level, the gubernatorial level, and as a composite (an average of the former three).[51] We lag the Whiteness Index one time period (presidential election year), believing that four years was enough time for a Southern voter to assess the "respectability" of the Republican Party when he went to the polls.[52] Thus, given the distribution of our convention data (1868 through 1952), our dependent variable extends from 1872 through 1956.

We also incorporate a *Disfranchisement* variable, which takes a value of 1 if voting restrictions (intended to disenfranchise black voters) were in place, and 0 otherwise. These voting restrictions took various forms and were adopted in different Southern states at different times. Table 2.3, based on data collected by J. Morgan Kousser, summarizes disfranchisement provisions by state.[53] Some (like the grandfather clause) were eliminated in fairly short order, but

---

[51] We use the David "Party Strength" data and measures here.

[52] Note that our results hold if we lag Whiteness Index two or three time periods, or use the average of the last three time periods.

[53] See Kousser, *The Shaping of Southern Politics*, 238–40. Note that we choose to begin our count of disfranchisement provisions with the first "high tide" (per Kousser) in the disfranchisement movement, which extended from 1888 to 1893. This ignores a small number of provisions enacted in Georgia, South Carolina, and Virginia before then (between 1871 and 1882).

most were in place during the entirety of our time period.[54] As blacks were the GOP's core constituency in the South after the Civil War, disfranchisement provisions should significantly cut into the Republican Party's electoral vote totals (or $\beta_2 < 0$).

A key variable will be the interaction of the *Whiteness Index* and *Disfranchisement*. This interaction allows us to examine how the whiteness of the Republican Party affected the GOP's electoral vote totals, *once voting restrictions were in place and most blacks were effectively disenfranchised*. Prior to the onset of voting restrictions, during Reconstruction and Redemption, we should observe a negative relationship between the *Whiteness Index* and our measures of GOP vote percentage (or $\beta_1 < 0$). This is because black electoral participation, and support for the Republican Party, should be reflected in a greater proportion of black delegates serving as Republican National Convention delegates. After the adoption of voting restrictions, however, black electoral participation approached zero in much of the South. Thus, for the GOP to regain electoral support, it had to come from the *eligible electorate* – Southern whites. And Southern whites, per our hypothesis about respectability, would consider voting Republican only if the GOP took steps to cast itself as a white party. And the GOP did this in a visible way, by making sure its public leaders – such as Republican National Convention delegates – were exclusively (or nearly so) white. Thus, after the onset of voting restrictions, we should observe a positive relationship between the *Whiteness Index* and our measures of GOP vote percentage (or $\beta_3 + \beta_1 > 0$). Finally, we include fixed effects to control for unobserved variation at the state level (α_s) and by presidential-election year (δ_t).

Ordinary least squares (OLS) regression results appear in Table 2.4, in four columns. We find evidence to support all of our hypotheses – regardless of which dependent variable we use. First, the years in which disfranchising provisions were in effect had a significant, negative effect on the average Republican vote tally – reducing the GOP vote between 26 and 31.5 percentage points, depending on the model. This decline can be interpreted almost exclusively as the elimination of the black vote in the South. Second, the relationship between the whiteness of the Republican Party and its share of the vote is consistent with our hypotheses: negative and significant before the advent of voting restrictions and positive and significant after. For ease of interpretation, we explore this relationship visually in Figures 2.8 and 2.9, based on the first column of regression results (presidential vote).

The average marginal effects of the Whiteness Index (Lagged) on GOP presidential vote are illustrated in Figure 2.8. Prior to disfranchisement, there was a −0.23 percentage-point change ($p < .01$) in GOP presidential vote for a one percentage-point increase in Whiteness Index (Lagged). After

---

[54] The US Supreme Court found the grandfather clause to be unconstitutional in *Guinn* v. *United States* (1915).

TABLE 2.4 *Estimating Republican electoral support in the South, 1872–1956*

	Presidential vote	Congressional vote	Governor vote	Composite vote
Whiteness Index (Lagged)	-0.23**	-0.29***	-0.23*	-0.23***
	(0.08)	(0.08)	(0.11)	(0.07)
Disfranchisement	-26.42***	-31.52***	-22.98***	-26.04***
	(4.75)	(4.66)	(6.79)	(4.35)
WI (Lagged) * Disfranchisement	0.35***	0.45***	0.35***	0.36***
	(0.07)	(0.07)	(0.11)	(0.07)
Constant	84.31***	85.01***	74.95***	77.76***
	(7.75)	(7.60)	(11.09)	(7.10)
N	242	242	242	242
F	27.50***	29.67***	13.58***	29.78***
R^2	0.82	0.83	0.69	0.83

Note: OLS coefficients with standard errors in parentheses. All models include both state and year fixed effects (excluded categories: Virginia, 1872).

$*p < .05, **p < .01, ***p < .001$

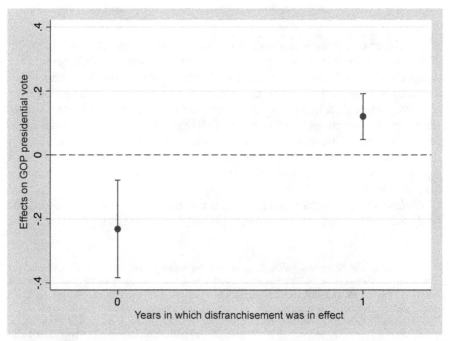

FIGURE 2.8 Average marginal effects of Whiteness Index (Lagged) on GOP presidential vote

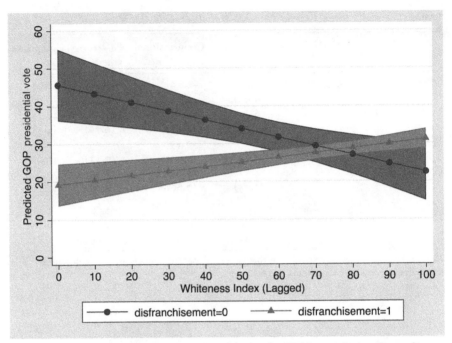

FIGURE 2.9 Predicted GOP presidential vote by level of Whiteness Index (Lagged)

disfranchisement, there was a 0.12 percentage-point change ($p < .001$) in GOP presidential vote for a one percentage-point increase in Whiteness Index (Lagged). The predicted GOP presidential vote by level of the Whiteness Index (Lagged) is illustrated in Figure 2.9. The two data series cross, based on their negative (before disfranchisement) and positive (after disfranchisement) slopes. After voting restrictions were in place, a change from one standard deviation below the mean Whiteness Index (Lagged) to one standard deviation above it resulted in a 5.98 percentage-point increase in GOP presidential vote.[55] This represents more than one-third of a standard deviation change in GOP presidential vote.[56]

We find similar results when looking at the marginal effects and plotting the predicted GOP support for congressional vote, governor vote, and the

[55] The mean of the Whiteness Index (Lagged) for the entire period (N=242) is 71.51 and the standard deviation is 23.83. The mean of the Whiteness Index (Lagged) under disfranchisement (N=171) is 75.18 and the standard deviation is 24.91. The mean of the Whiteness Index (Lagged) prior to disfranchisement (N=71) is 62.67 and the standard deviation is 18.34.
[56] The mean of GOP presidential vote for the entire period (N=242) is 29.07 and the standard deviation is 16.01. The mean of GOP presidential vote under disfranchisement (N=171) is 25.25 and the standard deviation is 15.86. The mean of GOP presidential vote prior to disfranchisement (N=71) is 38.27 and the standard deviation is 12.26.

composite vote. (See Figures A2.2 to A2.7 in the Appendix to this chapter.) Overall, the model fits are better for the federal elections (president and Congress) than the state elections (governor). This makes sense, as scholars have noted that white Southern movement to the Republican Party occurred first at the federal level before trickling down to the state and local levels.[57]

We can also disaggregate the presidential vote results by area within the South. Historians and political scientists typically subclassify the region as Deep South (Alabama, Georgia, Louisiana, Mississippi, and South Carolina) or Outer South (Arkansas, Florida, North Carolina, Tennessee, Texas, and Virginia).[58] The differences between the two subregions were extensive. As Robert Mickey elaborates:

For most of the twentieth century, the populations of the Deep South states were more rural and featured a greater share of blacks, their economies were more dominated by labor-repressive agriculture and were less industrialized, their politics were marked by almost a total absence of Republican or other ruling party challengers, their white populations seemed the most committed to white supremacy, and they had the weakest infrastructure for black insurgency.[59]

These differences between the states of the Deep South and the Outer South thus may have led to differences in the ways they reacted to changes in the Republican Party during the Jim Crow era. That is, a GOP that was eschewing Reconstruction-era traditions and establishing a new (lily-white) approach to leadership may have led white voters in different subregions to react differently from an electoral perspective. V. O. Key, for example, writing around the middle of the twentieth century, did not believe the South – as a unit – was as "solid" for the Democrat Party as many observers believed. Key saw the states of the Deep South to be "the bulwarks of Democratic strength."[60] In contrast, he noted that the states of the Outer South "manifest a considerably higher degree of freedom from preoccupation with the race question than do the states of the Deep South."[61]

---

[57] See, for example, David Lublin, *The Republican South: Democratization and Partisan Change* (Princeton, NJ: Princeton University Press, 2004), 33–65.

[58] See Robert Mickey, *Paths Out of Dixie: The Democratization of Authoritarian Enclaves in America's Deep South, 1944–1972* (Princeton, NJ: Princeton University Press, 2015), 25. The Outer South is sometimes called the Peripheral South. See Earl Black and Merle Black, *The Rise of Southern Republicans* (Cambridge, MA: Harvard University Press, 2002), 17.

[59] Mickey, *Paths Out of Dixie*, 25. V. O. Key makes a similar argument about the Deep South states, via a discussion of the "black belt," those counties in which blacks constituted a substantial proportion of the population. Key states: "It is the whites of the black belts who have the deepest and most immediate concern about the maintenance of white supremacy." V. O. Key, Jr., *Southern Politics in State and Nation* (New York: Knopf, 1949), 5.

[60] Key, *Southern Politics*, 9.   [61] Ibid., 669.

TABLE 2.5 *Estimating GOP presidential vote in the South by region, 1872–1956*

	Outer South	Deep South
Whiteness Index (Lagged)	−0.05	−0.42[**]
	(0.11)	(0.14)
Disfranchisement	−35.16[***]	−24.73[***]
	(9.09)	(7.22)
WI (Lagged) Disfranchisement	0.37[**]	0.45[**]
	(0.13)	(0.15)
Constant	57.60[***]	99.42[***]
	(10.22)	(13.05)
N	132	110
F	17.67[***]	13.93[***]
R^2	0.83	0.83

Note: OLS coefficients with standard errors in parentheses. All models include both state and year fixed effects (excluded categories: Virginia, 1872).
$^*p < .05, ^{**}p < .01, ^{***}p < .001$

Thus, we estimate the same OLS regression model on presidential vote as before, but now on two subgroups: the states of the Deep South and the states of the Outer South. Regression results appear in Table 2.5, in two columns. The relationship between the whiteness of the GOP and its share of the presidential vote is more complex than before, and not simply negative and significant (in both Southern subregions) before the advent of voting restrictions and positive and significant after. For ease of interpretation, we explore this relationship visually in Figures 2.10, 2.11, and 2.12.

The average marginal effects of the Whiteness Index (Lagged) on GOP presidential vote for both the Deep South and the Outer South are illustrated in Figure 2.10. For the Deep South, prior to disfranchisement, there was a −0.42 percentage-point change ($p < .01$) in GOP presidential vote for a one percentage-point increase in the Whiteness Index (Lagged). After disfranchisement, there was a 0.03 percentage-point change ($p < .46$) in GOP presidential vote for a one percentage-point increase in the Whiteness Index (Lagged). Thus, in the Deep South – with a higher percentage of blacks in the population – a whiter party was an extreme disadvantage before disfranchisement, but a whiter party provided no significant advantage after disfranchisement. The opposite proves to be true for the Outer South. Prior to disfranchisement, there was a −0.05 percentage-point change ($p < .63$) in GOP presidential vote for a one percentage-point increase in the Whiteness Index (Lagged). After disfranchisement, there was a 0.32 percentage-point change ($p < .001$) in GOP presidential vote for a one percentage-point increase in the Whiteness Index (Lagged). Thus, for states in the Outer South, a whiter party provided no significant advantage (or disadvantage) before disfranchisement,

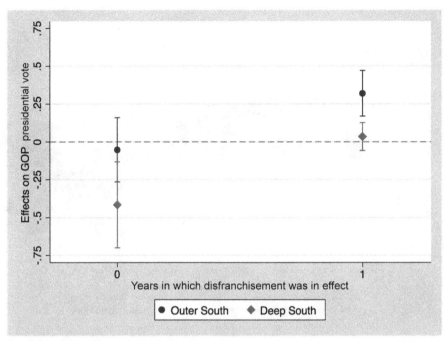

FIGURE 2.10 Average marginal effects of Whiteness Index (Lagged) on GOP presidential vote, Outer South versus Deep South

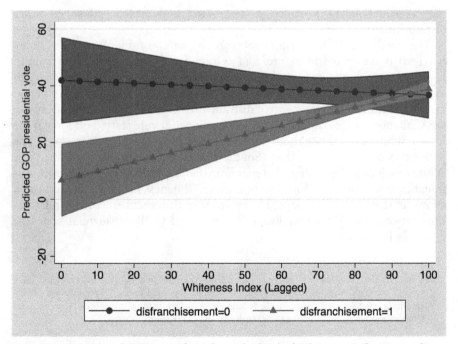

FIGURE 2.11 Predicted GOP presidential vote by level of Whiteness Index (Lagged), Outer South

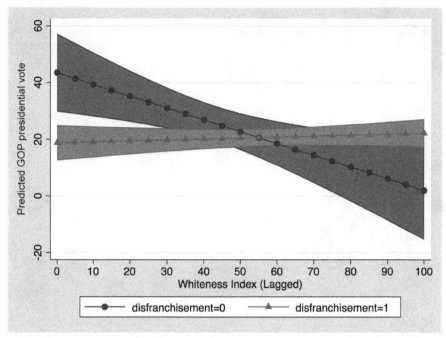

FIGURE 2.12 Predicted GOP presidential vote by level of Whiteness Index (Lagged), Deep South

but a whiter party provided a significant and sizable advantage after disfranchisement.[62]

The predicted GOP presidential vote by level of the Whiteness Index (Lagged) is illustrated in Figure 2.11 (Outer South) and 2.12 (Deep South). For the Outer South, the relationship between the Whiteness Index (Lagged) and Republican Party presidential vote was relatively high and flat before disfranchisement. However, after disfranchisement, the relationship between the Whiteness Index (Lagged) and GOP presidential vote started off low (at the lowest Whiteness Index values) and had a relatively steep, positive slope. The opposite was true in the Deep South. There, the relationship between the Whiteness Index (Lagged) and Republican Party presidential vote before disfranchisement started off high (at the highest Whiteness Index values) and had a relatively steep, negative slope. However, after disfranchisement, the relationship between the Whiteness Index (Lagged) and GOP presidential vote was relatively low and flat.

---

[62] We find similar results when looking at the marginal effects and plotting the predicted GOP support for congressional vote and governor vote. See Table A2.2 for the OLS regression results. Overall, the model fits are better for the federal elections (president and Congress) than the state elections (governor) in both the Outer South and the Deep South.

Overall, in the Outer South, after voting restrictions were in place, a change from one standard deviation below the mean Whiteness Index (Lagged) to one standard deviation above it resulted in an 8.32 percentage-point increase in Republican Party presidential vote.[63] This represents more than one-half of a standard deviation change in GOP presidential vote. By contrast, in the Deep South, after voting restrictions were in place, a change from one standard deviation below the mean Whiteness Index (Lagged) to one standard deviation above it resulted in a 1.84 percentage point increase in Republican Party presidential vote. This represents just over one-tenth of a standard deviation change in GOP presidential vote.

These results comport with the historical expectations of Key and others. Prior to disenfranchisement, a whiter GOP hurt the party in the states of the Deep South, where black voters were a much larger part of the population than in the states of the Outer South. After disfranchisement laws were introduced, the whitening of the Republican Party had its greatest impact in the states of the Outer South, where the baggage of the Reconstruction era was not as entrenched. White voters in the Outer South were more willing to vote for the GOP based upon a visible change in the racial composition of the party leadership. This was not true in the Deep South, where a deeply ingrained racial consciousness was present and white voters had long viewed the GOP as the party of "Negro domination." A whitening of the Republican Party leadership was not going to easily wipe away those long-standing beliefs. More had to happen before voters in the Deep South would view the GOP as a viable electoral option.

To summarize, variation in both the onset of disfranchisement and the Whiteness Index among the Southern states allows us to identify the effect of GOP leaders "whitening" the party in the post-disfranchisement era. The takeaway is this: a whitening of the party – by moving toward Lily-Whiteism – produced a significant vote gain for the GOP after disfranchisement. Once voting restrictions effectively removed blacks from the eligible Southern electorate, the Republican Party was able to slowly reemerge as a viable electoral party – more so in the Outer South – by excluding blacks from leadership positions, thus satisfying the "respectability" condition of the new, nearly exclusively white Southern electorate.[64]

[63] The mean of the Whiteness Index (Lagged) for the Outer South under disfranchisement (N=94) is 87.78 and the standard deviation is 13.78. Thus, we actually measure the high end up through 100 (whereas a one standard deviation move above the mean would extend beyond 100). The mean of the Whiteness Index (Lagged) for the Deep South under disfranchisement (N=77) is 59.80 and the standard deviation is 26.82.

[64] We also find a similar relationship when looking beyond GOP vote totals and focusing on a particular set of GOP electoral "wins." Note, though, that the Republican Party only began winning consistently in the South after our period of analysis here (see Figures 6.3 through 6.6 in Chapter 6). But there were enough GOP wins in presidential elections through 1956, by state, to perform a systematic analysis. We thus replicated our presidential-election model, but instead of

More generally, we consider this whitening of the Republican Party in the South as a necessary condition in the GOP's electoral growth and eventual dominance in the former Confederacy. By becoming a Lily-White party, the Republicans achieved some electoral gains, especially in the Outer South. But this move to Lily-Whiteism, by itself, was not sufficient. In order for those electoral gains to spread to the Deep South and grow generally such that the GOP could command a majority of votes throughout *all* areas of the South, a number of other things had to occur. For example, the national Democratic Party had to move leftward on the issue of civil rights. And the national Republican Party had to continue emphasizing its economic-conservatism credentials while moving rightward on civil rights (first explicitly in 1964 during Goldwater's presidential campaign and implicitly thereafter). Indeed, the Republicans had to become the broadly accepted party of racial conservatism before they could make a significant electoral breakthrough in the Deep South.

CONCLUSION

Our goal in this chapter was to set the stage for the analytical history that we present in Parts I and II of the book. We first discussed the various data and measures that we will use, from the standard party strength measures to our original racial composition measure of the Southern state delegations to the Republican National Convention. We then explained how apportionment of Southern delegates was determined (and why the slave states of the South received convention delegates at all in an anti-slavery party), discussed how the size of Southern delegations fluctuated over time, and explained why the South was able to maintain a sizable presence at Republican National Conventions while not providing the party with anything on election day. Finally, we engaged the basic "so what?" question, by explaining why a focus on factional GOP politics in the South in the late nineteenth and early twentieth centuries

GOP vote percentage as the dependent variable, we specified a binary variable for whether the Republican Party candidate won the election in the state (1) or not (0). A linear probability model reveals the same relationship between the Whiteness Index (Lagged), conditioned by disfranchisement, and the likelihood of the GOP winning: negative before disfranchisement and positive after. The average marginal effects, however, do not meet standard levels of statistical significance ($p < .173$ for the pre-disfranchisement era and $p < .175$ for the post-disfranchisement era). Digging deeper, we do find, though, that the predictive margins reach statistical significance ($p < .05$) for Whiteness Index (Lagged) values of 55 percent and greater. In effect, for every 5 percentage-point increase in the Whiteness Index (Lagged), the probability of a Republican winning a Southern state in the period after the introduction of disfranchisement laws increases by 0.79 percentage points. At a Whiteness Index (Lagged) of 100 percent in this period, a Republican presidential candidate has a 15.13 percent chance of winning a Southern state. While not a huge likelihood, the ability of the GOP to win in the South during this era – when the party was long seen by generations of Southerners as the "black party" and the party that initiated the "War of Northern Aggression" – is meaningful. And it was achieved by the Republican Party going Lily-White.

matters. Our answer was: to understand the rise of the Republican Party as an electoral force in the South in the second half of the twentieth century, we must understand the development of the Southern GOP in the prior decades. And, more to the point, we find in a multivariate analysis that the Republican Party in the South grew electorally more quickly the "whiter" it became – especially in the Outer South. In effect, the GOP started to become a viable second option to (white) voters in the Jim Crow South once it became "respectable" (i.e., "white") in their eyes.

With these preliminaries completed, we now turn to the meat of the book: an analytical history of the Republican Party in the South at the federal level (Part I: Chapters 3 to 6) and within the individual states (Part II: Chapters 7 to 9).

Appendix to Chapter 2

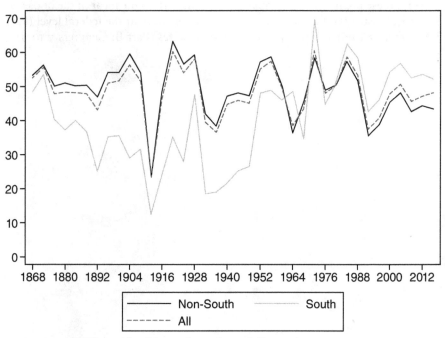

FIGURE A2.1 GOP presidential vote by region, 1868–2016

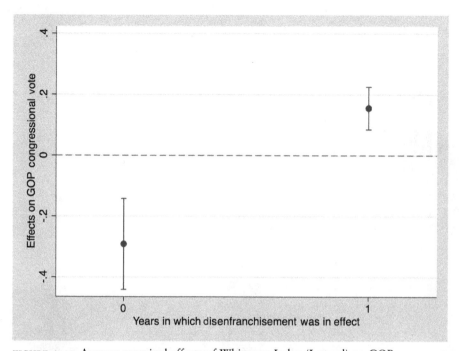

FIGURE A2.2 Average marginal effects of Whiteness Index (Lagged) on GOP congressional vote
Note: This figure corresponds to the second column of regression results in Table 2.4.

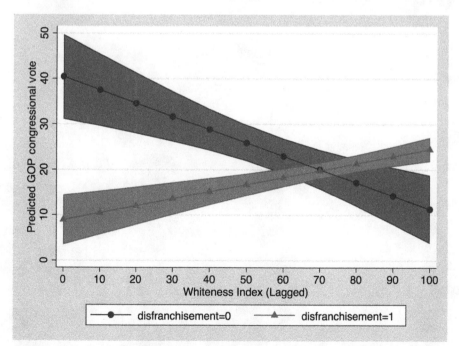

FIGURE A2.3 Predicted GOP congressional vote by level of Whiteness Index (Lagged)
Note: This figure corresponds to the second column of regression results in Table 2.4.

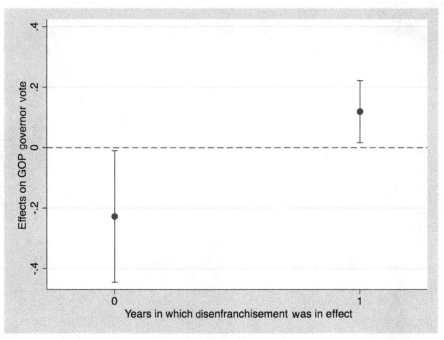

FIGURE A2.4 Average marginal effects of Whiteness Index (Lagged) on GOP
governor vote
Note: This figure corresponds to the third column of regression results in Table 2.4.

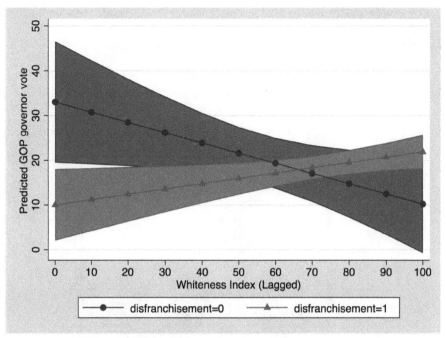

FIGURE A2.5 Predicted GOP governor vote by level of Whiteness Index (Lagged)
Note: This figure corresponds to the third column of regression results in Table 2.4.

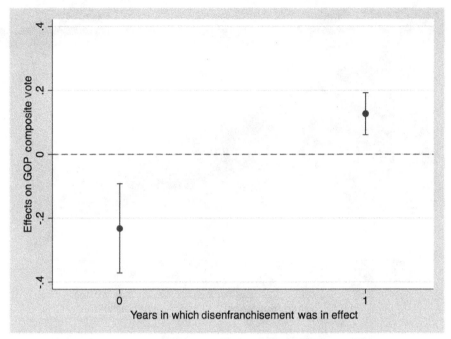

FIGURE A2.6 Average marginal effects of Whiteness Index (Lagged) on GOP composite vote
Note: This figure corresponds to the fourth column of regression results in Table 2.4.

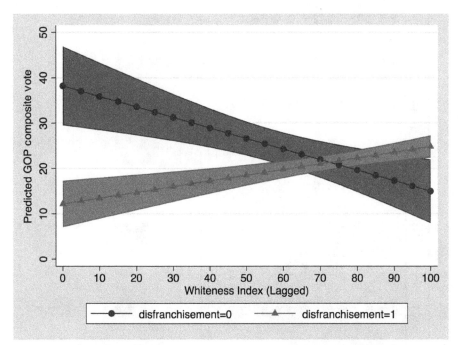

FIGURE A2.7 Predicted GOP composite vote by level of Whiteness Index (Lagged)
Note: This figure corresponds to the fourth column of regression results in Table 2.4.

TABLE A2.1 *Southern Republican National Convention delegates by state, 1856–1968*

	1856	1860	1864	1868	1872	1876	1880	1884	1888	1892	1896	1900	1904	1908	1912
Alabama				18	20	20	20	20	20	22	22	22	22	22	24
Arkansas			10	10	12	12	12	14	14	16	16	16	18	18	18
Florida				6	8	8	8	8	8	8	8	8	6	10	12
Georgia				18	22	22	22	24	24	26	26	26	26	26	28
Louisiana			14	14	16	16	16	16	16	16	16	16	18	18	20
Mississippi				14	16	20	16	18	18	18	18	18	20	20	20
North Carolina				18	20	20	20	22	22	22	22	22	24	24	24
South Carolina				12	14	14	14	18	18	18	18	18	18	18	18
Tennessee			15	20	24	24	24	24	24	24	24	24	24	24	24
Texas		6		12	16	16	16	26	26	30	30	30	36	36	40
Virginia		23		20	22	22	22	24	24	24	24	24	24	24	24
South Total	0	29	39	162	190	190	190	214	214	224	224	224	236	240	252
Total Delegates	567	466	519	650	752	756	756	820	832	906	924	926	994	980	1078
Percent South	0.0	6.2	7.5	24.9	25.3	25.1	25.1	26.1	25.7	24.7	24.2	24.2	23.7	24.5	23.4

	1916	1920	1924	1928	1932	1936	1940	1944	1948	1952	1956	1960	1964	1968
Alabama	16	14	16	15	19	13	13	14	14	14	21	22	20	26
Arkansas	15	13	14	11	15	11	12	12	14	11	16	16	12	18
Florida	8	8	10	10	16	12	12	15	16	18	26	26	34	34
Georgia	17	17	18	16	16	14	14	14	16	17	23	24	24	30
Louisiana	12	12	13	12	12	12	12	13	13	15	20	26	20	26
Mississippi	12	12	12	12	11	11	11	6	8	5	15	12	13	20
North Carolina	21	22	22	20	28	23	23	25	26	26	28	28	26	26
South Carolina	11	11	11	11	10	10	10	4	6	6	16	13	16	22
Tennessee	21	20	27	19	24	17	18	19	22	20	28	28	28	28
Texas	26	23	23	26	49	25	26	33	33	38	54	54	56	56
Virginia	15	15	17	15	25	17	18	19	21	23	30	30	30	24
South Total	174	167	183	167	225	165	169	174	189	193	277	279	279	310
Total Delegates	987	984	1109	1089	1154	1003	1000	1059	1094	1206	1323	1331	1308	1333
Percent South	17.6	17.0	16.5	15.3	19.5	16.5	16.9	16.4	17.3	16.0	20.9	21.0	21.3	23.3

TABLE A2.2 *Estimating Republican electoral support in the South by region, 1872–1956*

	Outer South		Deep South	
	Congressional vote	Governor vote	Congressional vote	Governor vote
Whiteness Index (Lagged)	−0.19	−0.30	−0.43[***]	−0.24
	(0.11)	(0.20)	(0.12)	(0.15)
Disfranchisement	−49.21[***]	−49.59[**]	−23.79[***]	−17.25[*]
	(9.17)	(16.81)	(6.00)	(7.67)
WI (Lagged) [*] Disfranchisement	0.60[***]	0.68[**]	0.48[***]	0.24
	(0.17)	(0.23)	(0.12)	(0.16)
Constant	62.28[***]	71.00[***]	99.48[***]	79.19[***]
	(10.30)	(18.89)	(10.84)	(13.87)
N	132	132	110	110
F	19.80[***]	4.62[***]	19.94[***]	10.46[***]
R^2	0.85	0.57	0.87	0.78

Note: OLS coefficients with standard errors in parentheses. All models include both state and year fixed effects (excluded categories: Virginia, 1872).

[*]$p < .05$, [**]$p < .01$, [***]$p < .001$

PART I

THE SOUTH AND NATIONAL REPUBLICAN PARTY POLITICS, 1865–1968

During and after the Civil War, the process of determining how the ex-Confederate states would be reincorporated into the Union was largely an intra-Republican Party question. While several approaches were proposed – among them, by Presidents Abraham Lincoln and Andrew Johnson – the eventual outcome was the approach preferred by Radical Republicans in Congress, in which the Southern states had to comply with a number of requirements in order to be readmitted, including drawing up new constitutions that guaranteed voting rights for freedmen and (often) placing restrictions on political participation and office holding for those whites who had been directly involved in the Confederacy. This approach to Reconstruction briefly served the GOP well in electoral terms: for a few years the Republican Party was dominant in the South, winning unified control of government in nearly all Southern states in the late 1860s.

However, this Republican electoral success was largely the product of the artificial majorities created by the Reconstruction design. Indeed, GOP success in the South proved fleeting; as white Southern voters were reincorporated into the franchise, and Democrats framed political conflict along racial lines, Republicans saw their electoral performance decline dramatically. This decline was also affected by terror groups who aligned with Southern Democrats – such as the White League and the Red Shirts – who attacked black voters and Republican politicians with the goal of keeping blacks from the polling place. As a result, Democrats regained ground quickly: by 1877 the party had won back unified control of every ex-Confederate state.

In the two decades that followed this Democratic "redemption" of the South, national Republican leaders – in particular presidents – did not give up on the region. Indeed, Presidents Hayes, Arthur, and Harrison all engaged in attempts at turning the electoral tide for the Southern GOP. While their strategies were different, their goal was the same: to make the Republican Party acceptable to white Southerners. Such attempts proved futile, however, and those same presidents often abandoned their Southern strategies in advance of elections, when they readopted "Bloody Shirt" rhetoric aimed at mobilizing Republican voters in the North.

While Southern GOP organizations struggled to compete in elections, Southern party leaders remained relevant in one crucial way: their continued presence at national conventions. Under the rules as they existed in the nineteenth century, states' representation at the Republican National Convention was based on the size of their congressional delegation – regardless of whether those members of Congress were Republicans or Democrats. As a result, the South maintained sizable representation at GOP national conventions – generally around 25 percent of all Republican delegates – while providing little to nothing to the party on election day.

The combination of sizable Southern representation at national conventions and a lack of electoral strength at home introduced a new political possibility: presidential candidates (including presidents up for reelection) could attempt to win support from Southern delegates by providing them with federal patronage or bribes and thereby gain a reliable and substantial basis of votes at the national convention. After the election of 1896, with the Republican Party in ascendancy nationally but with its electoral performance declining in the South, this perception of Southern party organizations as a set of "rotten boroughs" became commonplace. Indeed, during the "System of 1896" a consistent image emerged: presidential candidates, including William McKinley, Theodore Roosevelt, William Howard Taft, Calvin Coolidge, and Herbert Hoover, all relied on this version of a Southern strategy to help ensure their (re-)nomination at often unpredictable national conventions. In response, their political opponents within the party began to openly call for a reduction in the size of Southern delegations. Thus, the South became an often controversial, but always relevant, element in national Republican politics.

At the same time, national leaders never entirely abandoned hope for a Southern resurgence, though their (frequently half-hearted) attempts at reinvigorating the party in the former Confederacy were rarely successful. In particular, Presidents Warren G. Harding, Hoover and, to a lesser extent, Roosevelt attempted to replace some of the corrupt party organizations with new ones built around handpicked local leaders who were deemed "high quality" and were nearly always white. While those attempts largely failed, they did place these presidents at the center of major clashes between Black-and-Tan and Lily-White factions over control of state party organizations.

After the 1932 election, with the Republican Party in significant decline nationally, the South became less relevant to the GOP's intra-party politics. Without federal patronage, Republican presidential candidates had fewer tools to appeal to local party bosses, and with the party facing broader electoral difficulties, improving its performance in the South was not a priority. This changed by the end of the 1940s. With black voters now a considerable (and growing) part of the national Democratic Party's electoral coalition, the Southern Democrats' position in the party had become increasingly difficult to maintain. National Republicans sought to take advantage of this Democratic schism by, once again, appealing directly to white Southerners. The GOP achieved some success in this regard, as it began to actively compete in – and win some – Southern states in presidential elections from 1952 onwards. But Republicans also found that this strategy involved risk: appealing to Southern whites in practice meant, at the very least, condoning segregation, which was highly controversial within the party and unappealing to many GOP voters outside of the South. By 1968, however, Richard Nixon's campaign finally found a Southern strategy that managed to appeal to Southern whites but did not alienate voters elsewhere: rather than support segregation, Nixon promised to slow down the civil-rights process while engaging in a broader law-and-order campaign that appealed to both Southerners and non-Southerners alike. This created a Southern-strategy blueprint that the GOP would follow in the 1970s and beyond.

3

The Rise and Fall of a Republican South, 1865–1877

The dozen years following the Civil War were an eventful time for the Republican Party in the South.[1] In that relatively short period, Southern Republican fortunes changed dramatically, as the party went from being effectively non-existent in the war's immediate aftermath, to being electorally supreme across much of the ex-Confederacy during the late 1860s and early 1870s, to being driven into minority status in all of the Reconstructed states by the late 1870s. Undergirding that electoral roller-coaster ride was a genuine revolutionary experience, as the Southern GOP emerged and developed as a biracial coalition – with blacks (the majority of whom were former slaves) and whites (both Southern-born and Northern expatriates) coalescing into a fragile but hopeful partnership – in a region whose political and economic system prior to that time had been built around slavery and white supremacy. By 1877, that hope had been largely extinguished, as the traditional "White South" (as embodied in the Democratic Party) had regained control of all state governments in the former Confederacy.

The contours of Republican Party development in the South along with the legitimate successes that were achieved for black citizens and black civil rights more generally – before it all came crashing down – is the subject of this chapter. How a Republican South came to be – as a *political strategy* – is not widely known. In fact, for a time after the war, a majority of Republicans in Congress did not consider building a Southern wing to be a realistic endeavor. It only became the party's plan of action because of other political and electoral

---

[1] The best general account of Southern Reconstruction is Eric Foner, *Reconstruction: America's Unfinished Revolution, 1863–1877* (New York: Harper & Row, 1988). The best account of the politics of Southern Reconstruction is Richard M. Valelly, *The Two Reconstructions: The Struggle for Black Enfranchisement* (Chicago: University of Chicago Press, 2004). Other more specialized accounts will be noted, as they pertain to events covered.

events. In addition, understanding why the Republicans' "grand experiment" in the South failed – and why it failed in different states at different times – also merits attention. Finally, we examine how the GOP's racial structure at the *elite level* developed by state across the Reconstruction era, as well as the role that the South would play in Republican National Conventions.

We focus first on the development of a Republican South after the Civil War. At first, Republican leaders were resistant to the creation of a Southern wing of the party, mainly because moderate members believed that enfranchising blacks – a necessary condition for the creation of a Southern GOP – was too radical for the Northern public to accept. They only came around to the idea reluctantly, after President Andrew Johnson broke with the Republicans on Reconstruction and the protection of black civil rights, and the Northern public sided with the GOP in the elections of 1866. Once invested in the notion of creating a Southern wing, Republican leaders stacked the deck by dividing the South into military districts, enfranchising blacks, and requiring new constitutions to be drafted before states would be readmitted to the Union. Combined, this led to some initial GOP electoral successes in the former Confederacy.

These successes were not sustainable, however, despite strong and loyal black support, as a consistent and large proportion of white Southerners could not be persuaded to vote Republican. Without a true biracial foundation, the Southern wing of the GOP – confronted with violence and intimidation by white paramilitary groups working on behalf of the Democrats, as well as intra-party conflict – steadily collapsed, and Republican politicians were systematically driven from power. By 1877, white Southern Democrats had effectively "redeemed" all of the ex-Confederate states, and Reconstruction – despite its very real achievements, like the wealth of office-holding experience it provided for black citizens – had come to an end.

THE MAKING OF A REPUBLICAN SOUTH

In the wake of the Civil War, two prominent questions were at the forefront of national policy-making: (1) how would the conquered states of the Confederacy be reintegrated into the Union (or how would reconciliation between North and South be achieved)? and (2) who would be in charge of critical decision-making? Indeed, answers to those questions had been proposed and debated by Northern politicians even before the war had been won.

As early as 1861, President Abraham Lincoln had outlined a plan for "restoration," which left the decision to pro-Union loyalists in the states themselves; in doing so, he sought to avoid federal guidelines and allow the states to manage the task of returning to the fold.[2] By late 1863, he laid out

---

[2] Lincoln's views on Reconstruction, along with congressional Republicans' reactions to them, are covered in Herman Belz, *Reconstructing the Union: Theory and Policy during the Civil War* (Ithaca, NY: Cornell University Press, 1969); Michael Les Benedict, *A Compromise of Principle:*

more specifics: amnesty would be provided to Confederate supporters who pledged allegiance to the United States and agreed to support federal decisions with regard to emancipation. When the number of voting-age white males taking the oath of allegiance achieved 10 percent of the number of votes cast in the 1860 presidential election, the state would be ready to form a state government that could then be organized for purposes of federal recognition.[3] A return to the Union would then follow.

Lincoln's plan was meant to restore the ex-Confederate states to the Union as quickly as possible. And it was clear that he envisioned white-only governments to form. While he insisted that states explicitly abolish slavery in their new constitutions as a precondition for readmittance, for example, he also placed the onus of decision-making – including rebuilding social and economic arrangements in the states – in whites' hands. Republicans in Congress had other ideas, however. Led by Radicals in both chambers, the Republican majority sought more stringent terms for readmission, which included a stronger federal (that is, congressional) role in Reconstruction policy, the confiscation of slaveholders' land, and permanent rights restrictions for most whites who actively participated in the Confederacy.

As Lincoln's popularity plummeted in the spring of 1864 amid stalemate on the battlefield, the Radicals were emboldened and sought to up the ante with legislation. In July, the Wade–Davis Bill – named after Senator Benjamin Wade (R-OH) and Representative Henry Winter Davis (R-MD) – passed in both chambers, and stipulated that Congress (and not the president) was in charge of Reconstruction and 50 percent of a state's white voting population was required to take an oath of allegiance (not the 10 percent under Lincoln's plan) before procedures for executive recognition and a return to the Union were operable. Such procedures included the calling of constitutional conventions and the drafting of new constitutions that proscribed both slavery and the ability of high-ranking civilian and military Confederates to vote or hold political office. Additional provisions would make it difficult for many whites who supported secession and the Confederacy to participate in the constitutional conventions, which would thereby tilt political control in the states significantly toward Union loyalists.

Lincoln considered the Wade–Davis Bill to be both extreme and punitive, and refused to sign it. And since there were fewer than ten days left in the

Congressional Republicans and Reconstruction, 1863–1869 (New York: Norton, 1974); William C. Harris, *With Charity for All: Lincoln and the Restoration of the Union* (Lexington: University Press of Kentucky, 1997); Paul D. Escott, *Lincoln's Dilemma: Blair, Sumner, and the Republican Struggle over Racism and Equality in the Civil War Era* (Charlottesville: University of Virginia Press, 2014); Louis P. Masur, *Lincoln's Last Speech: Wartime Reconstruction and the Crisis of Reunion* (New York: Oxford University Press, 2015).

[3] Lincoln laid out these details in his Proclamation of Amnesty and Reconstruction (December 3, 1863). See Roy Prentice Basler, ed., *The Collected Works of Abraham Lincoln*, Vol. VII (New Brunswick, NJ: Rutgers University Press, 1953), 53–56.

congressional session when it passed, his inaction resulted in a "pocket veto." While Wade and Davis were livid – and issued a manifesto in early August 1864, which accused Lincoln of usurping Congress's authority and seeking Southern readmission in such a way to further his own ambitions – most Republicans downplayed the conflict in the months leading up to the November elections. This was effectively where the issue of reconciliation/reconstruction stood at the time of Lincoln's assassination in April 1865, just after the 38th Congress (1863–65) adjourned.[4]

Andrew Johnson, a War Democrat from Tennessee, ascended to the presidency after Lincoln's death,[5] and his plan for sectional reconciliation was more in line with Lincoln's than that of congressional Republicans.[6] Moreover, Johnson took advantage of Congress's adjournment – the 39th Congress (1865–67) would not officially convene until December 1865, and he had no intention of calling them into special session beforehand – to take control of Reconstruction and dictate its direction via proclamation.

Johnson sought a swift sectional reconciliation, and envisioned white-led governments in the South voluntarily making arrangements (per certain conditions) to rejoin the Union. He appointed a provisional civilian governor for each state to arrange Lincoln-like constitutional conventions that would only allow whites to participate. In terms of amnesty and pardon, Johnson articulated a basic oath of allegiance that required acceptance of emancipation.[7]

---

[4] At that point, Union loyalists in four Southern states (Arkansas, Louisiana, Tennessee, and Virginia) had established new governments in line with Lincoln's conditions and sought to rejoin the Union, only to be rebuffed by the Republican-controlled Congress. See David Herbert Donald, Jean Harvey Baker, and Michael F. Holt, *The Civil War and Reconstruction* (New York: Norton, 2001), 516–18.

[5] In 1864, the Republican Party took on the broader label of "National Union Party" to accommodate both pro-War Democrats (who sought to break with the anti-War Democrats, or "Copperheads," who controlled the national party and supported George McClellan) and border-state Unionists of various stripes, who wished to support the national ticket but did not want to formally vote Republican. Lincoln chose Johnson to replace Republican Hannibal Hamlin (ME) as Vice President to broaden his electoral coalition in advance of what he believed would be a difficult election. In 1862, Lincoln had chosen Johnson as military governor of Tennessee, after much of the state was under Union-army control.

[6] Johnson's views on Reconstruction, along with congressional Republicans' reactions to them, are covered in Eric L. McKitrick, *Andrew Johnson and Reconstruction* (Chicago: University of Chicago Press, 1960); Benedict, *A Compromise of Principle*; Foner, *Reconstruction*, chapter 5; Hans L. Trefousse, *Andrew Johnson: A Biography* (New York: Norton, 1997).

[7] The oath was: "I, _____, do solemnly swear (or affirm, in presence of Almighty God), that I will henceforth faithfully support, protect, and defend the Constitution of the United States and the Union of the States thereunder, and that I will in like manner abide by and faithfully support all laws and proclamations which have been made during the existing rebellion with reference to the emancipation of slaves. So help me God." See Andrew Johnson, Proclamation 134 – Granting Amnesty to Participants in the Rebellion, with Certain Exceptions (May 29, 1865), Online by Gerhard Peters and John T. Woolley, The American Presidency Project: www.presidency.ucsb.edu/node/203492 (accessed June 1, 2019).

He did, however, specify exceptions to try to eliminate the antebellum planter elite from returning to political power.[8] More generally, Johnson imagined a political realignment occurring, wherein extreme elements (Southern secessionists and Northern Copperheads on one side, and Radical Republicans and punitive Southern Unionists on the other) would be marginalized and a new party of the center (which would include pro-War Northern Democrats and moderate Republicans, along with border-state Unionists and anti-secession Southerners) would be created that would elect him president in 1868. Key to this realignment plan was a moderate South, "chastened" in defeat, which would rejoin the Union and provide him with a base of electoral support from which he could build his broader "National Union Party."[9]

Johnson's plan dissolved through the remainder of 1865, however, as Southern state conventions and governments proved recalcitrant in the war's aftermath. Alabama, Florida, Georgia, Mississippi, North Carolina, South Carolina, and Texas all adopted new constitutions and organized new state governments (thus joining Arkansas, Louisiana, Tennessee, and Virginia from the Lincoln era), and elected new US representatives and senators. However, the white Southerners who formed the conventions and the new state governments departed from Johnson's (and Republican) wishes in a variety of ways – such as failing to ratify the Thirteenth Amendment, to nullify prior secession ordinances, and to repudiate the Confederate debt, while electing some candidates who were prominent Confederates (and thus were not granted amnesty).[10]

Once in place, these white-dominated state governments sought to create a new social order in the South, mirroring the "white supremacy" of the antebellum era while acknowledging the reality of the Thirteenth Amendment. Wealthy planters – to whom Johnson eventually granted pardons – worked to keep black labor entrenched, first through threats and violence and then through more legal maneuvers.[11] Specifically, "Black Codes" – which restricted the rights of blacks and strongly incentivized them to return to plantation work

---

[8] This amnesty exception related to "All persons who have voluntarily participated in said rebellion and the estimated value of whose taxable property is over $20,000." In all, Johnson elaborated fourteen exceptions – seven that Lincoln had issued along with seven of his own. See ibid.

[9] See LaWanda Cox and John H. Cox, *Politics, Principle, and Prejudice, 1865–1866: Dilemma of Reconstruction* (Glencoe, IL: The Free Press, 1963).

[10] See Michael Perman, *Reunion without Compromise: The South and Reconstruction, 1865–1868* (New York: Cambridge University Press, 1973); Dan T. Carter, *When the War Was Over: The Failure of Self-Reconstruction in the South, 1865–1867* (Baton Rouge: Louisiana State University Press, 1985). A number of individuals who were chosen as convention delegates were also among those not granted amnesty.

[11] By fall 1865, Johnson had issued scores of individual pardons. As Eric L. McKitrick notes: "The Southern elections, upon which [Johnson] depended to set civil governments in motion were at hand; and the possibility that numbers of unpardoned men might be elected to office promised embarrassments for his entire program." McKitrick, *Andrew Johnson and Reconstruction*, 146. On this point, see also Jonathan Truman Dorris, *Pardon and Amnesty under Lincoln and*

through draconian vagrancy laws and a penal code that promoted peonage and convict leasing – were passed in most Southern states in 1865–66, with Mississippi, South Carolina, and Alabama leading the way.[12] While many provisions of the Black Codes were vetoed by Union military commanders associated with the Freedmen's Bureau, their passage signaled a white South that was defiant in the wake of military defeat.

The Northern public was horrified by these developments, and Republicans in Congress responded in kind. Arguing that Southern governments were trying to nullify the Union victory – and thereby dishonor the memory of the Northern troops who sacrificed their lives to win the war – GOP lawmakers sought to prevent Johnson's Reconstruction policy from taking effect. They made their move at the opening of the 39th Congress in December 1865. Under instructions from Rep. Thaddeus Stevens (R-PA), Edward McPherson, the Clerk of the US House and a Stevens protégé, skipped over the names of Southern representatives when calling the roll of members elect, thereby invalidating their election credentials.[13] McPherson's action was crucial, as Jeffery Jenkins and Charles Stewart explain: "If a congressional committee was to take charge of Southern Reconstruction, it was imperative that the Clerk not recognize Southern representatives in his roll of members-elect prior to the organization of the 39th Congress; otherwise, a precedent for readmission would be set."[14] Shortly thereafter, a Joint Committee of Fifteen – six from the Senate and nine from the House – was appointed to investigate conditions in the former Confederacy and advise on the issue of Southern representation in Congress.[15] In early 1866, the committee began collecting testimony from witnesses regarding civil atrocities that occurred in the South in prior months.[16] At the same time, Republicans in the Senate took the lead in offering a congressional response to Johnson, one that would guarantee rights and protections for blacks in the hostile Southern environment.

Johnson: The Restoration of the Confederates to Their Rights and Privileges, 1861–1898 (Chapel Hill: University of North Carolina Press, 1953), 316.

[12] On the Black Codes, see Theodor B. Wilson, *The Black Codes of the South* (University: The University of Alabama Press, 1965); Eric Foner, *Nothing but Freedom: Emancipation and Its Legacy* (Baton Rouge: Louisiana State University Press, 1983).

[13] Trefousse, *Andrew Johnson*, 174–76; Jeffery A. Jenkins and Charles Stewart III, *Fighting for the Speakership: The House and the Rise of Party Government* (Princeton, NJ: Princeton University Press, 2013), 252. McPherson had been a Republican member of the US House in the 36th and 37th Congresses, but was defeated for reelection to the 38th. He would go on to be elected House Clerk eight different times.

[14] Jenkins and Stewart, *Fighting for the Speakership*, 252.

[15] The Joint Committee of Fifteen was the brainchild of Stevens. He moved its creation in the Republican caucus prior to the convening of the 39th Congress, and it was adopted unanimously. See "From Washington," *Baltimore Sun*, December 4, 1865. The Committee comprised twelve Republicans and three Democrats.

[16] Foner, *Reconstruction*, 239, 246–47.

1866: A YEAR OF INSTITUTIONAL CONFLICT

The Republicans' efforts to revise Johnson's Reconstruction plan were based on two bills drawn up in the Senate Judiciary Committee: (1) a measure that extended the life of the Freedmen's Bureau and expanded its authority and activities[17] and (2) a civil rights bill that provided national citizenship to all persons born in the United States (except Indians) without regard to race, enumerated specific rights such citizens enjoyed, and provided federal protection of those rights. Moderate forces in the GOP shaped each bill, as Radicals' hope of a more extreme response – one that included some form of black suffrage – was rejected. Each bill was consistent with Republican Party philosophy and public positions, and few GOP members of Congress felt that Johnson would take any issue with them. Indeed, Johnson was consulted prior to the drafting of the bills, and he gave no indication of resistance.[18]

On February 19, 1866, Johnson vetoed the Freedmen's Bureau Bill, based on a variety of arguments: that the Bureau had served its purpose and was no longer needed (as the freedmen could now take care of themselves); that the bill as written was unconstitutional (imposing military jurisdiction when civil courts were available); and that such decisions should not be made while a segment of the country (the eleven states of the ex-Confederacy) was without representation in Congress. Republicans were shocked by Johnson's actions, but they were unable to muster the votes to override his veto.[19]

While Radicals saw Johnson's veto as a "declaration of war," moderate elements in the party sought to tread lightly. Moderate Republicans believed the freedmen's Bureau was an invaluable institution, but they were also aware that bankers and merchants opposed it, arguing that it made commerce more difficult.[20] Moderate Republicans, at their core, were pragmatists. While they believed in establishing a constructive and protected environment in the South for

---

[17] The Freedmen's Bureau was created by an act of Congress on March 3, 1865, with the mandate to aid former slaves (freedmen) in a variety of ways. Such aid typically took the form of helping the freedmen to secure food, clothing, health care, and housing, teaching them to read and write, and assisting them in entering into employment contracts with private landowners. Its charter was initially intended to last for one year. See Herman Belz, *A New Birth of Freedom: The Republican Party and Freedmen's Rights, 1861–1866* (New York: Fordham University Press, 2000).

[18] Donald, Baker, and Holt, *The Civil War and Reconstruction*, 530–32; Foner, *Reconstruction*, 246–47.

[19] Brooks D. Simpson, *The Reconstruction Presidents* (Lawrence: University Press of Kansas, 1998), 93–95. The House override vote was successful, but the Senate vote fell just short of the necessary two-thirds: 30–18, with 8 (moderate) Republicans voting to sustain Johnson based on constitutionality concerns. In July 1866, Congress passed a revised Freedmen's Bureau Bill, which Johnson again vetoed – but this time, Congress was able to successfully override. Simpson, *The Reconstruction Presidents*, 104.

[20] As Eric Foner states, such interests charged the Bureau with "interfering with the plantation discipline essential for a revival of cotton production." Foner, *Reconstruction*, 249.

the freedmen, they were also vigilant in tracking Northern public opinion. Johnson remained popular despite his recent actions, and many moderate Republicans were frightened by his goal of initiating a realignment of the parties.

These fears aside, moderate Republicans joined with Radicals in their support of a civil rights bill. Both sets of Republicans believed that the guarantees of equal rights and accompanying federal protections inherent in the bill were necessary to safeguard the lives of the freedmen and (relatedly, and perhaps more importantly) honor the sacrifices made by Northern soldiers (and their families) during the war. To allow the South to effectively create a racial caste system would surrender the fruits of victory and invalidate the moral basis of the war. On this, moderate Republicans believed they were on safe footing with their constituents back home. And they hoped Johnson would see things the same way.[21]

On March 27, 1866, Johnson followed his veto of the Freedmen's Bureau with a veto of the Civil Rights Bill. He argued that the bill was unconstitutional, as it extended the jurisdiction of federal courts into an area where states were supreme. More generally, Johnson saw the bill as the first salvo in a great "centralization effort" (or federal encroachment into local affairs). He thus set himself up as the champion of states' right and limited government – and, indirectly, of white supremacy in the South. Congressional Republicans again attempted to override Johnson, and unlike their effort on the Freedmen's Bureau Bill this time they were victorious.[22] The successful override demonstrated that Congress could in fact set the tone for Reconstruction, and indeed would for the foreseeable future. Moreover, it signaled a clear rift between the president and the Congress. While moderate Republicans may have wanted to avoid a public break with Johnson, his actions forced the issue and presented the public with broad and differing positions that they would have to evaluate in advance of the fall 1866 elections.

While the Republicans were fighting to enact the Freedmen's Bureau and Civil Rights Bills, the Joint Committee of Fifteen was designing a constitutional amendment to govern the means by which the Southern states would be restored to the Union.[23] Both Radicals and moderates felt that this was necessary, given the lax terms that Johnson had laid out. The two factions disagreed, however, as to how stringent the provisions in the amendment should be. And

---

[21] On the thinking and beliefs of moderate Republicans, see Foner, *Reconstruction*, 241–43. On the degree to which Reconstruction policy was shaped by moderates with an eye toward their Northern constituencies, see William Gillette, *Retreat from Reconstruction, 1869–1879* (Baton Rouge: Louisiana State University Press, 1979). On the moderates' relationship with the Radicals in the GOP, see Benedict, *A Compromise of Principle*.

[22] For details of the presidential–congressional politics surrounding the Civil Rights Bill, see Simpson, *The Reconstruction Presidents*, 95–99. The Senate override vote was 33–15, while the House override vote was 122–41. The earlier votes to pass the bill were 33–12 in the House and 111–38 in the Senate.

[23] For a narrative account of the politicking behind the Fourteenth Amendment, see Garrett Epps, *Democracy Reborn: The Fourteenth Amendment and the Fight for Equal Rights in the Post-Civil War America* (New York: Henry Holt, 2006).

after some internal politicking, the amendment tilted more in a moderate direction. Both Radicals and moderates approved of the first and fourth sections – the first mirrored the recent Civil Rights Act of 1866, by protecting the (civil) rights of all citizens, with guarantees of due process and equal protection of the laws, while the fourth repudiated all Confederate debt – but locked horns over the second and third. The third prevented any Confederate supporter, who prior to 1861 had held any United States office that required an oath of allegiance, from holding any state or national office. Radicals thought that these individuals should also have their voting rights stripped, while moderates disagreed – and the moderate position won out.

The intra-party disagreement over the second section of what became the Fourteenth Amendment was the most heated, and it foreshadowed decisions that would be made in subsequent years. With the abolition of slavery (via adoption of the Thirteenth Amendment) came the elimination of the three-fifths clause in the Constitution. As a result, the black population in the South would be fully counted toward Southern states' representation in the US House and Electoral College. Neither moderates nor Radicals wanted the Democrats to benefit from this increase, but they disagreed on how to respond. Radicals wanted blacks enfranchised, which would give them the ability to represent themselves. Moderates were not willing to support black suffrage – fearing that their Northern constituents would consider such a move to be too radical – and instead preferred language that would strip states of representation (on a proportionate basis) if any adult, male citizens were denied the right to vote. From the Radicals' perspective, this language provided the white South with a license to discriminate as long as they were willing to accept the accompanying representational penalty.[24] Nonetheless, the moderates' position won out.

The Republicans – via the Joint Committee of Fifteen – pursued a constitutional amendment (rather than a statute) to more permanently embed civil rights protections and other Reconstruction policies in the body politic. Should temporary Democratic majorities emerge at some point in the future, for example, they would not be able to erase the Republicans' policies with basic legislation. In June 1866, the Fourteenth Amendment received the necessary two-thirds vote in both chambers.[25] An accompanying bill to tie ratification of the Fourteenth Amendment to a return to the Union (and representation in the House and Senate) was debated but not passed. While Tennessee ratified the Fourteenth Amendment in July 1866, and subsequently regained its congressional representation in a week's time, Republicans were unwilling at that point to make it a binding precedent.[26]

---

[24] Donald, Baker, and Holt, *The Civil War and Reconstruction*, 545–46.
[25] The vote was 33–11 in the Senate (June 8, 1866) and 138–36 in the House (June 13, 1866).
[26] The Fourteenth Amendment was ratified by the requisite three-quarters of the states (twenty-eight in all) in July 1868, and officially became part of the Constitution.

Thus, as the 1866 elections approached, the Republicans' *partisan* view of the South was conflicted. While Radicals had been pushing for black suffrage, which would have been a step toward making the GOP a truly national party, the moderates were unwilling to go along. As David Donald, Jean Harvey Baker, and Michael F. Holt argue: "In 1866 ... Moderates had no intention of building a southern wing of the Republican party based on black votes. Rather, they would protect the fruits of northern victory by reducing the South's potential power in national politics and preserve federalism to boot by stopping Radicals from nationalizing suffrage standards."[27] The moderates' view on these matters would change in short order.

The 1866 congressional elections would be a referendum on the course of Reconstruction policy, as Johnson and congressional Republicans framed it in very different terms. Johnson argued that the Republican Congress was standing in the way of a speedy sectional reconciliation and pursuing unconstitutional actions in order to favor blacks at the expense of whites. Republicans countered that their actions were intended to protect the country's hard-won achievements in the Civil War and ensure that the freedmen were guaranteed their basic rights as US citizens.

In the wake of his two vetoes and the passage of the Fourteenth Amendment, Johnson went all-in on his party realignment strategy. He called for a National Union convention to meet in August in Philadelphia and hoped to use it as a springboard to build his broad, centrist coalition. However, aligning the different partisan types proved harder than he had anticipated. Former Democratic Unionists from the border states and current Democrats mistrusted former Whigs and current Republicans, and eventually the convention narrowed to a set of Democrats and Democratically leaning Unionists. Moreover, extreme Democrats – Copperheads from the North, and ex-Confederate officials from the South – actively participated, thus negating Johnson's former goal of a centrist-only National Union Party. In short, the partisan realignment Johnson hoped to create did not materialize.[28] So the choice for voters in 1866 would once again come down to Democrats vs. Republicans.

Two other events helped frame the contest for voters.[29] First, Johnson took actions that greatly reduced his popularity. He fired more than 1,600 Republican postmasters in the North, for example, and replaced them with men loyal to him. More troubling, however, was his behavior in the run-up to the election. Johnson actively campaigned against Republican congressional candidates in a ten-city, three-week tour known as the "swing around the circle."[30]

---

[27] Donald, Baker, and Holt, *The Civil War and Reconstruction*, 547.
[28] These events are best told by Cox and Cox, *Politics, Principle, and Prejudice*. See also Benedict, *A Compromise of Principle*, 191–96.
[29] See Foner, *Reconstruction*, 261–66; Simpson, *The Reconstruction Presidents*, 105–09.
[30] The tour included Philadelphia, New York, Albany, Buffalo, Cleveland, Chicago, Indianapolis, Louisville, Cincinnati, and Pittsburgh. For a description of events during the tour, see McKitrick,

On multiple occasions during this swing, Johnson made embarrassing verbal gaffes that were reported widely in the press, which demeaned both him and the presidency in the eyes of the Northern public. Second, events in the South made it clear that the region was unrepentant and institutionally unable (or unwilling) to protect the rights of the freedmen. Racial violence broke out in two cities of the old Confederacy – Memphis in May and New Orleans in July – which left dozens of blacks dead, many more injured, and countless homes, churches, schools, and businesses destroyed; more troubling, local law enforcement appeared to participate in the white-mob behavior.[31] This race-based violence seemed to suggest that the "old white South" was being allowed to "win the peace" by Johnson and his Democratic supporters.

This, then, was the setting as voters throughout the North went to the polls: Johnson had effectively become aligned with the Democratic Party; his popularity had taken a nose-dive thanks to his own words and actions; and Republicans were able to point to events in the South, claim that Reconstruction was far from over, and tie support for Democrats to support for rebellion and lawlessness. As a result, the GOP won nineteen of twenty-one states (the exceptions being Delaware and Maryland) and picked up a net of eight House seats.[32] These gains provided the Republicans with even stronger veto-proof majorities, and thus guaranteed that they would be able to continue to control the direction of Reconstruction.

THE RECONSTRUCTION ACTS AND BLACK SUFFRAGE

The Republicans sought to take advantage of their electoral momentum before the 39th Congress even adjourned. In the lame-duck session, they actively pushed Southern Reconstruction into a new phase. Disagreements continued to exist within the party, however, as Radicals and moderates envisioned different paths to success. Radicals still preferred a revolutionary set of policies, like broad confiscation and redistribution of Confederates' property, permanent removal of Confederates' voting rights, federal-led biracial education reform, and semi-permanent (or prolonged) military-led rule and oversight of the rebellious states. Moderates continued to be pragmatic, however, and thought more in terms of what would appeal to Northern constituents.

Both groups did agree on some general things, principally that the Democratic governments in the South organized under Johnson's purview needed to

Andrew Johnson and Reconstruction, 429–30; Simpson, *The Reconstruction Presidents*, 107–09.

[31] Donald, Baker, and Holt, *The Civil War and Reconstruction*, 551–53.

[32] Election results and partisan information are taken from Michael J. Dubin, *United States Congressional Elections, 1788–1997* (Boston: McFarland, 1998) and Kenneth C. Martis, *The Historical Atlas of Political Parties in the United States Congress, 1789–1989* (New York: Macmillan, 1989).

be removed and replaced with freedmen-friendly governments. This agreement was forged largely as a result of Southern state action; between October 1866 and February 1867, legislatures in all of the former Confederate states (save for Tennessee) voted to reject the Fourteenth Amendment.[33] Moderates had thus come around to an idea pushed by Radicals in recent years: black suffrage. And this signaled a profound shift in how they viewed the South in the postwar Union. Less than a year earlier, moderate Republicans had focused on limiting Democratic representation (the second section of the Fourteenth Amendment) in the event that Southerners proved unwilling to protect the rights of the freedmen. Now, faced with Southern intransigence and buoyed by the Northern electorate's rejection of Johnson and the Democrats, they saw an opportunity for *Republican* representation in the South. As Donald, Baker, and Holt state: "In 1867, for the first time, [moderate Republicans] decided to build up a southern wing of the Republican party based on freedmen, anti-Confederate white loyalists, and any ex-Confederates who could be persuaded to cooperate with them."[34]

Moderates would join with Radicals to design a structure that would produce black-friendly Republican governments in the South.[35] This would be embodied in a set of four Military Reconstruction Acts – the first of which was adopted over Johnson's veto at the end of the lame-duck session[36] – which judged the current governments in the ten ex-Confederate states to be "provisional" (and thus temporary), called for constitutional conventions to form new governments, enfranchised blacks in convention-delegate elections and set up procedures for new voter registration, maintained candidacy restrictions for whites per the stipulations of the Fourteenth Amendment and imposed accompanying voting restrictions in convention-delegate elections, and required new constitutions to guarantee black suffrage in all state and federal elections.[37] Upon ratification of its new constitution (following the stipulations above) by a majority of voters, a state could begin the process of rejoining the Union –

---

[33] Joseph P. James, "Southern Reaction to the Proposal of the Fourteenth Amendment," *The Journal of Southern History* 22 (1956): 477–97.

[34] Donald, Baker, and Holt, *The Civil War and Reconstruction*, 563.

[35] See Richard H. Abbott, *The Republican Party and the South, 1855–1877* (Chapel Hill: University of North Carolina Press, 1986), chapter 4; Foner, *Reconstruction*, 271–80.

[36] The remaining three Reconstruction Acts would be adopted during the 40th Congress, which convened in March 1867, immediately after the 39th Congress adjourned. The second and third were also vetoed by Johnson and overridden by Congress. The fourth became law without Johnson's signature.

[37] In describing these provisions, Donald, Baker, and Holt assert: "to ensure that Republicans, rather than Johnson's Union supporters or Democrats, gained initial control of the new state governments created by the new state constitutions their program required, Republicans rigged the rules of the game. They not only enfranchised blacks; they disfranchised an unknown number of whites." Donald, Baker, and Holt, *The Civil War and Reconstruction*, 563.

which would require ratifying the Fourteenth Amendment – and regaining representation in the US Congress.[38]

The military played a vital role in overseeing the various steps outlined in the Reconstruction Acts. To create a context for the establishment of new Southern governments, the ten ex-Confederate states were divided into five military zones. Five military commanders and a smattering of Union troops would oversee the electoral machinery in the various states, by registering voters, calling conventions, scheduling delegate elections, and securing an orderly and peaceful governmental transition. The goal was to establish new Southern governments that would allow the states to rejoin the Union before the presidential election of 1868. Republican moderates believed that sectional reconciliation was necessary to convince Northern voters that the postwar peace had been settled and the Nation was moving forward; otherwise, they felt the GOP would be punished at the polls. As such, one additional provision of the Reconstruction Acts was that Union troops would be removed from a state once its legislature ratified the Fourteenth Amendment. The Radicals were strongly opposed to this provision and felt that a much lengthier troop presence was needed to protect the new state governments (in the face of presumed rearguard actions by intransigent whites), but they lacked majority support in the caucus. So they held their noses and supported the Acts as the best policies that could be achieved.

By the early months of 1867, therefore, the Republicans in Congress had set the stage for a GOP South to emerge. The Congress could only do so much, however. That is, by enfranchising blacks, disenfranchising many whites, and directing the military to ensure that voter registration and subsequent elections operated smoothly throughout the former Confederacy, the Reconstruction Acts placed the onus squarely *on the states* to make a Republican South happen. It was now up to Southern state voters and convention delegates to do their part.

INITIAL REPUBLICAN SUCCESSES IN THE SOUTH

The first hurdle for the development of a Republican South occurred with the state-level constitutional conventions in 1867–68. Should these conventions trend in the correct direction, succeeding decisions – the election of state governments and the ratification of the Fourteenth Amendment – represented the next hurdle. The Republican Congress had stacked the deck for successful party development in the South, but state political actors would need to stay on script and perform the heavy lifting.

Per the guidelines of the Reconstruction Acts, the Southern states would choose first whether to hold a constitutional convention and, if decided in the affirmative, whether to elect delegates to it. In keeping with the suffrage

---

[38] The Reconstruction Acts would not be applied to Tennessee, which had ratified the Fourteenth Amendment in July 1866 and regained congressional representation shortly thereafter.

extension to the freedmen, a movement was initiated to quickly register black voters in the South. The Army, the Freedmen's Bureau, and the patriot-club Union Leagues were at the forefront of these efforts; however, blacks themselves were proactive and sought to secure their place in the nation. In the end, black registration was significant,[39] and black turnout in the convention elections was high: roughly 80 percent of registered black voters went to the polls, and their support was crucial to the conventions being approved.[40] Many whites did not vote – with many conservatives abstaining in protest – and the percentage of those that both voted *and* supported the conventions was small. This raised some red flags.[41] Northern Republicans believed that for a Southern wing of the party to be viable, it needed to comprise more than just the region's newly enfranchised blacks. However, the initial electoral efforts of the ex-Whig planters and businessmen, along with other anti-secessionist Southern Unionists from the hill-country, left a lot to be desired.

Nonetheless, the high black turnout bore fruit, as conventions in all ten states were approved.[42] These conventions convened at various times in late 1867 through early 1868 (see Table 3.1).[43] And while white mass participation in the convention elections was modest, white elite success was another story.[44] As Table 3.2a indicates, whites constituted a majority (72.5 percent) of the convention delegates, with white Southerners controlling the lion's share (77.8 percent) of those seats. Only in South Carolina did black delegates outnumber white delegates.

Overall, Republicans dominated the convention proceedings, which is illustrated through an examination of the state delegations. As Table 3.2b suggests, Radicals – those with a high "Republican Support Score" (RSS), based on their convention voting – represented a majority (58.7 percent) of convention delegates,[45] and a Radical contingent controlled every state delegation except one

---

[39] See Valelly, *The Two Reconstructions*, 32–34.
[40] Abbott, *The Republican Party and the South*, 137.
[41] Martin E. Mantell, *Johnson, Grant, and the Politics of Reconstruction* (New York: Columbia University Press, 1973), 47–49; Abbott, *The Republican Party and the South*, 137–38.
[42] The best coverage of the politics of the Southern constitutional conventions (or "black and tan" conventions, as they were commonly called) is Richard L. Hume and Jerry B. Gough, *Blacks, Carpetbaggers, and Scalawags: The Constitutional Conventions of Radical Reconstruction* (Baton Rouge: Louisiana State University Press, 2008). But see, also, Foner, *Reconstruction*, 316–33; Abbott, *The Republican Party and the South*, 139–49.
[43] The exception was Texas, which did not convene until June 1868.
[44] All data and statistics related to the conventions and convention delegates in this subsection come from Hume and Gough, *Blacks, Carpetbaggers, and Scalawags*.
[45] The Republican Support Score (RSS) "reflects the percentage of votes each delegate cast with Republicans on a series of votes in each issue category." The issue categories were: (1) economics, (2) government structure, (3) racial issues, (4) suffrage, and (5) miscellaneous. From these issue-based scores, an overall RSS was computed. See Hume and Gough, *Blacks, Carpetbaggers, and Scalawags*, 277–81.

TABLE 3.1 *Dates of Southern constitutional conventions*

State	Dates of convention	Days in session
Alabama	November 5, 1867–December 6, 1867	28
Louisiana	November 23, 1867–March 9, 1868	81
Virginia	December 3, 1867–April 17, 1868	103
Georgia	December 9, 1867–March 11, 1868	67
Arkansas	January 7, 1868–February 14, 1868	31
Mississippi	January 7, 1868–May 18, 1868	114
North Carolina	January 14, 1868–March 16, 1868	54
South Carolina	January 14, 1868–March 17, 1868	53
Florida	January 20, 1868–February 25, 1868	30
Texas	June 1, 1868–February 6, 1869	127

Source: Hume and Gough, *Blacks, Carpetbaggers, and Scalawags*, 3

TABLE 3.2 *Demographics of Southern constitutional conventions*

(A) *Delegate groups*

Convention	Southern whites	Blacks	Outside whites	Unclassified whites	Total
Alabama	56	17	24	2	99
Arkansas	48	8	17	0	73
Florida	17	19	13	1	50
Georgia	114	37	12	1	164
Louisiana	31	50	14	2	97
Mississippi	54	17	21	4	96
North Carolina	90	14	18	0	122
South Carolina	34	72	15	0	121
Texas	70	10	10	2	92
Virginia	60	24	20	0	104
Total	574	268	164	12	1018

(B) *Radical, swing, and conservative delegates*

Convention	Radicals	Swing voters	Conservatives	Total
Alabama	58	20	18	96
Arkansas	47	8	12	67
Georgia	66	28	48	142
Louisiana	55	19	14	88
Mississippi	47	12	19	78
North Carolina	90	15	11	116
Texas	24	23	36	83
Virginia	63	1	32	96
Total	450	126	190	766

(c) Radical delegates

Convention	Southern whites	Blacks	Outside whites	Unclassified whites	Total
Alabama	22	16	18	2	58
Arkansas	22	8	17	0	47
Georgia	22	35	9	0	66
Louisiana	10	36	9	0	55
Mississippi	12	17	16	2	47
North Carolina	59	13	18	0	90
Texas	13	5	6	0	24
Virginia	20	24	19	0	63
Total	180	154	112	4	450

Source: Hume and Gough, *Blacks, Carpetbaggers, and Scalawags*, 24, 271 (Tables 2.2, 8.1, and 8.2).

(Texas).[46] A closer look at the composition of those Radical delegates, per Table 3.2c, indicates that Southern white Republicans (or "scalawags") were the plurality coalition (40 percent). Outside whites (or "carpetbaggers") made up a quarter (24.9 percent) of the Radical delegates, while blacks represented just over a third (34.2 percent).

Scalawags were mostly former Whigs – planters and business leaders – who had been part of the antebellum social and economic elite.[47] They saw Reconstruction, and the decline of the Democratic Party, as an opportunity to regain political power. They also hoped that the GOP-controlled government, working within a new, competitive two-party system, would promote economic expansion and hasten the rebuilding of the war-ravaged Southern infrastructure. And while scalawags understood the necessity of working with blacks in the party, they often held racist views and blanched at notions of creating institutions that would promote blacks' social equality. Carpetbaggers were ex-Northern transplants – mostly farmers, businessmen, middle-class professionals (principally lawyers), or ex-military – who sought a fresh start in the South and were willing to make large up-front capital investments (such as those who attempted to enter the former-plantation economy) to seek their fortunes. Often their views dovetailed with the moral aspirations of Reconstruction, and thus their positions toward blacks were quite different from those of the scalawags.

---

[46] Florida and South Carolina are excluded, as support scores could not be calculated for these delegations.

[47] A useful summary of the backgrounds, beliefs, and policy positions of the scalawags and carpetbaggers is found in Donald, Baker, and Holt, *The Civil War and Reconstruction*, 582–85.

Black convention delegates were a heterogeneous group. A majority (52.5 percent) were, in fact, of mixed race. Most had been slaves at one time, but a sizable proportion (41.8 percent) was freeborn. The vast majority (88.4 percent) was literate. They were appreciably poorer than either scalawags or carpetbaggers, with property holdings around 20 percent of what white delegates combined possessed. Finally, their employment background was different, with a majority (almost 56 percent) working as ministers or laborers – occupations that only a small percentage of white delegates held. As a group, however, black delegates recognized the path for future black success in the South and voted unabashedly for Republican policies (87 percent could be classified as Radicals).

Northern Republican leaders – ever mindful of the need to attract Southern white supporters – actively worked to steer the conventions away from adopting extreme (punitive) policies that would divide the races and hamper the party's viability and growth.[48] In this endeavor, they were mostly successful, thanks in part to white delegates controlling all key convention committees. Most importantly, no constitutions made allowances for confiscation and redistribution of (ex-Confederate) property. All constitutions, by contrast, provided for universal manhood suffrage, equal protection under the law, and public education. Radical initiatives, like integrated public schools, were mostly defeated. Moderate pleas to avoid disenfranchisement were only partially heeded, however, as voting and office-holding restrictions against former Confederates were adopted in Alabama, Arkansas, Louisiana, Mississippi, and Virginia. Those limitations aside, all constitutions adopted moderate-approved economic initiatives, like tax reforms and economic-development provisions.

The new state constitutions having been written, Southern voters would now go to the polls to approve them (or not), while also electing state and federal officials. The Republicans were largely successful in their efforts to have new Southern state constitutions adopted, Republican state governments elected, and conditions for returning to the Union (ratification of the Fourteenth Amendment) satisfied. By the end of June 1868, seven of the ten Reconstructed states – Arkansas, Florida, North Carolina, Louisiana, South Carolina, Alabama, and Georgia – had adopted new constitutions, elected unified Republican governments (except Georgia),[49] and would be readmitted to the Union.[50] And by the end of July, all seven had representation in Congress once again,

---

[48] For examples of such efforts, see Abbott, *The Republican Party and the South*, 139–49.

[49] Partisan control of the Georgia House was disputed; the best account identified 88 Democrats, 84 Republicans, and 3 of unknown partisanship.

[50] The seven states would be readmitted in two separate acts in June (one act for Arkansas specifically, and one omnibus act for the other six states).

which would result in 28 House seats and 12 Senate seats being added to the Republican column against only 4 Democratic/Conservative House seats.[51] (See Tables 3.3 through 3.6 for individual state results in these and subsequent years.) And, finally, all seven – along with Tennessee – would participate in the 1868 presidential election in November.

These GOP successes were tempered by some more troubling elements. For example, the building of a broad biracial electoral coalition saw limited success. Per the advice of Northern leaders, state GOP organizations throughout the South nominated whites (scalawags and carpetbaggers) predominantly for state office, as a way to limit conservative attempts to use race (and white supremacy) as a wedge issue to split the burgeoning biracial Republican coalition. Despite these efforts, white support for Republican tickets and the newly drafted constitutions was tepid, and GOP victories and constitutional ratifications were achieved mostly because of strong black turnout (and continued, temporary disenfranchisement of some whites).[52]

More concerning, though, were constitutional ratification defeats in Mississippi and Virginia, the first by state referendum and the second by a scheduling failure.[53] In each case, continued policies of white disenfranchisement emboldened opposition and forestalled ratification success. These failures led Congress, early in 1869, to adopt a work-around, which called for separate votes on the constitutions and the disenfranchisement provisions. This led to both Virginia and Mississippi ratifying their constitutions (along with both the Fourteenth and Fifteenth Amendments) but voting down disenfranchisement. As a result, Virginia and Mississippi were restored to the Union in January and February 1870, respectively.[54] Texas, which had been much slower to convene and conclude a constitutional convention, would follow a month later.

More generally, the Democrats showed some electoral recovery as early as spring 1868, principally in Louisiana and Georgia, where GOP electoral success was weaker than everywhere else in the South. Republicans controlled both state houses in Louisiana, but by narrower margins than elsewhere, and could only muster majority control of the Georgia Senate. Moreover, three of the four

---

[51] Georgia would only have members seated in the House; one of its House seats and both of its Senate seats remained vacant through the remainder of the 40th Congress.

[52] Foner, *Reconstruction*, 332.

[53] See Donald, Baker, and Holt, *The Civil War and Reconstruction*, 707–08, fn. 26. Alabama had also initially rejected their constitution, which led to the Republicans changing the ratification requirements via a new (Fourth) Reconstruction Act. See Abbott, *The Republican Party and the South*, 162.

[54] See William C. Harris, *The Day of the Carpetbagger: Republican Reconstruction in Mississippi* (Baton Rouge: Louisiana State University Press, 1979), 115–27; Jack P. Madden, Jr., "Virginia: The Persistence of Centrist Hegemony," in Otto H. Olsen, ed., *Reconstruction and Redemption in the South* (Baton Rouge: Louisiana State University Press, 1980), 113–55.

TABLE 3.3 *Percentage of Republican seats in Southern state legislatures, 1867–1877*

State House

State/Elect year	1867	1868	1869	1870	1871	1872	1873	1874	1875	1876	1877
Alabama[a]	–	97	–	35	–	46	–	40	–	20	–
Arkansas	–	96	–	54	–	63	–	12	–	18	–
Florida[b]	–	71	–	53	–	56	–	46	–	40	–
Georgia	–	.	–	17	–	8	–	4	–	5	–
Louisiana[c]	–	55	–	73	–	.	–	.	–	38	–
Mississippi	–	–	77	–	57	–	59	–	16	–	7
North Carolina	–	68	–	35	–	45	–	28	–	30	–
South Carolina[d]	–	89	–	81	–	81	–	73	–	48	–
Tennessee	100	–	20	16	–	35	–	7	–	21	–
Texas	–	–	60	–	–	18	12	–	–	6	–
Virginia	–	–	30	–	25	–	24	–	20	–	7

State Senate

State/Elect year	1867	1868	1869	1870	1871	1872	1873	1874	1875	1876	1877
Alabama[e]	–	97	–	.	–	42	–	39	–	0	–
Arkansas	–	81	–	69	–	80	–	6	–	6	–
Florida[f]	–	67	–	52	–	54	–	50	–	38	–
Georgia	–	59	–	32	–	9	–	2	–	2	–
Louisiana[g]	–	56	–	81	–	.	–	.	–	44	–
Mississippi	–	–	79	–	62	–	62	–	30	–	5
North Carolina	–	76	–	28	–	36	–	22	–	20	–
South Carolina[h]	–	81	–	84	–	76	–	79	–	55	–

Tennessee	100	–	20	12	–	28	–	8	–	20	–
Texas	–	–	63	–	–	43	13	–	–	10	–
Virginia	–	–	30	–	23	21	–	14	–	–	9

Source: Michael J. Dubin, *Party Affiliations in the State Legislatures: A Year by Year Summary, 1796–2006* (Jefferson, NC: McFarland & Company, 2007).

Note: Dashes indicate years in which no elections were held, dots indicate that elections were held but no data on partisan division is available.

[a] Both parties disputed the results of the 1872 election in Alabama. Eventually, Republicans succeeded in placing several of their candidates in seats "won" by Democrats, resulting in a Republican majority in the House of 51 to 49 seats. This puts the "real" Republican percentage for 1873 and 1874 at 51 percent.

[b] The Florida legislature rejected returns from nine counties in the 1870 election. According to newspaper results the actual partisan division in the House was 28 Conservatives, 23 Republicans, and 1 Independent for the years 1871 and 1872. This would put the "real" Republican percentage at 44 percent for this period.

[c] The Louisiana elections of 1872 and 1874 produced two competing results – one in which Democrats controlled both chambers, one in which Republicans did. In this period, Louisiana effectively had two functioning legislatures.

[d] After the conclusion of the presidential election of 1876–77, when the South Carolina legislature convened in April 1877, a number of Republicans resigned or were expelled. Afterward, the actual partisan division in the House was 87 Democrats and 37 Republicans. This would put the "real" Republican percentage at 30 percent.

[e] There was no election of senators in 1870. Both parties disputed the results of the 1872 election in Alabama. Eventually, Republicans succeeded in placing several of their candidates in seats "won" by Democrats, resulting in a brief Republican majority in the Senate of 17 to 16 seats. This puts the "real" Republican percentage for 1873 and 1874 at 52 percent. The death of a Republican senator switched majority control back to the Democrats.

[f] The Florida legislature rejected returns from nine counties in the 1870 election. According to newspaper results the actual partisan division in the Senate was 12–12 for the years 1871 and 1872. This would put the "real" Republican percentage at 50 percent for this period.

[g] See note c.

[h] After the conclusion of the presidential election of 1876–77, when the South Carolina legislature convened in April 1877, a number of Republicans resigned or were expelled. Afterward, the actual partisan division in the Senate was 28 Democrats and 5 Republicans. This would put the "real" Republican percentage at 15 percent.

TABLE 3.4 *Percentage of Republican vote in Southern gubernatorial elections, 1867–1877*

State/Elect year	1867	1868	1869	1870	1871	1872	1873	1874	1875	1876	1877
Alabama	–	100	–	49.5	–	52.5	–	46.2	–	35.9	–
Arkansas	–	100	–	–	–	51.8	–	0	–	34.4	–
Florida	–	59.1	–	–	–	52.4	–	–	–	49.5	–
Georgia	–	52.2	–	–	0	30.5	–	–	–	23.1	–
Louisiana	–	63.1	–	–	–	56.9	–	–	–	47.9	–
Mississippi[a]	–	47.4	66.8	–	–	–	57.3	–	–	–	0
North Carolina	–	55.6	–	–	–	50.5	–	–	–	47.2	–
South Carolina	–	75.2	–	62.3	–	65.7	–	53.9	–	49.7	–
Tennessee[b]	76.8	–	31.8	34.5	–	46.3	–	35.1	–	5.0	–
Texas	–	–	50.6	–	–	–	34.4	–	–	24.9	–
Virginia[c]	–	–	45.8	–	–	–	43.9	–	–	–	0

Source: Michael J. Dubin, *United States Gubernatorial Elections, 1861–1911: The Official Results by State and County* (Jefferson, NC: McFarland & Company, 2010)

[a] Democratic candidate Benjamin Humphreys won the 1868 gubernatorial election. However, because the new constitution was rejected at the same time civil government was not restored and Humphreys did not take office.

[b] The 1869 gubernatorial election saw Dewitt W. Senter, a Republican-Conservative candidate, beat William B. Stokes, a Republican-Radical candidate; the percentage listed is the one received by Stokes.

[c] The 1869 gubernatorial election saw Gilbert C. Walker, a Conservative-Republican, beat Henry H. Wells, a Radical-Republican; the percentage listed is the one received by Wells.

TABLE 3.5 *Return to Democratic home rule ("Redemption") in the South, 1867–1877*

State/Elect year	1867	1868	1869	1870	1871	1872	1873	1874	1875	1876	1877
Alabama	–	R	–	.	–	D/R	–	D	–	D	–
Arkansas	–	R	–	R	–	R	–	D	–	D	–
Florida	–	R	–	R	–	R	–	D/R	–	D	–
Georgia	–	.	–	D/R	–	D	–	D	–	D	–
Louisiana[a]	–	R	–	R	–	.	–	.	–	D	–
Mississippi	–	–	R	–	R	–	R	–	D/R	–	D
North Carolina	–	R	–	D/R	–	D/R	–	D/R	–	D	–
South Carolina[b]	–	R	–	R	–	R	–	R	–	D/R	D
Tennessee	R	–	D	D	–	D	D	D	–	D	–
Texas	–	–	R	–	–	D/R	D	–	–	D	–
Virginia	–	–	D	–	D	–	D	–	D	–	D

Note: R indicates unified Republican control of state government on the basis of that year's elections, D indicates unified Democratic control of state government, and D/R indicates divided state government.

[a] The Louisiana elections of 1872 and 1874 produced two competing results – one in which Democrats controlled both chambers, one in which Republicans did. In this period, Louisiana effectively had two functioning legislatures.

[b] After the conclusion of the presidential election of 1876–77, when the South Carolina legislature convened in April 1877, a number of Republicans resigned or were expelled. Afterward, the actual partisan division in the Senate went from 18 Republicans and 15 Democrats to 28 Democrats and 5 Republicans. The Democrats would thus become the majority party in the South Carolina Senate.

TABLE 3.6 *Percentage of Republican seats in the US Congress, 40th–45th Congresses*

US House

Congress/ Years	40th (1867–69)	41st (1869–71)	42nd (1871–73)	43rd (1873–75)	44th (1875–77)	45th (1877–79)
Alabama	100	67	50	62.5	12.5	0
Arkansas	100	67	33	75	0	0
Florida	100	100	100	100	100	50
Georgia	57	43	43	22	0	0
Louisiana	80	100	100	83	50	33
Mississippi	–	100	100	83	17	0
North Carolina	83	83	29	37.5	12.5	12.5
South Carolina	100	100	100	100	80	60
Tennessee	100	100	25	70	10	20
Texas	–	75	25	0	0	0
Virginia	–	37.5	37.5	44	11	11

US Senate

Congress/ Years	40th (1867–69)	41st (1869–71)	42nd (1871–73)	43rd (1873–75)	44th (1875–77)	45th (1877–79)
Alabama	100	100	50	50	50	50
Arkansas	100	100	100	100	100	50
Florida	100	100	100	100	50	50
Georgia	–	50	50	0	0	0
Louisiana	100	100	100	50	50	50
Mississippi	–	100	100	100	100	50
North Carolina	100	100	50	0	0	0
South Carolina	100	100	100	100	100	50
Tennessee	50	100	50	50	0	0
Texas	–	100	100	50	50	0
Virginia	–	50	50	50	0	0

Source: Kenneth C. Martis, *The Historical Atlas of Political Parties in the United States Congress, 1789–1989* (New York: Macmillan, 1989).
Note: Percentages represent Republican totals at the *beginning* of a Congress, or upon first seating in a Congress. Dashes indicate years in which no elections were held.

US House seats from the South that the GOP failed to capture were from these states. This Democratic recovery became more pronounced in the November presidential election; while Republican Ulysses S. Grant – who was unopposed at the GOP convention and chosen by acclamation on the first ballot – carried Alabama, Arkansas, Florida, North Carolina, South Carolina, and Tennessee, both Georgia and Louisiana cast their electoral votes for Horatio Seymour (NY), the Democratic nominee.

The Democratic victories in Georgia and Louisiana were in part the result of increased white turnout – as conservative whites voted at much higher rates throughout the South, relative to the constitutional and state legislative elections earlier in the spring – but also the use of violence, threats, and intimidation by domestic terrorist organizations like the Ku Klux Klan, a secret society of ex-Confederates and like-minded others who were intent on restoring white supremacy and rule, against potential black voters.[55] Klan activities reduced black turnout considerably, which drew the attention and concern of national Republican leaders. In addition, political activities in Georgia – where two months before the presidential election some white Republican state legislators joined with Democratic state legislators to oust twenty-five black members of the state House and three black members of the state Senate on the grounds that the new Georgia constitution did not provide blacks with the right to hold office – grew so dire that Congress in December 1869 denied the state further representation and returned it to military rule. Georgia would rejoin the Union in July 1870, after the black legislators were reinstated and all the white legislators with Confederate backgrounds were removed.[56]

THE COLLAPSE OF RECONSTRUCTION

The difficulties in Louisiana and Georgia were extreme cases of a more general pattern throughout the South. As historian William Gillette notes:

Although the election of 1868 was a Republican victory, it revealed undercurrents of white conservatism and indications of black vulnerability that could endanger Republicanism. It was to be expected that Democratic voters would succumb to the pandering to white prejudice; but the number of reports indicating the disenchantment of white Republican voters with the course of reconstruction was ominous.[57]

Republican strategy, in response, took two forms. First, the national party sought to shore up black support by adopting a constitutional amendment that would guarantee and extend black suffrage rights. Similar to their

---

[55] On the use of violence in Southern elections, along with the rise of the Klan, see Allen W. Trelease, *White Terror: The Ku Klux Klan Conspiracy and Southern Reconstruction* (Baton Rouge: Louisiana State University Press, 1971), 3–188; George C. Rable, *But There Was No Peace: The Role of Violence in the Politics of Reconstruction* (Athens: University of Georgia Press, 1984), 74–79.

[56] See Alan Conway, *The Reconstruction of Georgia* (Minneapolis: University of Minnesota Press, 1967), 162–81.

[57] Gillette, *Retreat from Reconstruction*, 16–17.

argument regarding the Fourteenth Amendment, GOP leaders contended that an amendment would protect black voting rights for all time, and not leave them vulnerable to any temporary majorities that might seek to eliminate them with a simple statute. Moreover, an amendment would extend black voting rights *outside* of the South, into Northern areas that had been resistant to the granting of such rights. Republican leaders believed that additional black votes would help preserve the narrow Northern victories the party enjoyed in 1868, while perhaps opening up portions of the border states (where the GOP was competitive but could not break through) for electoral success.[58]

The legislation that would become the Fifteenth Amendment, which stipulated that "the right of citizens of the United States to vote shall not be denied or abridged by the United States or by any State on account of race, color, or previous condition of servitude" and provided Congress with power to enforce the right, passed in late February 1869, during the lame-duck session of the 40th Congress, and was ratified just under a year later. Amid more Klan violence in 1870, which led to Republican electoral losses in Alabama and North Carolina, Congress subsequently passed a series of Enforcement Acts in 1870–71 – empowering the federal judiciary and the president – to protect the sanctity of voting and black rights more generally.[59]

Second, Republican leaders sought to reach out, yet again, to ex-Whigs in the South in order to increase the party's white support. This would be accomplished by downplaying black interests – while trumpeting the symbolic benefit of the Fifteenth Amendment – and convincing would-be black politicians to step aside for the good of the party. Economic development, especially the promotion of railroads, would be emphasized instead, in an attempt to shift the basis of politicking away from race. Democratic leaders also, for a time, shelved distinctly racial appeals, in the hopes of eliminating their party's negative image (as an unrepentant, violent group of white supremacists), which they believed helped promote Republican unity.[60]

Thus, a more normal period of two-party politics took hold in 1871–73 – helped along by the US army's defeat of the Klan, following the passage of the

---

[58] William Gillette, *The Right to Vote: Politics and the Passage of the Fifteenth Amendment* (Baltimore: Johns Hopkins University Press, 1965).

[59] See Foner, *Reconstruction*, 454–59. The best legislative history of the various Enforcement Acts is Xi Wang, *The Trial of Democracy: Black Suffrage and Northern Republicans, 1860–1910* (Athens: University of Georgia Press, 1998), 49–92.

[60] On the move away from racial appeals by both parties and the courting of white ex-Whigs, see Michael Perman, *The Road to Redemption: Southern Politics, 1869–1879* (Chapel Hill: University of North Carolina Press, 1984).

final Enforcement Act in April 1871. White (Democratic) turnout declined, as distinctly racial appeals (which had been used to mobilize many whites) dried up, while Democratic leaders realigned their party's image and message. Republicans did not control the entire South, as they never gained a majority foothold in Virginia and (by that time) had lost Tennessee and Georgia, but they remained either competitive or solidly in control everywhere else.

The high tide of the Republican Party in the South may have come in the fall of 1872. With all Southern states back in the Union, Republican President Ulysses S. Grant – who again was nominated unanimously at the GOP convention – defeated Horace Greeley, the editor and publisher of the *New-York Tribune*, who was the fusion candidate of the Liberal Republicans and Democrats.[61] Grant won in a landslide, capturing thirty-one of thirty-seven states with an 11.8 percentage-point margin in the popular vote.[62] Moreover, Grant won eight of eleven Southern states, losing only Georgia, Tennessee, and Texas.[63] Grant's victory also increased the percentage of Republican House seats in the South (see Figure 3.1), thus reversing a trend and suggesting perhaps that the GOP had weathered the storm – that is, concerted efforts by white Democrats and paramilitary groups to regain control of the region – and positioned the party for long-standing Southern success.

This Republican optimism was dashed soon enough. In 1873, the GOP's economic strategy in the South collapsed, as the railroad development that was central to their plan failed. Corruption and over-chartering of lines led to widespread defaults. This left (mostly) Republican state governments holding the bag, as they directly subsidized the development with direct loans of bond issues. To meet the interest obligations on the bonds – now that the railroads were bankrupt – states had to raise taxes. This drew the ire of white taxpayers, and made them increasingly open to Democratic entreaties.[64]

As railroad bankruptcies spread across the country in 1873, banking collapses – including Jay Cook & Company – soon followed. Before long, a true economic panic took hold, which fed into a broader economic depression that persisted for the remainder of the decade (and beyond in some parts of the

[61] The Liberal Republican Party formed in May 1872 to oppose Grant's reelection. Members were mostly Republicans who championed reform and opposed the corruption that had permeated the Grant administration. They sought civil service reform and an end to Southern Reconstruction. Greeley was the choice of the Liberal Republicans, and the Democrats subsequently nominated him as well (believing that this was the only reasonable strategy to beat Grant). See Earle Dudley Ross, *The Liberal Republican Movement* (New York: Henry Holt, 1919); Andrew L. Slap, *The Doom of Reconstruction: The Liberal Republicans in the Civil War Era* (New York: Fordham University Press, 2006).

[62] Grant received 55.6 percent of the popular vote, with Greeley garnering 43.8 percent.

[63] When Congress counted the electoral vote on February 12, 1873, they threw out the returns from Arkansas and Louisiana due to irregularities. See "The Electoral Vote," *New-York Tribune*, February 13, 1873.

[64] See Valelly, *The Two Reconstructions*, 86–87.

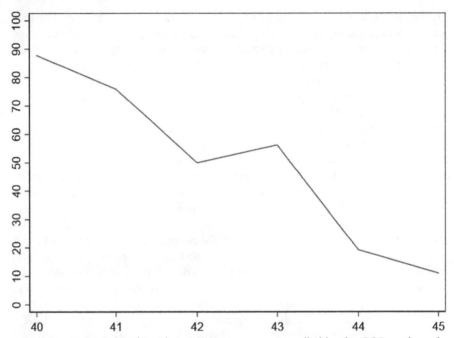

FIGURE 3.1 Percentage of Southern US House seats controlled by the GOP, 40th–45th (1867–1879) Congresses
Source: Jeffery A. Jenkins, "Partisanship and Contested Election Cases in the House of Representatives, 1789–2002," *Studies in American Political Development* 18 (2004): 112–35, Table 11

country).[65] The economic crash was particularly destructive for the GOP in the South, where the party's economic agenda was seen as the cause of this calamity. As a result, the balance of power within the Southern GOP establishment shifted, and the party did a quick about-face – eschewing its Whiggish economic strategy for a more pragmatic one. Specifically, Republican leaders refocused on maintaining and mobilizing the party's base – black voters – amid the growing economic turmoil. In addition to pushing state-level civil rights reforms,[66] Republican leaders also began actively recruiting blacks for public office. In very short order, the Scalawag-led Republican Party of the early

---

[65] See Nicolas Barreyre, "The Politics of Economic Crises: The Panic of 1873, the End of Reconstruction, and the Realignment of American Politics," *Journal of the Gilded Age and Progressive Era* 10 (2011): 403–23.

[66] National GOP leaders would also attempt to do their part, by adopting a new civil rights law (the Civil Rights Act of 1875).

1870s gave way to the carpetbagger–black-led Republican Party of the mid 1870s.[67]

The Republicans' turn toward the protection and promotion of blacks' rights also led the Democrats to alter their strategy, as they once again sold themselves as the party of white supremacy. With Southern elections becoming primarily about race, both parties focused on voter turnout. Republicans continued to receive blacks' votes but began losing the support of scalawags, who faced increasing pressure – threats of both violence and social ostracism – from white Democrats. In addition, Democrats were successful in re-mobilizing whites who had disengaged in the early 1870s, when the parties grappled over economic policy. Finally, various paramilitary groups like the Red Shirts and the White League, acting on behalf of the Democratic Party, used violence and terror to depress black turnout in strategic parts of the South.[68] Such organized violence was possible because President Grant – who had used the army and the Justice Department to crush the Klan in the early 1870s – had become less willing to intercede in such a fashion toward the middle of the decade. This was because the Northern public's view of Republican policies – amid the nation's financial difficulties and reports of widespread corruption within the Grant administration – had soured, especially those policies like Reconstruction that were not directed at addressing *their* most pressing concerns. Grant and GOP leaders worried that further military intervention in the South would result in voters punishing Republican politicians in the North and backed off.[69]

As a result, Republican governments in the South began to fall. By 1874, the GOP maintained full control only of Mississippi and South Carolina and partial control only of Florida, Louisiana, and North Carolina – the Southern states with the largest black populations. (See Table 3.5.) The Republicans would lose their majorities in the Mississippi legislature a year later, amid an electoral environment fraught with intimidation and violence, and Republican Governor Adelbert Ames would resign from office shortly thereafter, in advance of being impeached.[70] The GOP maintained an institutional foothold in the remaining four states until the elections of 1876, and three of them – Florida, Louisiana, and South Carolina – would play a critical role in both the outcome of the presidential election and a compromise to end Reconstruction.

The presidential election of 1876 pitted two reform-minded governors – Republican Rutherford B. Hayes of Ohio and Democrat Samuel Tilden of

---

[67] Donald, Baker, and Holt, *The Civil War and Reconstruction*, 599–602.

[68] The Red Shirts were active in Mississippi, North Carolina, and South Carolina, while the White League operated in Louisiana. See Rable, *But There Was No Peace*.

[69] See Gillette, *Retreat from Reconstruction*.

[70] The systematic use of intimidation and violence by the Red Shirts (and other paramilitary groups) to retake the elections for the Democrats became known as the "Mississippi Plan." See Warren A. Ellem, "The Overthrow of Reconstruction in Mississippi," *Journal of Mississippi History* 54 (1992) 175–201; Nicholas Lemann, *Redemption: The Last Battle of Reconstruction* (New York: Farrar, Straus and Giroux, 2007).

New York – against one another, and electoral momentum seemed to be running in the Democrats' favor.[71] Thus, Democratic leaders ambitiously set their sights on capturing the White House and perhaps wresting full control of the federal government from the GOP.[72] When all votes were cast, the result appeared to favor Tilden. But the electoral votes of three yet-to-be-redeemed Southern states (Florida, Louisiana, and South Carolina) were called into question,[73] with ballot fraud at the heart of the dispute, and the winner of these states would determine the election. Crucially, the Republicans still controlled the state canvassing board in all three states. Moreover, rival slates of partisan candidates claimed victory in state elections in Louisiana and South Carolina, but national Republican leaders were well past the point of using the military to support Republican governments in the South.[74] Still, as Donald, Baker, and Holt state: "if northern Republicans were prepared to allow the Democrats to resume control of state governments in Louisiana, Florida, and South Carolina in 1877, they were not ready to do so until the electoral votes in each had been cast in December and sent to Washington."[75]

In time, the GOP-controlled canvassing boards threw out a sufficient number of Democratic votes (based on fraudulent ballot design) to award the electoral votes of Florida, Louisiana, and South Carolina to Hayes. With these electoral votes in hand, Hayes had a one-vote majority. Democrats cried foul, and rival political actors in the three Southern states moved to certify results that would award the disputed electoral votes to Tilden. To settle the crisis, Congress set up a fifteen-member Electoral Commission to investigate and render a decision – with the eventual outcome favoring Hayes on an eight–seven vote.

Underlying the dispute-settlement process was a range of backdoor politicking, which culminated in the (presumed) Compromise of 1877.[76] The negotiations

---

[71] Hayes won the GOP nomination on the seventh ballot at the Republican National Convention. The South did not play a strategic role in his nomination. On the first ballot, Senator Oliver Morton of Indiana, a ruthless purveyor of "Bloody Shirt" politics, commanded a plurality of Southern delegates (80 of 190, or 42.1 percent) with Senator James Blaine of Maine coming in second (with 49). On the seventh and final ballot, the Southern delegation split their vote almost evenly between Blaine and Hayes (who emerged as a compromise candidate, starting on the fifth ballot): Blaine received 92 votes, Hayes 94, with 4 scattering. The balloting breakdown by state can be found at *Proceedings of the Republican National Convention, Held at Cincinnati, Ohio, June 14, 15, and 16, 1876* (Concord, NH: Republican Press Association, 1876), 84, 108–09. For a description of Republican nomination politics in 1876, see Michael F. Holt, *By One Vote: The Disputed Presidential Election of 1876* (Lawrence: University Press of Kansas, 2008), 67–95.

[72] See Keith Ian Polakoff, *The Politics of Inertia: The Election of 1876 and the End of Reconstruction* (Baton Rouge: Louisiana State University Press, 1973); Holt, *By One Vote*.

[73] One electoral vote in Oregon was contested as well.

[74] Such a technique was viewed by this time as illegitimate by nearly all local whites.

[75] Donald, Baker, and Holt, *The Civil War and Reconstruction*, 633.

[76] The standard account of the Compromise of 1877 is C. Vann Woodward, *Reunion and Reaction: The Compromise of 1877 and the End of Reconstruction* (Boston: Little, Brown, 1951). Whether the Hayes camp and Southern Democrats settled on a true quid pro quo

underlying the compromise were secret, but ultimately the Democrats agreed to give up their leverage – for example, the Democratically controlled House needed to validate the Electoral Commission's decision, and the minority Democrats in the Senate could have pursued a filibuster – and acquiesce to Hayes's election, in exchange for assurances from the Republicans that (among other things) they would no longer use the army to prop up GOP governments in the three remaining unredeemed states and instead allow "home rule" to operate.[77] Subsequent behavior by Grant, who withdrew the army in Florida in January 1877, when a new Democratic governor took office, and Hayes, who once inaugurated refused to support the entrenched but under-fire Republican governors in Louisiana and South Carolina and directed the army guarding the statehouses back to their barracks (thus nudging the Republican governors into giving up their office claims and stepping aside), was consistent with GOP leaders keeping up their end of the deal.

Thus, by late April 1877, the entire ex-Confederate South had been "redeemed" by the Democrats, and the Republicans' ambitious policy of Reconstruction had come to an end.[78] The collapse had not occurred all at once, as some states returned to white Democratic home rule as early as 1869 (Tennessee) while others (Louisiana and South Carolina) held out for considerably longer. Yet, the end result was the same, and the dream of creating a Republican South – which began so promisingly in 1867 – was dealt a near-fatal blow. National Republicans would continue to hold out (some) hope for a viable Southern wing for the better part of the next two decades – a point we will return to shortly – but little would be achieved to make that a reality.

ASSESSING BLACK GAINS DURING RECONSTRUCTION

Apart from tracking the rise and fall of the Republican Party in the South from 1867 to 1877, culminating in the failure of Reconstruction as a congressional program, a separate pursuit would be to assess the gains that Southern blacks

arrangement (such that it could be considered a "compromise") is discussed and debated in Polakoff, *The Politics of Inertia*; Allen Peskin, "Was There a Compromise of 1877?" *The Journal of American History* 60 (1973): 63–75; C. Vann Woodward, "Yes, There Was a Compromise of 1877," *The Journal of American History* 60 (1973): 215–23; Michael Les Benedict, "Southern Democrats in the Crisis of 1876–1877: A Reconsideration of *Reunion and Reaction*," *The Journal of Southern History* 64 (1980): 489–524.

[77] Both Grant and Hayes also demanded that blacks' rights be respected in the new Democratically controlled governments and received assurances of compliance.

[78] After the conclusion of the presidential election of 1876–77, the South Carolina Senate was the last state-level institution to be captured by the Democrats. When the South Carolina legislature convened in April 1877, a number of Republicans resigned or were expelled. Afterward, the actual partisan division in the Senate went from 18 Republicans and 15 Democrats – wherein the GOP had a majority – to 28 Democrats and 5 Republicans. In addition, the South Carolina House went from having a small Democratic majority (65–59) to a large one (87–37). See William J. Cooper, *The Conservative Regime: South Carolina, 1877–1890* (Baltimore: Johns Hopkins University Press, 1968), 24–25.

made during these years. At the individual level, due process, equal protection of the laws, and voting rights (guaranteed by the Fourteenth and Fifteenth Amendments) were major steps forward, and provided blacks with important civil and political rights. Over time, of course, these rights were eroded through extralegal means (i.e., violence, intimidation, fraud, and social pressure).[79] And rights of social equality – in public transportation and accommodations – never really came to fruition, despite the passage of the Civil Rights Act of 1875, due to lack of enforcement provisions and overall GOP weakness by that time.[80]

At the elite level, black success was quite tangible. Despite the national Republican strategy of limiting black office holding – in order (per their argument) to attract enough Southern whites to build a true and lasting biracial coalition in the South – blacks sought and won political office from the beginning of Reconstruction. Black participation in the state constitutional conventions has already been covered. Once the Southern states adopted new constitutions and began the process of electing new governments (and being readmitted to the Union and regaining representation in Congress), blacks claimed a sizable number of state legislative seats immediately. This is illustrated in Table 3.7. Black office holding was especially strong in the state Houses, where blacks tallied a significant number of seats beginning in 1868 – and constituted a third of the entire chamber in Florida and Louisiana and a majority in South Carolina. By the early 1870s, the Mississippi state house also emerged as a locale for strong black participation, with blacks comprising a chamber majority after the 1873 elections. Black speakers of the House would also be elected in both South Carolina and Mississippi.[81]

Overall, more than 630 blacks would be elected as state legislators in the ex-Confederate states during Reconstruction.[82] The high-water mark for several states, in terms of raw numbers, was 1873–74, coinciding with the GOP's desperate push to maintain a firm foothold in the South by actively courting blacks for office. Beyond the state legislature, blacks were elected to prominent state-level positions, including Lieutenant Governor (Louisiana, Mississippi, and South Carolina), Treasurer (Louisiana and South Carolina), Superintendent of Education (Arkansas, Florida, Louisiana, and Mississippi), and Secretary

---

[79] It is important to remember, though, that the voting rights provided by the Fifteenth Amendment were national in scope, and these rights were enjoyed by Northern blacks even as extra-legal means were infringing upon those of Southern blacks.

[80] On the Civil Rights Act of 1875, see "Abolitionists and the Civil Rights Act of 1875," *The Journal of American History* 52 (1965): 493–510; Bertram Wyatt-Brown, "The Civil Rights Act of 1875," *Western Political Quarterly* 18 (1965): 763–75; Gillette, *Retreat from Reconstruction,* 259–79. The Civil Rights Act of 1875 would be declared unconstitutional by the Supreme Court in 1883 (in the *Civil Rights Cases*).

[81] These individuals would be Samuel J. Lee (1872–74) and Robert B. Elliott (1874–76) in South Carolina, and John R. Lynch (1872–73) and I. D. Shadd (1874–76) in Mississippi. See Foner, *Reconstruction,* 354 fn. 15.

[82] Foner, *Reconstruction,* 354–55, fn. 15, complemented by Tennessee data.

TABLE 3.7 *Percentage of black legislators in Southern state legislatures, 1868–1877*

State House

State/Elect year	1868	1869	1870	1871	1872	1873	1874	1875	1876	1877
Alabama	26	–	19	–	21	–	27	–	7	–
Arkansas	6	–	7	–	10	–	16	–	5	–
Florida	37	–	40	–	25	–	25	–	15	–
Georgia	17	–	11	–	10	–	2	–	1	–
Louisiana[a]	35	–	36	–	.	–	.	–	18	–
Mississippi	–	29	–	37	–	48	–	14	–	5
North Carolina	15	–	16	–	10	–	11	–	6	–
South Carolina	60	–	61	–	60	–	65	–	57	–
Tennessee	–	0	0	–	1	–	0	–	0	–
Texas	–	10	–	–	7	7	–	–	3	–
Virginia	–	17	–	13	–	13	–	12	–	4

[a]The Louisiana elections of 1872 and 1874 produced two competing results – one in which Democrats controlled both chambers, one in which Republicans did. In this period, Louisiana effectively had two functioning legislatures.

State Senate

State/Elect year	1868	1869	1870	1871	1872	1873	1874	1875	1876	1877
Alabama	3	–	.	–	15	–	18	–	0	–
Arkansas	4	–	8	–	15	–	13	–	3	–
Florida	13	–	21	–	13	–	21	–	25	–
Georgia	7	–	9	–	11	–	0	–	0	–
Louisiana[a]	19	–	19	–	.	–	.	–	14	–
Mississippi	–	15	–	19	–	24	–	14	–	3
North Carolina	6	–	8	–	8	–	8	–	10	–
South Carolina	32	–	35	–	36	–	48	–	52	–
Tennessee	–	0	0	–	0	–	0	–	0	–
Texas	–	7	–	–	7	3	–	–	3	–
Virginia	–	14	–	7	–	7	–	7	–	7

[a]As noted above.

Sources: Data provided by J. Morgan Kousser; J. Mason Brewer, *Negro Legislators of Texas and Their Descendants* (Dallas: Mathis Publishing Co., 1935); Canter Brown, Jr., *Florida's Black Public Officials* (Tuscaloosa: The University of Alabama Press, 1998); Luther Porter Jackson, *Negro Office-Holders in Virginia, 1865–1895* (Norfolk, VA: Guide Quality Press, 1945)

Note: Dashes indicate years in which no elections were held, dots indicate that elections were held but no data on partisan division is available.

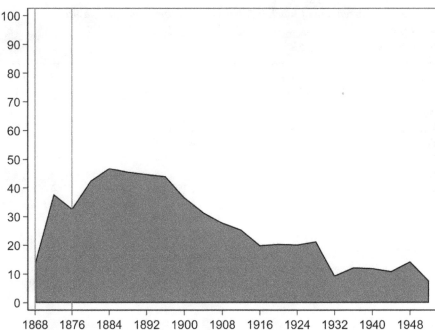

FIGURE 3.2 Percentage of Southern GOP convention delegates that were black, 1868–1876
Source: Data collected by authors.

of State (Florida, Mississippi, and South Carolina),[83] along with a range of lower offices like mayor, alderman, justice of the peace, county commissioner, and sheriff.[84] Blacks were also elected to the highest legislative positions at the federal level. As Figure 3.2 indicates, blacks constituted a sizable portion of Southern state delegates to the Republican National Convention; after a slow start in 1868, blacks accounted for around one-third of all GOP Southern delegates in the 1870s. And as Table 3.8 details, sixteen blacks were elected to the US Congress during Reconstruction – fourteen to the House and two to the Senate. More than half of them (9 of 16) had once been slaves, indicating the aspirational possibilities that emerged for blacks during a very short span of time.

Even as the Democratic consolidation of the South took hold, black political rights – and black office holding – were not eliminated immediately. The white

---

[83] P. B. S. Pinchback would also hold the governorship in Louisiana for a short time (between December 1872 and January 1873), having been elevated to the office due to the suspension of the sitting governor (Henry C. Warmoth).

[84] Foner, *Reconstruction*, 352–56.

TABLE 3.8 *Black members of the US Congress during Reconstruction*

Name (State)	Congress	Chamber	Former slave?
Joseph Rainey (SC)	41st–45th	House	Yes
Jefferson F. Long (GA)	41st	House	Yes
Hiram R. Revels (MS)	41st	Senate	No
Robert C. De Large (SC)	42nd	House	No
Robert B. Elliott (SC)	42nd–43rd	House	No
Benjamin S. Turner (AL)	42nd	House	Yes
Josiah T. Walls (FL)	42nd–44th	House	Yes
Richard H. Cain (SC)	43rd, 45th	House	No
John R. Lynch (MS)	43rd–44th, 47th	House	Yes
Alonso J. Ransier (SC)	43rd	House	No
James T. Rapier (AL)	43rd	House	No
Blanche K. Bruce (MS)	44th–46th	Senate	Yes
Jermiah Haralson (AL)	44th	House	Yes
John Adams Hyman (NC)	44th	House	Yes
Charles E. Nash (LA)	44th	House	No
Robert Smalls (SC)	44th–45th, 47th–49th	House	Yes

Source: *Biographical Directory of the United States Congress*

Reedemer governments tread lightly, not wanting to risk further federal government intervention (especially with a Republican in the White House). Their initial strategy to retain power was to use state registration and canvassing boards, along with the redrawing of legislative district boundaries, to keep black voting power in check. Thus, blacks continued to vote in large numbers in parts of the South through the latter part of the nineteenth century, and some blacks continued to be elected to office. Indeed, six additional blacks served in the US House between the end of Reconstruction and the turn of the twentieth century.[85] That said, these political "successes" were carefully calibrated and watched by Democratic leaders. Moreover, black civil rights suffered greatly with the onset of Redemption, as white Democratic sheriffs, judges, and other authorities in the South typically ignored black concerns involving due process and equal protection of the laws.

CONCLUSION

In this chapter, we trace the development of the Republican Party in the South in the years after the Civil War, during the period known as Reconstruction. As

[85] James E. O'Hara, North Carolina (48th and 49th Congresses); Henry P. Cheatham, North Carolina (51st and 52nd Congresses); John Mercer Langston, Virginia (51st Congress); Thomas E. Miller, South Carolina (51st Congress); George W. Murray, South Carolina (53rd and 54th Congresses); and George Henry White, North Carolina (54th and 55th Congresses).

national Republican leaders debated the best way to integrate the ex-Confederate states back into the Union, the issue of creating a Southern wing of the GOP evolved considerably. During the Civil War and early postwar years, a Southern GOP was little more than a Radical pipe dream, based on the enfranchisement of blacks – an idea that was too extreme for its time. In somewhat short order, moderate Republicans came around to the idea – after the GOP's successful battle with President Johnson and the positive results from the congressional elections of 1866 – and building a Republican South became a legitimate party strategy by 1867.

Southern Republicanism started well but never took firm hold anywhere in the ex-Confederate states. This was because the GOP was never able to establish a strong and consistent following among white Southerners – try as party leaders might to reach out to white ex-Whigs – something that was critical for building a lasting party organization. Early Republican successes were due mostly to strong black turnout and temporary disenfranchisement of some white Southerners. Over time, and at different rates in different states, GOP control of state governments melted away, often amid electoral environments fraught with violence, intimidation, and fraud, as white Democrats and paramilitary groups sought to regain the upper hand and the Northern public increasingly turned a blind eye. In the end, Republican politicians in the South were reliant almost exclusively on black votes, and the GOP held on the longest in those states (Mississippi, Florida, Louisiana, and South Carolina) where black voting power was the strongest.

While some national Republican leaders came to believe that Reconstruction was a failure, many still believed that a Southern wing of the party could be maintained (or re-made). This belief was in part a pragmatic one, as the Republicans in the immediate post-Reconstruction era could not hope to be the majority party nationally without some representation from the South. And over the next twenty years, multiple Republican presidents – Rutherford Hayes, James Garfield, Chester Arthur, and Benjamin Harrison – and GOP leaders in Congress would make concerted efforts to keep a Republican South alive. Different strategies would be employed at different times, but they would involve reaching out to Southern whites of various types, hoping yet again to expand the base of the party, as well as striving to protect black voting rights by ensuring a free ballot and a fair count.

4

The Attempt to Rebuild the Republican Party in the South, 1877–1896

While the Republicans' Reconstruction experiment in the South had come to an end following the presidential election of 1876, the GOP's belief in maintaining a viable party organization in the former Confederacy had not. As the Democratic Party returned to prominence in the North in the 1870s and actively contested elections in the region, Republican leaders recognized that ceding the South to the Democrats could not be a viable strategy for winning national majorities – either in congressional elections or in the Electoral College. At the same time, the last four years of the Grant administration had persuaded many Republican elites that using the military to prop up Carpetbag Republican governments in the South was a losing strategy. Doing so had helped make race the dividing issue in the region and forced together different groups of whites in solidarity against (as the rhetoric went) the GOP's heavy-handed desire to promote "Negro rule."

Thus, for a roughly twenty-year period, from 1877 through 1896, Republican national leadership sought a different strategy regarding the South. During this time – when partisan electoral battles were fierce and margins often narrow (see Table 4.1) – instead of building a party around the freedmen, as the Radicals had attempted to do, GOP leaders sought instead to reach out to select whites in the South and use them as the new building block in a Southern Republican Party. In extending this fig leaf to Southern whites, GOP leaders expected that black rights – embodied in the Fourteenth and Fifteenth Amendments – would be respected and protected. Indeed, the argument was that if there were two parties in the South, both led by whites, then black voters would be actively sought by each party. This electoral contestation and regular need for votes, so the logic went, would lead to the rational protection of black rights.

Over the course of this period, Republican presidents pursued different strategies of courting white Southerners. Hayes focused on conservative

TABLE 4.1 *Party control of House, Senate, and presidency, 1877–1897*

Congress	Years	House (%)	Senate (%)	Presidency (Pop %, EC %)
45	1877–79	Dem (51.5)	Rep (51.3)	Rep (Hayes, 47.9, 50.1)
46	1879–81	Dem (49.7)	Dem (56.0)	Rep
47	1881–83	Rep (50.2)	Rep (49.3)	Rep (Garfield, 48.3, 58.0)
48	1883–85	Dem (60.3)	Rep (49.3)	Rep (Arthur)
49	1885–87	Dem (56.0)	Rep (50.7)	Dem (Cleveland, 48.9, 54.6)
50	1887–89	Dem (51.4)	Rep (50.7)	Dem
51	1889–91	Rep (50.8)	Rep (51.3)	Rep (Harrison, 47.8, 58.1)
52	1891–93	Dem (71.7)	Rep (54.8)	Rep
53	1893–95	Dem (59.3)	Dem (51.8)	Dem (Cleveland, 46.0, 62.4)
54	1895–97	Rep (68.2)	Rep (48.3)	Dem
55	1897–99	Rep (57.7)	Rep (48.8)	Rep (McKinley, 51.0, 60.6)

Note: "Dem" or "Rep" in the House and Senate columns indicates the governing party in that Congress – which sometimes required assistance from third-party members – with percent size in parentheses. Partisan percentages calculated as of the beginning of the Congress. Note that Hayes in 1876 and Harrison in 1888 received fewer popular votes than their Democratic opponents (Samuel Tilden and Grover Cleveland).

Democrats with "Whiggish" preferences on matters of economic development; Arthur (and Garfield before him) backed anti-Democrat Independents; and Harrison first tried to build an alliance around the tariff issue and later (half-heartedly) to initiate a fusion alliance with the Populists. Republicans in Congress were also active, as they used contested election cases to "flip" seats to the GOP when fraud and violence characterized Democratic victories and, more ominously to Southern Democrats, pursued a new federal elections law to ensure the integrity of the electoral process.

All of these efforts, which required a significant amount of time and effort, came for naught. A new white-based Republican Party in the South did not develop. And while this was a perpetual disappointment to GOP leaders, by the end of the period the party had risen to dominance in every other region of the nation – the Northeast, Mid-Atlantic, Midwest, and West – such that a one-party Democratic South was no longer a meaningful concern to national Republican leaders. In effect, the GOP had emerged as the majority party in the nation *without* any assistance from the South. To be sure, later Republican presidents like Theodore Roosevelt, Warren G. Harding, and Herbert Hoover would continue to maintain some hope for a Republican resurgence in the South, and invest time and political capital in attempts to alter the existing Southern GOP organizations with this goal in mind (see Chapter 5). Beginning with William McKinley's election in 1896, however, regaining its electoral footing in the South would be less of a priority for the Republican Party.

Yet, while the Republicans struggled mightily in the South in presidential elections between 1880 and 1896 (see Table 4.2 for a breakdown of the

TABLE 4.2 *Republican vote percentage in presidential elections in the South, 1876–1896*

	1876	1880	1884	1888	1892	1896
Alabama	40.0	37.1	38.7	32.7	3.9	28.6
Arkansas	39.9	39.0	40.7	38.0	31.8	25.1
Florida	51.0	45.8	46.7	39.9	0.0	24.3
Georgia	28.0	34.6	33.8	28.3	21.6	36.8
Louisiana	51.6	37.3	42.4	26.5	23.6	21.8
Mississippi	31.9	29.8	35.7	26.0	2.7	6.9
North Carolina	46.4	48.0	46.6	47.1	35.8	46.8
South Carolina	50.2	34.1	23.4	17.2	18.9	13.5
Tennessee	40.2	44.3	47.7	45.8	37.8	46.3
Texas	29.7	23.8	28.6	25.9	18.3	31.7
Virginia	40.4	39.3	48.9	49.5	38.7	45.9

Source: *Congressional Quarterly's Guide to U.S. Elections*, 3rd edn. (Washington, DC: Congressional Quarterly, 1994)
Note: Harrison's performance in 1892 was dampened by the inclusion of a strong third-party challenger, the Populist (and former Republican) James Weaver.

popular vote by state), to the point where the South did not provide a single electoral vote to any GOP presidential candidate in those five elections, the South continued to play a meaningful role in Republican National Convention politics. While the Republican Party declined electorally in the South as Reconstruction ended, the region retained a considerable position of power at the party's national conventions.[1] As Figure 4.1 illustrates, between 1880 and 1896 the South accounted for around 25 percent of the GOP's total convention delegates. Yet this level of representation was considerably higher than the South's contribution to the party's performance in presidential elections – which was between 10 and 14 percent of the GOP's popular presidential vote during this period. This continued, and outsized, level of representation at conventions had important consequences: most notably, Southern support at the 1892 convention was pivotal to Benjamin Harrison winning the Republican presidential nomination.

Southern representation at the Republican National Convention during this period was sometimes controversial.[2] But actual challenges to the South's oversized influence were rare. This was partly because the party, as noted,

---

[1] A considerable portion of this section is derived from Boris Heersink and Jeffery A. Jenkins, "Southern Delegates and Republican National Convention Politics, 1880–1928," *Studies in American Political Development* 29 (2015): 68–88.
[2] Among the controversies were several major debates regarding the seating of competing delegations at the 1880 (Louisiana), 1884 (Virginia), 1888 (Virginia), 1892 (Alabama), and 1896 (Texas) conventions.

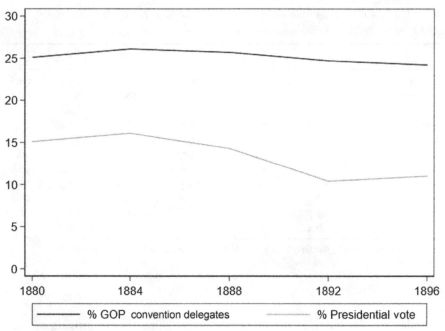

FIGURE 4.1 Southern percentage of delegates at Republican National Convention and Republican popular vote, 1880–1896

Source: *Congressional Quarterly's Guide to U.S. Elections*, 3rd edn. (Washington, DC: Congressional Quarterly, 1994)

Note: The figure above represents the percentage of delegates at the Republican National Conventions in this period that were from the South, and the percentage of the total popular vote received by Republican presidential candidates in each election that came from Southern states.

hoped that the region might still be redeemable through some form of cooperation between local Republican organizations and whites who were disenchanted with the Democratic Party. A subset of Republican leaders was also genuinely concerned about the exclusion of blacks from voting and believed that representation at the convention was an important way for them to continue to participate in democratic politics. Race in this regard was important. In the late 1890s, Southern GOP organizations began to be coopted by white supremacist Republicans (the Lily-Whites), who worked to exclude blacks from positions of authority in the party. Until then, however, Southern state party organizations were still under the control of black Republicans and their white allies (the Black-and-Tans). Thus, while the percentage of black delegates from the South would drop dramatically in the early twentieth century, blacks constituted between 40 and 50 percent of the South's delegation at the GOP national convention in the 1880–96 period (see Figure 4.2). By the

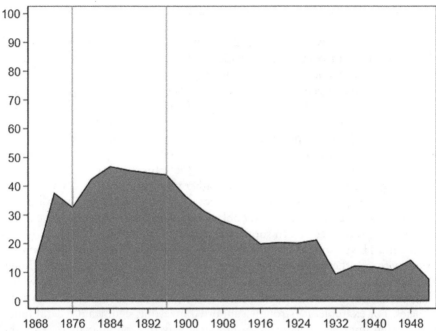

FIGURE 4.2 Percentage of Southern GOP convention delegates that were black,
1880–1896
Source: Data collected by authors.

end of the period, though, the noble interests had withered away, as a Republican South was no longer viable or urgently sought, and the instrumental interests had become the sole interests – as the South became a "rotten borough" full of patronage seekers and vote sellers.

HAYES'S FAILED ATTEMPT AT SOUTHERN OUTREACH

As Rutherford Hayes began his presidency in 1877, he and other national Republican leaders felt their party was on the defensive. The GOP had seemed dominant as recently as 1872, when Ulysses Grant won an easy reelection and the Republicans controlled both chambers of Congress. However, the Panic of 1873 ushered in a depression that lasted until the end of the decade and helped the Democrats take majority control of the US House following the 1874 midterms. By 1877, the GOP had barely held onto the White House – and did so, many believed, via an explicit deal (the Compromise of 1877) that ended the military oversight that remained in Florida, Louisiana, and South Carolina and thereby conceded the governments in those states to the Democrats. Now, the Republicans had to reassess their position and develop a new strategy going forward, lest the Democrats continue to make gains and drive them from power altogether.

Hayes's strategy was to rebuild the Republican brand in the South around the "Whiggism" of years past.[3] Specifically, Hayes sought to recreate Southern Republicanism around issues of economic development, rather than civil rights, and in so doing hoped to convince white Southerners that their future was better invested in the GOP than the Democratic Party. In this way, Hayes sought to rekindle the GOP's economic-based program from the early 1870s, before railroad bankruptcies and bank panics halted it in its tracks (see Chapter 3). Such a policy was not predicated on a rejection of the freedmen and their concerns – as Hayes made clear the importance of preserving and protecting the rights of all citizens – but rather was a pragmatic recognition that a mostly black party in the South was not a winning strategy. The fall of the scalawag and carpetbagger Republican governments in all eleven ex-Confederate states seemed to support that view.

In sum, Hayes sought to shift the focus away from race, promote concili-ation with Southern whites (and emphasize his readiness to accept "home rule"), and make the case that the South as a society (both black and white) had more to gain from Republican economic policies than similar Democratic policies. For example, he strongly supported investing significant federal funds for internal improvements in the South, as a way to economically develop the region. This Whiggish policy was a hit with Southern Democrats, who quickly suggested a range of possible plans – like a tunnel through the Allegheny Mountains and the construction of a canal across the state of Florida from the Atlantic Ocean to the Gulf of Mexico. Indeed, as Vincent De Santis describes, "From October to December in 1877, southern Democrats intro-duced forty bills in the Senate and 267 in the House asking for federal funds in their prospective states."[4]

As a way to build goodwill and potentially shift allegiances, Hayes made a concerted effort to bestow executive patronage positions on Southern Demo-crats. For example, Hayes chose David Key, former Confederate officer and Democratic senator from Tennessee, to be postmaster general, which was considered the most important patronage-dispensing position in the govern-ment. Key used his discretion to distribute a host of postmasterships to South-ern Democrats. Overall, as C. Vann Woodward notes, "one third of all the Southern appointments during the first five months of the [Hayes]

---

[3] See Vincent P. De Santis, *Republicans Face the Southern Question: The New Departure Years, 1877–1897* (Baltimore: Johns Hopkins University Press, 1959); Stanley P. Hirshson, *Farewell to the Bloody Shirt: Northern Republicans and the Southern Negro, 1877–1893* (Bloomington: Indiana University Press, 1962); Charles W. Calhoun, *Conceiving a New Republic: The Repub-lican Party and the Southern Question, 1869–1900* (Lawrence: University Press of Kansas, 2006).

[4] De Santis, *Republicans Face the Southern Question*, 88.

administration went to Democrats."[5] This was a blow to the existing GOP organizations in the South, which normally would have been the beneficiary of this executive windfall. Northern patronage politicians in the Republican Party – known as the Stalwarts – were outraged but could do nothing about it.

To hasten his policy of conciliation with the white South, Hayes undertook a nineteen-day whistle-stop tour of the former Confederacy, visiting cities and towns in Kentucky, Tennessee, Virginia, Georgia, and Alabama. Taking his family, along with Key and Democratic Governor Wade Hampton of South Carolina, Hayes spoke on the subject of reunion, sectional reconciliation, and racial cooperation before a range of crowds – some white, some black, and some biracial. While newspaper editorials in both the North and South were often critical of the tour and its objectives, crowds – especially white crowds – were often celebratory. A common interpretation of the tour among white Southerners was that Reconstruction was indeed over (and that they had emerged victorious).[6]

While Hayes believed his new strategy would yield quick returns for the GOP – he predicted that eight Southern states would move into the Republican column by 1880[7] – it proved to be a failure. Southern Democrats gladly took the patronage opportunities offered to them but continued to spurn the GOP and hold it in contempt. The 1878 midterms, which were the first test of Hayes's strategy, made this clear.[8] Southern Democrats used violence toward blacks, and electoral fraud (widespread use of "tissue ballots" and false counts), to consolidate their hold on the region.[9] As a result, the GOP vote in

---

[5] C. Vann Woodward, *Reunion and Reaction: The Compromise of 1877 and the End of Reconstruction* (Boston: Little, Brown, 1951), 226.

[6] For an extensive description and analysis of the tour, see Edward O. Frantz, *The Door of Hope: Republican Presidents and the First Southern Strategy, 1877–1933* (Gainesville: University of Florida Press, 2011), 22–54.

[7] Hirshson, *Farewell to the Bloody Shirt*, 40–41.

[8] In actuality, an earlier test of Hayes's strategy came in the House speakership election to the 45th Congress. Hayes believed he could organize a Republican House, despite the fact that the Democrats had a majority of members. Specifically, Hayes believed his appeals to the South on economic matters (the promise of federal funding for internal improvements), his appointment of David Key as postmaster general, and his executive patronage strategy had convinced a pivotal group of Southern Democrats (at least nine) to break ranks and support Republican James Garfield (OH) over Democrat Samuel Randall (PA). Hayes apparently received secret pledges in this regard and was offered assistance in rounding up votes by key Democratic figures (like Governor Wade Hampton of South Carolina). However, when the speakership vote was held, on October 15, 1877, Randall defeated Garfield, and every Democrat – North and South – supported Randall. As Allan Peskin notes: "Even though the President had kept his part of the bargain, the Southerners deserted him at the first opportunity." See Allan Peskin, *Garfield* (Kent, OH: Kent State University Press, 1978), 414, 425–26. Quote on p. 426.

[9] A tissue ballot, per Robert Goldman, "looked like a single normal Democratic ballot, but in reality was a number of thin identical ballots made of tissue and stuck loosely together. After the polls had been closed, it was contrived at some point to make sure that the ballot box was vigorously shaken or handled, causing the tissue ballots to separate. One hundred Democratic

both black and white counties in the South dropped from 1876.[10] Republicans, in the end, would hold only 3 of 73 House seats in the former Confederate states when the 46th Congress (1879–81) convened in December 1879 – down from 8 seats in the 45th Congress.[11] The GOP also lost 4 Southern seats in the Senate – leaving them with only 2 seats among the 22 – and would lose majority control of the institution in the 46th Congress.[12]

Why did Hayes's strategy fail? One reason was that his attempt to re-brand the Republican Party was not persuasive. From a white Southerner's perspective, the GOP was the "Negro party" – more specifically, the party that elevated blacks to the level of whites (or above the level of whites, in the minds of many Southern Democrats) by force, at the point of a bayonet. Any whites that belonged to such a party – per this view – were Yankee opportunists (carpetbaggers) or Southern traitors to their race (scalawags). As a result, "respectable" Southern whites could not envision becoming Republicans. It was conceivable, some held, that a Whiggish Republican brand could have been established in the South after the Civil War, built around white businessmen, yeoman white farmers, and freedmen – in opposition to the white planter class. And such a party might have been successful. But Radical Republican strategies and the military-led Reconstruction of the South created a general anti-GOP white identity (irrespective of economic interests) in the region that would prove impervious to new Republican entreaties.[13]

Now in control of both the House and the Senate, the Democrats sought in the 46th Congress to further establish home rule in the South by repealing the Civil War-era Enforcement Acts (which provided some federal oversight over the conduct of elections). Five times the Democrats passed repeal legislation – principally by attaching it as a rider to the Army Appropriations Bill – and five

---

ballots, for example, suddenly became five hundred Democratic votes." Robert M. Goldman, *"A Free Ballot and a Fair Count": The Department of Justice and the Enforcement of Voting Rights in the South, 1877–1893* (New York: Fordham University Press, 2001), 68.

[10] De Santis, *Republicans Face the Southern Question*, 99–101; Hirshson, *Farewell to the Bloody Shirt*, 47–48.

[11] The 3 seats were one each in North Carolina, Tennessee, and Virginia. The Republicans lost 3 seats in South Carolina, one in Tennessee, and 1 in Louisiana. (In fact, the Republicans gained a seat in North Carolina [in the 1st district] and also lost one [in the 2nd district].) Over the course of the 46th Congress, two contested election cases were decided by the Democratic House that kept the GOP's net seat total at 3 – one in favor of the Republicans (seating Horatio Bisbee over Democrat Noble Hull in the 2nd district of Florida) and one in favor of the Democrats (seating Jesse Yeats over Republican Joseph Martin in the 1st district of North Carolina). See Kenneth C. Martis, *The Historical Atlas of Political Parties in the United States Congress, 1789–1989* (New York: Macmillan, 1989), 130–33. On the partisan use of the contested election procedure, see footnote 21 in this chapter.

[12] The four GOP losses came in Alabama, Arkansas, Florida, and South Carolina. The two remaining seats were in Louisiana and Mississippi.

[13] See, for example, David Herbert Donald, Jean Harvey Baker, and Michael F. Holt, *The Civil War and Reconstruction* (New York: Norton, 2001), 584, 598–601.

times Hayes successfully vetoed the attempt.[14] These repeal efforts, along with the Democrats' active rejection of Hayes's efforts, led Republicans to jettison conciliation as an electoral strategy in 1879 and 1880 and coordinate instead around "Bloody Shirt" politics.

SOUTHERN STRATEGIES VERSUS THE BLOODY SHIRT, 1880–1884

The 1880 presidential election was the first after the disputed outcome of 1876–77, and the first after the South as a whole had fallen back into Democratic hands. As the 1880 Republican National Convention approached, former two-term president Ulysses S. Grant and Senator James Blaine of Maine were the front-runners.[15] Grant was being pushed for a third (nonconsecutive) term by Roscoe Conkling, leader of the anti-civil-service Stalwart faction of the GOP, while Blaine was the leader of the moderate Half-Breed faction. The Grant and Blaine forces were fighting for delegates in every part of the country, but Grant – given his past patronage policies and support of the former Reconstruction governments – was extremely popular in the South and looked to have a great advantage there. Yet he did not have the South, and its 25 percent of the convention delegates, wrapped up. This was due to John Sherman, a third candidate for the Republican nomination. Thanks to his position as Treasury Secretary under Hayes, Sherman controlled a massive patronage operation, which he used to keep the Southern wing of the GOP alive and tied to his own presidential ambitions.[16] As Kenneth D. Ackerman notes: "Sherman ... had used Treasury Department employees – all political appointees under his thumb – to pack local caucuses across the South and guarantee a harvest of friendly delegates."[17]

As the voting neared, Sherman understood that Grant and Blaine had considerably more support, but this did not trouble him. Sherman believed that if he could stay in the race long enough, he would become a compromise candidate.[18] He made sure that he remained on friendly terms with both Grant and Blaine, and worked to keep his stable of delegates – especially those from

---

[14] Xi Wang, *The Trial of Democracy: Black Suffrage and Northern Republicans, 1860–1910* (Athens: University of Georgia Press, 1997), 159–79; Jeffery A. Jenkins and Justin Peck, "The Erosion of the First Civil Rights Era: Congress and the Redemption of the White South, 1877–1891," working paper, 2015.

[15] Hayes did not seek re-nomination in 1880.

[16] On Sherman's patronage-based advantage, see Herbert John Clancy, *The Presidential Election of 1880* (Chicago: Loyola University Press, 1958), 30–31; Calhoun, *Conceiving a New Republic*, 170.

[17] Kenneth D. Ackerman, *Dark Horse: The Surprise Election and Political Murder of President James A. Garfield* (New York: Carroll and Graf, 2003), 32–33.

[18] John Sherman, *Recollections of Forty Years in the House, Senate, and Cabinet: An Autobiography*, Vol. II (Chicago: The Werner Company, 1895), 772–75.

the South – from scattering. On the first convention ballot, Grant and Blaine were neck and neck with 304 and 284 delegates, respectively, and 379 needed for the nomination. In the South, Grant commanded 120 of the 190 delegates, but Sherman held 42 (of his total of 93) and Blaine 26 with two scattering. This general breakdown of support would continue through thirty-four ballots, before Rep. James Garfield, Sherman's Ohio colleague, emerged on the 35th ballot as the convention dark horse. On the 36th ballot, nearly all of Blaine's support leaked to Garfield – giving him 399 overall – which was enough to nominate him.[19] In the end, Grant's delegates stuck by him, as he still commanded 306 delegates on the last ballot. But Sherman's Southern delegates largely hung with him as well, rather than moving to Grant.[20] Southern loyalty to Sherman, at least in part, was the product of his reputation as a strong civil rights advocate and, before that, a strong opponent of slavery.

The GOP retained the presidency in 1880, electing Garfield narrowly over Democrat Winfield Scott Hancock, and won back majority control of the House. These successes, however, were accomplished largely without help from the South, as Garfield lost every Southern state and the Republicans captured only seven House seats in the former Confederacy.[21] Thus, condemning the outrages (i.e., violence, intimidation, and fraud) by white Democrats in Southern elections, and calling for an "honest ballot and fair count" so as to promote and protect the interests of black citizens, may have firmed up some GOP support in the North, but yielded little benefit below the Mason–Dixon Line.

As the presidency shifted from Hayes to Garfield and then Chester A. Arthur – after Garfield's assassination in 1881 – the GOP strategy vis-à-vis the South changed, but only in degree, not in kind. That is, it was clear that

---

[19] For a breakdown of the ballots, see *Proceedings of the Republican National Convention, Held at Chicago, Illinois, June 2, 3, 4, 5, 7, and 8, 1880* (Chicago: The Jno. B. Jeffery Printing and Publishing House, 1881), 197–98 (first), 270–71 (thirty-sixth).

[20] See Leon Burr Richardson, *William E. Chandler: Republican* (New York: Dodd, Mead, 1940), 256. On the 34th ballot, for example, Sherman still had 35 delegates from the South. Eventually, these delegates would move to Garfield on the 35th and 36th ballots.

[21] These 7 Republican House seats were an increase over the 3 in the prior (46th) Congress, and more in line with the 8 from the 45th Congress. Moreover, Republicans used the stipulation in Article I, Section 5, Clause 1 of the United States Constitution – "Each House shall be the Judge of the Elections, Returns, and Qualifications of its own Members" – to add five additional GOP House seats via contested (disputed) election cases. Indeed, "flipping seats" via contested election cases would be a way that the Republicans during this era would attempt to counter Democratic efforts to disenfranchise black voters and fraudulently count ballots (and thus "steal" elections). In the next two Houses that the GOP would control – the 51st (1889–91) and the 54th (1895–97) – they would add 5 and 4 House seats in the South via contested elections. The Democrats also used contested election cases aggressively during this era, but predominantly as a way to increase their share of House seats in the *North*. See Jeffery A. Jenkins, "Partisanship and Contested Election Cases in the House of Representatives, 1789–2002," *Studies in American Political Development* 18 (2004): 112–35.

Hayes's dalliance with white Southern Democrats was not successful. However, a segment of the white South – forced into taking on the Democratic label because of the "stain" of Republicanism – was unhappy with the conservative policies of the "Bourbon" Democratic establishment. This populist element emerged in the late 1870s and early 1880s, and ran under various Independent labels. In their identity as Independents, they were able to align with Republicans in "fusion" arrangements in order to seek electoral success and share in the spoils of office. In effect, some Southern whites discovered that they could claim another partisan identity and collaborate with Republicans – and be successful.

Garfield and especially Arthur were open to aligning with the Independents, as a way to break the solid Democratic South.[22] They believed winning white votes was necessary to make inroads in the South and saw the Independent movement as a viable solution – whereas Hayes tried to convince conservative Democrats to switch to the GOP, Garfield and Arthur saw fusion with Democratic opponents (of any stripe) as an easier road to hoe. The prototype for a fusion arrangement was with the Readjuster movement in Virginia, a biracial coalition organized around the goal of repudiation of a portion of the state's pre-Civil War debt (by shifting it to West Virginia). Led by former Confederate General William Mahone, the Readjusters took control of the state legislature and elected a US senator (Mahone himself) in 1879; two years later they elected a governor and a second US senator.[23] The Readjuster movement led to other populist movements across the South, and Garfield and Arthur saw this as the key to rebuilding Republican influence in the former Confederacy. To promote fusion, they used the carrot of executive patronage.[24] Garfield (grudgingly) agreed to split such patronage between the Independents and regular Repub-

---

[22] Vincent P. De Santis, "President Arthur and the Independent Movements in the South in 1882," *The Journal of Southern History* 19 (1953): 346–63; Justin D. Doenecke, *The Presidencies of James A. Garfield and Chester A. Arthur* (Lawrence: University Press of Kansas, 1981), 114–23.

[23] On Mahone and the Readjuster movement, see Allen W. Moger, *Virginia: Bourbonism to Byrd, 1870–1925* (Charlottesville: University of Virginia Press, 1968); Jane Dailey, *Before Jim Crow: The Politics of Race in Postemancipation Virginia* (Chapel Hill: University of North Carolina Press, 2000); Richard M. Valelly, *The Two Reconstructions: The Struggle for Black Enfranchisement* (Chicago: University of Chicago Press, 2004), 57–59; Brent Tartar, *A Saga of the New South: Race, Law, and Public Debt in Virginia* (Charlottesville: University of Virginia Press, 2016).

[24] Mahone had optimal leverage to secure such patronage, as he was the pivotal voter in giving the Republicans organizational control of the Senate in the 47th Congress (1881–83). When the Congress assembled, there were 37 Republicans, 37 Democrats, 1 Independent (David Davis of Illinois), and 1 Readjuster (Mahone). Davis agreed to caucus with the Democrats, which meant the GOP needed Mahone (and Vice President Arthur as the eventual tiebreaker) to achieve majority control. In exchange for his support, Mahone received four key committee assignments and a share of executive patronage for his party from the GOP. See Dailey, *Before Jim Crow*, 53–54.

lican organizations,[25] while Arthur was willing to hand over full patronage authority to the Independents. Southern Republicans were also encouraged to actively support viable Independent candidates and accept fusion as their best route for political success.

In going all-in on fusion, Arthur directed his attorney general, Benjamin Brewster, to protect the ballot box in the South. And Brewster worked to do so, instructing federal authorities that "the right of suffrage must be protected, no matter who suffers."[26] As a result, prosecutions in the South more than tripled between 1880 and 1881 – increasing from 53 to 177 – and remained high (154, 201, and 160) for the next three years.[27] Prosecutions did not often lead to convictions, however, as prejudiced local juries would typically result in mistrials. For example, while the conviction rate in 1881 was a modest 53.7 percent, it quickly fell to 14.9 percent in 1882 and 6 percent in 1883. Nonetheless, Arthur and Brewster hoped active prosecutorial oversight and the *threat* of conviction might help reduce ballot fraud.

In advance of the 1882 midterms, Arthur supported Independent movements and fusion arrangements in nearly every Southern state.[28] These fusion efforts bore some fruit, with meaningful Republican and Independent gains (thanks largely to Readjuster success in Virginia) in Southern House elections. In all, "non-Democrats" won a total of 17 seats in 1882.[29] Arthur was pleased, as he saw these Southern gains as validating his fusion strategy; he also considered them important for his own election chances in 1884 (and, more immediately,

---

[25] Garfield was a more reluctant supporter of Mahone, believing (like Hayes before him) that Readjuster efforts to repudiate a portion of Virginia's debt flew in the face of Republican economic principles. Garfield was more far-sighted in his approach to the South than Arthur (who reacted instrumentally, consistent with the machine politician that he was) and believed that Republican fortunes would be tied to greater education of the populace (blacks and whites as well). Prior to his assassination, he had been considering federal aid for common schools in the South. See Hirshson, *Farewell to the Bloody Shirt*, 78–98. This general policy theme – federal financing of the common schools – would be picked up by Senator Henry Blair (R-NH) and became a major issue in Congress through the 1880s. See Gordon B. McKinney, *Henry Blair's Campaign to Reform America: From the Civil War to the U.S. Senate* (Lexington: University Press of Kentucky, 2013), 77–130; Jeffery A. Jenkins and Justin Peck, "The Blair Education Bill: A Lost Opportunity in Public Education," working paper, 2018.

[26] Quoted in Hirshson, *Farewell to the Bloody Shirt*, 100. For a detailed discussion of enforcement efforts in the South under Arthur, see Goldman, *"A Free Ballot and a Fair Count,"* 89–117.

[27] Overall, prosecutions more than doubled under Arthur relative to Hayes. Data on prosecutions and convictions by region can be found in Wang, *The Trial of Democracy*, 300.

[28] Only in Florida and Louisiana did Arthur reject the Independents and throw his full weight behind the regular Republican organizations. See De Santis, *Republicans Face the Southern Question*, 164–66.

[29] De Santis, "President Arthur and the Independent Movements in the South in 1882," 361–62. Relying upon data collected by Walter Dean Burnham, De Santis undercounts the Independents by one – missing Thomas Ochiltree from the 7th district of Texas. For more on Ochiltree, see Claude H. Hall, "The Fabulous Tom Ochiltree: Promoter, Politician, and Reconteur," *Southwestern Historical Quarterly* 71 (1968): 347–76.

for gaining the Republican convention nod), as he viewed Southern support to be fundamental for his own personal success. However, a deeper analysis of these non-Democratic gains suggests Arthur's optimism was misplaced – of the 17 non-Democratic seats, 8 were won by Republicans. (Republicans had ended the 47th Congress with 11 total seats in the South, thanks to four successful election contests.) Of the remaining 9 Independent pickups, 6 were Readjusters from Virginia, who were already in the midst of a successful run before Arthur unfurled his strategy. Thus, his efforts to help Independents in seven other Southern states resulted in the addition of only 3 seats.[30] Overall, the Republicans suffered significant defeats nationally in 1882 and lost control of the House in the upcoming 48th Congress (1883–85).

Despite his hopes, Arthur would be disappointed soon enough. In the state-level races in 1883, Democrats used threats and violence – which included a racial brawl that left two whites and seven blacks shot in Danville, Virginia, and the vigilante murder of a Republican county chairman in Hazlehurst, Mississippi – in advance of the elections to successfully depress Independent/fusion vote totals.[31] As a result, Democrats won smashing victories throughout the South, including wresting majority control from the Readjusters in both chambers of the Virginia General Assembly. These defeats effectively broke the back of the Independent/fusion movement.

Arthur and other GOP leaders then went on the attack, unfurling a new round of Bloody Shirt rhetoric. Republicans in the House and Senate held investigations into the murders in Virginia and Mississippi, as a way to keep Southern atrocities in the news. However, other Northern GOP constituencies – manufacturers, merchants, and Mugwumps (Northern Republican intellectuals focused on good government issues) – sought to move past sectionalism and Bloody Shirt appeals. Business interests had been pushing for sectional reconciliation from the end of the Civil War, as a way to provide stability and eliminate uncertainty in the economic marketplace. Now, business interests ramped up their push: manufacturers wanted a focus on the tariff, which could be used to reach out to Southern industrialists who had grown in number and importance since the Civil War, while merchants were concerned about keeping Southern markets open and hospitable to Northern goods. Mugwumps, on the other hand, believed that only time and education would improve race relations in the South, and thus argued against further political intervention.[32]

At the same time, the 1880 election – and the Republicans' lack of success in the South – increased criticism within the party over the influence Southern delegates had at national conventions. As a result, some party members called

---

[30] These seat additions included 1 in Mississippi, 1 in North Carolina, and 1 in Texas.

[31] Hirshson, *Farewell to the Bloody Shirt*, 118–20.

[32] The Mugwumps were the successors to the Liberal Republicans of the early 1870s. See John G. Sproat, *"The Best Men": Liberal Reformers in the Gilded Age* (New York: Oxford University Press, 1968), 112–41.

for a reconsideration of the electoral apportionment rules that governed GOP representation at the national convention. If the South was lost to the Republicans, these individuals argued, shouldn't those states that *could* support the party on election day have a stronger hand in the selection of the party's nominees and the design of its platform?

The first major challenge to the equality+size status quo arrangement (see Chapter 2) at the Republican National Convention occurred in 1883–84, as some Northeastern Republicans sought to tie a portion of a state's delegate allotment to its GOP presidential vote total in the previous election. Senator William P. Frye (ME) – a friend and supporter of Blaine – introduced the new initiative at an RNC meeting in December 1883.[33] Frye's plan would provide each state with four at-large delegates, one for each congressional district, and one for each 10,000 votes (or majority fraction thereof) cast for the Republican nominee at the last presidential election. If implemented, Frye's plan would have had an immediate, negative impact on the ex-Confederate South's level of representation at the 1884 convention, reducing its delegate percentage from 26.1 percent (214 of 820 delegates) to 18.4 percent (160 of 870).[34] After debating the plan, RNC members voted 25–18 to refer the decision to the convention, forestalling any change.[35]

Arthur was opposed to such a change. The consummate machine politician, Arthur believed his best chance at receiving the Republican nomination in 1884 – as a first step toward holding onto the presidency – was to establish a clear following among some element of the GOP. He considered the South to be his best bet and, as noted, invested considerable time trying to build (or rebuild) a Southern wing of the party.[36] Arthur believed that the attention he showed Southern GOP leaders would yield direct benefits at the 1884 convention. As a fundamental part of this strategy, Arthur added William E. Chandler of New Hampshire – a favorite of Southern Republicans for his condemnation of white Democrats' actions in the South – to his cabinet. As Vincent De Santis notes, Arthur chose Chandler in part "to conduct the 1882 congressional elections in the South," but perhaps more importantly,

Chandler was also given the job of rounding up southern delegates for Arthur at the 1884 national convention. The Washington correspondent of the New York *Age*

---

[33] In 1877, for example, Blaine had lobbied President Hayes to add Frye to his cabinet, to no avail. See Clancy, *The Presidential Election of 1880*, 22.

[34] See "Republican Representation," *New York Times*, December 7, 1883; "Republican Representation," *Washington Post*, December 7, 1883. Note that both newspapers, in characterizing "southern states," also include Kentucky, Maryland, Missouri, and West Virginia. Only Kentucky, of these four, would have lost convention delegates under the Frye plan.

[35] "A Convention Called," *Washington Post*, December 13, 1883; "Republican Plans for '84," *New York Times*, December 13, 1883.

[36] Vincent P. De Santis, "President Arthur and the Independent Movements in the South in 1882," *The Journal of Southern History* 19 (1953): 346–63.

reported that it was an open secret that Arthur had taken Chandler into the cabinet for this express purpose ... Chandler had the full authority to barter away federal patronage and to use southern offices where they would do the most good in picking up delegates for the President.[37]

Thus, while Frye's motion resonated with many in the party, Arthur and Chandler worked to ensure that it would not be implemented. At the time, important segments within the GOP still believed that Republican electoral success in the South was possible. These party members could point to the victories achieved in Tennessee in 1880, when a split within the Democratic Party allowed a Republican governor (Alvin Hawkins) and a GOP majority in the state House to be elected, and in Virginia by William Mahone and his Readjuster organization, which in alliance with the state Republicans success-fully elected a governor, a majority in the General Assembly, and two US senators between 1879 and 1883. Arthur and Chandler used these victories, and highlighted their own (somewhat successful) efforts to back fusion tickets in other states in 1882, to counter Frye's challenge.[38]

Frye's initiative was proposed once again at the Republican National Convention in 1884. It was first considered by the convention's Committee on Rules, which voted 21–14 to keep the present rules in place (and thus reject the initiative).[39] Table 4.3 breaks down the vote: committee members from all eleven ex-Confederate states opposed Frye's initiative.[40] The majority and minority on the committee then submitted their separate reports to the full convention, where a vigorous debate was had. Both sides – those who believed that state representation at the convention should better mirror state influence on election day and those who sought to avoid blaming Southern Republicans for the disenfranchising efforts of Southern Democrats – raised the issue of fairness. But the most pointed comments came from delegates who supported the majority report (and thus resisted a change). For example, William O'Con-nell Bradley, a white delegate from Kentucky and future governor and US senator, strongly argued in favor of maintaining Southern representation and accused the supporters of delegate reapportionment of trying "for the first time in the history of the Nation" to "disfranchise a portion of the people."[41]

---

[37] Ibid., 354.

[38] On these efforts by Arthur and Chandler across the various Southern states, see Justin D. Doenecke, *The Presidencies of James A. Garfield and Chester A. Arthur* (Lawrence: University Press of Kansas, 1981), 114–23.

[39] See "Committee on Rules," *Chicago Tribune*, June 5, 1884. A second initiative, offered by George Chahoon of New York, was also rejected as part of the vote. Chahoon's initiative would become the basis of the minority report that was sent to the convention. The actual vote was 20–13, with a set of pairs.

[40] This includes the committee member from South Carolina, who paired with the committee member from Vermont.

[41] *Proceedings of the Eighth Republican National Convention, Held at Chicago, June 3, 4, 5, and 6, 1884* (Chicago: Rand, McNally, 1884), 85.

TABLE 4.3 *Rules Committee vote to maintain delegate apportionment rules, 1884 GOP convention*

Yea		Nay	
Alabama	Maryland	Colorado	New Hampshire
Arkansas	Mississippi	Connecticut	New Jersey
California	Missouri	Indiana	New York
Delaware	Nevada	Kansas	Ohio
Florida	North Carolina	Maine	Pennsylvania
Georgia	Oregon	Massachusetts	West Virginia
Illinois	Tennessee	Michigan	Vermont (P)
Iowa	Texas		
Kentucky	Virginia		
Louisiana	Wisconsin		
	South Carolina (P)		

Source: *Chicago Tribune*, June 5, 1884, 5. Committee members from South Carolina and Vermont paired on the vote.

John Lynch, a black delegate from Mississippi, former member of the US House, and the temporary chairman of the convention, spoke passionately about maintaining the South's level of representation in the GOP convention:

> Those of us who come from States where elections are not pure and free will be materially injured by [the Frye proposal]. When you adopt that minority report, you simply say to the ballot-box stuffer at the South, and to the shot-gun holder at the South, that we will let them have the benefit in the Electoral College of each colored man's vote, but we will give him another blow in addition to that, by turning him, the colored man, out of the Republican Convention.[42]

Lynch suggested instead that Southern representation *in Congress* should be reduced because of disfranchisement, in accordance with the provisions of the Fourteenth Amendment. Finally, Powell Clayton, a white delegate from Arkansas and former governor of the state, argued that the South provided no electoral votes to the GOP presidential nominee not because of any failure of Republicanism, but because the federal government was unable to ensure that the votes cast in the Southern states were actually counted. In the end, supporters of Frye's plan sensed they lacked a majority and dropped their challenge. The convention then adopted the majority report, thus maintaining the status-quo arrangement.[43]

With state apportionment reform defeated, Arthur focused on retaining his hold on the presidency. Thanks to his and Chandler's strategic use of patronage

---

[42] Ibid., 87.
[43] For coverage of the debate on the apportionment of delegates, see ibid., 84–91, and "The Routine Work Completed," *New York Times*, June 6, 1884.

appointments, he entered the convention with strong Southern support.[44] On the first convention ballot, Arthur commanded 163 of the 214 delegates from the South, or 76.2 percent. However, he failed to muster much of a following outside of the South, as James Blaine led the count – 334.5 to 278 for Arthur, with 207.5 scattering.[45] Over the next two ballots, Blaine picked up more than 40 votes, while Arthur held virtually steady. And on the fourth ballot, Blaine won the nomination, collecting most of the votes that had scattered to that point along with almost 150 from Arthur.[46] Nevertheless, Arthur's support among Southern delegates largely held until the end. From the first ballot to the fourth, 82 percent of Arthur's supporters from the ex-Confederate states stayed with him.[47]

DEMOCRATIC INTERLUDE, THE HARRISON PRESIDENCY, AND THE LODGE BILL, 1884–1892

During the 1884 presidential election campaign, Blaine continued the Republican Party's alternation between sectionalism and economics as the primary electoral theme in his eventual loss to Democrat Grover Cleveland. Subsequent weak electoral showings in Northern states in 1885, in which Bloody Shirt rhetoric was dominant amid almost constant criticism from Mugwump newspaper editors, finally turned the tide. For the next several years, Republicans would emphasize economics – specifically, the tariff – in their political messaging. In doing so, they would try, once again, to build a Southern Republican Party around a form of Whiggism; whereas Hayes emphasized federal funding for internal improvements a decade earlier, the Republicans of the mid-to-late 1880s saw protection (and a high-tariff platform) as the mechanism to move portions of the white South into the GOP column.

As national Republican leaders increasingly focused on winning the votes of white southerners, organizational GOP politics in the South evolved. The old Black-and-Tan arrangement of freedmen, carpetbaggers, and scalawags, which had been the key to Republican success during Reconstruction, increasingly displayed rifts. White Republicans in various states began to complain about

---

[44] Richardson, *William E. Chandler*, 346–48.

[45] As Leon Richardson states, "Arthur did not have the national appeal of Blaine; his strength, so far as he had any, aside from his creditable record as President was derived from his control of patronage." See Richardson, *William E. Chandler*, 347. Thomas C. Reeves makes a similar point, noting "Arthur was virtually a President without a party. Each of the GOP's warring factions [the Half-Breeds and the Stalwarts] found him objectionable." See Thomas C. Reeves, *Gentleman Boss: The Life and Times of Chester Alan Arthur* (New York: Alfred A. Knopf, 1975), 371.

[46] For a breakdown of the ballots, see *Proceedings of the Eighth Republican National Convention*, 141–63.

[47] Calhoun, *Conceiving a New Republic*, 204. Arthur commanded 134 delegates from the former Confederate states on the fourth ballot.

"Negro domination" and made the case that the only reasonable (and realistic) future for a Southern GOP was to re-create the brand around a more respectable image – namely "whiteness." That is, as this argument went, the only way that the Republican Party in the South would become an electorally viable entity once again would be to increase its white membership – but that was only possible by making the party more hospitable to whites. And a party comprised of blacks, especially one where blacks held leadership positions, was anathema to "upstanding" Southern whites. Thus, as the Southern GOP foundered in the 1880s, many national Republican leaders and Northern intellectuals saw advantages in a Southern wing that moved away from its Reconstruction roots and composition.

The Lily-White movement – which sought to eliminate blacks from positions of leadership in the Republican Party – would officially start in Texas, when in 1886, Norris Wright Cuney, a black Republican, was elected state party chairman.[48] White Republicans, who had been feuding with blacks in the party since the late 1870s, resented Cuney and rejected any black holding such a leadership role. In 1888, at the state party convention in Fort Worth, they fought to expel several blacks, and proceedings degenerated considerably thereafter.[49] Cuney held onto his position, but the general Lily-White vs. Black-and-Tan feud in Texas began spreading to other states in the South – with white Republicans in South Carolina, Alabama, and Louisiana forming white high-tariff parties.[50] This white-party "contagion" was due partly to the white supremacy arguments discussed earlier. However, it was also the case that Lily-White organizations emerged as a way for Southern whites to vie for influence, when such influence was harder to achieve by working within traditional Southern GOP organizations – where blacks had played an active and meaningful role for a generation. Thus, by 1888, while Republican politicians continued to mention the protection of civil and voting rights, the basis of national party politics had turned to substantive differences on major economic policies, like the tariff.

---

[48] On the conflict between the Black-and-Tans and Lily-Whites, see Hanes Walton, Jr., *Black Republicans: The Politics of the Black and Tans* (Metuchen, NJ: The Scarecrow Press, 1975). And while some Lily-Whites wanted to throw all blacks out of the Republican Party, most understood the importance of keeping blacks within the organization (but out of leadership roles). As Ralph Bunche explained some years later: "The lily-white Republican organizations do not generally exclude Negroes entirely. There is no such thing as a pure white Republican primary in the South. In some states ... the Negro Republican registrants are needed in order to give the party sufficient representation in the state to continue the party's legal recognition and keep its place on the ballot." See Ralph Bunche, *The Political Status of the Negro in the Age of FDR* (Chicago: University of Chicago Press, 1973), 82.

[49] Alwyn Barr, *Reconstruction to Reform: Texas Politics, 1876–1906* (Austin: University of Texas Press, 1971); Paul D. Casdorph, *A History of the Republican Party in Texas, 1865–1965* (Austin: Pemberton Press, 1965).

[50] Hirshson, *Farewell to the Bloody Shirt*, 175–76, 179–81.

John Sherman of Ohio (now back in the Senate) was the front-runner for the Republican nomination in 1888. His long history of support for black civil rights again gave him an edge in the South.[51] However, with Cleveland in the White House, Southern Republicans had been denied executive patronage since early 1885. As a result, they were a beleaguered group, which made some Republican leaders concerned that they would sacrifice long-term loyalty for short-term benefit.

And this is indeed what occurred: while Sherman led the field for the first six ballots, he could not get much beyond the halfway mark in terms of winning the nomination. Moreover, he saw the Southern share of his delegate total decline, to the benefit of Russell A. Alger – lumber baron, former Union general, and former governor of Michigan, who possessed an "ample wealth [that] gave him the wherewithal to court delegates outside of Michigan, especially in the South."[52] On the first ballot, Sherman commanded 111 of the 214 Southern delegates, or 51.9 percent. Alger, by comparison, had the support of only 27 Southern delegates. By the sixth ballot, Sherman's Southern delegate count had dropped to 97, while Alger's had increased to 60.

That Alger "bought" Southern delegates previously committed to Sherman (and others) became a core narrative that emerged from the 1888 convention. As James A. Kehl recounts,

In explaining Sherman's decline in the South, a subordinate complained that Alger "bought our Negro delegates like sheep." Under the guise of purchasing gallery tickets from southern blacks who desperately needed expense money, Alger literally purchased the delegates who transferred their allegiance from Sherman.[53]

Sherman himself also subscribed to this narrative. In his memoirs, published in 1895, Sherman made clear that he believed Alger and his lieutenants were corrupt: "I believe and had, as I thought, conclusive proof that the friends of General Alger substantially purchased the votes of many of the delegates of the Southern states who had been instructed by their conventions to vote for me."[54] Alger responded by saying such charges had "no foundation" and noted that

---

[51] Calhoun also notes that one of Sherman's lieutenants was former Illinois congressman Green R. Raum, who was "long an ardent advocate of blacks' civil rights [and] was particularly proficient at persuading southern delegates to enlist in Sherman's cause." Calhoun, *Minority Victory*, 95.

[52] Ibid., 85.

[53] James A. Kehl, *Boss Rule in the Gilded Age: Matt Quay of Pennsylvania* (Pittsburgh: University of Pittsburgh Press, 1981), 87.

[54] Sherman, *Recollections of Forty Years in the House, Senate, and Cabinet*, Vol. II, 1029. In discussing whether he harbored any resentments toward those who may have contributed to his defeat in 1888, Sherman said the following: "The only feeling of resentment I entertained was in regard to the action of the friends of General Alger in tempting with money poor negroes to violate the instructions of their constituents." Ibid., 1032.

Sherman's brother, General William T. Sherman, harbored no ill will toward him.[55]

Prior to 1888, there had been a general belief that Southern delegates could be plied with patronage appointments, and that established loyalties would be honored during the balloting process for the nomination. Beginning in 1888, a more negative belief about Southern delegates emerged: that they were available continuously to the highest bidder. More generally, as the viability of the Southern wing of the GOP declined, the degree to which the Southern state organizations became rotten boroughs increased significantly.

Benjamin Harrison, Senator from Indiana, would eventually take the lead on the seventh convention ballot and win the nomination on the eighth (drawing delegates from Blaine, Alger, and all other candidates).[56] Now, looking ahead to November, GOP leaders sought to structure the campaign to win back the White House. Specifically, they intended to use the tariff to break up the Solid South and denounced strongly any attempts by party members to raise sectional concerns.[57] Harrison was fully behind the high-tariff strategy. And with Democratic President Grover Cleveland strongly in favor of tariff reform (reduction), the tariff thus became the central issue in the campaign.[58]

In the 1888 presidential election, Harrison came out on top, winning the electoral vote while losing the popular vote. The Republicans also won majority control of both chambers of Congress. Harrison's performance in the South, however, did not match the ambitious pre-election forecasts – many in the party believed that emphasizing protection and downplaying sectionalism would lead

[55] See "Alger Makes a Reply," *Washington Post*, November 22, 1895; "Ire of Alger Aroused," *Chicago Tribune*, November 22, 1895; "Alger Answers Sherman," *New York Times*, November 22, 1895. According to Alger, he was told by William T. Sherman: "You made a good show of votes, and if you bought some, according to universal usage, I don't blame you. I laughed at John for trying to throw off on anybody. He was fairly beaten at the convention."

[56] For a breakdown of the ballots, see *Proceedings of the Ninth Republican National Convention, Held at Chicago, Illinois, June 19, 20, 21, 22, 23, and 25, 1888* (Chicago: The Blakely Printing Co., 1888), 163–205.

[57] Senator William Chandler (R-NH) was a thorn in the GOP leadership's side during this time, as he (and a small group of like-minded colleagues) worked to keep sectionalism (and the plight of blacks in the South) at the party's forefront. During the 50th Congress (1887–89), for example, he successfully sponsored a resolution to have the Judiciary Committee investigate allegations of black voter suppression in recent municipal elections in Jackson, Mississippi. He also sought unsuccessfully to block the Supreme Court nomination of Lucius Q. C. Lamar of Mississippi (Secretary of the Interior at the time), on the basis that Lamar was a known racist and a ringleader in the "Mississippi Plan" of 1875, an organized effort to use violence and intimidation to suppress the black vote and "redeem" the state. See Leon Burr Richardson, *William E. Chandler, Republican* (New York: Dodd, Mead, 1940): 390–91; Hirshson, *Farewell to the Bloody Shirt*, 152–56.

[58] Joanne R. Reitano, *The Tariff Question in the Gilded Age: The Great Debate of 1888* (University Park: Pennsylvania State University Press, 1994); Charles W. Calhoun, *Minority Victory: Gilded Age Politics and the Front Porch Campaign of 1888* (Lawrence: University Press of Kansas, 2008).

enough white Southerners to vote Republican that several states would move into the GOP column.[59] That did not happen: Harrison was unable to win even one Southern state. He came very close in Virginia, and reasonably close in North Carolina.[60] But in nine of the other eleven ex-Confederate states, Harrison actually performed worse than Blaine in 1884 – and in some, like Louisiana, considerably worse. The Solid Democratic South was still crack-free.

Nevertheless, the GOP leadership pressed on in their efforts to use protectionism to split the Democrats' control in the South. A concerted attempt would be made in two Southern elections in late 1889 – a House race in Louisiana (3rd district) and the gubernatorial race in Virginia – that Republican leaders viewed as a litmus test for the continued high-tariff strategy. Moreover, GOP leaders made clear that they favored the growth of white parties in the South, and President Harrison agreed that patronage should be distributed in accordance with that mission.[61] Thus, in the fall of 1889, the Republican establishment went all-in on their "white protectionist" message, and marshaled men and resources to back it up.

In each election, the Republicans were beaten badly.[62] In Louisiana, there was evidence of Democratic suppression of the GOP vote. In addition, blacks responded negatively to the white-party theme and loss of patronage, and many either stayed home or voted Democratic in protest. In Virginia, the GOP candidate was former Senator William Mahone, and a number of high-profile Republicans – House Speaker Thomas B. Reed (ME), Sen. J. Donald Cameron (PA), Rep. William McKinley (OH), Sen. John Sherman (OH), Sen. Matthew Quay (PA; and chairman of the Republican National Committee), Rep. Julius Ceasar Burrows (MI), and James S. Clarkson (RNC member) – backed him and invested time in his campaign. The RNC also provided $25,000 in support, a significant sum for the time. And, in the end, it was all for naught. The Democrats ran a campaign of "Negro domination," playing up racial fears, and emphasized the importance of local self-government as a counter to the GOP's campaign of protectionism. As a result, Mahone was soundly defeated,

---

[59] See Hirshson, *Farewell to the Bloody Shirt*, 168–76; Calhoun, *Conceiving a New Republic*, 223–24.

[60] Harrison also came very close in West Virginia, a border state (and former slave state). He received 49.03 percent of the vote, compared to Cleveland's 49.35 percent.

[61] As Stanley Hirshson writes: "In [June 1889] the country learned the details of the administration's Southern policy, which had been worked out after a series of conferences with important senators and Southern Republicans of both races. A white, high-tariff party would be formed in the South. The Negro was to be kept in the background and given only minor posts and an attempt would be made to detach states like West Virginia, North Carolina, and Louisiana, where there were large numbers of protectionists and former Whigs, from the Democratic fold. The administration was sure the colored men would remain loyal Republicans when they realized that the party intended to restore tranquility in the South." Hirshson, *Farewell to the Bloody Shirt*, 182.

[62] For an overview, see ibid., 182–89.

with the Democrats also taking both chambers of the state legislature. GOP leaders cried foul, holding that "Democratic machines using a combination of intimidation and fraud had successfully prevented Republican victories."[63]

In the aftermath of these losses, the Republicans who had so strongly advocated for protectionism in place of sectionalism now did an about-face. Building a white party was out, and aiding Southern blacks was back in. As Stanley Hirshson states: "The defeats in Louisiana and Virginia finally convinced [them] that the Bourbons were not to be trusted and that only federal regulation of elections could solve the sectional problem."[64] What was needed, GOP congressional leaders now believed, was new and forceful legislation. And President Harrison, who had previously been a supporter of black civil rights during his years in Congress, agreed.[65]

Rep. Henry Cabot Lodge (R-MA) answered the call. Lodge, a strong advocate of black voting rights and honest elections, introduced his Federal Elections Bill, which would have placed the federal government – principally US district and circuit court justices – in charge of supervising federal elections.[66] The bill stipulated that a set of three federal supervisors, appointed by US district judges, would be placed at every polling place to check registration books, observe the vote, participate in the count, and (most importantly) make their own returns. A three-man federal canvassing board, appointed by US circuit courts, would then certify the election results. If the results provided by state officials and the federal supervisors differed, a majority decision of the canvassing board would serve as prima facie evidence of election.[67] And the army and navy would be charged with enforcing the law. Lodge's bill thus had the potential to eliminate a considerable degree of fraud, which state officials in the South routinely allowed and often participated in.

Democrats dubbed Lodge's bill "the Force Bill" and likened it to the Enforcement Acts of the early 1870s. They decried the GOP's attempt to federalize what they argued was a local matter and lambasted their heavy-

---

[63] McKinney, *Henry W. Blair's Campaign to Reform America*, 125. For example, Rep. Joseph Cheadle (R-IN), who was on the ground in Virginia, claimed that "Democrats had deleted 20,000 Republican names from the registration lists and had barred from voting or had refused to count the votes of another 25,000." See Calhoun, *Conceiving a New Republic*, 233.

[64] Hirshson, *Farewell to the Bloody Shirt*, 205.

[65] See Vincent De Santis, "Benjamin Harrison and the Republican Party in the South, 1889–1893," *Indiana Magazine of History* 51 (1955): 279–302.

[66] For a lengthy discussion of the politics surrounding the Lodge Bill, see Richard M. Valelly, "Partisan Entrepreneurship and Policy Windows: George Frisbie Hoar and the 1890 Federal Elections Bill," in Stephen Skowronek and Matthew Glassman, eds., *Formative Acts: American Politics in the Making* (Philadelphia: University of Pennsylvania Press, 2007), 126–52; Calhoun, *Conceiving a New Republic*, 226–59; Rayford W. Logan, *The Betrayal of the Negro: From Rutherford B. Hayes to Woodrow Wilson* (New York: Da Capo Press, 1997), 61–73; Richard E. Welch, Jr., "The Federal Elections Bill of 1890: Postscripts and Preludes," *The Journal of American History* 52 (1965): 511–26.

[67] A contestant (the ostensible loser in the election) could appeal the decision to a circuit court.

handedness in trying to impose their preferences on the white citizens of the South. Deflecting these criticisms and accompanying dilatory actions, Speaker Reed – after a week of debate in late June and early July 1890 – steered the bill successfully through the House, winning a close (155–149) vote near the end of the first (regular) session of the 51st Congress. The vote was almost perfectly party-line, with no Democrats supporting the bill and only two Republicans opposing it.[68]

The problem would be the Senate, where the Republican majority factionalized – some GOP senators sought to pass a new tariff bill (which had been under debate for weeks) before considering the Federal Elections Bill, others wanted a new silver policy first, while still others feared the Lodge Bill's negative effect on North–South commerce. Eventually, Republican Senator Matthew Quay (PA) negotiated a deal with Democratic leaders to postpone consideration of the Lodge Bill until after the 1890 elections – and thus until the lame-duck session of the 51st Congress – in exchange for ending debate on the tariff and bringing the matter to a vote. Quay was chairman of the RNC and had made the tariff issue instrumental in the 1888 election, and he now felt compelled to deliver for Pennsylvania industrialists and other national business leaders. While many Republican senators, like George Frisbie Hoar (MA) and John Spooner (WI), criticized Quay and thought postponement meant the death of the Federal Elections Bill, Quay was unmoved. Eventually, a deal was struck among Senate Republicans that the Lodge Bill would be the first matter dealt with when the lame-duck session convened in December – and would remain at the top of the agenda, to the exclusion of all other matters, until resolved. With this, Quay and his pro-business Republican allies got their tariff hike – known as the Tariff Act of 1890 – before the election.[69]

When Congress reconvened in December 1890, the Republicans were smarting after a major electoral defeat – the Democrats had routed them and would be the majority party in the House in the 52nd Congress (1891–93). And while many held that the Tariff Act of 1890 was the reason behind the rout, as it increased average duties across all imports from 38 percent to 49.5 and thus resulted in consumer prices shooting up and the governing party (the GOP) being blamed,[70] Southern Democrats also used the "fear of the Force Act" to attack Republican House members in the South. As Charles Calhoun notes: "[The Lodge Bill] proved a godsend for southern Democrats, who revived the

---

[68] The two Republicans who voted against the Lodge Bill were H. Dudley Coleman (LA) and Herman Lehlbach (NJ). Also, one Independent, Lewis Porter Featherstone, a member of the Union Labor Party from Arkansas, supported the bill. See *Congressional Record*, 51st Congress, 1st Session (July 2, 1890): 6940–41.

[69] The Tariff Act of 1890 was otherwise known as the McKinley Tariff, after sponsor Rep. William McKinley (R-OH).

[70] See, for example, Reitano, *The Tariff Question in the Gilded* Age, 129–30.

specter of a revived Reconstruction."[71] As a result, the number of GOP House seats in the ex-Confederate states went from 13 to 3, as most Republican incumbents were defeated soundly.[72]

With these Republican electoral defeats, the Lodge Bill's momentum was halted. The Democrats were emboldened and set about on a filibuster (or protracted debate) to expend the short session's remaining time. Over the next month, Republican supporters of the bill in the Senate considered pursuing a new measure to bring the debate to a close – that is, adopting a cloture or previous question rule – but were ambushed when one of their own, Sen. William Stewart of Nevada, was recognized and proposed taking up a free coinage bill (and thus bypassing consideration of the Lodge Bill). This was shocking, as Stewart had a long Senate history of being a champion of black voting rights; he was a major contributor to the passage of the Fifteenth Amendment and the Enforcement Acts. Now, he argued that the Lodge Bill was unworkable in its current form, as it would require the active use of the military to enforce – something that had been shown to be a failure and was no longer supported by the Northern public. The Senate adopted Stewart's motion on a 34–29 vote, with eight Republicans (seven of whom were from silver states) joining all Democrats against the majority of Republicans.[73]

Nine days later, the free coinage bill was passed – the vote cut across both parties, but all eight Republicans who had supported Stewart's motion joined with a majority of Democrats to adopt the measure. With free coinage out of the way, Sen. Hoar immediately moved to take up the Lodge Bill once again – which produced a 33–33 vote. Six of the eight Republicans who had supported Stewart's motion voted with the Democrats to reject taking up the Lodge Bill. The Republicans were only successful because Vice President Levi Morton cast a tiebreaking vote in favor.[74] Debate on the Lodge Bill then commenced and continued for nearly a week, and GOP supporters of the bill were once again considering a cloture motion. Republican Senator Edward Wolcott (CO), however, was recognized and moved to consider an apportionment bill instead.

---

[71] Calhoun, *Conceiving a New Republic*, 252.

[72] At the end of the 51st Congress, Republicans held 1 House seat in Alabama, 1 in Louisiana, 3 in North Carolina, 1 in South Carolina, 3 in Tennessee, and 4 in Virginia. (Of these 13 seats, 4 – in Alabama, South Carolina, and 2 in Virginia – were generated by the Republicans flipping seats via the contested election procedure during the 51st Congress.) All but 1 of these 13 Republican incumbents ran for reelection. The only 3 that were successful were Henry P. Cheatham (NC), Alfred Taylor (TN), and Leonidas Houk (TN).

[73] See *Congressional Record*, 51st Congress, 2nd Session (January 5, 1891): 912–13. The eight Republicans were John P. Jones (NV), William J. McConnell (ID), George L. Shoup (NV), Leland Stanford (CA), William Stewart (NV), Henry M. Teller (CO), William D. Washburn (MN), and Edward O. Wolcott (CO).

[74] See *Congressional Record*, 51st Congress, 2nd Session (January 14, 1891): 1323–24. The six Republicans were Jones (NV), Stanford (CA), Stewart (NV), Teller (CO), Washburn (MN), and Wolcott (CO).

And Wolcott's attempt to bypass the Lodge Bill was successful, as the Senate voted 35–34 to take up the apportionment bill. Six Republicans voted with all Democrats in support of Wolcott's motion against the rest of the GOP. Five of these six Republicans were part of Stewart's previous coalition. They were joined by Sen. J. Donald Cameron of Pennsylvania, "who was speculating in silver at the time."[75]

Senate Republicans could not muster the votes to reverse this decision. As a result, the Lodge Bill died. According to Stanley Hirshson: "The Lodge bill had been buried by a bargain between the Democrats and the free silverites." He notes that prior to moving his coinage bill on January 5, Stewart conferred with Albert Pue Gorman, the leader of the Senate Democrats. And they joined forces to push the Lodge Bill off the agenda in favor of the currency bill. Then, on January 20, "six Silver Republicans [repaid] their debt to Gorman ... and joined with the Democrats... to sidetrack the election bill and consider an apportionment act."[76] In the parlance of modern political science, the silver Republicans and Democrats agreed upon – and carried out – an inter-temporal vote trade. Regular Republicans were incensed, but in the end could not prevent the Lodge Bill's defeat.

While the "silver alliance" between the South and West was an obvious culprit in the Lodge Bill's demise, other forces were also in play. Northern businessmen, seeking to maintain a stable economic environment in the South, also opposed the Lodge Bill. And the behavior of their advocates in Congress – Quay and Cameron – provides some evidence of this.[77] In addition, during the summer and fall of 1890, public opinion in the country turned against the Lodge Bill.[78] Special interests, like the Farmers' Alliance, Manufacturers' Clubs, and Republican Party clubs at the state level, came out against the bill. Negative editorials also appeared in leading party papers. And informal polls of party members revealed considerable opposition to the bill and its (perceived) federal encroachment. Which of these factors was most important is unclear. But what was clear was the effect of the bill's failure. As Charles Calhoun asserts: "Defeat of the Lodge bill dealt a devastating blow to Republican efforts to fulfill their republican aims in the South."[79]

The Lodge Bill would be the Republicans' last serious attempt in the nineteenth century to build a viable Republican Party in the South. As Stanley Hirshson notes:

Never again did the party leaders of this generation adopt an aggressive Southern policy. Aware that in the past fifteen years all of their plans to build Republicanism in the South had failed, almost all Republicans now conceded that their party was destined to be a

---

[75] Hirshson, *Farewell to the Bloody Shirt*, 233.   [76] All quotes from ibid., 233.
[77] De Santis, *Republicans Face the Southern Question*, 214.
[78] Ibid., 210–14; Hirshson, *Farewell to the Bloody Shirt*, 234–35; Calhoun, *Conceiving of a New Republic*, 258–59.
[79] Calhoun, *Conceiving of a New Republic*, 260.

Northern, not national, organization. The day of education bills, of election laws, of investigations of Bourbon atrocities, and of campaigns run on the race question was gone. The Southern problem hereafter became largely a matter of dispensing patronage and of obtaining delegates for national conventions.[80]

All else equal, Harrison – as an incumbent president – should have considered his re-nomination in 1892 to be a mere formality. However, he presided over a party in a state of disarray, as the GOP was slaughtered in the 1890 midterms and lost their House majority. In addition, Harrison's cold, impersonal style and unwillingness to "play ball" with GOP party bosses like Tom Platt of New York and Matt Quay of Pennsylvania on patronage matters created significant dissension within the Republican ranks. Finally, Harrison became estranged from James Blaine, his secretary of state, who resigned days before the 1892 convention. As a result, a movement – led by Quay – to replace Harrison gained momentum, and Blaine appeared ready to accept the nomination if it came to him.[81]

In the end, Southern delegates saved Harrison's re-nomination, as Platt, Quay, and others could not overcome the president's ability to control Southern delegates with patronage. The first hint of Harrison's convention strength came on a contest involving the seating of delegates from Alabama, which Harrison's side won.[82] On the basis of this vote, Quay concluded that "the Harrison people have bought up the colored fellows, and we must try to get them back."[83] Quay then frantically tried to convince enough delegates to back either Blaine or William McKinley, then the governor of Ohio, to prevent Harrison from winning a first ballot majority. Quay hoped to extend the contest, and in so doing steadily build a coalition against Harrison. But his gambit failed, as Harrison received a 59 percent majority on the first ballot and won the nomination.[84]

Table 4.4 provides a breakdown of the balloting by region. As the numbers indicate, Harrison dominated the South, winning 164.16 of 224 delegate votes,

---

[80] Hirshson, *Farewell to the Bloody Shirt*, 236.

[81] For an overview of Republican pre-convention politics, see George Harmon Knoles, *The Presidential Campaign and Election of 1892* (Stanford, CA: Stanford University Press, 1942), 34–48; Donald Marquand Dozer, "Benjamin Harrison and the Presidential Campaign of 1892," *The American Historical Review* 54 (1948): 49–77.

[82] The outcome of this dispute resulted in the seating of an all-white delegation, rather than a biracial delegation of whites and blacks. See Iric Nathanson, "African Americans and the 1892 Republican National Convention, Minneapolis," *Minnesota History* 61 (2008): 76–82. This was the first hint of the Lily-White versus Black-and-Tan dispute that would plague the Southern GOP for the next several decades. For a detailed history of this internal Republican dispute in the South, see Walton, *Black Republicans*.

[83] Quoted in Kehl, *Boss Rule in the Gilded Age*, 172.

[84] For a breakdown of the ballot, see *Proceedings of the Tenth Republican National Convention Held in the City of Minneapolis, Minn., June 7, 8, 9, and 10, 1892* (Minneapolis, MN: Harrison & Smith, 1892), 141.

TABLE 4.4 *Balloting at the 1892 Republican convention, by region*

Delegate region	Total votes	Harrison	Blaine	McKinley
Non-South	682	371	141	166
South	224	164.16	41.16	16
Total	906	535.16	182.16	182

Source: Proceedings of the Tenth Republican National Convention, Held in the City of Minneapolis, Minn., June 7, 8, 9, and 10, 1892 (Minneapolis: Harrison & Smith, 1892), 141

or 73.3 percent. Moreover, those 164.16 votes constituted just under 31 percent of Harrison's entire delegate total. Given that 454 votes were necessary to win the nomination, Harrison's support in the South was crucial, as he was only able to manage 371 votes outside of the former Confederacy. As James Kehl notes, "Harrison's patronage power, particularly in the South, was the decisive factor … In the South, Blaine could attract only 10 percent of the delegate support necessary to acquire the nomination and had no asset comparable to patronage when he went forth to corner the other 90 percent." Summing things up – with an assist from Quay himself – Kehl states: "with the Republican electoral potential of the South almost nonexistent, Quay commented that 'the President has been re-nominated by the powers which cannot give him an electoral vote.'"[85]

During the convention, regional animosity surfaced. Southern Republicans were often referred to derisively as "office holders," and criticized for the transactional way they went about determining their support. For example, Colorado delegate and former US Senator Edward Wolcott challenged "the office-holding contingent, who are bringing a Solid South against us, to at least conduct their side of the case in common decency, and common honor, so that we won't be ashamed to vote the ticket."[86]

This animosity and the controversial nature of Harrison's nomination victory resulted in Republican party bosses providing only tepid support in mobilizing voters during the general election campaign. Additionally, the Lodge Bill played a major role in the election but as a tool of the Democrats. Grover Cleveland was once again the Democratic presidential nominee – setting up a rematch with Harrison – but the Democrats were internally divided on some key issues (chiefly the tariff and currency). Thus, they coordinated around a campaign of fear, by warning that reelecting Harrison (and voting for

[85] Quotes from Kehl, *Boss Rule in the Gilded Age*, 174.
[86] After Arkansas delegate Powell Clayton responded to Wolcott by noting that he himself had "never filled a Federal office in my life, and none that come from my own State," Wolcott responded by noting his "desire to remind the distinguished gentleman from Arkansas that if he does not hold office, he drags a beautiful lot of them always in his train." All quotes from *Proceedings of the Tenth Republican National Convention Held in the City of Minneapolis*, 54–57.

Republicans generally) would lead to "Negro domination." The "return of the Force Bill" became the Democrats' bogeyman in the run-up to the election, and GOP leaders' attempts to dispel that concern were unsuccessful. The result was that Cleveland regained the presidency and carried in Democratic majorities in both congressional chambers on his coattails. In the subsequent (53rd) Congress, the Democrats acted quickly to repeal the Reconstruction-era Enforcement Acts – which they failed to do during the Hayes administration – and Cleveland signed the repeal into law.[87] Meanwhile, Republicans were left looking ahead to 1896 as the "out party" once again.

WILLIAM MCKINLEY AND THE NEW "SOUTHERN STRATEGY," 1892–1896

In the next few years, the Republicans made only token party-building efforts in the South. The major initiative – which itself was half-hearted – was a new fusion effort with the Populist Party.[88] The Populists began as an agrarian membership organization – first called the Grange and then later the National Alliance – that tried to initiate change in the Democratic Party from within. When this failed, a break occurred and the Populists tried to build their own party. The Republicans saw in the Populists a chance to break the Democrats' grip on the South, and devoted resources in several Southern states to build an alliance.[89] But "fusion" in this case was nothing more than expedience, as the Republicans and Populists had no common issue agenda. As Vincent De Santis notes: "The only unifying element for these two groups was their opposition to the Democratic party in the South. Going it alone, each despaired of victory over the Democrats, but the prospects of winning through a combination of forces proved to be too tempting."[90] Yet the strategic alliance yielded little payoff. The only place where a Republican–Populist alliance generated success was in North Carolina, where the Populists won control of the upper house and the Republican–Populist alliance won control of the lower house – and the state legislature would then select a Populist and a Republican to represent the state in the US Senate (see Chapter 7).[91]

Even as a Solid Democratic South remained in place, the Panic of 1893 and the subsequent depression that included countless bank closings, business

---

[87] See Wang, *The Trial of Democracy*, 253–59.
[88] See C. Vann Woodward, *Origins of the New South, 1877–1913* (Baton Rouge: Louisiana State University Press, 1951), 275–82; De Santis, *Republicans Face the Southern Question*, 227–62.
[89] A Republican–Populist alliance did not develop in Arkansas, Florida, Georgia, South Carolina, Texas, and Virginia. De Santis, *Republicans Face the Southern Question*, 247.
[90] Ibid., 229.
[91] The two US senators were Populist Marion Butler and Republican Jeter C. Pritchard. The Populists and Republicans would also control seven of nine US House seats (after one Democratic seat was flipped to Populist, thanks to a contested election procedure). And in 1896, Republican Daniel L. Russell was elected governor.

failures, and farm foreclosures helped the Republicans regain control of the House and Senate in the 1894 midterms. The GOP front-runner for the 1896 presidential nomination was William McKinley, who had been a (reluctant) candidate for the nomination in both 1888 and 1892. Mark Hanna, McKinley's campaign manager, had been positioning him for the presidency for some time and set out to build a secure convention majority for him well in advance. Hanna, having witnessed Harrison's strategy in successfully defeating his re-nomination challenge in 1892, understood that "cultivating a strong relationship with southern Republicans [needed to be] a large part of his plan."[92] As a result, Hanna and McKinley decided to "hunt where the ducks were" (almost seventy years before Barry Goldwater would make this quip) and rented a house in Thomasville, Georgia for several weeks in the winter of 1895.[93] During this time, Hanna and McKinley hosted Southern GOP delegates – both black and white – and discussed "patronage and other political possibilities in a relaxed atmosphere."[94] For those Southern delegates who could not make the trek to Thomasville, McKinley had lieutenants fan out across the region to talk to them individually.[95] Hanna and McKinley hoped to keep their Thomasville strategy as inconspicuous as possible, but word leaked out and other Republican nomination hopefuls attempted to counter-mobilize. Such efforts, however, were in vain, as Hanna and McKinley's first-mover advantage paid off. New York GOP party boss Tom Platt showed Hanna some (grudging) respect in his assessment that "[he] had the South practically solid before some of us awakened."[96]

In addition to courting existing party organizations, Hanna and McKinley succeeded in controlling the South by fundamentally restructuring those that refused to support them. The most notable example of this concerned the state party organization in Texas, which had been under the control of Norris Wright Cuney since 1884. Cuney's hold on federal patronage combined with his race (black) earned him the hostility of Lily-White Republicans in the state. The Lily-Whites began organizing local Republican clubs in an attempt to replace Cuney's organization with their own as early as 1888. However, with Harrison continuing to provide Cuney with federal offices, the Texas GOP

---

[92] William T. Horner, *Ohio's Kingmaker: Mark Hanna, Man and Myth* (Athens: Ohio University Press, 2010), 141.

[93] For more on the Thomasville rental strategy, see Clarence A. Bocote, "Negro Officeholders in Georgia under President McKinley," *The Journal of Negro History* 44 (1959): 217–39; Stanley L. Jones, *The Presidential Election of 1896* (Madison: The University of Wisconsin Press, 1964), 112–13; Walton, *Black Republicans*, 57–60; Horner, *Ohio's Kingmaker*, 142–43.

[94] Kehl, *Boss Rule in the Gilded Age*, 198. In terms of "other political possibilities," R. Hal Williams speculates: "In light of later events, it is likely that in some conversations, McKinley hinted at a softer federal policy toward white southerners if he were elected." R. Hal Williams, *Realigning America: McKinley, Bryan, and the Remarkable Election of 1896* (Lawrence: University Press of Kansas, 2010), 57.

[95] Williams, *Realigning America*, 57.   [96] Quoted in Kehl, *Boss Rule in the Gilded Age*, 197.

remained under his control. Harrison's loss in 1892 cut off Cuney's organization from federal patronage, but he remained Texas's representative on the Republican National Committee. Hanna initially attempted to convince Cuney – who had already lined up behind the candidacy of Sen. William Allison (IA) – to throw his support to McKinley.[97] When Cuney refused, Hanna and McKinley – in the assessment of Cuney's daughter – "found it necessary to place the McKinley organization in other hands."[98] At the Republican National Convention in 1896, the Credentials Committee – dominated by supporters of McKinley – did exactly that by voting to seat a set of (black and white) Texas delegates pledged to support McKinley.[99]

As a result of this mix of strategies, McKinley received the support of 196.5 of 224 delegates from the South (or 87.7 percent) in his landslide victory at the 1896 convention.[100] McKinley, with help and guidance from Hanna, had achieved what other GOP presidential hopefuls in the late nineteenth century had long sought: firm control over the large group of convention delegates from the former Confederate South, as a means of building a successful majority coalition. What Harrison had begun to accomplish in 1892, McKinley had seemingly perfected in 1896. And the rotten-borough nature of the South, which had become the status quo for the Republicans by 1896, would make the pre-convention hunt for Southern delegates the go-to strategy for GOP presidential aspirants going forward.

The presidential election of 1896 was largely fought on economic terms, with McKinley supporting high tariffs (after a Democratic reduction under Cleveland) and hard money, and Rep. William Jennings Bryan (D-KS) advocating a populist agenda of low tariffs and free silver (and the inflation that it would bring).[101] With regard to the South, McKinley pursued a conciliatory strategy, cautiously staying away from any bloody-shirt themes. He often made references to the free and fair elections enjoyed by Americans in all regions, and how the country had truly become a "nation" after decades of bitter North–South conflict. McKinley and Hanna hoped such a strategy could make inroads

---

[97] Paul Douglas Castorph, "Norris Wright Cuney and Texas Republican Politics, 1883–1896," *The Southwestern Historical Quarterly* 68 (1965): 455–64; Douglas Hales, *A Southern Family in White and Black: The Cuneys of Texas* (College Station: Texas A&M University Press, 2003), 87–91.

[98] Maud Cuney Hare, *Norris Wright Cuney: A Tribune of the Black People* (New York: The Crisis Publishing Company, 1913), 181.

[99] And with McKinley in the White House, Cuney's control over the Texas Republican Party was gone for good. As Douglas Hales states, "Cuney lost his hold on leadership, not at the hands of the Lily Whites, but because he backed the wrong presidential candidate." Hales, *A Southern Family in White and Black*, 90.

[100] McKinley won 661.5 of 902 delegates on the first convention ballot. See *Republican National Convention, St. Louis, June 16–18, 1896* (St. Louis: I. Haas Publishing and Engraving Company, 1896), 158.

[101] See Williams, *Realigning America*.

into the white South, but more generally believed it was the winning strategy for an election in 1896, given the country's economic condition. And while the ex-Confederate South stayed solid for the Democrats, McKinley was able to win the (former-slave) border states of Maryland, Kentucky, Delaware, and West Virginia.

McKinley's victory in 1896 set up a series of presidential elections in which Republicans would dominate without Southern success. As a result, the party became less interested in reaching out to Southern voters (though, as we discuss in Chapter 6, the dream of a two-party South never faded away entirely). Following Democrats' formal disfranchisement of black voters and Northern Republicans' loss of interest in bloody-shirt politics, the Southern wing of the GOP remained relevant in only one respect: within the Republican National Convention itself, specifically in the choice of the GOP presidential nominee. That is, by the late 1890s, as the Democrats methodically locked down the electoral arena in the South, the only benefits that a Southern Republican could hope to achieve were limited to patronage and side payments associated with presidential politics. Thus, Lily-White and Black-and-Tan factions began to ignore organizational issues at home and increasingly fought over the more pragmatic issue of which group should represent their state at the national convention. And national Republican leaders, in turn, began to view the Southern states simply as a set of rotten boroughs.

CONCLUSION

During the latter half of the Reconstruction era, Republicans in the South faced major electoral defeats due to the enfranchisement of white voters, dismal economic conditions, and Democratic Party-sponsored terror against black voters. As a result, by 1877 the Democrats won unified control of state governments across the region – and largely held it for the succeeding two decades. Yet this decline in Republican electoral strength did not reduce the South's influence at the GOP national convention. Indeed, from 1877 to 1896, the eleven states of the former Confederacy made up around 25 percent of Republican convention delegates. There were three reasons for this.

First, many Republican national leaders remained hopeful that the end of Reconstruction was not the final word on the GOP's role in the South. Some, like Presidents Hayes and Harrison, thought conservative Southern whites could be enticed to become Republicans based on economic matters (internal improvements and tariffs). Others, like President Arthur, thought that fusion arrangements with third parties in individual states could keep the GOP competitive. And still others – like Republicans in Congress – felt that a new federal elections bill could successfully "reconstruct" the South again by ensuring a free ballot and a fair count. Regardless of the particular strategy, prior to the full onset of Jim Crow-style disenfranchisement, some national Republican leaders believed that a winning electoral strategy could be devised for the party to remain a viable political force in the South.

Second, Southern delegates passionately – and, to a large extent, correctly – argued that their states' inability to produce electoral votes and congressional seats for the GOP was due to Democratic sabotage of the electoral process. Additionally, throughout this period, Southern delegations included a substantial number of blacks. With Southern blacks increasingly excluded from the democratic process at home, the Republican National Convention was one of the few remaining political arenas in which they could participate. For the Party of Lincoln to try and strip these delegates of their role within the party was, for some, problematic.

Finally, Southern delegates were very helpful to presidential hopefuls from other parts of the country, because their support could be easily acquired through patronage and other forms of bribery. Thus, whoever could afford to court the South could go into the convention with a sizable bloc of votes. Certainly, Southern support was no guarantee of victory. However, the South was pivotal in Harrison's successful re-nomination effort in 1892. And McKinley's nomination strategy in 1896 was based in part on ensuring that he would "own" the South going into the national convention. While opponents of these candidates openly charged Southern delegates with selling their votes in exchange for federal offices, their value to presidential candidates outweighed any possible reputational cost.

The 1896 election would fundamentally change this equation. By the early twentieth century, all the Southern states had passed legislation or made changes to their constitution to effectively disenfranchise black voters. As a result, the lingering hope of a competitive GOP largely disappeared. And, with the Republican Party in ascendance elsewhere in the nation during the "System of 1896," national party leaders also had less of an incentive to try to alter this status quo. That is, while the GOP could not compete for electoral votes and congressional seats in the South, it also did not need them to win the presidency and majorities in the House and Senate. Thus, in the post-1896 period two developments that had begun prior to the McKinley presidency would develop further: first, Southern delegations became fully understood and treated as rotten boroughs. Second, with black Southerners excluded from electoral politics, Lily-White GOP organizations began to appear across the South – or grow stronger in areas where they already existed – and sought to exclude blacks from any meaningful leadership role in Republican Party politics.

5

The System of 1896 and Republicanism in the South, 1897–1932

The presidential elections of 1896 and 1900 established the GOP as the majority party across most of the United States for the better part of the next three decades. But while the Republicans expanded their dominance in the Northeast, Midwest, and West, the South remained almost exclusively Democratic throughout this period. As a result, the traditional argument that a GOP revival in the Solid South remained a possibility – which, in part, validated the sizable Southern presence at Republican national conventions – rang increasingly hollow. As Richard M. Valelly has argued, the Republican Party's ability after 1897 to win the presidency and Congress without achieving electoral success in the South produced an "abrupt change in the costs and benefits of the party's historical southern policy."[1] That is, Republican leaders mostly concluded that the cost of maintaining a party organization in the South that was fit to compete electorally with an implacable (and very hostile[2]) Democratic majority outweighed the increasingly slim chances at GOP electoral success there.[3]

In this context, the intra-party struggle over the South increased after the 1896 election, and the GOP saw a series of clashes between national leaders,

---

[1] Richard M. Valelly, "National Parties and Racial Disenfranchisement," in Paul E. Peterson, ed., *Classifying by Race* (Princeton, NJ: Princeton University Press, 1995), 209.

[2] Valelly recounts an incident in North Carolina in 1898 during which Republican Governor Daniel Russell "was nearly lynched by a Democratic mob that stopped his train; he escaped death only because he managed to find a good hiding place on the train." Richard M. Valelly, *The Two Reconstructions: The Struggle for Black Enfranchisement* (Chicago: University of Chicago Press, 2004), 131.

[3] An additional reason for the Republican Party's shift in interest in competing in Southern elections was based on a shift in the racial diversity of its voting base in the North: "the black–white North–South coalition of 1867–1868 was supplanted by a new white–white North–West coalition" that placed no value in continuing to contest Southern elections that the party was bound to lose. See ibid., 134.

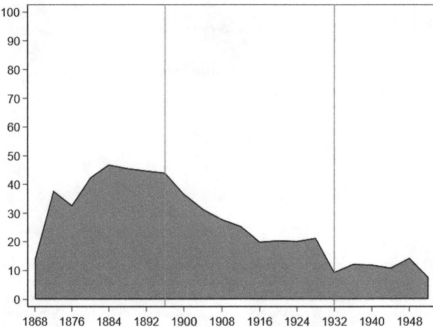

FIGURE 5.1 Percentage of Southern GOP convention delegates that were black,
1897–1932
Source: Data collected by authors.

some of whom benefited from the presence of Southern convention delegates. Republican administrations continued to use their control of patronage in the South to produce a reliable and sizable voting bloc that played a significant role in the selection of presidential candidates in 1908 and 1912, and the selection of the vice-presidential candidate in 1900. At the same time, however, several moves were made by competing factions to reduce the size of the Southern delegations. Not all of these moves were sincere; rather, some were threats to (successfully) force compliance on other issues. Additionally, Republican leaders were far from consistent in their support of Southern delegates and were prone to changing their positions depending on whether they were the ones who controlled federal patronage. Thus, as the GOP moved into a position of national political domination, its Southern political organizations increasingly became pawns in a game of national-level party politics.

In the same period, within a large number of Southern states, the ruling Black-and-Tan factions were challenged – and, in a number of cases, replaced – by Lily-Whites who argued that the rise of disenfranchisement laws across the region required the GOP to adjust its image to fit the new white electorate. The result was a clear decline in the percentage of black convention delegates from the South during this period (see Figure 5.1). Republican presidents also intervened in this process. For example, Theodore Roosevelt's refusal to accept a Lily-White takeover in Mississippi allowed the Black-and-Tans to stay in power there. Warren G. Harding and Herbert Hoover, however, sought to intervene in intra-GOP politics in the South with an eye toward replacing Black-and-Tan leaders with whites. Hoover, in particular, worked hard to replace existing (and, in his eyes, corrupt) biracial party organizations with ones led by local handpicked whites, who he believed would help create competitive local parties in states like South Carolina, Mississippi, and Georgia. In most cases, such presidential interventions failed to achieve their intended goals. However, they did help weaken a number of the remaining Black-and-Tan organizations in the South.

PRESIDENTIAL POLITICS AND SOUTHERN PARTY ORGANIZATIONS, 1897–1908

After the 1896 election, McKinley and Hanna increased their control over the Southern GOP through the use of federal patronage. Appointments to federal offices in the South were made largely in consultation between Hanna and local Republican party leaders. In cases of particularly important offices, the administration relied on advice from the three local Republicans seen as controlling the state party organization: the most recent Republican candidate for governor, the state chairman of the party, and the member of the RNC for the state. If the specific Southern state lacked acceptable local Republicans to take on the position, McKinley would occasionally appoint non-locals and have them move to the state in question. Still, as H. Wayne Morgan has noted, "both McKinley and Hanna were anxious to reward [Southern] pre-convention support and to try to build a Republican party there."[4]

Crucially, however, the building of such a Southern party would not rely on McKinley protecting the voting rights of blacks. Around the same time that national Republican leaders were losing interest in sectional concerns (and in protecting blacks' political rights), a pivotal institutional change was occurring at the state level, first in Mississippi in 1890 and then in other states of the former Confederacy by 1908.[5] A series of disfranchisement provisions – such as literacy tests, residency requirements, and poll taxes, among others – were put in place, through statutes or constitutional changes, which severely restricted

---

[4] H. Wayne Morgan, *William McKinley and His America* (Kent, OH: Kent State University Press, 2003), 220.

[5] See J. Morgan Kousser, *The Shaping of Southern Politics: Suffrage Restriction and the Establishment of the One-Party South* (New Haven, CT: Yale University Press, 1974); Michael Perman, *Struggle for Mastery: Disfranchisement in the South, 1888–1908* (Chapel Hill: University of North Carolina Press, 2001).

the voting rights of blacks (and many poor whites).[6] The new Mississippi constitution was challenged, but the Supreme Court in *Williams v. Mississippi* (1898) ruled in a 9–0 decision that the suffrage provisions (restrictions) did not, on their face, discriminate by race. This led other Southern states to follow Mississippi (see Table 2.3). The result of these restrictions was that black registration and turnout rates dropped significantly in affected states, to the point of effectively wiping out blacks as a voting bloc. And as blacks constituted the bulk of Republican voters in most places in the South, the disenfranchising provisions effectively drove the GOP's electoral viability in the region to zero.

During a tour through Georgia and Alabama in December 1898 – mere weeks after elections that saw considerable violence against blacks and Democratic campaigns based largely on messages of white supremacy – McKinley failed to address the issue. According to Charles Calhoun: "McKinley's administration marked the effective abandonment of blacks' rights by the GOP."[7] In office, he promoted sectional harmony and emphasized "self-help" and industrial training for Southern blacks. And while he distributed some patronage to Southern blacks, he was careful to balance these with positions given to whites – especially positions of prominence. McKinley, however, did not embrace the Lily-White movements within Southern party organizations, which had begun to call for the complete exclusion of blacks from the local GOP. To the extent that the Lily-Whites relied on an electoral argument for such exclusion, the belief was that an all-white GOP would be able to compete in local elections by appealing to white Populists. But since many of these Populists had supported William Jennings Bryan in the 1896 election, McKinley did not view this as the most obvious coalition to throw his weight behind. Thus, as Michael Perman concludes, "[with] southern politics so unstable and the outlook so uncertain, McKinley no doubt preferred to wait and see what transpired."[8]

While McKinley's re-nomination was never in doubt, the 1900 Republican National Convention and the period leading up to it saw two major attempts by party bosses to reduce Southern delegation size. The first attempt came in December 1899, during a two-day RNC meeting at which the 1900 convention city was to be selected. Henry Clay Payne, an RNC member from Wisconsin and an important figure in McKinley's 1896 campaign, sought to replace the existing division of delegates (in which states received two delegates for each senator and representative they had in Congress, regardless of partisan

---

[6] Many states also adopted "grandfather clauses," which allowed poor whites to vote (despite their illiteracy and/or poverty), while still excluding blacks.

[7] Charles W. Calhoun, *From Bloody Shirt to Full Dinner Pail: The Transformation of Politics and Governance in the Gilded Age* (New York: Hill and Wang, 2010), 167. For more on McKinley's Southern policy in office, see Charles W. Calhoun, *Conceiving a New Republic: The Republican Party and the Southern Question, 1869–1900* (Lawrence: University Press of Kansas, 2006), 281–87.

[8] Perman, *Struggle for Mastery*, 119.

affiliation) with a new scheme in which each state would receive four at-large delegates and one additional delegate for each 10,000 votes that it had contributed to the Republican presidential ticket in the most recent election. If adopted, Payne's plan would have significantly reduced Southern representation at the 1900 convention, from 224 delegates (25 percent of the total) under the existing rules to 126 delegates (14 percent of the total), based on the 1896 presidential vote totals.[9]

From Payne's perspective (at least as stated publicly), this reduction in Southern representation was simply a case of fairness. He wondered "why the states of Alabama, Arkansas, Florida, Georgia, Louisiana, Mississippi, South Carolina, casting 200,076 Republican votes at the last Presidential election, should have 124 delegates in the National Convention, while New Jersey, casting 221,367 Republican votes, should have but twenty delegates?"[10] Unsurprisingly, Southern Republicans were strongly opposed to Payne's proposal; black RNC members from the South, in particular, charged Payne with attempting to drive black delegates out of the party entirely.[11] Nonetheless, many non-Southern party leaders considered Payne's proposal to be reasonable, given that, as the *Charlotte Observer* noted, "the counsels of white Southern Republican delegates are lightly esteemed in the national conventions of their party and the colored delegates are regarded as so many chattels to be purchased by the highest bidder."[12]

While black Republican leaders had little hope of success in opposing Payne's proposal, it never came to a vote during the RNC meeting.[13] Instead, the selection of the 1900 convention city and the decision on Payne's delegate plan – the two crucial issues of the meeting – were settled as part of a logroll between the different regional camps. The committee members from Pennsylvania were willing to oppose the Payne plan if Philadelphia were chosen as the 1900 convention city. Meanwhile, Southern members of the RNC decided to

[9] "The South; Too Many For 'Em," *Columbus Enquirer Sun*, November 28, 1899. Note that Payne's proposal was introduced around the same time that Republicans in Congress attempted to demand enforcement of Section 2 of the Fourteenth Amendment, which would result in a decrease in Southern House seats commensurate with the number of black voters that were denied the right to vote. The first attempt to bring such a Fourteenth Amendment challenge against a Southern state came in October 1899, just two months before the RNC meeting that considered Payne's proposal to reapportion Southern delegates. See Jeffery A. Jenkins, Justin Peck, and Vesla M. Weaver, "Between Reconstructions: Congressional Action on Civil Rights, 1891–1940," *Studies in American Political Development* 24 (2010): 57–89.
[10] Cited in William Ward Wight, *Henry Clay Payne: A Life* (Milwaukee: Burdick and Allen, 1907), 102.
[11] Ibid., 118.
[12] "To Reduce Southern Representation," *Charlotte Daily Observer*, November 29, 1899.
[13] "Opposed to Mr. Payne's Plan," *Washington Post*, December 13, 1899.

vote as a unit on the selection of a convention city "in such a way as will win for them the most support in their fight against reapportionment."[14]

These negotiations were concluded successfully, as Philadelphia was selected over Chicago by a single vote. The Southern bloc played a crucial role in this process, as Pennsylvania would have lost its bid to Illinois without unanimous Southern support. The next day, the RNC was scheduled to vote on the Payne proposal. However, after the selection of Philadelphia, Payne was shuttled to the White House for late-night meetings with McKinley and Hanna, during which he came to understand that "committeemen who had favored [the reapportionment plan] in private correspondence ... had been stormed into opposition by letters and telegrams from every source."[15] As a result, Payne withdrew his proposal the following day, stating that while he had not "in the slightest degree changed [his] conviction as to its justice,"[16] the opposition to the plan had convinced him not to offer it to a committee vote. Whether Payne himself understood the proposal to be a mere bargaining chip all along remains unclear, but by the end of the two-day meeting Philadelphia had been named the host of the 1900 convention with Southern support and Payne's plan for reducing Southern representation had been abandoned – at least temporarily.

During the 1900 Republican National Convention, Pennsylvania's GOP boss Matt Quay resuscitated the Payne plan. However, here too the size of future Southern delegations was used as a bargaining chip to achieve a different goal: in this case, to influence the choice of the Republican vice-presidential candidate. With McKinley's re-nomination assured, the only major issue before the convention was the question of who would become the vice-presidential candidate after Garret Hobart's death in 1899. Among the most discussed options was New York Governor Theodore Roosevelt, although he was on record as having no interest in the nomination. Nonetheless, Roosevelt's candidacy was pushed by machine politicians from New York, as they sought to rid themselves of their increasingly powerful and independent governor.[17] While McKinley and Hanna had expressed no interest in having Roosevelt on the ticket either, New York's GOP boss, Tom Platt, sought Quay's help to ensure that Roosevelt would be nominated.[18] Quay believed Roosevelt's selection was possible, but only if he could win over Western and Southern delegates. The latter, however, were firmly under Hanna's control.

---

[14] "Cities in a Fight," Los Angeles Times, December 14, 1899; "Quakers Make a Deal," Washington Post, December 14, 1899.
[15] Wight, Henry Clay Payne, 104; "Philadelphia June 19: Place and Date Fixed for Republican Convention," Washington Post, December 16, 1899.
[16] Wight, Henry Clay Payne, 105.
[17] Herbert Croly, Marcus Alonzo Hanna: His Life and Work (Hamden, CT: Archon Books, 1965).
[18] James A. Kehl, Boss Rule in the Gilded Age: Matt Quay of Pennsylvania (Pittsburgh, PA: University of Pittsburgh Press, 1981), 225.

At the end of the second day of the convention, Quay introduced the Payne proposal to reapportion delegates. Admitting that it "involves a very radical change in the base of representation,"[19] Quay called for a vote on the proposal to be postponed until the next day. This delay, as he explained it, would give delegates time to educate themselves on the specifics of the plan. With black Southern Republicans already frustrated at the seating of several rival Lily-White slates (reportedly due to pressure from Quay and Payne[20]), Quay's proposal was met with "manifest uneasiness" and the belief that its passage would result in the "death of Republicanism in the South" altogether.[21] With only hours before a scheduled vote on the matter, Southern delegates lobbied other regional delegations in an attempt to prevent the proposal's passage.

By proposing a change but immediately postponing further debate, Quay successfully stirred discontent among Northern delegates vis-à-vis the South, while simultaneously threatening Southern delegates with a loss of influence in the future. With Southern desperation rising, "Quay quietly leaked to Southern delegates the idea that he was prepared to withdraw the resolution if they swung their support to the New York governor."[22] The move worked as planned: Southern delegates traded their votes for vice president in exchange for Quay dropping his reapportionment proposal.[23] Sensing imminent defeat, Hanna and McKinley accepted Roosevelt as the vice-presidential nominee. At the beginning of the third day of proceedings, Quay withdrew the delegate proposal without further comment and Theodore Roosevelt was selected as McKinley's running mate.

After McKinley's assassination in September 1901, Roosevelt was elevated to the presidency. And while maintaining a cordial relationship with Hanna, Roosevelt understood that he faced a potential challenge to the Republican nomination from the Ohio senator in 1904.[24] To build majority support at the convention, Roosevelt sought to follow McKinley's example and gain control over Southern delegates through federal patronage – mostly by distributing postmaster positions. Notably, Roosevelt (like Hayes before him) also attempted to improve the standing of the GOP in the South through his willingness "to appoint Democrats rather than some of the old party hacks."[25] This strategy proved to be controversial in the South, as it meant that Roosevelt

[19] *Official Proceedings of the Twelfth Republican National Convention*, (Philadelphia: Press of Dunlap Printing Company, 1900), 99.
[20] "Hard Blow for Hanna," *Daily Picayune*, June 16, 1900.
[21] "Quay's Rap at the South," *New York Times*, June 21, 1900.
[22] Kehl, *Boss Rule in the Gilded Age*, 227.
[23] "Theodore Roosevelt to be the Unanimous Choice for Vice-President," *Los Angeles Times*, June 21, 1900.
[24] Herbert David Croly, *Marcus Alonzo Hanna: His Life and Work* (New York: Archon Books, 1912), 415–16.
[25] Richard B. Sherman, *The Republican Party and Black America: From McKinley to Hoover, 1896–1933* (Charlottesville: University of Virginia Press, 1973), 31.

did not provide all traditional Southern party organizations with access to patronage. He also waded into the (by then increasingly complicated) racial dynamics within local Southern party organizations. For starters, Roosevelt had dinner with Booker T. Washington at the White House just weeks after taking over as president.[26] To many white Southerners, the mere act of a white president sharing a meal with a black man was unacceptable.[27] Roosevelt further alienated many white Republicans by relying on Washington's advice in the distribution of patronage during his first term, and appointing a number of black public officials. In late 1901, for example, Roosevelt appointed two black federal office-holders – one in Alabama and one in the District of Columbia – on Washington's advice. Roosevelt's goal in this regard was to "placate many Negroes and, at the same time, deliver a blow to the Hanna organization."[28]

The following year, Roosevelt's conflict with the Lily-White movement reached a fever pitch. In August 1902, Roosevelt met with Republican Senator Jeter Pritchard of North Carolina. Days after this meeting, Pritchard appeared at the North Carolina and Alabama state Republican conventions and called for black delegates to be banned from participation; this move was presented as being in line with the president's own views. Roosevelt initially did not challenge this account and even made several appearances in the South with Pritchard in September, during which he did not raise the issue of race relations. By October, however, Roosevelt attacked the Lily-Whites by appointing a number of blacks to office in the South. The Lily-Whites, in turn, strongly criticized Roosevelt and began floating the possibility of supporting Hanna in 1904. In the end, Roosevelt cut his losses in North Carolina, by abandoning his attempt at appointing a black man to a postmastership there, and instead followed Pritchard's recommendation. In Alabama, however, Roosevelt refused to give up: between 1902 and the early months of 1904, he insisted on ignoring the existing Lily-White-dominated party organization and relied instead on a committee of black and white local Republicans to propose acceptable candidates for federal offices. In trying to manage the Republican Party in the South, Roosevelt therefore found himself ensnared in the expanding conflict between Lily-Whites and Black-and-Tans.[29] As a result, Hanna, while no longer in direct

---

[26] Deborah Davis, *Guest of Honor: Booker T. Washington, Theodore Roosevelt, and the White House Dinner That Shocked a Nation* (New York: Atria Books, 2012).

[27] Roosevelt initially defended his meal with Washington but later concluded that it had been a mistake. See Seth M. Scheiner, "Theodore Roosevelt and the Negro, 1901–1908," *The Journal of Negro History* 47 (July 1962): 169–82. On both Southern and Northern reaction generally, see Davis, *Guest of Honor*, 203–17.

[28] Scheiner, "Theodore Roosevelt and the Negro," 172.

[29] Lewis L. Gould, *The Presidency of Theodore Roosevelt* (Lawrence: The University Press of Kansas, 1991), 118–22.

control of patronage, remained popular in the South and a potential challenger to Roosevelt.[30]

Hanna's sudden death in February 1904, however, cleared the way for Roosevelt's reelection. His personal popularity left no credible challengers, and he was nominated unanimously at the 1904 convention. During his second term, Roosevelt largely abandoned any attempts at challenging the Lily-White organizations that were now dominant in many Southern states. Instead, in his last four years in the White House, Roosevelt expanded his control of Southern GOP organizations and, in advance of the 1908 convention, pushed Southern delegates to support William Howard Taft's candidacy. The Roosevelt administration's use of (Southern) patronage was a key factor in Taft's successful nomination. Postmaster General George von Lengerke Meyer in particular played an important role in this regard: recipients of postmaster positions in the South were "selected with Mr. Taft's nomination in mind," and while postmasters were "discouraged from being officers of the conventions or of the committees ... they could work behind the scenes and could also attend, as delegates, the national convention."[31] Indeed, a congressional investigation of the Roosevelt administration in 1909 concluded that "the officeholders in the South practically control the Republican party organization in their respective states" and that "nearly one in three [Southern delegates], and of some Southern states more than half" at the 1908 Republican convention were federal office-holders.[32]

Taft himself had been critical of the Southern rotten boroughs and held that votes at the Republican convention should be proportional to the party's vote share. During a speech in Greensboro, North Carolina, in July 1906, Taft had warned that "as long as the Republican party in the Southern states shall represent little save a factional chase for federal offices in which business men and men of substance in the community have no desire to enter, we may expect the present political conditions of the South to continue."[33] Additionally, in a private letter written in January 1908, Taft stated that

the South has been the section of rotten boroughs in the Republican national politics and it would delight me if no southern votes were permitted to have a vote in the National Convention except in proportion to its Republican vote ... But when a man is running for the presidency, and I believe that is what I am now doing, he cannot afford to ignore the tremendous influence, however undue, that the southern vote has.[34]

---

[30] Croly, *Marcus Alonzo Hanna*, 421; Horace Samuel Merrill and Marion Galbraith Merrill, *The Republican Command, 1897–1913* (Lexington: University Press of Kentucky, 1971), 181.

[31] Dorothy Ganfield Fowler, *The Cabinet Politician: The Postmasters General, 1829–1909* (New York: Columbia University Press, 1943), 293.

[32] "Civil Service Charges," *New York Tribune*, April 5, 1909.   [33] Ibid.

[34] See Henry F. Pringle, *The Life and Times of William Howard Taft: A Biography*, Vol. I (New York: Farrar & Rinehart, 1939), 347.

Despite Taft's opposition to the Southern rotten boroughs, Southern delegates proved to be a reliable base for him: of the 240 Southern delegates at the 1908 convention, 223 (or 93 percent) voted for Taft on the first (and only) presidential ballot. Meanwhile, delegates from other regions that Roosevelt controlled defended the South against an attempt by anti-Taft forces to reduce Southern representation. This was done with long-term rather than short-term consequences in mind – Taft could have been nominated without this Southern support on the first ballot – as Roosevelt "was not prepared to see his successor deprived of so useful a political device"[35] as a reliable Southern voting bloc at national conventions. This was sensible political mentorship in 1908, but it would have dramatic consequences for Roosevelt himself in the future: while the outcome of the 1908 convention was one of party unity behind its new leader, the 1912 convention would see Southern delegates play a crucial role in preventing Roosevelt from regaining control of the GOP.

STANDING AT ARMAGEDDON: THE SOUTH AND THE 1912 CONVENTION

The 1912 convention presented a major test of a Republican administration's ability to control Southern delegates and use them to produce a majority. With President Taft up for reelection but facing a challenge from the progressive wing of the party, his lieutenants in 1911 began organizing the Republican "Old Guard" conservatives. By early 1912, Taft's reelection came to face a critical test when Roosevelt announced that he would challenge him for the nomination. While Roosevelt had anointed Taft as his chosen successor in 1908, their relationship had soured during that campaign and Taft's subsequent presidency. Roosevelt believed that Taft had thrown in with the conservatives in the party and rejected many tenets of progressivism. Thus, in 1911, Roosevelt, increasingly restless and frustrated in his exile from power, began to consider challenging Taft's re-nomination.[36] In February 1912, on the urging of his supporters, Roosevelt finally decided to insert himself into the race, stating that he would not be "unresponsive to a plain public duty."[37]

Roosevelt's ability – realistically speaking – to prevent Taft from being re-nominated at the Republican convention was limited. While in 1912 states for the first time began organizing primaries as a means of instructing their delegates how they should vote at conventions, only thirteen states held a primary. Of those, the New York primary election was controlled by the local

---

[35] Sherman, *The Republican Party and Black America*, 92.

[36] Victor Rosewater, *Backstage in 1912: The Inside Story of the Split Republican Convention* (Philadelphia: Dorrance & Company, 1932), 29–33.

[37] Sidney M. Milkis, *Theodore Roosevelt, the Progressive Party, and the Transformation of American Democracy* (Lawrence: The University Press of Kansas, 2009), 53.

Republican machine, which was hostile to Roosevelt.[38] All other states relied on the traditional approach of delegates being controlled by local party organizations and bosses. Roosevelt also struggled to unite GOP progressives due to his clash with Senator Robert La Follette (R-WI), who claimed Roosevelt had encouraged him to challenge Taft before Roosevelt himself jumped in the race. This clash made a coherent progressive coalition during the delegate-selection period or the subsequent Republican National Convention unlikely. Nonetheless, Taft's ability to survive the progressive challenge would rest, at least in part, on his capacity to control the South. As these party organizations "were kept alive on a diet of federal patronage in order to secure favorable delegates at national conventions,"[39] and because Roosevelt posed a serious threat, Taft needed near unanimous Southern support.

Charles D. Hilles, Taft's private secretary and campaign manager, was tasked with securing the South and sought to forestall the Roosevelt campaign by compelling the state committees to select their delegates as early in the election year as possible. Hilles's endeavor proved successful, with eight Southern committees opting to select their delegates in February and March of 1912, and two others following suit in early April. In contrast, only four non-Southern committees held their state conventions before April.[40] This approach resulted in a predominantly pro-Taft Southern delegation, as the *New York Times* reported that (prior to both the convention and the RNC's decisions on contested delegates) 569 delegates had been pledged to Taft or had been instructed to support him, of which 214 came from Southern states. Based on these numbers, Taft had received the support of 85 percent of all Southern GOP delegates.[41]

Taft's control of Southern delegates appears to have followed mainly from the distribution of federal patronage.[42] Indeed, evidence that the South's support for Taft was closely linked to the federal government's provision of employment is suggested by Wilensky's study of 884 Taft supporters – defined as "men and women who gave their time and money to the regular Republican cause"[43] – in the contest for the Republican nomination. As Table 5.1 indicates, while no more than 12 percent of Taft's supporters from the Northeast,

[38] Ibid., 76–77, 83.
[39] Norman M. Wilensky, *Conservatives in the Progressive Era: The Taft Republicans of 1912* (Gainesville: University of Florida Press, 1965), 17.
[40] Ibid., 29.
[41] These numbers include the delegates the Roosevelt campaign contested (112 delegates, of whom 66 were from the South). "Taft's Certain List Goes up to 325," *New York Times*, June 9, 1912.
[42] As Casdorph notes, Roosevelt outperformed Taft in the South during the 1912 presidential election. Paul D. Casdorph, *Republicans, Negroes, and Progressives in the South, 1912–1916* (Tuscaloosa: The University of Alabama Press, 1981), 151.
[43] Norman M. Wilensky, *Conservatives in the Progressive Era: The Taft Republicans of 1912* (Gainesville: University of Florida Press, 1965), 33.

TABLE 5.1 *Occupation of Republican activists supporting Taft in 1912, divided by region*

Occupation	Northeast %	Midwest %	South %	West %
Federal officials	9	12	44	12
US senators and representatives	13	12	6	19
State and local officials	9	7	4	10
Businessmen, lawyers, and bankers	42	45	35	36
Newspapermen	15	17	4	11
Unknown / Other	12	7	7	12
TOTAL	100	100	100	100

Source: Norman M. Wilensky, *Conservatives in the Progressive Era: The Taft Republicans of 1912* (Gainesville: University of Florida Press, 1965), 36

Midwest, and West held federal positions, 44 percent of his Southern supporters were federal officials.[44]

Roosevelt, in advance of the convention, decried the role Southern delegates would play for exactly this reason. Writing in the progressive publication *Outlook*, Roosevelt argued that the Southern delegates "represent nothing but Mr. Taft's own office-holders and the survivors of the carpetbag regime."[45] In the same vein, historian William Garrott Brown, a native of Alabama and a strong advocate of a competitive Republican Party in the South, asserted in *Harper's Weekly* that "the mass of Southern Republican delegates chosen this year are not merely products of the same old methods employed in 1908" but represented a scandal that "has been flagrant for decades, but this year it is so very flagrant that one cannot help hoping something will at last be done about it."[46]

With Taft seemingly controlling more delegates than the 540 needed for a majority, the Roosevelt campaign attempted to forestall defeat by challenging a large number of Taft's pledged Southern delegates. The Roosevelt camp also proposed a reduction in the total number of Southern delegates that would be admitted to the convention. Both approaches failed: with Taft in control of the RNC, only 19 of the 254 contested delegates were awarded to Roosevelt in

---

[44] A more detailed analysis of "the 292 most politically active Old Guardsmen" also shows that Southern Taft supporters were more likely to have had prior political experience: 97.4 percent of Southern Taft men did, while in the Northeast, Midwest, and West these numbers were lower (respectively, 82.7 percent, 84.5 percent, and 75.7 percent). See ibid., 33, 38.

[45] "A Naked Issue of Right and Wrong," *Outlook*, June 14, 1912.

[46] Cited in Bruce L. Clayton, "An Intellectual on Politics: William Garrott Brown and the Ideal of a Two-Party South," *North Carolina Historical Review* 42 (1965): 319–34.

advance of the convention, while the proposal to reduce Southern representation was voted down 39–14.[47] The next crucial test of Taft's strength was the selection of a temporary chair at the beginning of the convention. On a close vote (570–501), conservative Senator Elihu Root (R-NY) was elected. Taft's control of the South was crucial to this success: 199 of the delegates that voted for Root were from ex-Confederate states (constituting 79 percent of all Southern delegates).[48] On a subsequent vote to refer all debate regarding contested delegates to the convention's Credentials Committee, the South again largely aligned with Taft: 78 percent of Southern delegates voted in favor of tabling discussion on the contested delegates.[49] Root's selection was consequential: in his role as temporary chairman, he helped the Taft camp by deciding that contested delegates had the right to vote on *all* of the convention's decisions, even those confirming the RNC's prior decisions on contested delegates (except those that concerned themselves).[50] This decision resulted in a majority approving the national committee's support for the Southern Taft delegates.

There remains scholarly debate as to whether the decision to seat Taft's Southern delegates was fair or not. In certain cases, there is reason to doubt that the Taft delegates represented the "true" party in their state. For example, the regular Texas GOP – led by RNC member Cecil A. Lyon – supported Roosevelt. However, a different Republican group formed to support Taft instead. Both groups sent delegations to the national convention, with the Taft delegates being seated by the RNC.[51] Still, while Taft's control of the convention may have hurt Roosevelt in this regard, many of Roosevelt's Southern delegations had questionable claims of legitimately representing their state party as well. For one thing, as the *Washington Times* reported, the challenges of delegates selected before Roosevelt could build a campaign machine were largely intended for "psychological effects" so that "a tabulation of delegate strength could be put out that would show Roosevelt holding a good hand"[52] by inflating the number of contested delegates. Along similar lines, Robert La Follette claimed in his autobiography that the Roosevelt campaign picked up many delegates in advance of the convention "because of the false claims put

---

[47] Milkis, *Theodore Roosevelt, the Progressive Party, and the Transformation of American Democracy*, 109.

[48] *Official Report of the Proceedings of the Fifteenth Republican National Convention* (New York: The Tenny Press, 1912), 61–88.

[49] Casdorph, *Republicans, Negroes, and Progressives in the South*, 115.

[50] Hanes Walton, Jr., *Black Republicans: The Politics of the Black and Tans* (Metuchen, NJ: The Scarecrow Press, 1975), 156.

[51] Paul D. Casdorph, *A History of the Republican Party in Texas, 1865–1965* (Austin, TX: The Pemberton Press, 1965) 99–101.

[52] "Figures to Date Fail to Show Taft Victory," *Washington Times*, June 9, 1912.

forth by his managers that he had a large lead in the contest, claims which they well knew to be false."[53] In addition, Paul Casdorph notes that Roosevelt supporters voted with Taft supporters on many of the decisions regarding contested delegates because it was their strategy "not to stand by any cases from the South or elsewhere that did not have genuine merit."[54] However, historian Lewis L. Gould presents a different view in his study of Texas delegate politics, arguing that a correct division should have given Roosevelt twenty-four delegates to Taft's sixteen. If this would indeed have been the division, Taft's total would have dropped to only a handful of votes above the 540 majority line.[55]

Regardless, with Taft's victory all but assured, Roosevelt called upon his delegates to bolt the convention and leave the Republican Party for a new progressive alternative. As a result, Taft was easily re-nominated on the first convention ballot, while many of Roosevelt's supporters who remained in attendance voted "present" in protest.[56] In the general election that followed, Roosevelt's Progressive Party campaign would succeed in pushing the Republican Party to third place, as Taft ran behind Democratic candidate Woodrow Wilson and Roosevelt, and received only 8 electoral votes and a mere 23.2 percent of the national vote. And by splitting the Republican vote, Roosevelt not only denied Taft reelection but helped Wilson win a landslide victory in the Electoral College.

THE GOP AND THE SOUTH UNDER WILSON, HARDING, AND COOLIDGE

While Taft succeeded in winning the GOP presidential nomination in 1912, thanks in part to his "solid" Southern delegate bloc, the contentious Republican convention and subsequent general election disaster would trigger the long-debated reapportionment of delegates. In the aftermath of the election, both conservatives and many of the progressives that had bolted the GOP for Roosevelt realized that some form of unification between the two camps was needed to prevent permanent Democratic government. Shortly after Wilson's inauguration, Republican members of Congress gathered to discuss reorganization of the party and, in the words of Senator Lawrence Sherman (R-IL),

---

[53] Robert La Follette, *La Follette's Autobiography: A Personal Narrative of Political Experiences* (Madison: The University of Wisconsin Press, 2013), 668.

[54] Casdorph, *Republicans, Negroes, and Progressives in the South*, 95.

[55] Lewis L. Gould, "Theodore Roosevelt, William Howard Taft, and the Disputed Delegates in 1912: Texas as a Test Case," *Southwestern Historical Quarterly* 80 (1976): 33–56.

[56] It is important to note, however, that during procedural votes on the first days of the convention, Taft's majority remained slim. Had La Follette and Roosevelt managed to overcome their intra-progressive squabbling, Taft would have lacked the votes necessary to select Root and to decide the contested delegate races. See Milkis, *Theodore Roosevelt, the Progressive Party, and the Transformation of American Democracy*, 114.

"agreed that Southern representation in the convention should be cut down according to the strength of the party in each Southern state."[57]

In December 1913, the RNC followed the GOP congressional recommendation and voted unanimously to reduce Southern representation by adopting a new apportionment scheme. This new division of delegates presented a radical change from how convention delegates were determined previously. Up until then, each state was assigned delegates in relation to the size of its congressional representation regardless of the Republican Party's electoral strength in the state, resulting in a dramatic overvaluing of the South. In the new scheme, each state would receive two at-large delegates, but congressional districts would only receive a delegate if the GOP vote in the 1914 midterms was 7,500 or greater. The committee's decision required ratification by those states that had voted Republican in the 1908 election (of which two-thirds would be required to support the proposed reapportionment).[58] Without a Republican president in the White House, Southern delegates could not fend off the proposal. And in October 1914, RNC Chairman Hilles announced that the plan had been ratified and thus the division of delegates at the 1916 convention would be based upon the new apportionment rule.[59] As a result, Southern representation at the 1916 convention declined significantly relative to 1912: every ex-Confederate state lost delegates (a total of seventy-eight for the region as a whole), and the South's proportion of convention delegates decreased from 23.4 percent to 17.6 percent (see Figure 5.2).

During the 1916 GOP convention, with the Republicans in exile from the executive branch and unable to control patronage, Southern delegates played a muted role, and Supreme Court Justice Charles Evans Hughes was nominated on the third ballot with little controversy. Additionally, with the new delegate apportionment plan in place, there was little new debate regarding the size of the Southern delegations. While Hughes was defeated in the 1916 general election, the Republicans regained control of both chambers of Congress in the 1918 midterms. This recovery also allowed the party some space to reconsider its role in the South. RNC chairman Will Hays visited North Carolina in 1919 and Virginia in 1920 – two states where the GOP had been competitive longer than in other ex-Confederate states. In both states, Hays urged local party leaders to organize and compete in elections. In private correspondence

[57] "Republicans Meet; Plan Party Reform," *New York Times*, May 12, 1913. Sherman represented a logical choice as one of the negotiators between progressives and conservatives: he had supported Roosevelt as a delegate to the 1912 convention, but he later backed Taft in the general election. See Aaron Chandler, "Senator Lawrence Sherman's Role in the Defeat of the Treaty of Versailles," *Journal of the Illinois State Historical Society* 94 (2001): 279–303.
[58] "Republicans Vote Delegate Reforms," *New York Times*, December 17, 1913; "Plan Cut in South in G.O.P. Delegates," *New York Times*, April 8, 1914.
[59] "Republicans Cut Down Delegates," *New York Times*, October 26, 1914.

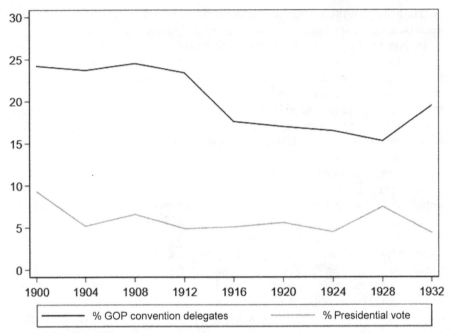

FIGURE 5.2 Southern percentage of delegates at Republican National Convention and
Republican popular vote, 1900–1932
Source: Congressional Quarterly's Guide to U.S. Elections, 3rd edn. (Washington, DC:
Congressional Quarterly, 1994)
Note: The figure above represents the percentage of delegates at the Republican National
Conventions in this period that were from the South, and the percentage of the total
popular vote received by Republican presidential candidates in each election that came
from Southern states.

with party leaders in Florida, South Carolina, and Texas, Hays expressed
similar views.[60]

In 1920, in the run-up to the GOP national convention, the Republicans
faced a highly divided field with as many as nine presidential candidates. Of
these, Frank Harris Hitchcock, the postmaster general under Taft, invested the
most in trying to buy a Southern bloc for the 1920 convention; after ending his
campaign in early 1920, Hitchcock transferred his Southern operation to
General Leonard Wood.[61] While Hitchcock's investments meant Wood could

---

[60] Robert Ellwood Hauser, "Warren G. Harding and His Attempts to Reorganize the Republican
Party in the South, 1920–23" (Dissertation, Pennsylvania State University, 1973), 41–43.

[61] In a testimony to the US Senate's Subcommittee on Privileges and Elections in May 1920,
Senator George H. Moses (R-NH), who functioned as one of Wood's campaign managers,
detailed the kind of expenses he was personally responsible for distributing in the South

count on a substantial number of Southern delegates throughout most of the balloting – ten ballots would prove necessary to select a presidential nominee – at no point did he control the South to the extent that previous candidates had.[62] After four ballots on the fourth day of the convention, the body adjourned. Frustrated party bosses met in the proverbial "smoke-filled room" and decided that Senator Warren G. Harding of Ohio would be the compromise candidate if the deadlock were not broken early the next day. After four ballots on the fifth day of the convention (and eight ballots overall), an adjournment was called; when the body reconvened later that afternoon, states began switching their votes to Harding, who achieved a majority on the sixth ballot of the day (and tenth overall).[63]

Harding's nomination, and his subsequent presidency, resulted in two separate attempts at significantly altering the relationship between the national party and the South. First, Republicans tried to cut the size of the South's delegation at future conventions. Second, Harding himself tried to change the party organizations in two states: Georgia and Louisiana. In the end, each of these attempts failed and the status quo as it was in 1920 remained in place. These failures were due in part to Harding's death in 1923, and his successor Calvin Coolidge's need to ensure enough support to be nominated at the 1924 national convention. But the cases also illustrate the limited power presidents and national committees had in forcing a change in their party's organizations at the state level.

The fact that Harding's victory at the 1920 convention occurred without him personally investing in Southern party organizations raised the possibility of a further reduction in Southern delegation size. That is, because Harding owed Southern party bosses nothing for winning the presidential nomination, and because he had not yet invested any capital himself in maintaining a relationship with them, he appeared at least open to reducing the South's

---

(additional money was invested through other sources), which included payments to Republican party leaders in Virginia ($1,000), North Carolina ($8,000), South Carolina ($600), Georgia ($5,000), Alabama ($4,000), and Tennessee ($1,000). See US Congress, Senate, *Presidential Campaign Expenses: Hearings before a Subcommittee of the Committee on Privileges and Elections*, 66th Congress, 2nd Session (May 24–October 18, 1920), 456–69. These donations were subsequently used to purchase the necessary votes: for example, in Georgia one of the local party leaders "spent money with a recklessness that you could scarcely believe" and "gave $500 to the delegates from Emanuel County to vote for instructions." See *Presidential Campaign Expenses: Hearings*, 465.

[62] Wood never received more than 40 percent of support from the ex-Confederate states on any of the ten ballots.

[63] Southern states voted for Harding at a higher rate and were quicker to embrace his candidacy than the rest of the convention: on the ninth ballot, Harding received 38 percent of the total vote, but 61.1 percent of the Southern vote. On the tenth ballot, Harding received 70.3 percent of the total vote and 90.1 percent of the Southern vote. See *Official Report of the Proceedings of the Seventeenth Republican National Convention* (New York: The Tenny Press, 1920), 213–14, 220.

representation at future conventions. Southern delegates had been protected from such attempts in most previous conventions, due to their inclusion in a majority coalition that had (frequently) been dependent upon their support. Harding's outsider status left the South without such cover. Immediately after the selection of Harding and Coolidge, the convention passed a resolution calling on the RNC to "adopt a just and equitable basis of representation in future National Conventions," which was to ensure that "proper and necessary changes in the present apportionment of delegates in proportion to the Republican vote actually cast at general elections throughout the various States of the Union" be achieved, as well as "to inspire a greater effort to erect and maintain substantial party organizations in all the States."[64] Despite initial protests by Southern delegates, the resolution was passed by acclamation.[65]

After Harding's comfortable victory in the 1920 general election, the national GOP intended to follow through on the convention's resolution. In January 1921, RNC Chairman Hays announced the creation of the Committee on Reconstruction,[66] which was chaired by C. Bascom Slemp, a Republican congressman from Virginia who represented the Lily-White movement.[67] On the basis of the Slemp committee's recommendations, the RNC in June of 1921 voted to reduce Southern representation. Per the Slemp proposal, at-large district representation would be eliminated, and congressional districts would receive (a) one delegate if at least 2,500 votes had been cast for the Republican candidate in the last presidential or congressional election and (b) a second delegate if 10,000 or more votes had been cast, or if the Republican candidate had won.[68] While the effects would be relatively minor and could have even increased the number of delegates for some Southern states,[69] based on the 1920 election results the South as a whole would lose an additional fourteen delegates to the 1924 convention (representing an 8.4 percent decrease relative to 1920). As a result, black Southern members of the RNC accused the committee of trying to "penalize people of the South whose only crime has been the voting for such men as McKinley, Roosevelt and Harding."[70]

The Slemp proposal, however, never went into effect. In December 1923, the RNC voted to restore the basis of representation that had been agreed upon in 1913, while expanding the number of delegates for states that had voted for Harding in 1920. As Richard B. Sherman notes, there were several reasons for

[64] *Official Report of the Proceedings of the Seventeenth Republican National Convention*, 233.
[65] Ibid., 234.
[66] "Republicans Move for Reform in South," *New York Times*, January 31, 1921.
[67] Guy B. Hathorn, "The Political Career of C. Bascom Slemp" (Doctoral dissertation, Duke University, 1950), 160.
[68] Richard B. Sherman, *The Republican Party and Black America: From McKinley to Hoover* (Charlottesville: University of Virginia Press, 1973), 157.
[69] Based on 1920 election results, Arkansas would gain one delegate, Florida two, and Virginia one. See "Republicans Cut Quota from South," *New York Times*, June 9, 1921.
[70] Ibid.

this change in strategy toward the South.[71] First, the Republican losses in the 1922 congressional elections would have meant a decrease in delegate numbers for non-Southern states. Additionally, black Republicans remained strongly opposed to the change, and some Republican leaders feared that a drop in black votes in other parts of the country would occur if the plan was implemented.[72] Most important, however, was the traditional control of Southern delegates by a president up for reelection. While Harding had earned the Republican nomination in 1920 without reliance on Southern support and may therefore not have appreciated the importance of controlling Southern delegates, his death in the summer of 1923 left Calvin Coolidge with less than a year to secure his own nomination at the 1924 convention.[73] While Coolidge would go on to win the nomination easily, in 1923 it was far from certain that he would. Facing a challenge by Senator Hiram Johnson of California, who announced his candidacy in November 1923,[74] Coolidge calculated that controlling "as large a block of southern delegates as possible"[75] would be the most effective way to maximize his chances of winning the nomination. The issue of reapportionment was thus debated extensively during the December 1923 RNC meeting, and the committee members in the end voted to reinstate the previous delegate proportions.[76] Unsurprisingly, Johnson opposed the return to pre-1921 Southern delegate levels, calling it "an act repugnant to

[71] Sherman, *The Republican Party and Black America*, 157–58.

[72] During the debate that took place in the RNC meeting of December 1923, Harmon L. Remmel, RNC member from Arkansas, noted that black voters "are the balance of power" in states like Illinois, Missouri, and Indiana, and additionally "they are nearly the balance of power in the state of Ohio. They have a large vote in the state of Pennsylvania, and I understand that in the state of New York they have got perhaps 150,000 colored men in the city of New York, and the Democratic party is flirting with them." Paul Kesaris et al., *Papers of the Republican Party* (Frederick, MD: University Publications of America, 1987), Reel 1, Frame 596.

[73] Among the first decisions Coolidge made as president was to select Slemp as his personal secretary. The move was instantly regarded by Democrats as an indication that Coolidge would run for president in 1924, and that the appointment was the "first step to round up the delegates from Southern States." Cited in Hathorn, "Political Career of C. Bascom Slemp," 195. Whether or not this was the intention behind Slemp's appointment, the former Virginia congressman would become responsible for the Coolidge campaign's outreach in the South in advance of the 1924 convention. See Hathorn, "Political Career of C. Bascom Slemp," 205–07.

[74] "Johnson Enters Presidential Race as Foe of Reaction," *New York Times*, November 16, 1923.

[75] Sherman, *The Republican Party and Black America*, 158; Hathorn, *Political Career of C. Bascom Slemp*, 208.

[76] During the debate, RNC member and Senator Robert B. Howell (R-NE) insinuated that proponents of the 1921 decision were not informed that the issue would be brought up, stating that "we would not merely have delegations from the southern states here in reference to this matter if it had been thought in the northern states that this question was going to be reopened at this time. I had not an idea when I came to Washington that there would be a thought of re-opening this matter." Kesaris et al., *Papers of the Republican Party*, Reel 1, Frame 609. Based on the roll call taken on the second day of the RNC meeting (during which the debate on overturning the 1921 decision was concluded), this does not appear to have resulted in a notably higher presence of Southern RNC members: 58 percent of members from the fifty-three states and territories that

every sense of fair dealing," while describing the Southern states as having "nothing Republican in them except a few office-holders, absolutely under the direction and control of the Administration."[77]

Separate from the attempts at reducing the South's representation at national conventions, Harding also engaged in a direct attempt at changing the party organizations. During the 1920 campaign, the RNC had created a Southern Headquarters (in Washington, DC) with Slemp in charge. In October 1920, Coolidge engaged in a multi-day speaking tour of the South, while Harding – who engaged in limited campaign appearances – also made an appearance in the former Confederacy, giving a speech in Chattanooga, Tennessee. The Republican attention to the South – at least in Harding's estimation – paid off, as Tennessee for the first time since Reconstruction went for the GOP. In other Southern states, the party failed to win but saw higher vote totals than in recent memory. Thus, once again, Republican national leaders faced the all-too-tempting possibility that a breakthrough in the South could be at hand. Indeed, after the 1920 election, Harding received a number of letters from Southern Republicans urging him to invest in major party-building activities in the South. Specifically, as a friend of his from Texas suggested, Harding should announce "that in the distribution of political patronage, no faction or party organization would be recognized as entitled to consideration, that did not maintain a continuous local organization."[78]

As Robert E. Hauser has argued, such suggestions were in line with Harding's existing views that a competitive Republican Party in the South would not just be good politically for the GOP, but also for the region itself. Once in office, Harding began a process aimed at radically altering the structure of Southern party organizations. His first step was to change the way patronage would be distributed. Like Theodore Roosevelt before him, Harding sought to replace the existing (and corrupt) party machines with new organizations assembled by handpicked local leaders. Those new organizations subsequently would control local patronage and thus become the "true" Republican Party in the state. By appointing capable, white men to the offices – the theory went – voters in the South would come to see the local GOP as a responsible party worthy of their support.[79]

Harding pursued such reform in two states: Georgia and Louisiana. In Georgia, the existing party organization was a long-standing Black-and-Tan coalition led by a black man, Henry Lincoln Johnson – though at the time Johnson's organization was challenged by other factions. Harding selected John Louis Philips, a local white businessman, to organize a new Republican

---

made up the RNC were present during the meeting, but only 45 percent of Southern members were in attendance. See Kesaris et al., *Papers of the Republican Party*, Reel 1, Frame 623–25.

[77] "The Southern Delegate 'Scandal'," *Literary Digest* 80 (January 5, 1924), 14.

[78] Hauser, *Warren G. Harding*, 94.   [79] Ibid., 92–99.

Party in Georgia. The attempt failed miserably, in part because the existing factions refused to cooperate with Philips, but also because Philips himself became enmeshed in a number of legal scandals – including allegations that he had been a war profiteer during World War I. In the 1922 midterms, the GOP performed as poorly in Georgia as it did before Philips began his reorganization attempts (see Chapter 9).[80]

In Louisiana, where the Democratic Party faced a variety of factional splits, Harding had done moderately well in the 1920 election. However, the local GOP was also divided between a resurgent Black-and-Tan organization – led by (white) RNC committeeman Emile Kuntz – and a competing Lily-White group. With the 1920 election suggesting a possible path toward genuine electoral success in Louisiana, the Lily-Whites intensified their attacks on Kuntz. Harding's stated belief that Southern party organizations needed to reflect the majority of a state's voting population further encouraged the Lily-Whites in this regard. A lobbying effort by a number of Louisiana politicians – including former Republican Governor Henry Warmoth – pushed Harding to withhold patronage until the existing Kuntz faction was redesigned to include white business leaders. Throughout the spring and summer of 1921, Harding navigated between Kuntz and businessman Warren Kearney, promising both sides some access to patronage in exchange for cooperation between the two factions. Such cooperation failed when Kearney demanded the resignation of all blacks from the state party organization as well as the right of new white party leaders to remain registered as Democrats. In the end, negotiations between the two groups broke down due to Kearney's unwillingness to compromise with the Kuntz faction (see Chapter 8).[81]

In the end, both the Georgia and the Louisiana experiments were abandoned after the 1922 midterms. To be sure, the lack of progress by then in both states made success unlikely, but the Republican Party's dreadful performance across the country meant Harding had neither the interest nor the luxury to continue focusing on the South. Additionally, after Harding's death in 1923, Coolidge realized he could help secure his own nomination at the 1924 national convention both by maintaining the size of the Southern delegation and by keeping the existing party organizations in place in exchange for loyalty at the convention. Thus, at the 1924 convention, both the Johnson and the Kuntz delegations were seated.[82]

---

[80] Robert E. Hauser, "'The Georgia Experiment': President Warren G. Harding's Attempt to Reorganize the Republican Party in Georgia," *The Georgia Historical Quarterly* 62 (Winter 1978): 288–303.

[81] Hauser, *Warren G. Harding*, 221–54.

[82] *Official Report of the Proceedings of the Eighteenth Republican National Convention* (New York: The Tenny Press, 1924), 57, 62.

HERBERT HOOVER AND THE SOUTH, 1928–1932

Four years later, with Coolidge's decision not to run for reelection in 1928, the Republican presidential nomination was up for grabs. Herbert Hoover, who was Coolidge's secretary of commerce, devised a pre-convention strategy that relied on an informal campaign organization to collect delegates on his behalf. Hubert Work, the secretary of the interior, played an important role in this regard and focused much of his attention on lining up support for Hoover in the South. Hoover was by no means an illogical candidate in this regard. After the Great Mississippi Flood of 1927, Coolidge had chosen Hoover to direct the administration's response, and Hoover had built up a genuine level of popularity among Southern businessmen based on his efforts.

Nonetheless, the Hoover campaign organization had little qualms about buying Southern support in the McKinley/Hanna tradition: Rush Holland, a close associate of Work's, who "specialized in factional squabbles and patronage,"[83] was sent to Arkansas, Louisiana, Florida, and South Carolina with $10,000 to dole out among local party leaders.[84] Thanks to this Southern strategy, as well as participation in carefully chosen primary elections, Hoover began the Republican convention with a sizable lead in delegates and was elected on the first ballot, receiving 77 percent of the total delegate tally and more than 96 percent of Southern delegates.

Hoover used the likelihood of New York Governor Al Smith – a Catholic – becoming the Democratic candidate to make inroads into the South for the general election, by favoring Lily-Whites over black Republicans. As Allan J. Lichtman has argued, Hoover "saw a unique opportunity to garner the electoral votes of the normally Democratic South by shrewdly directing appeals to religious bigotry, prohibitionism, and racism."[85] During the convention, Hoover actively supported the Lily-White movement and ensured that black Republican leaders were denied credentials. Hoover's associate Mabel Walker Willebrandt, Assistant Attorney General of the United States, used her influence as chairman of the Credentials Committee to ensure that Southern delegations were packed with Hoover supporters.[86] The Credentials Committee refused to seat delegations from the South that were not seen as guaranteed Hoover votes. As a result, the pro-Hoover Mississippi delegation (controlled by local black

---

[83] Donald J. Lisio, *Hoover, Blacks, and Lily-Whites: A Study of Southern Strategies* (Chapel Hill: University of North Carolina Press, 1985), 39.

[84] In subsequent testimony before the Special Senate Committee Investigating Presidential Campaign Expenditure, Holland admitted that he disbursed $10,200 in the South in the run-up to the 1928 convention but denied Hoover had been aware of these expenses (ibid., 52–53).

[85] Allan J. Lichtman, *Prejudice and the Old Politics: The Presidential Election of 1928* (Lanham, MD: Lexington Books, 1979), 151.

[86] Charles Rappleye, *Herbert Hoover in the White House: The Ordeal of the Presidency* (New York: Simon & Schuster, 2016), 24–26.

party boss Perry Howard) was seated, while Black-and-Tan delegates from Louisiana and Texas, who were not obvious Hoover votes, were rejected in favor of Lily-Whites.[87]

Hoover would dramatically improve the GOP's performance in the former Confederacy,[88] cracking the Democratic Solid South by winning Texas, Tennessee, North Carolina, Virginia, and Florida.[89] Because Jim Crow institutions in the South restricted black electoral participation almost to zero, Hoover's significant vote totals – he won 47 percent of the popular vote in the eleven ex-Confederate states[90] – meant that white Southerners had supported his candidacy at historically high rates. These results suggested a possible breakthrough for the Republican Party in future elections.

To be sure, Hoover's performance likely overestimated his influence on the vote. Indeed, multiple studies have argued that part of the Republican success in 1928 was due to the intense religious bigotry against Smith – the first Catholic on a national ticket.[91] Rather than interpret his Southern victories as an anti-Smith backlash, however, Hoover chose to attribute them to his popularity in the South, stemming from his successful management of the (overwhelmingly Southern) relief effort following the Great Mississippi Flood of 1927.[92] Yet his Southern success produced little in the way of coattails. In the 70th Congress (1927–29), the GOP controlled only three House seats in the former Confederacy and no Senate seats. In the 71st Congress (1929–31), which would convene after the 1928 election, the GOP controlled eight House seats and no Senate seats.[93] Thus, Hoover's five-state victory in the South carried with it only five additional House seats for the party. Still, Hoover viewed his Southern success as an opportunity to rebuild a serious Southern wing of the GOP.

As Donald J. Lisio has argued, characterizing Hoover's strategy to rebuild the South as being based simply on elevating Lily-Whites in states where the

---

[87] Lisio, *Hoover, Blacks, and Lily-Whites*, 59.

[88] Lichtman, *Prejudice and the Old Politics*, 151–53.

[89] By comparison, Harding won one Southern state (Tennessee) and Coolidge won none.

[90] James L. Sundquist, *Dynamics of the Party System: Alignment and Realignment of Political Parties in the United States* (Washington, DC: Brookings Institution Press, 1983), 189.

[91] See Mark K. Bauman, "Prohibition and Politics: Warren Candler and Al Smith's 1928 Campaign," *Mississippi Quarterly* 31 (1977): 109–17; Herbert J. Doherty, Jr., "Florida and the Presidential Election of 1928," *The Florida Historical Quarterly* 26 (1947): 174–86; Edmund A. Moore, *A Catholic Runs for President: The Campaign of 1928* (Gloucester, MA: Peter Smith, 1968); Robert A. Slayton, *Empire Statesman: The Rise and Redemption of Al Smith* (New York: Free Press, 2001).

[92] Note that Hoover actually performed worse in those counties affected by the Mississippi Flood. See Boris Heersink, Brenton D. Peterson, and Jeffery A. Jenkins, "Disasters and Elections: Estimating the Net Effect of Damage and Relief in Historical Perspective," *Political Analysis* 25 (April 2017): 260–68.

[93] The same three House seats (two in Tennessee and one in Texas) were in both Congresses. Of the five that were added after the 1928 election, two were in North Carolina and three were in Virginia.

Black-and-Tans were still dominant is too simple. Instead, a more realistic assessment is that Hoover tried to replace local Republican leaders accused of corruption with new "clean" leaders. That is, Hoover wanted a "higher type of citizen" to play a leadership role in the Southern GOP organizations.[94] In practical terms, however, this meant that Hoover called for either the replacement of existing Lily-Whites with different Lily-White leaders or the replacement of existing Black-and-Tan groups with Lily-Whites. The one exception concerned Hoover's (failed) attempt to replace Perry Howard as the Republican party boss in Mississippi in the summer of 1928. While Howard had supported Hoover at the GOP convention, he was subsequently charged with selling federal offices. Hoover instructed his campaign manager and RNC chair Hubert Work to replace Howard "with some colored representation and leadership that cannot be questioned."[95]

Still, during the fall campaign, Hoover provided further indication that race could become an issue in his actions as president when it came to the South. During a speech in Elizabethton, Tennessee, targeted specifically toward (white) Southern voters, Hoover discussed a number of issues related to the South. One sentence of this speech, however, stood out. Hoover stated that "I believe in the merit system of the Civil Service and I believe further that appointive offices must be filled by those who deserve the confidence and respect of the communities they serve."[96] While vague enough to allow Hoover considerable leeway, many interpreted this sentence to suggest that, once elected, he would upend the traditional patronage system on which Southern Republican parties relied for their survival.

Once in office, Hoover followed through on his promise to try to reshape the GOP in the South, though he dismissed reports that he was engaging in an explicitly racial strategy. Indeed, Hoover dropped a number of political actors that had assisted him in his 1928 presidential campaign but were accused of supporting an exclusively Lily-White Republican South after the election – this included Work, Slemp, and Horace A. Mann, a Tennessee Republican who had helped shape his campaign in the South.[97] Initially, Hoover's decisions pleased black Southern Republicans like Tennessee's Robert R. Church, Jr., who received guarantees from Hoover that he would not offer any appointments to Lily-Whites in his state.[98]

However, the relationship between Hoover and the Black-and-Tans declined considerably thereafter. In March 1929, Hoover issued a declaration on the actions necessary to rebuild the GOP in the South, stating that "[it] has been the aspiration of Republican Presidents over many years to build up sound Republican organization in the Southern States of such character as would commend

[94] Joshua D. Farrington, *Black Republicans and the Transformation of the GOP* (Philadelphia: University of Pennsylvania Press, 2016), 19.
[95] Cited in Lisio, *Hoover, Blacks, and Lily-Whites*, 70.   [96] Cited in ibid., 88.   [97] Ibid., 117.
[98] Ibid., 120.

itself to the citizens of those States." He specifically praised the Republican organizations in Virginia and North Carolina – both Lily-White-dominated groups – for their ability to elect Republicans to Congress. Notably, Hoover also praised Republican organizations in Alabama, Arkansas, Louisiana, Texas, and Florida for recently showing "increasing strength" and stated that he highly approved and welcomed

the movement of the leaders of Texas, Alabama, Florida, and other States to broaden the basis of party organization by the establishment of advisory committees of the highest type of citizenship to deal with administrative questions and who will also cooperate with independent Democrats. This movement, springing as it does from within the States themselves, insures its strength, permanence, and constant improvement in public service.[99]

Each of these states had previously been dominated by a Black-and-Tan organization, but in the first decades of the twentieth century had seen Lily-White groups come to power. On the other hand, Hoover explicitly criticized Republicans in Georgia, South Carolina, and Mississippi for misleading the government in the appointment process for federal jobs. Hoover stated that such actions

obviously render it impossible for the old organizations in those States to command the confidence of the administration, although many members of these organizations are not subject to criticism. But such conditions are intolerable to public service, are repugnant to the ideals and purposes of the Republican Party, are unjust to the people of the South and must be ended. The duty of reorganization so as to correct these conditions rests with the people of those States, and all efforts to that end will receive the hearty cooperation of the administration.[100]

At the time, Georgia, South Carolina, and Mississippi were the only remaining states in which local Republican Party organizations were controlled by Black-and-Tans.

Hoover concluded his proclamation with the warning that his government would "adopt other methods to secure advice as to the selection of Federal employees" if these states did not form new Republican organizations.[101] In particular, Hoover threatened to cut off patronage to the existing GOP organizations in Georgia, South Carolina, and Mississippi. The Hoover proclamation thus sent a clear message to all Republicans in the South, by praising the (new) Lily-White organizations while declaring war on the few remaining Black-and-Tan groups. As the *New York Times* summarized the proclamation, Hoover "clearly foreshadows a Republican party in the South almost as purely a white man's party as is the Democratic party there."[102]

[99] Herbert Hoover, *Statement on the Reorganization of the Republican Party in the South*. Online by Gerhard Peters and John T. Woolley, The American Presidency Project: www.presidency.ucsb.edu/node/211022 (accessed June 1, 2019).
[100] Ibid.   [101] Ibid.   [102] "Mr. Hoover to the South," *New York Times*, March 27, 1929.

To achieve this radical change in the South, Hoover created a national patronage advisory committee, consisting largely of two of his most influential advisors: Postmaster General Walter F. Brown and Walter Newton, his political secretary. Brown and Newton were supposed to work with state-level patronage committees – staffed with both Republican politicians and independent non-political leaders – who could vouch for the quality of any proposed candidates. In practice, this approach was mostly ineffective. As Lisio notes, the warring Republican factions within each state (including a number of competing Lily-White groups) would propose their preferred appointees while slandering those of the opposition. The independent leaders quickly grew tired of the battles and abandoned the committees, leaving only the local Republican leaders to provide advice. Newton and Brown then had to assess the many fault lines that divided the different party groups within each state – often with mixed success.[103]

This approach also represented a threat to many of the existing Lily-White organizations. While Lily-White Republicans had interpreted Hoover's proclamation as supporting Lily-Whiteism in general, his call for cooperation with independent Democrats in the South suggested that these state party organizations might see an end to *their* monopoly on federal patronage as well. Indeed, one of the GOP state organizations that saw its patronage requests denied consistently early on was Florida – by then under Lily-White control. Despite the fact that its party boss, Glenn A. Skipper, had been acknowledged as the state party's leader at the 1928 national convention and had supported Hoover's candidacy, Hoover sided with Skipper's (Lily-White) competitors.[104]

Hoover's attempts at changing the existing party structures in the South quickly experienced difficulties. In Louisiana, Hoover and RNC chairman Claudius Huston – a Lily-White from Tennessee – sought to forge a new state party organization combining two Lily-White groups. But Hoover's unwillingness to remove the former Black-and-Tan party leader from a prominent patronage position slowed down the process – in a state where the Black-and-Tans were already on their way out. In Virginia, Hoover attempted to replace Slemp with a coalition of Republican reformers. While Slemp was forced to show outward support for the efforts, he successfully undermined them behind the scenes and remained in control. In Alabama, the corrupt Lily-White organization survived another challenge to its authority. In Mississippi – where the party's black leader Perry Howard was acquitted twice on corruption charges – Hoover's attempts at creating a Lily-White party also failed. Howard, in cooperation with Democratic politicians who preferred the status quo of a

---

[103] Lisio, *Hoover, Blacks, and Lily-Whites*, 159–62. [104] Ibid., 161–65.

non-competitive local GOP, remained Mississippi's representative on the RNC and legally in control of the state party organization.[105]

Hoover's lack of success at radically altering the party structures in the South was largely the product of strong opposition from nearly every existing party organization in the region. However, it was also partly due to a lack of consistent party leadership at the national level. Hoover left much of the direct responsibility for restructuring the party's role in the South to his RNC chairmen. But the RNC during the Hoover administration was in constant turnover. Hubert Work, who served as Hoover's campaign manager in 1928 and his first RNC chair, had become alienated from Hoover early on. In the fall of 1929, Work was replaced as RNC chair by Claudius Huston. However, Huston's time as chairman proved to be limited as well: facing a financial scandal and grilled before a Senate subcommittee, Huston was forced to resign in the summer of 1930.[106] And Huston's precipitous fall had sullied Hoover along the way. As Charles Rappleye argues: "Hoover had raised up Huston as the arbiter of patronage, the man who would clean up the corrupt party organizations in the South. Now Huston was the object of scorn, and his sponsors – Hoover, principally, but also the Republican Party – appeared his dupes."[107]

Huston's successor was Republican Senator Simeon D. Fess of Ohio, who initially intended to stay on only through the 1930 midterms. Fess's designated successor after the midterms was Robert Lucas, the executive director of the RNC. But Lucas became embroiled in a political scandal of his own when it turned out he had campaigned actively against the reelection of Republican Senator George W. Norris of Nebraska. As a result, Lucas became too controversial to take over as chairman, and Fess remained chair through the 1932 national convention, despite a clear lack of interest in the position.

[105] Ibid. David J. Ginzl, "Lily-Whites versus Black-and-Tans: Mississippi Republicans during the Hoover Administration," *Journal of Mississippi History* 42 (1980): 194–211; Neil R. McMillen, "Perry W. Howard, Boss of Black-and-Tan Republicanism in Mississippi, 1924–1960," *The Journal of Southern History* 48 (1982): 205–24.

[106] Charles Rappleye, *Herbert Hoover in the White House: The Ordeal of the Presidency* (New York: Simon & Schuster, 2016), 145–47.

[107] Ibid., 147. W. E. B. Du Bois, writing in the May 1930 issue of *The Crisis*, commented at length on this scandal and Southern Republicans in general: "Mr. Claudius H. Huston, Chairman of the Republican National Committee, Southern gentleman from Tennessee, appointed for the express purpose of cleansing these Augean stables for the benefit of Hoover majorities at the next president elections, is suddenly discovered to have deposited some $36,000 which he received as a lobbyist, working for the sale of Muscle Shoales to private interests, to his own banking account in New York! Here, it was used to cover his gambling operations in Wall Street, and then, as he firmly asserts, it was 'returned'. All of which convinces us of the spotless purity of the white Republicans of the South and the unforgiveable perverseness of Negroes in not following their able teachings and shining example" (171–72).

TABLE 5.2 *Senate roll call on Judge Parker's nomination, 71st Congress*

Party	Official Tally		Tally with Pairs	
	Yea	Nay	Yea	Nay
Northern Democrat	1	13	2	14
Southern Democrat	9	10	11	12
Republican	29	17	34	22
Farmer-Labor	0	1	0	1
Total	39	41	47	49

Source: *Congressional Record*, 71st Congress, 2nd Session (May 7, 1930): 8487

Combined, the GOP's national political leadership lacked focus and consistency to successfully redesign its Southern wing.[108]

Hoover himself became further disillusioned in his ability to radically change the South's party structure by the failed nomination of John J. Parker to the Supreme Court. On March 21, 1930, Hoover nominated Parker to fill the vacancy created by the death of Edward Terry Sanford. Parker served on the US Court of Appeals for the Fourth Circuit in Richmond and had a long career in Republican Party politics in his home state of North Carolina, serving as a delegate to the GOP national convention in 1924 and earlier running unsuccessfully for governor and Congress. The North Carolina GOP was a Lily-White organization, and Hoover saw Parker as the kind of fresh, high-caliber leader to help promote a new Southern wing of the Republican Party. Parker met quick resistance from unions, based on some prior anti-labor decisions, and the National Association for the Advancement of Colored People (NAACP), based on comments that he made about the fitness of black voters when he ran for governor in 1920.[109]

The politics surrounding Parker's nomination were national news, and senators in both parties faced a variety of pressures – partisan, regional, state, and interest group – as they considered whether to consent or not.[110] Finally, on May 7, 1930, the Senate voted on Parker's nomination, and it failed 39–41.[111] The vote breakdown appears in Table 5.2. There were considerable divisions in each party. Democrats as a whole mostly voted against Parker, but Northern Democrats were almost unanimously opposed while Southern

---

[108] Boris Heersink, "National Party Organizations and Party Brands in American Politics" (Doctoral dissertation, University of Virginia, 2017), 67–68.

[109] Kenneth W. Goings, *"The NAACP Comes of Age": The Defeat of Judge John J. Parker* (Bloomington: Indiana University Press, 1990); Rappleye, *Herbert Hoover in the White House*, 142–45.

[110] Rappleye, *Herbert Hoover in the White House*, 144.

[111] *Congressional Record*, 71st Congress, 2nd Session (May 7, 1930): 8487.

Democrats were nearly evenly split. Republicans were mostly in favor of Parker, but a significant minority was opposed.

The NAACP took credit for defeating Parker, citing its concerted lobby of Republicans and threats of the GOP losing black votes on election day. Kenneth Goings, based on a survey of various sources, claims "the NAACP campaign may have affected from 10 to 13 votes" in the Senate.[112] But Southern Democrats were also critical to Parker's defeat. While they did not want to go along with the NAACP, they also did not want to strengthen the Lily-White movement in the South.[113] Ultimately, Southern Democrats broke relatively evenly, and enough voted "nay" to cost Parker his confirmation. Hoover was furious but made no public comments on the matter. But as Simon Topping notes, "Hoover later admitted that the Parker defeat had damaged the prestige of his presidency, and he put the blame for this defeat squarely at the door of African Americans in general and the NAACP in particular."[114] Hoover also largely dropped his Southern Strategy at that point. He made no attempt to replace Parker with another Southerner – selecting Owen Roberts of Pennsylvania instead, who was confirmed quickly and easily – and focused his attention on the economic difficulties arising in the wake of the recent stock market crash and the early stages of the Great Depression.

All told, Hoover's attempts at a Southern strategy were largely a failure. His efforts at reconfiguring existing party organizations in the South alienated those Lily-Whites already in charge. And his attempts at forcing out the Black-and-Tan organizations in Mississippi, Georgia, and South Carolina further alienated black Republicans already frustrated with the president on a number of other issues. Hoover's sole successes were in undermining the rule of the existing Black-and-Tan coalitions in South Carolina and Georgia. At the 1932 convention, Mississippi's Perry Howard was easily recognized as the legitimate leader of the state party, and challenges by rival Lily-White delegations were rejected by the Credentials Committee. However, South Carolina's "Tieless Joe" Tolbert and his delegation were rejected at the convention (see Chapter 9).[115] Meanwhile, a new party organization from Georgia – which combined Lily-White and Black-and-Tan groups in an unstable coalition that nonetheless had been successful in getting the Hoover administration to appoint its preferred candidates to federal offices – was seated.

[112] Goings, *"The NAACP Comes of Age,"* 48.
[113] Simon Topping, *Lincoln's Lost Legacy: The Republican Party and the African American Vote, 1928–1952* (Gainesville: University of Florida Press, 2008), 22.
[114] Ibid.
[115] After Hoover's reelection loss in 1932 and the decline of Republican federal patronage, Tolbert regained control of the South Carolina GOP and successfully seated his delegation at the 1936 national convention. However, without patronage, Tolbert's machine declined rapidly and was soon replaced by a Lily-White organization.

CONCLUSION

After the election of 1896, with the Republican Party in ascendancy nationally but in further decline in the South, national GOP leaders became less concerned with finding ways to revitalize the party's electoral prospects in the former Confederacy. Instead, presidents and presidential hopefuls began to increasingly rely on the strategy introduced by McKinley and Hanna in 1896: using Southern state party organizations as rotten boroughs to ensure delegate support at the national convention. With Southern state party organizations often not running candidates in local elections, much of their infrastructure became focused exclusively on distributing patronage for financial gain and controlling the national convention delegation. In response to this, several attempts to reduce the size of the South's convention delegation were made – in 1899, 1900, 1913, and 1920 – but only one of these – in 1913 – proved successful.

While some of the criticism of the South's role in national party politics was based on genuine frustration with (what many non-Southerners believed to be) a corrupt group of politicians, the vantage points of different political actors also shaped their view of the South. That is, those actors that were able to obtain Southern support defended the region, while their opponents attacked it. In the case of Theodore Roosevelt, a change in vantage point also resulted in a change in position: while Roosevelt relied on patronage to ensure Southern convention support for himself in 1904 and Taft in 1908, he charged the system as corrupt when those same party leaders supported Taft (instead of him) in 1912.

While the South may not have been an electoral priority during this period, Republican leaders never fully gave up on the region's potential. Most notably, both Harding and Hoover, during their respective presidencies, invested considerable time and political capital in trying to reshape some of the Southern party organizations into new groups that would be electorally competitive. In both cases, the main strategy amounted to the replacement of black party leaders with handpicked white leaders. This approach failed to significantly alter the GOP's electoral competitiveness in the region, though in some cases it would serve to undermine the survival of existing party organizations.

6

Toward a Modern Southern Strategy, 1933–1968

Despite the attempts by Herbert Hoover to radically redesign a number of Southern state parties during his one term in the White House, a Southern breakthrough appeared even further away after the Democratic wave elections of 1930 and 1932. Indeed, at the dawning of the New Deal era, the GOP faced a decidedly new political environment: with the party experiencing major defeats across the nation. Recovery in former-GOP strongholds thus became the party's top priority and revitalization of the South was put on the back burner. But starting in the late 1940s, with the GOP beginning to recover from the string of New Deal defeats, national Republican leaders – including RNC chairman Guy Gabrielson between 1948 and 1952 and President Dwight Eisenhower during his two terms in office (1953–61) – began to refocus their attention on the South.

With black voters becoming an increasingly important element of the Democratic coalition, Republican leaders saw white Southerners grow increasingly alienated from the national Democratic Party. If Republicans could convince these white Southerners to join their party, they believed, the end of single-party rule in the South could finally be achieved. Taking advantage of this Democratic schism, however, proved to be complicated. Attempts by national Republicans to cater to white Southerners between 1949 and 1964 proved successful, as the GOP's performance in the South began to improve considerably – with Goldwater's performance there in 1964 a particular high point (see Figure 6.1). Yet, to achieve this, the national party frequently relied on (at the very least) condoning segregation. Such an approach alienated many within the GOP – including elected officials in the Northeast – and produced multiple internal clashes over the national party's political strategy. Opponents of the Republicans' Southern Strategy argued that the party ought to focus instead on black voters in major cities in the Northeast.

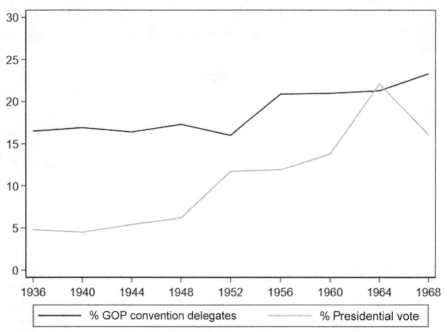

FIGURE 6.1 Southern percentage of delegates at Republican National Convention and Republican popular vote, 1936–1968
Source: *Congressional Quarterly's Guide to U.S. Elections*, 3rd edn. (Washington, DC: Congressional Quarterly, 1994)

While the GOP for a time would walk a tightrope between appealing to whites in the South and to black voters in major northern cities,[1] Richard Nixon's 1968 presidential campaign provided the party with an electoral blueprint to appeal to Southern whites but not alienate voters in other parts of the country in the process. With the last remaining Black-and-Tan party organizations disappearing during this period and black delegates at the GOP convention thus reaching a new numerical low (see Figure 6.2), the Republican Party nevertheless found itself positioned to emerge as the new dominant party in the South on the basis of white votes.

THE MARGINALIZATION OF SOUTHERN REPUBLICANISM, 1932–1948

The Democrats scored significant victories in the 1930 midterms and would – when the 72nd Congress convened in December 1931 – enjoy majority control

---

[1] For arguably the most extensive assessment of GOP outreach to black voters in the post-1968 period, see: Leah Wright Rigueur, *The Loneliness of the Black Republican: Pragmatic Politics and the Pursuit of Power* (Princeton, NJ: Princeton University Press, 2015).

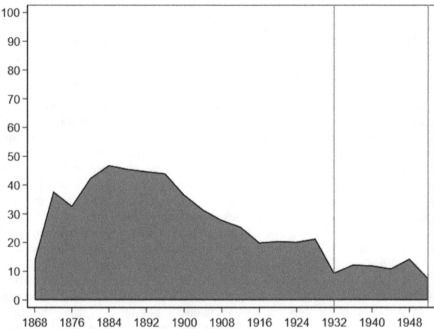

FIGURE 6.2 Percentage of Southern GOP convention delegates that were black,
1933–1952
Source: Data collected by authors.

in the House. As the Great Depression deepened, and Hoover made little attempt to envision the federal government as a provider of relief, Democrats also won the 1932 elections in a landslide. Southern whites who had supported Hoover in 1928 – the so-called "Hoovercrats" – returned home to the Democratic Party in 1932, as Franklin Delano Roosevelt (FDR) swept the ex-Confederate states. While black voters in the North were unhappy with Hoover and his Lily-White tendencies, they continued to largely support the GOP at the polls – and Hoover himself still received a majority of black votes. Soon, however, black voters reached a tipping point. FDR's New Deal, a federally based set of social welfare programs, provided a variety of relief opportunities during the troubled economic time. While these programs were tilted toward white recipients,[2] black Americans also enjoyed the benefits as well. Thus, while FDR offered no progress on civil or voting rights for blacks, his New Deal made day-to-day life tangibly better for many of them. This proved enough for a

---

[2] Ira Katznelson, *When Affirmative Action Was White: An Untold History of Racial Inequality in Twentieth-Century America* (New York: Norton, 2005).

majority of blacks to vote Democratic for the first time in 1936, in FDR's first reelection.[3]

The New Deal, for a time, negated any GOP strategy to court white voters in the South. During FDR's first term in office, the New Deal was wildly popular in the former Confederacy, as white Southern Democrats were able to temper the programs with disfranchisement restrictions. And even after FDR began to blanch at conservative limitations on his initiatives and began to butt heads with Southern Democrats during his second term, the New Deal was still a big net positive for the Southern states. Republicans, on the other hand, were put on the defensive. Some GOP leaders – like Hoover's allies – wanted to continue a reform program in the South. Others wanted to pay more heed to black voters in the North, believing that their move to the Democratic Party was actually a move to FDR; thus, it was potentially temporary and personal, and with some effort the GOP could bring them back to the party fold.

The 1936 Republican National Convention was thus a battle between these differing perspectives. Lily-White and Black-and-Tan factions contested control of the delegations in Florida, Louisiana, South Carolina, and Mississippi. The Credentials Committee initially seated the Lily-Whites in Florida, Louisiana, and South Carolina, while acceding to Perry Howard's Black-and-Tan faction in Mississippi. Black Republicans complained loudly about getting the short end of the stick, and various GOP leaders worried that the continued Hoover-esque Southern Strategy would cost the party black votes in the North. Thus, the decision on South Carolina was reversed, with "Tieless Joe" Tolbert's Black-and-Tan faction seated instead.[4]

In addition to (somewhat) evening out the factional disputes relating to the few remaining Black-and-Tan delegations, Republican leaders gave Roscoe Conkling Simmons, an important black party activist from Illinois, the prime position of seconding Republican presidential candidate Alf Landon's nomination. Democrats, however, were making their own changes, as they would seat their first set of black delegates ever in 1936. While the Republicans continued their outreach in the campaign – outspending the Democrats two to one in an attempt to woo black voters – the economics of the era and the introduction of

---

[3] Nancy J. Weiss, *Farewell to the Party of Lincoln: Black Politics in the Age of FDR* (Princeton, NJ: Princeton University Press, 1983), 206, 293. Note that Simon Topping claims that a majority of blacks first voted Democratic in the 1934 midterms but does not provide a source. See Simon Topping, *Lincoln's Lost Legacy: The Republican Party and the African American Vote, 1928–1952* (Gainesville: University Press of Florida, 2008), 2, 30. The data in Table XII.4 in Weiss (p. 293) seems to contradict Topping's claim. One House election in 1934 does suggest a transition was under way: Arthur Mitchell (IL), the first black Democrat in congressional history, defeated three-term Republican Oscar DePriest (IL), the sole black representative in the House.

[4] Topping, *Lincoln's Lost Legacy*, 39.

the New Deal was too much to overcome: FDR won the 1936 election easily and captured over 70 percent of the black vote.[5]

During much of the 1940s, Republican leaders and presidential aspirants no longer saw the South as an area that could be turned to the GOP. With white Southerners firmly back in the Democratic Party, Republicans felt that a more achievable goal was to siphon back the black voters in the North that the Democrats had won over in 1936. Thus, in 1940 and 1944, Republican National Convention politics mostly resembled the pre-1920s era, when the South was treated as a rotten borough.

In 1940, Senator Robert Taft of Ohio devoted a considerable amount of resources toward lining up delegates in the South.[6] Relying on his reputation as a vehement anti-New Dealer and friend to business interests, Taft successfully appealed to both conservative Republicans in the South and more "main street" co-partisans. Moreover, he hired Colonel Rentfro B. Creager, the white GOP boss in Texas, to be his floor manager at the convention and entered into an arrangement with Perry Howard in Mississippi. As Table 6.1 indicates, Taft's pre-convention work earned him a plurality of Southern delegates on the first convention ballot, in his attempt to stall the momentum of Thomas Dewey (NY), Manhattan District Attorney and buster of organized crime, who had emerged as the front-runner for the nomination. Taft largely held onto his Southern delegates through the entirety of the six convention ballots, but he eventually succumbed to businessman Wendell Willkie, who steadily built up support across the balloting.[7] In 1944, Dewey – by then governor of New York – had the field mostly to himself, thanks to Taft's decision not to run (and instead support Ohio Governor John Bricker) and Willkie's sudden death. In addition, Herbert Brownell, Dewey's new campaign manager, was a first-class organizer, and his efforts reduced Dewey's remaining GOP foes to minor annoyances at best. Dewey thus cruised to a huge first-ballot victory. But Dewey, like Willkie in 1940 and Landon in 1936, was no match for FDR in the general election.

By 1948, Republicans began to face a different political reality: with FDR dead, his successor Harry Truman deeply unpopular, and Republicans finally rebounding in the 1946 midterms – winning control of both the House and the Senate – the GOP appeared on the road back to political dominance. And both Taft and Dewey once again showed interest in the GOP presidential nomination. Taft had scored a major anti-union victory with the enactment of the Taft–Hartley Act in 1947, which banned the closed shop. Dewey,

---

[5] Joshua D. Farrington, *Black Republicans and the Transformation of the GOP* (Philadelphia: University of Pennsylvania Press, 2016), 22–24; Weiss, *Farewell to the Party of Lincoln*, 205–08.
[6] James T. Patterson, *Mr. Republican: A Biography of Robert A. Taft* (Boston: Houghton Mifflin, 1972), 208, 212, 225.
[7] Ibid., 224–28.

TABLE 6.1 *Republican National Convention balloting in the South, 1940*

State	First ballot			Fourth ballot			Fifth ballot		Sixth ballot	
	Dewey	Taft	Willkie	Dewey	Taft	Willkie	Taft	Willkie	Taft	Willkie
Alabama	53.8	46.2	0.0	53.8	38.5	7.7	53.8	38.5	53.8	46.2
Arkansas	16.7	58.3	16.7	25.0	58.3	16.7	83.3	16.7	83.3	16.7
Florida	50.0	8.3	0.0	75.0	16.7	0.0	25.0	58.3	16.7	83.3
Georgia	50.0	21.4	0.0	42.9	21.4	14.3	50.0	42.9	50.0	42.9
Louisiana	41.7	41.7	0.0	50.0	50.0	0.0	100.0	0.0	100.0	0.0
Mississippi	27.3	72.7	0.0	18.2	81.8	0.0	100.0	0.0	81.8	18.2
N. Carolina	39.1	30.4	8.7	26.1	26.1	39.1	47.8	52.2	34.8	65.2
S. Carolina	100.0	0.0	0.0	80.0	0.0	20.0	0.0	90.0	0.0	100.0
Tennessee	44.4	16.7	11.1	27.8	33.3	27.8	50.0	33.3	27.8	55.6
Texas	0.0	100.0	0.0	0.0	100.0	0.0	100.0	0.0	100.0	0.0
Virginia	11.1	50.0	27.8	0.0	38.9	61.1	38.9	61.1	11.1	88.9
All delegates	36.0	18.9	10.5	25.0	25.4	30.6	37.7	42.9	31.8	65.5
Southern delegates	34.9	44.4	6.5	30.8	42.0	18.9	60.9	34.3	52.1	45.6

Note: Support is reflected in percentage of delegates. The sixth ballot was redone after it became clear that Willkie would win the nomination, which resulted in him winning the nomination with unanimous support.

Source: CQ Guide to US Elections, 6th edn., 719

meanwhile, remained governor of New York – winning reelection in 1946 with the largest margin in the state's history.

Dewey sought to dominate the pre-convention stage of the 1948 campaign by undermining Taft in the South – in large part through activities by Herbert Brownell, who again served as his campaign manager.[8] Brownell sought to "out organize" the Taft forces and pursued a splinter campaign in the South.[9] He understood that Taft had strong relations with the leaders of the Southern GOP organizations and thus worked to recruit the under-leaders if possible. Sometimes, Brownell failed: in Texas, for example, Creager kept the state party apparatus firmly in his control and ensured delegates remained loyal to Taft. But often Brownell was successful, as in Alabama, where he worked around Lonnie Noojin, the state's national committeeman, and cut a deal with Claude Vardaman, the state party chairman. As Michael Bowen states, "by recruiting the second in command and offering to give him an increased stake in patronage notes, Brownell scored a strategic advantage at the national convention."[10] In the end, Brownell's organizing strength not only in the South, but throughout the country, was too great, and the Taft forces were no match.[11] After jumping out to a big lead on the first convention ballot, Dewey neared a majority on the second ballot – at which point Taft withdrew and asked his delegates to vote for Dewey for the sake of party harmony.

In the 1948 general election, Dewey was a heavy favorite. But in a remarkable turnaround, Truman emerged victorious. Truman survived a Southern Democratic walkout at the Democratic convention, after the inclusion of a civil rights plank in the party platform, and the loss of four Deep South states to Governor Strom Thurmond of South Carolina, the "Dixiecrat" presidential candidate.[12] Part of Truman's surprise victory was the product of his own hard work, through an extensive and invigorated election campaign.[13] But Truman's victory was also due in part to black voters in the North, who rewarded him for his positive stance on civil rights. Indeed, black voters proved to be a key swing

---

[8] In the years after 1940, Taft continued to maintain his strong conservative reputation, working to undermine organized labor (in the Taft–Hartley Act of 1947) and opposing fair employment legislation. These positions, along with hints that he was pro-states' rights, continued to endear him to many white Republican leaders in the South, like Boss Creager in Texas. See Topping, *Lincoln's Lost Legacy*, 124; Patterson, *Mr. Republican*, 416.

[9] Michael Bowen, *The Roots of Modern Conservatism: Dewey, Taft, and the Battle for the Soul of the Republican Party* (Chapel Hill: University of North Carolina Press, 2011), 61–66.

[10] Ibid., 63.

[11] As James Patterson notes, "[Taft's campaign manager] Clarence Brown seemed no match for Herbert Brownell, an affable, shrewd, and highly efficient lawyer who ran the governor's operations. While the Dewey forces were busy flattering delegates and hinting at promises of patronage, Brown was still worrying about such mundane matters as hotel rooms and seats in the gallery for his friends." Patterson, *Mr. Republican*, 410.

[12] The official name of the Dixiecrat Party was the States' Rights Democratic Party.

[13] Boris Heersink and Brenton D. Peterson, "Truman Defeats Dewey: The Effects of Campaign Visits on Election Outcomes," *Electoral Studies* 49 (October 2017): 49–64.

coalition in Ohio, California, and Illinois, three states that Truman won by less than one percentage point.[14]

The presidencies of FDR and Truman meant that the GOP lacked control over federal patronage for two decades. For the Republican Party in the South, this meant an entire generation without access to federal offices. Without this access, the battles between Lily-Whites and Black-and-Tans became less important at the state level. Additionally, as black voters in the North moved to the Democratic Party, blacks in the South also began to reassess matters. Of course, due to disfranchisement, Southern blacks could rarely vote, but they could associate vicariously through their brethren in the North – especially, as Northern Democrats became increasingly active in pushing for civil and voting rights for black Americans.[15] At the same time, the Dixiecrat walkout in 1948, and the clear schism the incorporation of black voters had created inside the Democratic Party more broadly, led many in the GOP to call for a greater investment in recruiting white conservatives in the South. As the Republican Party looked ahead to 1952, this seesaw thinking within leadership circles – whether to place more emphasis on black voters in the North or white conservatives in the South – began to tilt toward a revitalized Southern strategy.

DEMOCRATIC FRACTURES AND EISENHOWER'S SOUTHERN SUCCESS, 1948–1960

During the years when the GOP remained shut out of electoral competition in the South, the New Deal radically altered the makeup of the Democratic coalition. Roosevelt's landslide victories of the 1930s meant that the South's position within the Democratic Party changed from being a majority of a minority party to a minority in the majority party. Crucially, the New Deal coalition's success outside of the South also meant that the party had to please other constituent groups. Southern Democrats thus slowly came to realize that they had become "just one among many components in an alignment that included urban white ethnic and black voters."[16]

Throughout FDR's presidency, the relationship between the South and the rest of the Democratic Party was maintained in part by Roosevelt's reluctance to move aggressively on civil rights, as well as by his continuing personal

[14] Harvard Sitkoff, "Harry Truman and the Election of 1948: The Coming of Age of Civil Rights in American Politics," *The Journal of Southern History* 37 (1971): 597–616.
[15] See Eric Schickler, *Racial Realignment: The Transformation of American Liberalism, 1932–1965* (Princeton, NJ: Princeton University Press, 2016); Christopher Baylor, *First to the Party: The Group Origins of Political Transformation* (Philadelphia: University of Pennsylvania Press, 2018).
[16] Joseph E. Lowndes, *From the New Deal to the New Right: Race and the Southern Origins of Modern Conservatism* (New Haven, CT: Yale University Press, 2008), 13.

popularity among Southern voters. With FDR's death in 1945, Southern Democratic politicians were initially relieved that the more conservative Harry Truman – from the Border state of Missouri – would become president. However, Truman soon proved to be more open to civil rights than his predecessor. In 1947, Truman spoke to the NAACP and announced that "we cannot, any longer, await the growth of a will to action in the slowest state or the most backward community. Our national government must show the way."[17] By October of that year, Truman's Committee on Civil Rights issued a report calling for the enactment of a variety of civil rights measures – including anti-lynching and anti-poll tax laws. Truman endorsed the report in his 1948 State of the Union Address, and at the 1948 Democratic convention liberals succeeded in pushing through a strong pro-civil rights plank. In protest, Democrats from several Southern states bolted the party and organized their own ticket, with South Carolina governor Strom Thurmond as the Dixiecrat presidential candidate. The Dixiecrats would succeed in keeping Truman off the ballot in several Southern states, and Thurmond would carry Alabama, Louisiana, Mississippi, and South Carolina – but Truman's surprise success in the rest of the country meant that the Dixiecrats' attempt to either play a spoiler role (for Truman) or, at the very least, push the presidential election into the House of Representatives failed.[18]

An important subset of Republicans saw in the Dixiecrat movement an opportunity to capitalize on the disunity within the Democratic Party. RNC chairman Guy Gabrielson in particular believed that the GOP would need to break up the Solid South in order for the party to dislodge the Democrats' presidential and congressional majority coalitions. Speaking during an RNC meeting in December 1950, Gabrielson noted that the single-party system in the South meant that the Republican Party began every election with a considerable vote deficit. This, Gabrielson argued,

might not have been too serious ... when we had solid Republican states north of the Mason–Dixon line, but some of those states that were at one time very solidly Republican are now becoming marginal areas, and if we are going to build towards a stronger Republican Party that can carry a national election we must do some effective and constructive work south of the Mason–Dixon line.[19]

Thus, under Gabrielson, the RNC began to explore the possibility of rebuilding the party in the South, and he created a committee to investigate ways of improving the GOP's performance.[20] Gabrielson himself made several

---

[17] Cited in ibid., 26.
[18] Numan V. Bartley, *The New South, 1945–1980* (Baton Rouge: Louisiana State University Press, 1995), 85–96.
[19] Cited in Timothy N. Thurber, *Republicans and Race: The GOP's Frayed Relationship with African Americans, 1945–1974* (Lawrence: University Press of Kansas, 2013), 31.
[20] Ibid.

appearances in the South, speaking before audiences of both Republicans and Dixiecrats. During a Lincoln Day rally in Alabama in February 1952, Gabrielson explicitly linked the Dixiecrats' segregationist views to the Republicans' opposition to the New Deal state:

Our friends call themselves States' Righters and we call ourselves Republicans. But they oppose corruption in government and so do we. We want the Dixiecrats to vote for our candidate. The Dixiecrat movement is an anti-Truman movement. The Dixiecrat party believes in states' rights. That's what the Republican Party believes in.[21]

The South would again play an important role in the close contest between Senator Robert Taft and Dwight D. Eisenhower for the 1952 presidential nomination. Taft remained popular with many Lily-White party leaders and could count on friendly delegations from Arkansas, Florida, Mississippi, South Carolina, and Tennessee.[22] However, three Southern delegations were contested: Georgia (which had a pro-Taft Lily-White delegation and a pro-Eisenhower Black-and-Tan delegation), Louisiana, and Texas. The Texas case in particular drew attention because of the questionable approach that produced the "official" delegation. In advance of the convention, Eisenhower's team had worked hard to drum up local support and win at least some delegates in Texas. At the county level, Eisenhower supporters greatly outnumbered Taft supporters in local precincts. However, Henry Zweifel, the Texas Republican boss, preferred Taft, and at the state convention elected his own slate of delegates – arguing that Eisenhower's supporters were mostly Democrats and should not have a say in the GOP delegate-selection process.[23]

The "Texas steal" received considerable media attention and set up a major confrontation at the Republican National Convention. While Taft's supporters had a majority on the Republican National Committee and on the convention's Credentials Committee, Eisenhower proved to have a small but consistent majority of the total delegates – even with the contested Southern delegates voting with Taft. As a result, the Eisenhower forces successfully forced a number of adjustments in the seating of delegates. For example, while the RNC and the Credentials Committee voted to seat Georgia's Lily-White delegation, the decision was overruled through a floor vote – which resulted in the seating of a pro-Eisenhower Black-and-Tan delegation.[24]

With Eisenhower as the party's 1952 presidential candidate, the GOP found itself in a good position to take advantage of the growing schism between Southern and Northern Democrats. Eisenhower was a national hero, with an appeal that transcended traditional partisan lines. On the issue of race, while no

[21] Cited in Lowndes, *From the New Deal to the New Right*, 36.
[22] The Virginia delegation was mixed: on the first full convention vote – regarding the seating of the Georgia delegation – thirteen Virginia delegates voted in support of the Taft-preferred outcome, while ten supported the Eisenhower position. See *CQ Quarterly's Guide to US Elections*, 723.
[23] Bowen, *The Roots of Modern Conservatism*, 126–29.   [24] Ibid., 145–48.

supporter of segregation, Eisenhower believed that integration, whether it be in the military or in the South, was most likely to succeed without government interference. Speaking at a Senate hearing on the integration of the military in 1948, Eisenhower stated that "I do believe that if we attempt merely by passing a lot of laws to force someone to like someone else we are just going to get trouble."[25] Further anticipating a successful Southern breakthrough, Republican leaders designed the party's 1952 platform to be soft on civil rights. While it opposed lynching, the poll tax, and employment discrimination, the platform took no position on reforming the Senate filibuster rule (a necessary change to achieve much of anything on those issues) and embraced states' rights by affirming "the primary responsibility of each state to order and control its own domestic institutions."[26]

These GOP overtures in advance of the 1952 election largely paid off: Eisenhower won four Southern states (Florida, Tennessee, Texas, and Virginia), only one less than the five Hoover had captured in 1928, and received more votes in the South than any Republican presidential candidate since Reconstruction. While Eisenhower's biggest successes occurred in the more economically prosperous "outer-South," he also assembled considerable vote totals in "die-hard Dixiecrat states"[27] such as South Carolina (49 percent), Louisiana (47 percent), and Mississippi (40 percent). Eisenhower's success did not translate into major partisan shifts at the congressional level, however, as the Republicans added just one House seat in North Carolina and three in Virginia to two traditionally safe seats from Tennessee.[28]

As president, Eisenhower sought to balance his own opposition to segregation and his conviction that integration could only be achieved slowly and naturally (sans government interference) with the party's ongoing political goal of breaking the Solid Democratic South. On the one hand, Eisenhower pushed for the end of segregation in Washington, DC, and created a committee focused on ending discriminatory employment practices by contractors working for the federal government (the latter with considerably less success than the former).[29] On the other hand, on the biggest civil rights issue in Eisenhower's first term – the Supreme Court's unanimous ruling in *Brown* v. *Board of Education* – the administration moved slowly. Prior to the 1956 convention, Eisenhower demanded that the draft language of the platform's civil rights plank, which stated that the "Eisenhower Administration and the Republican Party have supported the Supreme Court" on the desegregation of schools, be scrapped. While Attorney General Brownell had filed a brief in support of desegregation,

[25] Cited in ibid., 38.   [26] Cited in ibid., 41.
[27] Kevin P. Phillips, *The Emerging Republican Majority* (New Rochelle, NY: Arlington House, 1969), 199.
[28] Kenneth C. Martis, *The Historical Atlas of Political Parties in the United States Congress, 1789–1989* (New York: Macmillan, 1989), 204–07.
[29] Thurber, *Republicans and Race*, 34–57.

Eisenhower now claimed that the administration itself never "took a stand in the matter."[30]

Throughout his first term, Eisenhower remained concerned about the party's electoral success in the South. As president-elect, Eisenhower ordered the creation of a Committee on the South within the RNC, which was tasked with producing a "long range program for expanding the Republican party in the South."[31] To Eisenhower's frustration, the committee acted slowly; though in analyzing the state of multiple Southern state party organizations in November 1953, the committee did identify a number of possibly competitive House races for the 1954 midterms. However, the Republican Party's brand across the South remained a concern throughout the early Eisenhower years. Some sought to expand the Citizens for Eisenhower groups across the South to connect Eisenhower's regional popularity to individual Republican candidates.[32] Other Southern Republicans argued that the best approach to rebuilding the GOP was to create a Committee for a Two-Party South, independent from existing Republican state party organizations and the RNC, but approved by Eisenhower.[33] In seeking to expand the GOP's reach in the South, Eisenhower even considered replacing his vice president, Richard Nixon, with a conservative Democrat in 1956, telling RNC chairman Leonard W. Hall that "if you did not have to answer the segregation problem, [the] answer would be to get a really good Southern Democrat" on the 1956 Republican ticket.[34]

Eisenhower's strategy of incremental civil rights reform while remaining sympathetic to Southern "sensibilities" meant that his personal popularity in the South remained high throughout his first term (see Table 6.2 for a comparison between national and Southern approval ratings in this period). In the 1956 presidential election, Eisenhower once again won Florida, Tennessee, Texas, and Virginia – while also adding Louisiana. But his personal popularity still did not produce a Republican breakthrough at the congressional level: the Southern Senate delegation remained solidly Democratic, while no new Southern House seats were won by Republicans (although all incumbent Southern Republicans won reelection).[35]

---

[30] Jim Newton, *Eisenhower: The White House Years* (New York: Anchor Books, 2011), 217.

[31] Cited in Daniel J. Galvin, *Presidential Party Building: Dwight D. Eisenhower to George W. Bush* (Princeton, NJ: Princeton University Press, 2010), 63.

[32] "McKillips to Chairman," November 24, 1953, in Southern Situation 1953–54, Box 166, RNC Office of the Chairman Records, Dwight D. Eisenhower Library (DDEL).

[33] "Report on the Citizens for Eisenhower Activity in the South," in Southern Situation 1953–54, Box 166, RNC Office of the Chairman Records, DDEL; "John Wisdom to Leonard W. Hall," September 26, 1953, in Southern Situation 1953–54, Box 166, RNC Office of the Chairman Records, DDEL.

[34] Cited in Robert Mason, *The Republican Party and American Politics from Hoover to Reagan* (New York: Cambridge University Press, 2012), 173.

[35] Martis, *The Historical Atlas of Political Parties in the United States Congress*, 208–11.

TABLE 6.2 *National and Southern approval ratings of Dwight Eisenhower*

Year	Month	National (%)	South (%)
1953	February	68	70
	May	74	74
	July	71	65
	September	75	71
1954	January	68	63
	June	61	57
	August	70	66
1955	January	69	64
	March	71	72
	May	64	71
	June	69	67

Source: George Gallup, *The Gallup Poll, 1949–1958* (New York: Random House, 1972)

To capitalize on Eisenhower's popularity in the South, the RNC in 1957 created a Southern Division – known as "Operation Dixie" – under the leadership of national committee operative I. Lee Potter. Throughout Eisenhower's second term, Potter went on speaking tours in the South and worked on recruiting candidates and enlisting new activists.[36] As Daniel Galvin has noted, the "principal objective of Operation Dixie was to lay an organizational foundation"[37] for the Republican Party in the South. In doing so, the RNC and Eisenhower hoped that viable candidates for local and statewide positions would be inspired to run for office and, step by step, break down the Democratic one-party system.

Operation Dixie experienced a setback almost immediately after its founding, when Eisenhower responded to the Little Rock school integration crisis in September 1957.[38] While the Supreme Court had ruled in *Brown* that Southern schools could no longer be segregated, it had not established a clear timeline for when desegregation would need to begin or be completed. The Little Rock school board had adopted a plan of gradual desegregation in 1955, and by 1957 the NAACP had selected nine students to attend Little Rock Central High. When the students attempted to begin their classes on September 23, however, white segregationist groups protested and blocked the school entrance. Under orders of Governor Orval Faubus (D-AR), the Arkansas National Guard did not intervene to ensure that the black students could attend

[36] Lowndes, *From the New Deal to the New Right*, 47–48.
[37] Galvin, *Presidential Party Building*, 65.
[38] For an overview of Little Rock and its aftermath, see Robert Frederick Burk, *The Eisenhower Administration and Black Civil Rights* (Knoxville: University of Tennessee Press, 1984), 174–203.

school. Thus, on September 24, Eisenhower federalized the Arkansas National Guard and ordered it to support the integration.[39]

"Little Rock" had a profoundly negative effect on the organizational efforts of the RNC's Southern division, in part because it undermined the one advantage the GOP had in the South: Eisenhower's personal popularity there. Potter believed that Little Rock had set the GOP's ability to organize in the South back immeasurably, particularly because the Dixiecrats (whom the Republicans had previously targeted) now backed away from the party: "I have been into every one of the Southern States and I can tell you that there has been severe damage done ... [Southern Democrats] feel that this is an invasion of the rights of the States."[40]

Potter's concern that Little Rock would set the GOP back "fifty years" in the South turned out to be an exaggeration.[41] In part, the Republican Party was assisted by a major leftward move within the Democratic Party around the same time. While Southern Democrats remained staunchly in favor of segregation, Northeastern liberals in the party – fearing that the Southern Democrats would push black voters back to the GOP – began using the Democratic National Committee (DNC) to promote the national party's pro-civil rights stance. With assistance from the Democratic Advisory Council (DAC) – a new party institution created to set national party policies – the DNC in early 1957 called on all Democratic politicians to support "legislation to end discrimination of all kinds."[42]

Thus, both parties in the late 1950s moved toward more active support of black civil rights, while also retaining some hope for success in the South. With Richard Nixon as the GOP's presidential candidate in 1960, and a prominent Southern Democrat (Lyndon Johnson) on the Democratic ticket running on a pro-civil rights platform, both parties sought to strike a balance between appealing to black voters in the North and white voters in the South.

CONSERVATIVES AND THE SOUTH, 1961–1965

The 1960 election was a mixed bag for the GOP.[43] In the House and Senate, Republicans won seats nationally but remained in the minority, while in the South the GOP remained largely ineffective. All seven GOP House incumbents in the South were reelected, but the party won no additional seats there. In the Senate, the Democrats' control of the region remained solid with no Republican

---

[39] See Newton, *Eisenhower*, 242–53; Thurber, *Republicans and Race*, 81–88.

[40] Cited in Galvin, *Presidential Party Building*, 65.   [41] Ibid.

[42] Cited in Boris Heersink, "Party Brands and the Democratic and Republican National Committees, 1952–1976," *Studies in American Political Development* 32 (April 2018): 89.

[43] Much of this, and the following section, is based on Heersink, "Party Brands and the Democratic and Republican National Committees," and Boris Heersink, "Party Leaders and Electoral Realignment: Democratic and Republican Southern Strategies, 1948–1968," *The Forum* 15 (2017): 631–53.

victories. Finally, in the presidential race, John F. Kennedy (JFK) defeated Richard Nixon in the popular vote by less than half a percentage point (while winning comfortably in the Electoral College). Still Nixon managed to win Florida, Tennessee, and Virginia, and came within three percentage points of winning South Carolina and Texas.[44]

Moderate and conservative Republicans interpreted the 1960 election in decidedly different ways.[45] Moderates focused on the party's poor performance in major cities (predominantly in the Northeast and Midwest) and argued that its failure to engage low-income black and ethnic voters there resulted in Nixon's defeat – since Kennedy significantly outpolled Nixon in those areas.[46] With Kennedy winning several states with major cities by razor-thin margins, the counterfactual of a Nixon electoral-vote victory based on a stronger Republican performance in major cities was certainly plausible.[47] As RNC chairman Thruston Morton told members of the national committee during its first post-election meeting, "when you lose in the cities by 1.8 [million votes] and you lose an election by 112,000 [votes] clearly we have a job in certain metropolitan areas."[48]

In contrast, conservatives pointed to the South as the only viable path for the GOP to rebuild itself. This argument was based on two lines of thinking. First, Nixon came within three percentage points of JFK in South Carolina and Texas, and had these electoral votes gone to the GOP, Kennedy's Electoral College tally would have dwindled to a mere 271 votes. With Senator Harry Byrd of Virginia winning 14 electoral votes in Mississippi and Alabama as an independent Dixiecrat, conservatives believed the Democratic presidential coalition in the South was weak enough that Nixon could have kept Kennedy from winning the presidency had he adopted a more principled Southern strategy. Second, conservatives argued that the Democrats' control of the

---

[44] There were widespread allegations that the Democratic machine in the Lower Rio Grande Valley committed voter fraud and provided the Kennedy–Johnson ticket with the votes necessary to win Lyndon B. Johnson's home state. Regardless, it appears that Johnson did aid Kennedy's performance in Texas – be it by inspiring local party bosses to engage in voter fraud or through his personal appeal. See Robert A. Caro, *The Years of Lyndon Johnson: The Passage of Power* (New York: Alfred A. Knopf, 2012), 150–55; Boris Heersink and Brenton D. Peterson, "Measuring the Vice-Presidential Home State Advantage with Synthetic Controls," *American Politics Research* 44 (July 2016): 734–63.

[45] See Heersink, "Party Brands and the Democratic and Republican National Committees."

[46] Mary C. Brennan, *Turning Right in the Sixties: The Conservative Capture of the GOP* (Chapel Hill: University of North Carolina Press, 1995), 40.

[47] Illinois went Democrat by a mere 0.2 percentage points under suspicions of major voting fraud in Chicago. JFK won Michigan by a little more than 2 points, and Pennsylvania by fewer than 3 points. In each of these states, Kennedy's performance in Chicago, Detroit, and Philadelphia provided him with the necessary margin of victory. Had Nixon won these three states, he would have won the presidency with 297 electoral votes.

[48] Paul Kesaris, Blair Hydrick, and Douglas D. Newman, *Papers of the Republican Party* (Frederick, MD: University Publications of America, 1987), Series B, Reel 1, Frame 88.

House and Senate was due to their ongoing control of the South. In the 1960 election, Democrats won a total of 262 seats in the House – 99 of which came from the former Confederacy. In the Senate, Democrats held 64 seats, of which 22 were from the South. To conservatives, these results suggested that the Republican Party would never be able to regain control of Congress without turning the South into a competitive two-party system.

Initially, the RNC followed the moderates' strategy and focused on improving the party's performance among black voters in major cities. Under Morton, the RNC in January 1961 created a committee, chaired by Ray C. Bliss, RNC member and chair of the Ohio Republican Party, and tasked it with investigating the GOP's performance in big cities. Bliss's committee took a full year to complete its work. Finally, in January 1962, the Bliss committee presented its findings at an RNC meeting in Oklahoma City, concluding that Nixon had lost the presidency because of the GOP's complete lack of organizational efforts in major cities.[49]

While the Bliss committee was working, the fortunes of the conservative wing of the party improved. In the spring of 1961, Morton announced his intention to resign as RNC chair. His replacement, William E. Miller, was a House member from New York and then chair of the Republican Congressional Campaign Committee (RCCC). Despite concerns that Miller was too conservative for the job, moderates failed to field a competitive alternative – and he was elected unanimously in June 1961.[50] Under Miller's chairmanship (1961–64), the RNC shifted its focus from appealing to minority voters in big cities to the South and Operation Dixie.

To be clear, the RNC did not drop the big-cities strategy entirely: under Miller, the RNC adopted a six-point plan to improve the GOP's performance among black voters in the 1962 midterms. The plan relied on incorporating black leaders into the GOP, increasing organizational activities in big cities with large black populations, and encouraging black women to volunteer for the party.[51] However, Miller brought a distinctly different perspective to the necessity of reaching out to black voters. While moderates believed an all-out attempt at convincing black voters to (re-)join the GOP was necessary, Miller stressed that a small improvement was more than enough: "all we need to do is get a fair percentage of the votes. If we get 25 or 30 percent of the vote in Philadelphia we can carry Pennsylvania."[52]

---

[49] See William L. Hershey and John C. Green, *Mr. Chairman: The Life and Times of Ray C. Bliss* (Akron: University of Akron Press, 2017), 125–28; Philip A. Klinkner, *The Losing Parties: Out-Party National Committees, 1956–1993* (New Haven, CT: Yale University Press, 1994), 45–47; "Stress Precincts, Republicans Told," *New York Times*, January 13, 1962.

[50] "G.O.P. is Expected to Name Miller," *New York Times*, May 27, 1961; "G.O.P. Elects Rep. Miller as Chairman," *Chicago Daily Tribune*, June 3, 1961.

[51] See "Stress Precincts, Republicans Told," *New York Times*.

[52] Kesaris et al., *Papers of the Republican Party*, Series B, Reel 3, Frame 8.

TABLE 6.3 *RNC campaign division expenditures, 1962*

Activity	Expenditures
Southern Division	$40,000
Special events	$20,000
Labor Division	$18,000
Minorities Division	$18,000
Business and professional groups	$15,000
Arts and Sciences Division	$15,000
Senior Citizens Division	$13,000
Nationalities Division	$10,000
Big City Panel	$ 4,000

Source: Philip A. Klinkner, *The Losing Parties: Out-Party National Committees, 1956–1993* (New Haven, CT: Yale University Press, 1994), 59

In contrast, Miller was far more concerned with building up a competitive party in the South. Philip Klinkner has argued that "Miller knew that the Republicans' only chance to capture the House was to win seats in the South and that a big city strategy offered no such hope."[53] The surprise victory of John Tower in the 1961 Senate race in Texas added to this Southern momentum: as the opponent of Lyndon B. Johnson (LBJ) in the 1960 Senate election, Tower received a respectable 41 percent of the vote. In 1961, with LBJ now the vice president and his former seat open, Tower won a run-off election with close to 51 percent of the vote, becoming one of the first, and biggest, examples of how Operation Dixie could deliver.

Thus, under Miller, the RNC refocused its attention on the committee's Southern Division and invested heavily in Operation Dixie. In April 1962, the Southern Division introduced a newsletter, *The Republican Southern Challenge*, a monthly publication that by 1964 had a distribution list of 39,000 people.[54] The RNC also began running ads in Southern newspapers and magazines, criticizing the Democratic Party and – in particular – the Kennedy brothers for their neglect of Southern needs.[55] The RNC spent considerable funds on its Southern Division in this period: during the 1962 midterm campaign, Southern expenditures outweighed what the committee spent on several other core budget items – including that of the big-city outreach program (see Table 6.3).

In the RNC's estimation, these investments in the South paid off in the 1962 midterms. Democrats won all Southern Senate seats up for reelection, but Republicans retained all of their seats in the House and defeated Democrats in four more races (one each in Florida, North Carolina, Tennessee, and

---

[53] Klinkner, *The Losing Parties*, 54.   [54] Ibid., 55.   [55] Ibid.

Texas).[56] In its assessment of the election results, the RNC's research division concluded that the "sharp increase in Republican strength in the South" had been the "most impressive" aspect of the 1962 election.[57] Specifically, the research division noted a 243.8 percent increase in the Republican vote in the South compared to the 1958 midterms. The big city program was far less effective: Republican candidates performed about as poorly in major cities in 1962 as they had in 1958. During the RNC's December 1962 meeting, the committee voted to continue Operation Dixie with the 1964 election in mind – approving a "massive 1964 GOP assault on Democratic strongholds in the segregationist South."[58]

While Miller defended the GOP's investments in the South – warning Northern Republicans not to adopt a "guilt complex"[59] over the party's new successes in the region – moderates remained uncomfortable with this Southern strategy. Several prominent Northeastern Republicans publicly stated their fear that, in Senator Jacob Javits's (R-NY) words, the GOP faced the likelihood of "[lapsing] into a permanent minority status as a the result of negativism."[60] Meanwhile, *Advance*, the magazine of the Young Republican party organization, criticized the RNC for stressing the party's successes in the South over the continued support of the GOP's black voters in big cities, and charged the party with "betraying [its] heritage"[61] to win in the South.

Moving into the 1964 campaign, the RNC and conservatives hoped the Democratic Party's embrace of civil rights and Kennedy's increasing unpopularity in the South would expedite the GOP's breakthrough there. In November 1963, Southern Republicans gathered in Charleston, South Carolina, for a Southern Regional Leadership Conference to prepare for the 1964 election. During the meeting, local leaders called for both the nomination of Barry Goldwater as the party's presidential candidate and further investments by the RNC in Southern party building, so as to create an "unprecedented drive to grab all Dixie away from the Democrats."[62]

JFK's assassination a few weeks later radically altered the political context. Most importantly, Texan native Lyndon Johnson – JFK's vice president – was now the likely Democratic candidate. By January 1964, reporters Rowland Evans and Robert Novak wrote in their column that "realistic Republican

[56] Martis, *The Historical Atlas of Political Parties in the United States Congress*, 214–17. A new apportionment helped create the context for these additional GOP seat pick-ups.

[57] *Congressional Quarterly Almanac*, 88th Congress, 1st Session, 1963, Vol. XIX (Congressional Quarterly Service, Washington DC, 1963), 1168.

[58] "GOP Leaders Approve All-Out Drive in South," *Los Angeles Times*, December 8, 1962.

[59] Kesaris et al., *Papers of the Republican Party*, Series B, Reel 2, Frame 577.

[60] "Javits Declares G.O.P. Right Wing is Peril to Party," *New York Times*, February 13, 1962.

[61] "G.O.P. is Attacked for Its Aid to Segregationists in the South," *New York Times*, November 26, 1962.

[62] "GOP is Turning to South in '64," *The Times-Picayune*, November 10, 1963. See also "Chairman Asks Effort for GOP," *The Times-Picayune*, November 9, 1963.

TABLE 6.4 *1964 Republican National Convention votes, by region*

Region	% of total delegates	% yea on pro-civil rights amendment	% support for Goldwater on 1st ballot
Northeast	22.9	90.0	14.7
Midwest	27.8	17.6	77.2
West	19.6	10.5	84.8
South	29.1	10.5	90.3

Source: *Congressional Quarterly's Guide to U.S. Elections* (Washington, DC: Congressional Quarterly Ltd., 1994)
Note: Regional classification is based on the standard US census regional division. Excluded from this assessment are Puerto Rico and the Virgin Islands, which had – respectively – five and three delegates each, all of whom voted in favor of the civil rights amendment and opposed Goldwater.

politicians" had now abandoned hope for 1964 to be the GOP breakthrough year in the South.[63] Yet the South would go on to dominate the 1964 presidential election within the Republican Party. First, Southern convention delegates supported Goldwater's presidential campaign by a significant margin. During the primaries, Goldwater participated in twelve state contests, winning six, including Texas and Florida – the only Southern states to hold primaries. More importantly, the pro-Goldwater campaign had specifically targeted Southern state organizations to ensure that nearly all of the 280 Southern convention delegates would support him for president.[64] The strategy paid off, with over 90 percent of Southern delegates at the Republican National Convention voting for Goldwater on the first presidential nomination ballot (see Table 6.4).

Second, Goldwater's opposition to the 1964 Civil Rights Act framed his candidacy in a way that appealed to Southern segregationists. Goldwater's victory in the California primary on June 2 provided him with a majority of delegates. Afterward, moderate Republicans expressed hope that Goldwater would be a team player. On June 10, however, the presumptive GOP nominee became one of only six Republicans in the Senate to vote against the Civil Rights Act. To be sure, Goldwater's vote was based at least in part on his belief in states' rights rather than direct support for segregation. Nonetheless, Goldwater's vote and his subsequent actions to ensure the 1964 Republican platform would include no support for the Civil Rights Act was a blow to moderate Republicans.[65] An attempt by moderates to pass a pro-Civil Rights Act amendment to the platform failed, in part due to strong opposition from the South.

---

[63] "GOP Break in South Seen Long Way Off," *Los Angeles Times*, January 1, 1964.
[64] "Southern GOP for Goldwater," *The Times-Picayune*, November 8, 1963.
[65] During a speech to the Republican convention's Platform Committee, Goldwater opposed a plank that would proclaim the new civil rights law as constitutional and warned that no one "should violate the rights of some in order to further the rights of others." See "South's GOP Chiefs Reassured on Rights," *Washington Post*, July 11, 1964.

Combined, these actions sent a clear signal that the Republican Party did not embrace the new civil-rights legislation – even though GOP support had been both strong and pivotal in the House and Senate. As a result, moderate Republicans received little of the credit they could (and should) have received for their pro-civil rights votes.[66]

The defection of Senator Strom Thurmond (SC) from the Democratic Party to the Republican Party in September 1964 – and Goldwater's support for his party switch – further framed the Goldwater campaign as appealing to Southern segregationists. Thurmond had been at odds with the Democratic Party since 1948, when, as governor of South Carolina, he ran as a third-party (Dixiecrat) candidate to protest the pro-civil rights plank in that year's Democratic platform. In subsequent election years, Thurmond had stayed out of presidential politics, though he frequently attacked his party for including pro-civil rights positions in its platform. With the passage of the Civil Rights Act, Thurmond switched his allegiance and argued that "the Democratic party has abandoned the people" and "repudiated the Constitution of the United States."[67] Thurmond linked his party switch directly to Goldwater's presidential campaign:

Fortunately, for those of us who cherish the traditional freedom entrusted to us by our forefathers, there is another choice this year. Altho [sic] the party of our fathers is dead, the principles of our forefathers live now in the cause of a Presidential nominee. The man who has gained the Republican nomination for President against all the odds and opinion polls, and who now has control of the Republican party, is one who believes in and abides by our Constitution.[68]

Conservatives welcomed Thurmond into the GOP with open arms. Goldwater, campaigning in Tennessee as Thurmond's switch became public, called Thurmond "one of the great Americans of this country"[69] and stated that he did not "blame the Democrats for leaving the party that no longer represents their views."[70] Dean Burch, Goldwater's handpicked RNC chairman who had been a member of his senatorial staff since 1955, described Thurmond as "a man of rare honesty, courage, and integrity."[71] Thurmond campaigned for, and with, Goldwater throughout the South in advance of the election. During their appearances together, neither Thurmond nor Goldwater specifically addressed civil rights –

---

[66] Geoffrey Kabaservice, *Rule and Ruin: The Downfall of Moderation and the Destruction of the Republican Party, from Eisenhower to the Tea Party* (Oxford: Oxford University Press, 2012), 101.

[67] "Democratic Party Forsakes the People, Thurmond Says," *Chicago Tribune*, September 17, 1964. See also: "Sen. Thurmond to Bolt Party, Support Barry," *Chicago Tribune*, September 16, 1964

[68] "Democratic Party Forsakes the People," *Chicago Tribune*.

[69] "Goldwater Woos Dixie Democrats," *Washington Post*, September 17, 1964.

[70] "One of South's Worst Racists Backs Barry, Quits the Democrats," *Chicago Daily Defender*, September 17, 1964.

[71] "Thurmond Given Praise and Scorn," *New York Times*, September 17, 1964.

but, as Walter Lippmann noted "there was no need for [Goldwater] to mention civil rights or to take notice of the existence of a large Negro population when he could consort publicly with Sen. Strom Thurmond."[72] Thus, Lippmann argued, the Goldwater campaign inaugurated "the so-called southern strategy in order to lay the foundations for a radically new Republican Party."[73]

This radically new party did not do particularly well in its first outing. Johnson beat Goldwater in an unprecedented landslide, receiving slightly more than 61 percent of the popular vote. Goldwater also proved to be a drag on the party in congressional races, as the Republicans lost 36 seats in the House and 2 in the Senate. In the South, however, the GOP performed much better. While Goldwater succeeded in winning only six states nationally, five were Southern states (Alabama, Georgia, Louisiana, Mississippi, and South Carolina) in addition to his home state of Arizona. Additionally, Goldwater came within four points of winning Florida and Virginia. In the House, Republicans gained a net of five seats in the South (most notably in Alabama, where Republicans won 5 out of 8 seats).[74] But while the RNC and Goldwater succeeded in continuing to dismantle the Solid South, they did so at the expense of the GOP's success nearly everywhere else in the nation.

NIXON'S SOUTHERN STRATEGY, 1965–1968

In the wake of Goldwater's epic defeat, Republican moderates called for the resignation of Burch as RNC chairman. Goldwater attempted to keep Burch on – stating that he would consider the dismissal of his conservative national committee chairman as "a repudiation of a great segment of our party and a repudiation of me."[75] Moderates countered that Goldwater's strategy of appealing to Southern whites by tacitly supporting segregation (albeit via genuine support for states' rights) had hurt the party elsewhere. Javits warned that the GOP faced "not only a major reconstruction job throughout the nation; it also faces the difficult task of exorcising the image which the 'Southern strategy' created – that of an impending transformation to a 'lily white' party."[76] After a series of meetings in January 1965, Burch and Goldwater realized that the vote at the upcoming RNC meeting to retain Burch as chair was likely to result in defeat. As a result, Burch announced his resignation and was succeeded by Ray Bliss.[77]

---

[72] "Goldwater Lays Foundation for a Radically New Republican Party," *Los Angeles Times*, September 23, 1964.
[73] Ibid.
[74] The GOP also picked up 1 seat in Mississippi and one in Georgia. But the Republicans lost the 2 seats they controlled in Texas in the previous Congress. Martis, *The Historical Atlas of Political Parties in the United States Congress*, 216–19.
[75] "Goldwater Appeals to GOP to Retain Burch," *Los Angeles Times*, December 30, 1964.
[76] "The Road Back for the G.O.P.," *New York Times*, November 14, 1964.
[77] Hershey and Green, *Mr. Chairman*, 155–58.

As RNC chair, Bliss, who had chaired the committee that investigated the Republican defeat in major cities in the 1960 election, moved the party away from the Southern strategy that had been the priority under Miller and Burch. Instead, the RNC now began to invest again in outreach efforts in major cities.[78] In February 1966, the RNC announced that it had created a new advisory committee of black Republican leaders to help the party strengthen support among black voters. Bliss saw some immediate gains from this new strategy. As William Hershey and John Green note: "[In 1966], the Republicans won a number of big city mayoral races, including John Ballards's reelection in Akron. The GOP candidate narrowly lost in Philadelphia, but cut the Democratic margin of victory from 65,000 four years earlier to 10,000."[79] In addition, Republican Edward Brooke, a black man, was elected to the US Senate from Massachusetts.

Bliss felt he now had momentum and upped the ante. In 1967, the RNC presented a new "blueprint" to attract black voters – with the goal of winning 30 percent of the black vote during the 1968 presidential election.[80] To be sure, the 1966 election *also* produced considerable success in the South. In Arkansas and Florida, Republican candidates Winthrop Rockefeller and Claude R. Kirk, Jr. won gubernatorial elections, and in Tennessee, Howard Baker won a Senate seat. Thurmond was also reelected in South Carolina. Additionally, Republicans expanded their number of Southern House seats to 24 (up from 16 in 1964). Yet the South – at least temporarily – was no longer the RNC's priority.

While the RNC moved its strategy away from the South, Richard Nixon began planning his own presidential comeback in the wake of Goldwater's defeat. Despite his failure to win the 1960 presidential election, and his embarrassing defeat in the 1962 California gubernatorial election, Nixon remained one of the best-known Republicans in the country. But he also lacked a clear constituency within the party to lift him to a second presidential nomination. Nixon understood both the important role that conservatives would play in selecting the next presidential nominee and the limitations of conservatism in general elections. Thus, Nixon – in Joseph Lowndes's assessment – attempted "to negotiate the distance between a party now committed to conservatism and a larger public that was wary of the Right."[81] In doing so, Nixon devised a Southern strategy that allowed the GOP to break through in the South while not alienating voters elsewhere.

Nixon reintroduced himself to active politics in the 1966 midterms, campaigning heavily for Republican candidates in the South.[82] While the RNC and the moderate wing of the party believed the 1964 election had shown that a

[78] Ibid., 209–15.   [79] Ibid., 209.

[80] "GOP Designs Blueprintto Snag Negro Vote," *Chicago Defender*, February 4, 1967.

[81] Lowndes, *From the New Deal to the New Right*, 108.

[82] Kabaservice, *Rule and Ruin*, 175; John A. Farrell, *Richard Nixon: A Life* (New York: Doubleday, 2017), 318–19.

purely Southern strategy amounted to electoral suicide, Goldwater's success in the South and the RNC's metric of providing states with convention delegates based in part on electoral performance meant that Southern states would be allocated more delegates to the 1968 convention than in previous years. And while Nixon used the 1966 campaign to ingratiate himself with Republicans in the South and praised segregationists like Strom Thurmond, he also explicitly opposed any pro-segregation plank in the national Republican platform.[83] The 1966 midterm elections not only represented an important improvement for the GOP, a mere two years after the devastating Goldwater defeat, but also made Nixon the front-runner for the 1968 nomination. Still, Southern Republicans remained unsure whether to support Nixon – whose conservative credentials were in doubt given his links to the Eisenhower wing of the party – or Ronald Reagan, who had won the California gubernatorial election in 1966 and, while inexperienced, was viewed as a true conservative. During a set of meetings between Southern party leaders and presidential hopefuls prior to the 1968 convention, which were organized by Thurmond aide Harry Dent, Nixon carefully built on his 1966 balancing act between support for Southern positions and rejection of segregation itself. Nixon promised the Southern Republicans that, while he did not oppose Brown, he would not insist on swift implementation of the ruling. Additionally, as Lowndes notes, Nixon

told them that he would appoint only strict constructionists to the bench, and that he opposed busing. He held that no federal funds would be given to school districts that practiced open segregation, but that such funds would not be withheld from schools for tardiness in implementing desegregation. He also assured leaders that he would have southerners in key positions in his administration and that the federal patronage would flow southward.[84]

The Southerners were largely convinced. While a considerable number of Southern delegates still supported Reagan on the first ballot at the convention, Nixon's strongest regional support would come from the South (see Table 6.5).

In the general election, Nixon's campaign continued to walk a fine line between trying to win Southern states and not repelling voters in other regions. In doing so, it received a crucial assist from disenchanted white voters in other parts of the country. While whites outside the South may not have supported segregation, many of them saw blacks as a threat to their jobs or believed they received undeserved governmental support.[85] Combined with significant racial unrest in major cities – including serious riots in Washington, DC, Baltimore, Chicago, and Kansas City after the assassination of Martin Luther King in April 1968 – Nixon's rejection of hardcore segregation but support for slowing down civil-rights reform, along with a general "law-and-order" message,

[83] Lowndes, *From the New Deal to the New Right*, 109.   [84] Ibid., 111–12.
[85] Thurber, *Republicans and Race*, 257.

TABLE 6.5 *1968 Republican National Convention votes, by region*

Region	% of total delegates	% support for Nixon
Northeast	22.2	10.4
Midwest	26.6	26.8
West	19.8	18.1
South	31.5	44.6

Source: *Congressional Quarterly's Guide to U.S. Elections* (Washington, DC: Congressional Quarterly Ltd., 1994)
Note: Regional classification is based on the standard US census regional division. Excluded from this assessment are Puerto Rico and the Virgin Islands. Puerto Rico had five delegates of which none voted for Nixon on the first ballot. The Virgin Islands had three delegates of which two voted for Nixon. The vote represented here are the "pre-switch" totals – that is, Nixon's performance before he was nominated (nearly) unanimously.

resonated. Former Alabama governor George Wallace's run as the pro-segregation, American Independent Party candidate meant that neither Nixon nor Democratic presidential candidate Hubert Humphrey were likely to be competitive in the Deep South. Thus, Nixon focused on major cities in the peripheral South where whites opposed segregation but preferred desegregation to be implemented slowly. And his focus on law and order – and protection against crime and disorder – connected to a general lack of safety felt by white voters outside of the South.[86]

Nixon would win a narrow popular-vote plurality over Humphrey – with the two separated by only slightly more than a half million votes, or 0.7 percentage points.[87] Nixon's victory in the Electoral College, however, was considerably more impressive: 301 electoral votes to Humphrey's 191 and Wallace's 46. Nixon's Southern Strategy did not result in an overwhelming breakthrough in the region; while Nixon won Florida, North Carolina, South Carolina, Tennessee, and Virginia, Wallace emerged victorious in Alabama, Arkansas, Georgia, Louisiana, and Mississippi.[88] Crucially, however, their combined performance meant that Humphrey succeeded in winning only one Southern state: Texas. In Congress, Republicans won 26 House seats in the South, along with a Senate seat in Florida. Thus, Nixon's Southern Strategy provided Republicans with a blueprint for a way to appeal to voters *inside* the South while not being punished for doing so by voters *outside* the region.

[86] Ibid., 277.
[87] Nixon would win 43.4 percent of the popular vote, compared to 42.7 percent for Humphrey and 13.5 percent for Wallace.
[88] Nixon's "Southern Strategy" is discussed at length in Phillips, *The Emerging Republican Majority*.

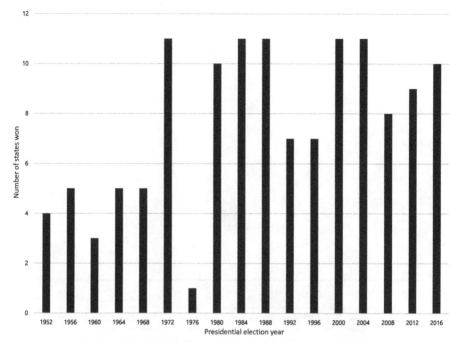

FIGURE 6.3 Number of Southern states won by Republican presidential candidates,
1952–2016
Source: *Congressional Quarterly's Guide to U.S. Elections*, 7th edn. (Washington, DC:
Congressional Quarterly, 2016)

THE REPUBLICAN SOUTH AFTER 1968

Nixon's Southern Strategy did not immediately turn the South into a Republican stronghold. Additionally, the GOP's electoral success in the South continued to differ quite dramatically across different levels of government. After
1968, the most obvious area of Republican Southern success was in presidential
elections. As illustrated in Figure 6.3, since 1972 – with the exception of 1976 –
the GOP nominee for president has carried a majority of Southern states in
every election. Indeed, in five elections (1972, 1984, 1988, 2000, and 2004) the
Republican candidate (Nixon, Reagan, Bush I, and Bush II twice) won every
single Southern state. Moreover, every Republican candidate since 1972 who
has won the presidency won at least ten Southern states.

Below the presidential level, Republican dominance in the South took longer
to develop. Figure 6.4 illustrates the proportion of Southern seats controlled by
the GOP in the US Congress from 1952 through 2016. In both the House and
Senate, the GOP started from single-digit percentages in the early 1960s and
gradually increased its vote share for the next fifteen years. Reagan's election in

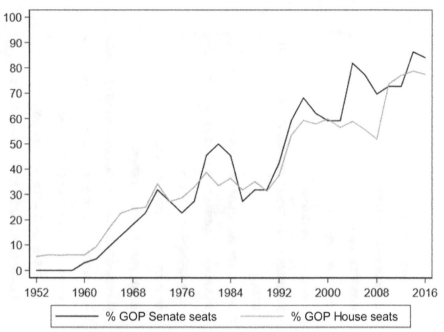

FIGURE 6.4 Percentage of US House and Senate seats in the South held by Republicans,
1952–2016
Source: *Congressional Quarterly's Guide to U.S. Elections*, 7th edn. (Washington, DC:
Congressional Quarterly, 2016)

1980 saw a spike in the Senate for three years, as the Republicans took majority
control of the institution. But by the late 1980s, the GOP share of Southern
seats hovered in the low 30s. A spike occurred in the 1992 elections, especially
in the Senate, before the Republicans became the majority party in the South
starting with the 1994 "Contract with America" election. Thus, as the GOP
took control of Congress, the South became its electoral bedrock. Since 1994,
the Republican Party has claimed a majority of Southern seats in every Congress – in both the House and the Senate. And in recent elections (2014 and
2016), the GOP yield has exceeded 75 percent in both chambers.

In terms of governorships in the South, Republican success roughly mirrored
the party's performance in US congressional elections. As Figure 6.5 illustrates,
the GOP was shut out entirely through the mid-1960s, but Winthrop Rockefeller (Arkansas) and Claude Kirk, Jr. (Florida) each broke through and were
elected in 1966. GOP governorships in the South hovered in the two to three
range until 1980, when five Republicans were elected. This was the high point
(achieved again in 1986 and 1988), until 1994, when six Republican governors
were elected – giving the GOP a majority of Southern governorships. And since
1994, the Republican Party has controlled at least six governorships, with their
high being ten in 2012 and 2014.

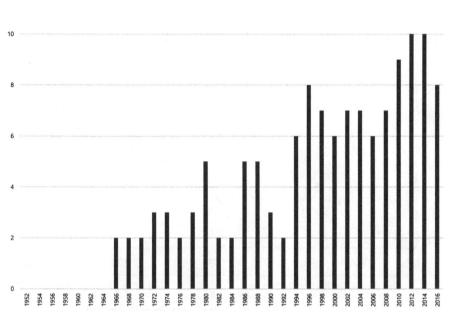

FIGURE 6.5 Number of Southern governorships held by Republicans, 1952–2016
Source: *Congressional Quarterly's Guide to U.S. Elections*, 7th edn. (Washington, DC: Congressional Quarterly, 2016)

The Republican Party's near-century of dominance in presidential elections and quarter-century of dominance in congressional and gubernatorial elections took time to filter down to the state legislative level. As Figure 6.6 illustrates, the GOP's share of seats in Southern state legislatures was quite weak through the 1980s. But Republican successes in congressional elections, starting in 1994, created coattails in state legislative elections. By the late 1990s, more than 40 percent of seats in Southern state legislatures were GOP-controlled. These successes continued to creep up through the George W. Bush years, until a majority breakthrough occurred in 2010 – when Democrats were "shellacked" across the board in President Obama's first midterm election. Since 2010, Republican state legislative gains have continued to increase; the 2016 elections represent the zenith, with the GOP controlling roughly two-thirds of both state House and Senate seats in the South. Thus, by the 2010s, Republican redemption of the South had been fully completed.

CONCLUSION

The 1932–1968 period represents a crucial era of change between the Republican Party and the American South. With the New Deal realignment, the GOP

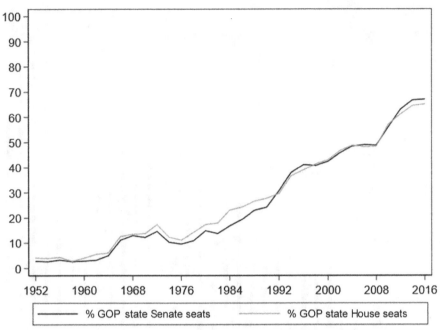

FIGURE 6.6 Percentage of state House and Senate seats in the South held by Republicans, 1952–2016
Source: Carl Klamer, "State Partisan Balance Data, 1937-2011," Harvard Dataverse, https://hdl .handle.net/1902.1/20403 (2013). Data updated by authors.

slowly but surely came to the realization that some form of electoral competition in the South could no longer be avoided for the party to have a chance at winning presidential elections and congressional majorities consistently. After FDR's death, and with liberals and conservatives in the Democratic Party divided on civil rights, Republicans – for the first time – had both the opportunity and the need to advance in the South.

In previous eras, the Republicans were incapable of breaking the Democratic hold on the Southern white vote (1880–1896, 1932–1948) and frequently were so strong electorally *outside* of the South (1896–1928) that the party lacked a real incentive to try to change this status quo. With Dixiecrat politicians and white Southern voters increasingly alienated from the national Democratic Party, Republican leaders saw an opening to rebuild a Southern wing of the party. Meanwhile, with the stable presidential and congressional majorities of the System of 1896 far behind it, the GOP also had a clear need to improve its performance in the South.

But how to take advantage of this opening in the South while simultaneously not alienating traditional Republican voters elsewhere proved to be a difficult puzzle to solve. In the wake of the Dixiecrat third-party challenge in 1948 and

Eisenhower's remarkable success in 1952 and 1956, the RNC attempted to connect with Southerners on the basis of a shared preference for states' rights. Conservative Republicans, who blamed the party's 1960 presidential defeat largely on its failure to appeal to Southern whites, went all in on this Southern strategy between 1961 and 1964 – opposing civil rights reform on the basis of strict constitutionalism, while coming dangerously close to endorsing the concept of segregation itself.

While the 1964 election showed that catering to Dixiecrats could open the South up to the Republican Party, Goldwater's dismal performance everywhere else temporarily scared the RNC and other Republican leaders from continuing with their "Operation Dixie" strategy. Instead, the national party switched gears and began investing in outreach to black voters in major cities. A breakthrough in the inherent conflict between (a) the party's failure to succeed in the South and (b) the price it paid outside of the South for *trying* was forged by Richard Nixon, in his efforts to win the 1968 presidential nomination. In assessing both the internal dynamics within the GOP as well as the national effects of previous Republican southern strategies, Nixon identified a winning strategy. By rejecting segregation, Nixon reassured voters outside of the South that he was not giving in to the worst elements in the Dixiecrat movement. Yet Nixon's support for the less extreme policies that Southern conservatives were demanding – a slowdown in the implementation of civil rights reforms – was tied to the broader sense of insecurity whites felt across the country with regard to job safety and crime.

In sum, Nixon's Southern Strategy not only produced electoral success inside and outside of the South in the 1968 election but also created a game plan for Republicans in the decades that followed. By sidestepping both the confrontational language of segregation and the broader question of racial conflict, and focusing instead on issues such as crime, job insecurity, and general unease among whites, the GOP found a way of connecting simultaneously with voters in the South and elsewhere.

PHOTOS

Perry W. Howard (left), the boss of the Republican party in Mississippi, pictured with Roscoe Conkling Simmons, a reporter and civil rights activist from Illinois, points at a portrait of President Herbert Hoover, at the 1932 Republican National Convention. At this convention, Hoover tried to unseat Howard and his Black-and-Tan delegates and replace them with Lily-Whites. Hoover failed and Howard would remain boss of the Mississippi GOP until 1960.
Source: Photo by NY Daily News Archive via Getty Images.

The first black Senator and Representatives in the 41st and 42nd Congresses. Top, standing left to right: Rep. Robert C. De Large (R-SC), Rep. Jefferson H. Long (R-GA). Seated, left to right: Sen. H.R. Revels (R-MS), Rep. Benjamin S. Turner (R-AL), Rep. Josiah T. Walls (R-FL), Rep. Joseph H. Rainy (R-SC), and Rep. R. Brown Elliot (R-SC).
Source: Lithograph by Currier and Ives, 1872, via Getty Images.

A political cartoon shows voter intimidation in the 1876 election. Two white men point their guns at a black voter with the description below stating: "Of course he wants to vote the Democratic ticket! Democratic 'Reformer': You're as free as the air, ain't you? Say you are, or I'll blow your black head off!"
Source: Stock Montage / Getty Images.

DELEGATES FROM SOUTH CAROLINA AND FLORIDA.
" Should auld acquaintance be forgot?"

African American Delegates
Illustration of black delegates from South Carolina and Florida at the 1880 Republican
National Convention in Chicago.
Source: American Stock Archive / Archive Photos / Getty Images.

A " READJUSTOR " CAJOLING A NEGRO VOTER.

A vintage engraving showing a Readjuster "cajoling" a black voter in Richmond, Virginia in 1882.
Source: Bettmann via Getty Images.

MEAN, BUT FUTILE.
President Harrison's Spite can not Disturb the Growing Harmony between the Whites and Negros of the South.

A cartoon from the satirical magazine *Judge* shows a black and white man walking hand in hand while President Benjamin Harrison tries to separate them. During the Harrison administration, Republican Party leaders tried – but failed – to pass legislation to ensure voting rights for black Southerners.
Source: Bettmann via Getty Images.

President William McKinley with his campaign manager Mark Hanna and family members in Thomasville, Georgia in 1899. McKinley and Hanna's "Southern strategy" of courting Southern delegates at the Republican National Convention in 1896 would be copied by other Republican presidential hopefuls in the decades that followed.
Source: Library of Congress / Corbis / VCG via Getty Images.

Rep. George Henry White (R-NC) was one of the leading black politicians in North Carolina. White declined to run for reelection in 1900 as the Democratic Party in North Carolina unleashed a wave of terror attacks against black voters.
Source: Photo by Corbis via Getty Images.

President Theodore Roosevelt speaking with a group of black children during a visit to Summerville, South Carolina in May 1902.
Source: Photo by George Rinhart / Corbis via Getty Images.

President Calvin Coolidge and his personal secretary C. Bascom Slemp at a World Series baseball game in Washington DC. Slemp was the head of a Lily-White Republican organization in Virginia and a long-time member of Congress.
Source: Photo by FPG / Getty Images.

Republican presidential candidate Herbert Hoover appearing in Tennessee during a stop in the 1928 campaign.
Source: Bettmann via Getty Images.

Joseph W. Tolbert – known as "Tieless Joe" – was the boss of the Republican Party in South Carolina, one of the longest surviving Black-and-Tan organizations in the South. Tolbert is pictured speaking to delegates from South Carolina at the 1944 Republican National Convention.
Source: Photo by Jack Wilkes / The LIFE Images Collection / Getty Images.

Robert R. Church Jr., the Republican Party boss in west Tennessee in the first half of the 20th century. Church's influence in Tennessee politics was based in part on his longstanding cooperation with Democratic party leaders. Church is pictured attending a convention of black Republicans in 1944.
Source: Photo by Gordon Coster / The LIFE Picture Collection / Getty Images.

A Georgia delegate receives a badge after being seated by the Credentials Committee at
the 1948 Republican National Convention.
Source: Photo by Ralph Morse / The LIFE Picture Collection / Getty Images.

Members of the Mississippi Republican state party meet in 1952 to elect delegates for the Republican National Convention that year.
Source: Photo by John Dominis / The LIFE Picture Collection / Getty Images.

Republican presidential nominee Dwight D. Eisenhower appears in Denison, Texas during the 1952 campaign.
Source: Photo by Hank Walker / The LIFE Picture Collection / Getty Images.

Senator Strom Thurmond – the Dixiecrat presidential candidate in 1948 – in September 1964 announced that he had joined the Republican Party. Thurmond campaigned with GOP presidential nominee Barry Goldwater in the South during the campaign.
Source: Bettmann via Getty Images.

PART II

SOUTHERN REPUBLICAN PARTY POLITICS
AT THE STATE LEVEL

As we have shown in Part I, the South was relevant to the GOP between 1865 and 1968, even though the party was not competitive in the former Confederacy for most of this period. In this part, we focus on state-level party politics by presenting case studies of each Southern state and discussing the history of the Republican Party there and the battles over organizational control that occurred.

We show that in all states there was frequent – and in some cases continuous – competition over control of the state party organization. In the 1870s, this competition largely concerned the question of which candidates were to be on the ballot representing the party. After the Democratic Party returned to power throughout the South, however, these intra-GOP conflicts still occurred, but party nominations become increasingly irrelevant. Indeed, in many states the Republican Party often failed to run candidates in statewide races. Instead, control of the state party remained important because it was the recognized institution through which national leaders delivered patronage – as well as the institution most likely to have its delegation seated at the national convention and its leaders represented in the Republican National Committee (RNC). Thus, local party leaders possessed something – convention support – that national leaders cared about, and they could exchange it for patronage and other forms of payments. As a result, rival factions in these organizational conflicts sought to claim that *they* represented the "true" state party – so that they could get their delegation seated at the national convention, support their given national patron, and receive a stream of resources in return.

Factions battling over organizational control of a state party often won or lost at the national convention due to the strength of presidential candidates whose supporters dominated the RNC or the relevant convention committees that decided seating disputes. In practice, this meant that if a delegation bet on the wrong horse – that is, a candidate who did not end up controlling the convention – they might not get seated. This was especially true if a competing delegation from that same state supported the dominant candidate – in which case *they* would likely be seated instead. Sometimes GOP presidents – most notably Theodore Roosevelt, Warren G. Harding, Calvin Coolidge, and Herbert Hoover – tried to influence the outcome of these conflicts during their time in office, though with mixed success.

During Reconstruction, the different factions that competed for control of the state party organizations were mostly biracial. In these clashes, the different groups often organized around different local leaders – typically (former) elected officials or office-holders in the state – but all of these coalitions tended to have both black and white members. By the late nineteenth century, these conflicts for party control became centered on race itself, with Black-and-Tan groups defending their position within the party against Lily-Whites who sought to replace them. These Lily-White groups' claim as to why they – rather than the existing biracial coalitions – ought to control the state party largely relied on a combination of two arguments: (1) that the existing party organizations were corrupt, and (2) that in a Jim Crow world – in which black voters were almost entirely disenfranchised, and in which racism was the norm – the GOP could never compete in elections as long as it was seen as the "black party." To be sure, these arguments were somewhat self-serving as most Lily-White groups, once in control, were just as corrupt and showed as little interest in electoral competition as their predecessors. Still, eventually, Lily-Whiteism succeeded in all Southern states. However, the timing and context of these victories differed. That is, some party organizations "flipped" to Lily-White control earlier than others. And the extent to which Lily-Whites excluded blacks from participation in the party varied as well.

In the chapters that follow, we detail the history of Republican Party organizations in each ex-Confederate state. In presenting these cases, we rely on primary and secondary historical sources as well as newspaper accounts. Additionally, we present figures for each state based on the data we collected measuring the size of black convention representation between 1868 and 1952, as well as data covering the GOP's strength at the federal and state levels between 1868 and 2012.[1] While the history of each state has its own unique context, this approach allows us to identify three broad categories of states. First, in Chapter 7, we discuss those states – Virginia, Texas, North Carolina,

---

[1] The party strength figures include two composite measures of the party's electoral performance within the state. The federal strength metric represents the average of the percentage of the presidential vote, the percentage of the combined House vote, and the percentage of the most recent Senate vote in a state that the Republican Party received. Note that for years in which senators were not elected by voters we exclude the senate vote and rely on an average of just the first two variables. Meanwhile, the state strength metric represents the average of the percentage of the gubernatorial vote, the percentage of state Assembly seats, and the percentage of state Senate seats the GOP received in a state.

and Alabama – in which the Lily-White takeover resulted in the eventual exclusion of (nearly) all blacks from intra-party political participation. In Chapter 8, we focus on those states – Arkansas, Louisiana, Florida, and Tennessee – in which the Lily-White takeover resulted in a clear reduction of black influence, but not complete exclusion. That is, in this "softer" version of Lily-Whiteism, the takeover of the state party resulted in whites controlling patronage appointments but allowing a small but consistent percentage of blacks to remain delegates to state and national conventions. Finally, in Chapter 9, we examine three states where the Black-and-Tans managed to hold on to control of the state party much longer than in the rest of the South. While the Lily-Whites did eventually take over in these states – in South Carolina (around 1940), Georgia (1950s), and Mississippi (1960) – the Black-and-Tan organizations survived longer and had considerably more black representation at national conventions than elsewhere.

7

Virginia, Texas, North Carolina, and Alabama

In four former Confederate states, the Lily-White movement not only succeeded in taking control of the local Republican party organization but subsequently used this control to exclude blacks from participating in the party either entirely (North Carolina and Alabama) or nearly so (Virginia and Texas). These white Republicans went the exclusion route despite many other Lily-White-controlled states allowing black Republicans to continue participating in the party to some extent. Why did white Republicans in these four states choose to implement Lily-Whiteism in such a "strong" way?

As the case studies presented here show, there is no consistent answer to this question. The path toward Lily-White control, and the subsequent nature of white rule in the state GOP, was dependent (at least in part) on the unique historical context in each state. For example, in Virginia, black Republicans were excluded from the party much earlier than in most other states. Local party leaders consistently kept black representation at national conventions close to zero and even criticized the local Democratic Party for becoming the "black party" during the New Deal era. In Texas, the Lily-White movement was a response to a black man – Norris Wright Cuney – controlling the state party organization in the 1880s and 1890s. After the end of Cuney's rule, Lily-Whites took control of the party and expelled nearly all blacks from participation in state and national conventions. In North Carolina, the Lily-White takeover followed the dramatic events of the 1898 and 1900 elections, in which extreme violence against (black) Republicans instigated the passing of new voter laws banning black participation. In response, white GOP leaders explicitly banned blacks from the party organization entirely in 1902. Finally, in Alabama, Lily-White control came in 1912 and resulted in a slow but consistent reduction of black delegates at the national convention until no blacks were left in the state's national convention delegation from 1924 onwards.

TABLE 7.1 *Descriptive Republican Party success in Virginia, 1865–1968*

	1865–1877	1878–1896	1897–1932	1933–1968
Presidential candidate won the state?	✓		✓	✓
Senatorial candidate elected?	✓	†		
Gubernatorial candidate elected?	✓	†		
At least one House candidate elected?	✓	✓	✓	✓

† A Republican–Readjuster alliance elected a governor in 1881 (William E. Cameron) and two US senators in 1879 (William Mahone) and 1881 (Harrison H. Riddleburger), respectively.

VIRGINIA: READJUSTERS AND EARLY LILY-WHITEISM

The development of the Republican Party in Virginia was unlike any other ex-Confederate state, in that the GOP experienced no period of electoral success immediately after the state's return to the Union. Even Tennessee, which had seen the Democrats return to power by the late 1860s, still enjoyed a brief period of Republican control during Reconstruction. On the other hand, the GOP would perform better in Virginia than in most other Southern states in terms of (occasional) presidential victories and seats in the House of Representatives in the early twentieth century and beyond (see Table 7.1 and Figure 7.1). Additionally, the Lily-White takeover of the Republican Party in Virginia resulted in the near complete exclusion of blacks from the party after 1912 (see Figure 7.2).

* * * * *

The lack of GOP success in Virginia during Reconstruction was the result of politics during and after the state's constitutional convention. Like those in other ex-Confederate states, the constitutional convention in Virginia, held in accordance with the first federal Reconstruction Act, produced a pro-Republican majority of delegates. Behind the voting strength of blacks, who turned out in larger numbers than whites, 72 of the 105 delegate seats were filled by Republicans (25 of whom were black). The remaining 33 seats were won by "conservatives" of various stripes.[1] This election result – and the sense that the convention and subsequent state politics could be dominated by

---

[1] Allen W. Moger, *Virginia: Bourbonism to Byrd, 1870–1925* (Charlottesville: University of Virginia Press, 1968), 6. Other sources provided slightly different party numbers. See, for example, Richard Lowe, *Republicans and Reconstruction in Virginia, 1856–70* (Charlottesville: University of Virginia Press. 1991), 126–27, 199–200.

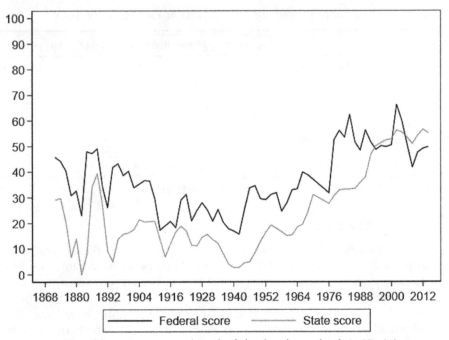

FIGURE 7.1 Republican Party strength at the federal and state levels in Virginia, 1868–2012

Radical Republicans – led to the founding of the Conservative Party in December 1867.[2]

The Conservative Party, at its inception, was a conglomeration of former Whigs and Democrats. As Jack Maddex notes: "Whiggery and Democracy had not lost their identities, but they had formed a common organization against Radicalism."[3] The party was largely led by ex-Whigs, with Alexander H. H. Stuart, a former Whig member of the US House, playing a prominent role. William Mahone, railroad president and former Confederate general, would also be an early and influential leader. As the constitutional convention convened in December 1867, the Radicals took charge – and over the course of the ensuing months drafted a reform-based document that provided for debt protection, public education, and a secret ballot in elections.[4] More troubling to Conservatives, however, were two provisions that threatened to bias the future electorate significantly in a pro-Republican direction: (a) a test-oath clause,

[2] The standard account of the Conservative Party in Virginia is Jack P. Maddex, Jr., *The Virginia Conservatives, 1867–1879: A Study in Reconstruction Politics* (Chapel Hill: University of North Carolina Press, 1970).

[3] Maddex, *The Virginia Conservatives*, 56–57.

[4] Moger, *Virginia*, 6–7; Lowe, *Republicans and Reconstruction in Virginia*, 144.

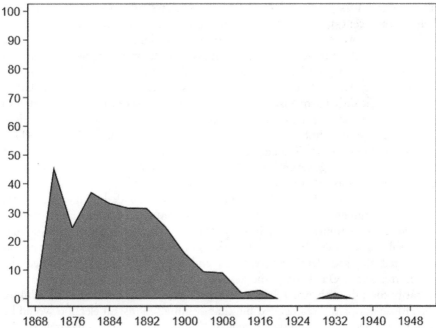

FIGURE 7.2 Percentage of GOP convention delegates from Virginia that were black, 1868–1952
Source: Data collected by authors.

which restricted jury and office-holding eligibility to those who could swear that they never supported the Confederacy, and (b) a disenfranchisement clause, which prohibited those who held civil or military office under the Confederacy from being able to vote.[5] A constitution adopted with these two clauses would, in the minds of Conservatives, exclude almost all Southern whites (except for a small group of Unionists) from the political process. A number of moderate Republicans also opposed the test-oath and disenfranchising clauses. Nonetheless, the Radical Republicans had the numbers, and in April 1868 pushed through the Underwood Constitution – named after Judge John Curtiss Underwood, the president of the convention – complete with the two disabling clauses.

Over the next year, Conservatives and their moderate Republican allies worked to frame the procedures and politics of the state referendum that would determine the Underwood Constitution's fate. Stuart organized a "Committee of Nine" influential Virginians (consisting of politicians, bankers,

[5] Maddex, *The Virginia Conservatives*, 58–59.

and industrialists), some of whom were associates of Mahone (who worked behind the scenes), to lobby President Grant and the Republican Congress regarding the process of Virginia's return to the Union. The Committee of Nine acceded to black suffrage – even though many Conservatives opposed it initially – but sought to have the Underwood Constitution voted on separately from the two disabling clauses. Stuart and his associates argued that the disabling clauses would significantly harm Virginia economically and make the state a burden to the remaining states in the Union.[6] Helping their cause was testimony by Brigadier General John Schofield, who commanded the First Military District, which comprised the state of Virginia. Schofield believed the disabling clauses would make organizing a government in Virginia impossible, because all competent candidates for important positions would be disqualified.[7]

On April 7, 1869, Grant indicated that he was persuaded by the Committee of Nine's arguments, as he asked Congress for money to conduct an election in Virginia and recommended separate votes on the Underwood Constitution and the disabling clauses. The next day, the Joint Committee on Reconstruction supported the president's suggestions, and the House quickly adopted the committee's bill. On April 9, the Senate amended the bill to require Virginia to ratify the Fifteenth Amendment before it could be readmitted to the Union; the House adopted the amended bill that evening.[8] Thus, an election would be held in July 1869, wherein the citizens of Virginia would vote separately on the Underwood Constitution and the two disabling clauses, as well as choose a new governor and state legislature.

While the Radicals dominated the elections to the constitutional convention in 1867, the succeeding politics had shifted the electoral dynamics in the state. Many conservative whites had sat out the 1867 vote in protest. Now, with the governing structure and regime on the line, conservative whites were energized. The Republican ticket included Henry H. Wells, a Michigan lawyer, former Union Army officer, and Radical, for governor and J. D. Harris, a black physician and native of the West Indies, for lieutenant governor.[9] Conservatives initially assembled their own ticket, but then – through the machinations of Mahone – rejected it in favor of a ticket headed by moderate Republicans.[10] This "True Republican" ticket – with Gilbert C. Walker, a Northern banker and former "Douglas Democrat," for governor and John F. Lewis, a wealthy Virginia farmer and nationalist Whig – would effectively be a shadow

[6] Richard Lee Morton, *The Negro in Virginia Politics, 1865–1902* (Charlottesville: University of Virginia Press, 1919), 66–68; Maddex, *The Virginia Conservatives*, 58–59.

[7] Moger, *Virginia*, 7–8.   [8] Lowe, *Republicans and Reconstruction in Virginia*, 170.

[9] Harris's nomination was a strategic maneuver made by moderate Republicans (with the unwitting help of black delegates) to cripple the Wells ticket and stymie the Radicals. As Richard Lowe notes: "the majority of native whites and many white carpetbaggers would never support any slate of officers with a black man in the second position." Lowe, *Republicans and Reconstruction in Virginia*, 166.

[10] Maddex, *The Virginia Conservatives*, 74–77.

Conservative ticket, solidifying the alliance between the moderate Republicans and the Conservatives.

On July 6, 1869, voters went to the polls – and more than 80 percent of both whites and blacks voted. And when the votes were counted, the Conservatives swept the elections. Walker beat Wells by more than 18,000 votes for governor, while Lewis defeated Taylor by more than 20,000 votes. The Underwood Constitution was adopted by more than 200,000 votes, while the two disabling clauses were each defeated by over 40,000 votes. Conservatives also won 30 of 43 state Senate seats and 97 of 138 House of Delegates seats.[11] Among the winners were six blacks in the state Senate (all Republicans) and twenty-one blacks in the House of Delegates (eighteen of whom were Republicans).[12]

Once in power, the Conservatives would dominate Virginia government through the 1870s. Republicans – while they did manage to win the state for President Ulysses S. Grant in 1872 – could only command a small number (usually a quarter or less) of seats in the state Senate, House of Delegates, and US House. As the GOP worked to build itself into a viable opposition, it took a biracial approach. For example, a sizable proportion of Republican National Convention delegates were black – nearly 46 percent in 1872, dropping to 25 percent in 1876. And black candidates continued to be elected to the state legislature. However, Conservatives actively sought to diminish black voting power, via gerrymandering (which occurred four times in the 1870s) and new laws that made certain crimes a barrier to voting.[13] As a result, the number of black legislators began dropping – to seventeen in 1871 and all the way down to five in 1878.[14] And by 1877, the state Republican Party was in such disarray that they failed to field candidates for governor and other state offices.

By the late 1870s, however, a ray of hope had emerged for the Virginia GOP. In 1871, the Conservatives passed the Funding Act, to address the $46 million debt the state had incurred (largely through investment in internal improvements) prior to the Civil War. Over the next several years, interest payments on the debt ate up a significant portion of the state's annual tax revenue, and chronic deficits were the result – which led to cuts in popular state programs, like the public school system the Conservatives had installed. Conservatives became increasingly split between continuing the current course (fully funding the debt and thus cutting money for programs, like the schools) and repudiating

---

[11] The detailed results were: Walker over Wells 119,535 to 101,204; Lewis over Harris 120,068 to 99,400; the Underwood Constitution was adopted 210,577 to 9,136; the test-oath clause was rejected 124,715 to 83,458; and the disenfranchising clause was rejected 124,360 to 84,410. Lowe, *Republicans and Reconstruction in Virginia*, 177. The Conservatives also controlled 5 of the 8 US House seats.

[12] Maddex, *The Virginia Conservatives*, 82; Moger, *Virginia*, 12.   [13] Moger, *Virginia*, 24.

[14] Charles Wynes, *Race Relations in Virginia, 1870–1902* (Charlottesville: University of Virginia Press, 1961), 9–10; Luther Porter Jackson, *Negro Office-Holders in Virginia, 1865–1895* (Norfolk, VA: Guide Quality Press, 1945), 79.

part of the principal of the debt so that state programs could be better financed. The former group of Conservatives would become known as "Funders," while the latter group would take on the label "Readjusters."[15] The Funders were made up of bankers, merchants, and businessmen, while the Readjusters largely comprised farmers and poor wage laborers. William Mahone was the leader of the Readjusters. The two groups were roughly even in size, but the Republicans in the state, led by blacks, largely supported the Readjusters. As a result, the Readjusters outperformed the Funders in the 1879 state legislative elections. They were, however, short of majorities in the General Assembly. Mahone thus secured a coalition-government arrangement with a small group of black Republican legislators. A more formal Readjuster–Republican alliance followed shortly thereafter, which led to Readjuster control of Virginia for the next four years. In that time, the Readjusters won control of the General Assembly outright and elected two US senators (Mahone and James Riddleberger), several US House members, and a governor (William Cameron). Mahone went on to caucus with the national Republicans in the Senate and used his pivotal status (he was the tiebreaker between the Republicans and Democrats) to extract a set of important committee assignments and an arrangement to distribute executive patronage to his Readjuster–Republican coalition back home.

In office, the Readjusters made good on their policy promises: they refinanced the public debt (shifting one-third of the principal to West Virginia), raised taxes on railroads and various businesses, reduced taxes on farmers, and increased spending on the public schools. Blacks fared well under Readjuster rule. Mahone made sure to work with black leaders and distribute patronage in a biracial way, with sizable numbers of blacks receiving positions in the Virginia Treasury and Post Office Departments. He also worked to ensure that black voters would be treated fairly and that their votes would be counted ("equal suffrage"). Blacks were also more successful politically, after a decline throughout the 1870s, with sixteen serving in the 1881–82 General Assembly. And issues important to black Virginians – like the creation of black asylums and colleges, and integrated public school boards – were addressed.[16]

In 1883, the Readjusters' successful run came to an end. The Funders had reorganized themselves as the Democratic Party, and they set their sights on regaining control of the state. They "drew the color line" by claiming that the Readjusters were propagating "Negro rule" in the state and pursuing policies of social equality. Shortly before the elections, a street fight in Danville, VA,

---

[15] On the funding issue and the Readjuster Party more generally, see Jane Dailey, *Before Jim Crow: The Politics of Race in Postemancipation Virginia* (Chapel Hill: University of North Carolina Press, 2000); Brent Tarter, *A Saga of the New South: Race, Law, and Public Debt in Virginia* (Charlottesville: University of Virginia Press, 2016).

[16] Dailey, *Before Jim Crow*, 67–76.

that involved serious racial conflict – which was framed (successfully) as the "Danville Race Riot" – was used by the Democrats to frighten white voters. And on election day, fraud and threats of violence were rampant, which the Democrats used to carry both chambers of the General Assembly. Once in power, they made changes to take control of the election administration throughout the state in order to perpetuate white rule.[17] In 1884, the Democrats carried the state for Grover Cleveland in the presidential election by a tiny majority. And in 1885, they won the governorship, retained majorities in the General Assembly, and replaced Mahone in the Senate. In 1887, they took control of the other Senate seat.[18]

By the mid-1880s, the Readjusters were effectively done as a party, and Mahone and most of the Readjusters became Republicans. Mahone became GOP boss in the state and held the title until his death in 1895. He made strong organizing efforts in 1888 (to carry the state for Republican presidential candidate Benjamin Harrison) and 1889 (to win the governorship for himself), but fell short each time. Repeated electoral defeats – brought about in part by the Democrats' white supremacist rhetoric – made him bitter, and he increasingly lashed out against blacks in the party. In 1888, he blocked the nomination of John Mercer Langston, a mixed-race lawyer and former US Minister to Haiti and Law School Dean at Howard University, for the 4th congressional district. Langston ran as an Independent Republican and lost a three-way race in a heavily fraudulent election; the Republican majority in the US House eventually seated him via a contested election procedure.[19] In 1889, Mahone stated that "[blacks in the party] have been made to understand that they must take a back seat and let their white bosses and political masters run the machine and have all the offices."[20] A number of Republican Party leaders had made trips to Virginia in 1889 to speak on behalf of Mahone. The hope was that the Old Dominion could be turned to the GOP on the tariff issue. Moreover, as Stanley Hirshson states: "Reasoning that the Negro would remain a Republican even if deprived of political patronage, these men reported that their purpose was to build up, as far as possible, a white man party's in the state."[21] Mahone's performance in 1889 was a great disappointment for the party, as his electoral tally was considerably worse than Harrison's in 1888.

Despite not having much to show from the Lily-White strategy in 1889, the Republicans in Virginia began to move headlong in that direction. As the

---

[17] Moger, *Virginia*, 56. [18] Ibid., 57–61.
[19] Wynes, *Race Relations in Virginia*, 42–43; Moger, *Virginia*, 62–63; Luis-Alejandro Dinnella-Borrego, *The Risen Phoenix: Black Politics in the Post-Civil War South* (Charlottesville: University of Virginia Press, 2016), 168–72.
[20] Wynes, *Race Relations in Virginia*, 42–43.
[21] Stanley P. Hirshson, *Farewell to the Bloody Shirt: Northern Republicans and the Southern Negro, 1877–1893* (Bloomington: Indiana University Press, 1962), 187. GOP leaders named by Hirshson included Thomas B. Reed, J. Donald Cameron, William McKinley, John Sherman, Thomas Quay, Julius Caeser Burrows, and James S. Clarkson.

Democrats in the state started working toward formally disenfranchising black voters – beginning with the Walton Act in 1894, which instituted a secret ballot and thus discriminated against illiterates – Republicans began to segregate party operations.[22] As Jane Dailey notes: "By 1896 white Republicans in Virginia had succeeded in Jim Crowing all party meetings, on one occasion allegedly resorting to stringing a clothesline down the center of an auditorium."[23] While the Walton Act reduced black voting significantly, Democrats wanted a more permanent change – and one that would both complete the disfranchisement of blacks and end the fraud that had developed in the preceding decade and found its way into Democratic politics (between establishment candidates and populists, after the Republicans were marginalized). After a couple of false starts, a constitutional convention was called, and delegates met in two sessions (in 1901 and 1902).[24] A constitution was eventually produced that phased in (over the course of three years) literacy tests (handwriting and understanding clauses) and poll taxes ($1.50 annually, paid in the three preceding years) as requirements in order to vote. These changes were effective: as Andrew Buni writes, of "the estimated 147,000 Negroes of voting age prior to the adoption of the 1902 constitution, only 21,000 remained on the registration lists by October 15, 1902." And by the time the full range of constitutional provisions was instituted in 1904, that 21,000 was reduced by half.[25]

As a result of these legal changes, and the growing Lily-Whiteism in the GOP, the share of black convention delegates at the Republican National Convention dropped significantly after 1892 (see Figure 7.2). By 1904, the share had fallen below 10 percent, and by 1912 it was effectively zero. And even as black voting power was largely eliminated beginning in 1902, the Democrats continued to successfully hang the "black party" label on the Republicans at election time. This was in response to Republican leaders fighting to compete in the now largely white electorate by emphasizing the party's "respectability" – i.e., that it was now a Lily-White party. Black voters in the GOP were told that this was now the way: for example, George Hanson, in the congressional nominating convention for the 3rd district in 1905 argued that the "time has come for the negro as a leader to take a back seat. He must be content to follow, not to lead, and if he cannot lead he must get behind the party and shove."[26]

---

[22] On the Walton Act, see J. Morgan Kousser, *The Shaping of Southern Politics: Suffrage Restrictions and the Establishment of the One-Party South* (New Haven, CT: Yale University Press, 1974), 173–75.

[23] Dailey, *Before Jim Crow*, 161.

[24] For a description of the 1901–02 convention proceedings and the politics involved, see Michael Perman, *Struggle for Mastery: Disfranchisement in the South, 1888–1908* (Chapel Hill: University of North Carolina Press, 2001), 195–223.

[25] Andrew Buni, *The Negro in Virginia Politics, 1902–1965* (Charlottesville: University of Virginia Press, 1967), 24.

[26] Quoted in ibid., 54.

In the aftermath of Mahone's death in 1895, after a short period of leadership turbulence, the Slemp family took control of the Republican Party in the state. Campbell Slemp and his son C. Bascom Slemp would represent the 9th district in the US House from 1903 (the 58th Congress) through 1922 (the 67th Congress). C. Bascom, who took over from his father after Campbell's death in 1907, was the GOP boss in Virginia until his own death in 1932.[27] Slemp's district was in the southwest region of Virginia, and was almost completely white. Democrats tried time and again to defeat Slemp – the lone Republican figure from Virginia left on the national scene – but he repeatedly beat back their attempts. To stay in power, he used federal patronage to its fullest effect and matched the Democrats in vote-buying activities.[28] The Slemp machine's success was in large part based on its racial strategy: Slemp (as well as his father) worked to make the GOP a Lily-White party, through the systematic exclusion of blacks from patronage lists and state and local conventions.[29] As Allen Moger notes: "Aware that his party suffered from its historical association with the Negro, Slemp bowed to public opinion and political expediency."[30]

Black Republicans fought against the Slemp machine, and in one case (in 1921) ran a "Lily-Black" slate of state-level candidates.[31] But these efforts proved futile, and they were essentially and effectively marginalized. Slemp went on to be Calvin Coolidge's personal secretary in 1923 and would play a significant role in the distribution of executive patronage throughout the South. He was also critical in carrying Virginia for Herbert Hoover in the presidential election of 1928, even as the RNC largely wrote off the state and distributed money elsewhere in the South.[32] But despite his efforts, Slemp never realized the cabinet appointment to which he aspired – as Hoover, who sought to reform and build up the party in the South, saw Slemp as little more than a political spoilsman and dropped him quickly after the 1928 election (see Chapter 6).[33]

After Slemp passed from the scene, the Republicans in Virginia continued to be Lily-White. Black voters began moving to the Democratic Party slowly. And

---

[27] Campbell Slemp was an officer in the Confederate Army during the Civil War and a member of the House of Delegates during the era of Readjuster dominance. He died in office in 1907, and C. Bascom won a special election to serve out his father's unexpired term.

[28] For a portrait of Slemp as Republican power broker, see Guy B. Hathorn, "C. Bascom Slemp – Virginia Republican Boss, 1907–1932," *The Journal of Politics* 17 (1955), 248–64.

[29] Buni, *The Negro in Virginia Politics*, 255. Allen Moger identifies 1909 as the year when the Lily-Whites took control of the party, by naming a full slate of Lily-White Republicans for the state offices. See Moger, *Virginia*, 219.

[30] Moger, *Virginia*, 349.

[31] The Lily-Black movement occurred in response to the Republican leadership publicly trumpeting the Lily-Whiteness of the party. See Moger, *Virginia*, 329. For more on the Lily-Black movement, see Buni, *The Negro in Virginia Politics*, 84–89.

[32] See Hathorn, "C. Bascom Slemp."

[33] Donald J. Lisio, *Hoover, Blacks, and Lily-Whites: A Study of Southern Strategies* (Chapel Hill: University of North Carolina Press, 1985), 171–72.

by the late 1930s, they had firmly made the move with their backing of FDR. Rather than compete for black votes, Republican leaders in Virginia tried to use the race issue against the Democrats – by claiming the Democrats were now the "black party."[34] The GOP would not have meaningful success in Virginia again until 1952, when a new group of voters – most having never cast a Republican vote before – supported Dwight D. Eisenhower for the presidency. Eisenhower's victory in 1952, and his carrying of Virginia and three other Southern states, began the development of the modern Republican Party in the South.

TEXAS: BLACK LEADERSHIP UNDER SIEGE

The Texas Republican Party organization was founded in July 1867. For the next four decades, the party remained under the control of a Black-and-Tan coalition.[35] Throughout this period, blacks made up a considerable percentage of the state's national convention delegation, though they were never the majority (see Figure 7.3). And while black Texans played a major role in the state party, their participation was a source of major and continuous conflict – with white-only Republican groups organizing throughout the state in an attempt to limit black influence. While such attempts were eventually successful, black Republicans in Texas were remarkably effective at ensuring their representation for a considerable period of time. Notably, Texas was one of a small number of states where a black man became the leader of the local Republican Party, with Norris Wright Cuney serving as Texas GOP boss in the 1880s and 1890s.

Black influence in the Texas Republican Party was due in large part to the work of the Texas Loyal Union League – a secret organization focused on registering black male voters, educating them on voting procedures, and promoting the GOP. The Union League's success in this regard meant that black voters made up a majority of the party's voting base at the state level. As whites would go on to leave the GOP in the 1870s, however, the party declined in electoral competitiveness. And as in many Southern states, the Republican Party in Texas was little more than a skeleton organization for decades. In the 1950s, the GOP in Texas would begin a resurgence, with Eisenhower winning the state in both 1952 and 1956. And in 1961, Republican John Tower emerged victorious in the election to fill Lyndon Johnson's Senate seat

---

[34] Buni, *The Negro in Virginia Politics*, 143.

[35] Paul Casdorph notes that the party was founded by a number of political radicals who opposed the 1866 constitution, which was adopted at a convention dominated by delegates who had previously been active in the Texas Democratic Party. Approximately one month after the Texas Republican Party was founded, its leader, Elisha M. Pease, was installed as governor by General William Techumseh Sherman. Thus, the GOP "had in essence taken office without having to undergo an election." Paul Casdorph, *A History of the Republican Party in Texas, 1865–1965* (Austin, TX: The Pemberton Press, 1965), 5.

TABLE 7.2 *Descriptive Republican Party success in Texas, 1865–1968*

	1865–1877	1878–1896	1897–1932	1933–1968
Presidential candidate won the state?			✓	✓
Senatorial candidate elected?	✓			✓
Gubernatorial candidate elected?	✓			
At least one House candidate elected?	✓	✓	✓	✓

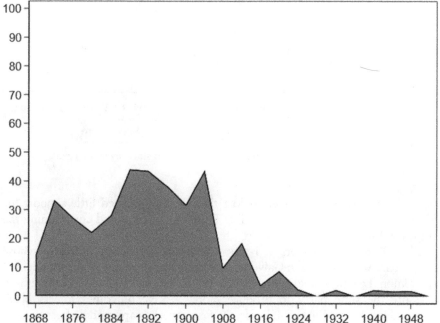

FIGURE 7.3 Percentage of GOP convention delegates from Texas that were black, 1868–1952
Source: Data collected by authors.

(see Table 7.2 and Figure 7.4). This was the first instance of a Republican winning a Senate seat in the South in the twentieth century.

* * * * *

In the immediate aftermath of the Civil War, whites controlled both the state GOP and the state convention called to draft a new version of the Texas state constitution. Many of the white "Republicans" involved in this process had

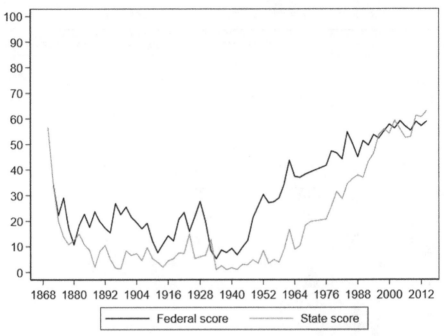

FIGURE 7.4 Republican Party strength at the federal and state levels in Texas, 1868–2012

been Democratic office-holders before the war and showed little support for black rights. Indeed, a subset of white Republicans proposed constraining the franchise for black Texans.[36]

Black Republican leaders in Texas – most notably George T. Ruby, whose power base was centered in Galveston and who had been one of the founders of the Union League – realized they needed to use their electoral strength to pressure the state party to produce more positive outcomes for its black constituents. Under Elisha M. Pease, the first governor appointed after the Civil War, black leaders were excluded from the party. But in advance of the 1869 election, the Texas GOP split over the question of whether all laws passed in Texas during the Confederacy should be declared null and void retroactively.[37] Ruby's leadership was fundamental in shaping the outcome of this clash. Notably, he based his actions on a desire for compromise with white Republicans: in supporting moderate Edmund J. Davis for the gubernatorial nomination, Ruby passed on the potential of a more radical version of the

[36] W. C. Nunn, *Texas under the Carpetbaggers* (Austin: University of Texas Press, 1962), 6–9.
[37] Casdorph, *A History of the Republican Party in Texas*, 9–11.

Texas GOP.[38] Ruby and other black leaders used the Loyal Union League to ensure that there would be high rates of registration and turnout of black voters. And these efforts were successful: Davis won the gubernatorial election, Republicans won majorities in the state legislature, and Ruby himself won a state Senate seat.[39]

With Davis as governor, Republicans used their control of the state government to create a state militia, a racially integrated state police force, and a public school system.[40] During the Davis administration, Ruby also expanded his influence within the party. Most notably, Ruby held considerable sway over the state's new public school system and its related patronage. As Carl Mahoney notes, Ruby also tried to work with white economic elites, in an attempt at "[developing] a new image, one of a conservative politician who looked after not only the interests of blacks, but also whites in his community."[41] Ruby functioned as a power broker between whites in the Galveston area and the Davis administration, and controlled the appointment of local state officials. Ironically, this new influence did not strengthen Ruby's political position. On the one hand, many black voters grew disillusioned with his appeals to wealthy whites. On the other hand, many whites grew increasingly hostile to the concept of a black man holding such political power.

With considerable white migration into Texas in the early 1870s, the GOP's electoral success in 1869 proved to be their last. In the state legislative elections of 1872, Republicans lost their majorities in both the Senate and the Assembly, and Grant lost Texas in the presidential election – receiving only 41 percent of the vote.[42] In 1873, Davis lost his reelection as governor in a landslide, and Democrats won 87 percent of seats in the state Senate and 88 percent in the Assembly.[43] By then, Ruby had already decided not to seek reelection. Shortly after Davis' loss, Ruby left Texas and moved to Louisiana where he continued to support Republican candidates and black causes.[44]

The Democratic takeover of the early 1870s placed black leaders in a complicated situation, and in the years that followed some of these leaders attempted to work with third parties or even Democrats.[45] However, most black Republicans remained within the party. Indeed, the changing demographics of the state and the decline of the GOP produced a peculiar political

---

[38] Alwyn Barr, *Black Texans: A History of Negroes in Texas, 1528–1971* (Austin, TX: Jenkins Publishing Company, 1973), 47.

[39] Carl H. Moneyhon, "George T. Ruby and the Politics of Expediency in Texas," in Howard N. Rabinowitz, ed., *Southern Black Leaders of the Reconstruction Era* (Urbana: University of Illinois Press, 1982), 366–78.

[40] Casdorph, *A History of the Republican Party in Texas*, 17.

[41] Moneyhon, "George T. Ruby and the Politics of Expediency in Texas," 379.

[42] Michael J. Dubin, *Party Affiliations in the State Legislatures: A Year by Year Summary, 1796–2006* (Jefferson, NC: McFarland & Company, 2007), 181.

[43] Ibid.   [44] Moneyhon, "George T. Ruby and the Politics of Expediency in Texas," 388.

[45] Barr, *Black Texans*, 71.

situation: in Texas as a whole, white migration meant that by 1880 blacks declined as a group to just 25 percent of the population.[46] Yet, because whites had abandoned the Republican Party, the Texas GOP's black wing *increased* its overall influence within the party in the 1870s, with blacks representing a reported 90 percent of the party's voting base by 1880.[47]

After Ruby's departure from Texas in 1873, one of his former protégés – Norris Wright Cuney – became the most important black Republican leader in the state. Like Ruby, Cuney would wield influence by working with white party leaders. However, unlike Ruby, Cuney would aspire to more – and, in time, he would go on to become the state party's leader. Cuney was born the son of Adeline Stuart, a black slave, and her owner, Philip Cuney, a white planter and Democratic politician. He was freed by his father as a teenager and educated at an all-black school in Pittsburgh.[48] Cuney remained in the North during the war but returned to Texas in the late 1860s and settled in Galveston. There, he began to build his political career through his participation in the local (black) Free Mason organization and his activities on behalf of the city's black dock-worker union movement.[49]

During the Ruby era, Cuney was named to the Texas school board and appointed customs inspector in Galveston – an important position in terms of patronage. Cuney also began to attend Republican National Conventions as a member of the Texas delegation for the first time in 1872. He would go on to attend every subsequent convention until his death in 1898. Cuney's career had flourished during the Davis–Ruby era, but after the 1873 elections the status of the Texas GOP became more complex. With Democrats now in control of the Texas state government, Republicans were excluded from political influence and access to state-level patronage.[50] However, with Grant in the White House, Texas Republicans still held sway through their control of federal patronage.

---

[46] *Statistics of the Population of the United States at the Tenth Census*, 4, 378.

[47] Douglas Hales, *A Southern Family in White and Black: The Cuneys of Texas* (College Station: Texas A&M University Press, 2003), 52.

[48] Philip Cuney served as a member of the Texas state Assembly and Senate. As a legislator he took particular interest in legislation intended to secure the rights of slave owners – including laws banning slaves from being provided with alcohol. Cuney had several children with multiple slaves and died shortly after the end of the Civil War. See ibid., 3–14.

[49] Ibid., 15–39.

[50] This period also saw a split within the Republican Party, with a number of Texas Republicans bolting the Davis–Cuney organization and forming the Greenback Party. In the 1878 gubernatorial election, Greenback candidate A. B. Norton and his black running mate Richard Allen (both former Republicans) received more votes than the Republican ticket. In the years that followed, the Texas GOP and the Greenback Party maintained a complicated relationship. The Greenback Party ran another gubernatorial candidate in 1880, but support dropped considerably and the Republicans regained their position as the state's second party. In the 1882 election, Republican leaders supported the Greenback gubernatorial candidate – Congressman George Washington Jones, who had built up considerable popularity among black voters – by not fielding a Republican ticket. See Casdorph, *A History of the Republican Party in Texas*, 38–45.

Former governor Davis remained the leader of the party in this regard and continued to support Cuney.[51] In 1877, a change occurred as President Hayes sought to rebuild a Southern Republican Party by currying favor with white Democrats. This "new departure" represented a temporary setback for Cuney, as it cost him his position as customs inspector.[52]

During the Hayes, Garfield, and Arthur administrations, Cuney remained active within the state party. After Davis' death in 1883, Cuney emerged as the party's new leader on the basis of black majorities at state conventions in the 1884 election year.[53] Cuney would remain in charge of the Texas GOP between 1884 and 1897, serving as Texas' representative to the RNC between 1886 and 1896. Throughout his leadership, the Republican Party was mostly a nonentity when it came to competing in elections. Indeed, Cuney's GOP regularly refused to field a ticket for statewide offices – with Cuney supporting fusion tickets, and in some cases even moderate Democrats.[54] Between 1882 and 1894, the GOP had zero state senators and its Assembly membership was consistently in single digits (out of over 100 seats).[55] In statewide races, the party did little better, frequently winning less than a quarter of the vote and occasionally getting outpolled by third parties.

But while the GOP achieved little to no electoral successes during this period, Cuney's control over the party did represent considerable political power in Texas as long as Republicans held the White House. This was particularly true during the presidency of Benjamin Harrison (1889–1893), during which time Cuney served as collector of customs in Galveston. This position provided Cuney with control over nearly all federal patronage in Texas.[56] Cuney also shrewdly used his power over party meetings – regularly dismissing opposing (white) critics, denying them credentials to participate in state conventions, or packing the crowd with black Republicans supportive of his agenda to ensure favorable outcomes.[57]

[51] Cuney faced considerable opposition from a newly appointed collector of customs at Galveston starting in 1875 who attempted to fire him from his position as inspector of customs. These attempts failed in part due to the support Cuney received from Davis, and even from elected Democratic officials in Galveston where Cuney's career in local politics had earned him considerable respect. See ibid., 47–48.

[52] Ibid., 49, 52.   [53] Ibid., 49.

[54] "The Republican Programme in Texas," *Dallas Morning News*, September 16, 1888; "Collector N. W. Cuney: His Views Fully Expressed on State Politics," *Dallas Morning News*, February 13, 1892.

[55] Dubin, *Party Affiliations in the State Legislatures*, 181.

[56] As Casdorph notes, when the GOP lost control of the White House during the Cleveland administration "the federal jobs in Texas had passed into the hands of the Democratic faithful, making the major prizes to be handed out" at Republican state conventions the membership of the RNC (which Cuney held) and the chairmanship of the state party's executive committee. See Casdorph, *A History of the Republican Party in Texas*, 51.

[57] Hales, *A Southern Family in White and Black*, 73.

Cuney's tenure as party leader coincided with increased hostility from Texas Democrats and the state government toward black political participation. Throughout the 1880s, black voters were terrorized by whites, resulting in a number of violent incidents. In areas where blacks were in the majority and won local elections, such violence and intimidation was particularly extreme. For example, in 1888 white Democrats in Fort Bend County instigated a riot after losing an election, resulting in a state-controlled reorganization of the county's political system that placed Democrats in control.[58] As Douglas Hales notes, Cuney's prominence was partly accepted because he was of mixed-race origins, and

[newspapers] and many individuals used this feature to account for Cuney's success, variously describing him as a "bright olive complexioned gentleman," of having an appearance "more like that of a Spaniard than a black man," or that "his features, hair and lanky figure seem to show a mixture of Indian and Spanish blood."[59]

Still, throughout his time as party leader, Cuney faced continuous challenges from the white GOP minority, who attempted to overthrow the existing party structure by organizing their own institutions. For example, white Republicans proposed a scheme in 1894 in which representation at state conventions would be proportionate to the black population in each Texas county. Unsurprisingly, Cuney rejected this proposal, arguing that "[such] a thing is against the policy or teachings of any party, and particularly of the republican [sic] party. In our public and political relations we know no color, no creed, no sect, and a proposition on a racial basis is just simply ridiculous and republicans [sic] will not hear to it."[60] In dismissing his white opponents, Cuney also coined a new term that would come to define white Republicanism in the South, describing them as "Lily Republicans" and "Lily-Whites."[61]

The Lily-White argument in Texas was similar to that employed elsewhere: as one local Republican leader argued, "the Negro is an incubus, a millstone on the back of the Republican Party. We must drop him. Give him his legal rights but let him remain in the background where he belongs."[62] The Lily-Whites were particularly active during the Harrison administration when Cuney was at his most powerful, although attempts at undermining Cuney's leadership continued during the second Cleveland administration, when Republican federal patronage dried up. For example, in 1894 Lily-White Republicans bolted the regular Republican Party and held their own state convention to nominate candidates for state-level elections. As a result, in the 1894 elections the

[58] Ibid., 71.   [59] Ibid., 62.
[60] "Clark's Committee," *Dallas Morning News*, January 15, 1894.
[61] Hales, *A Southern Family in White and Black*, 75.
[62] Darlene Clark Hine, *Black Victory: The Rise and Fall of the White Primary in Texas* (Columbia: University of Missouri Press, 1979), 75.

Democratic candidate for governor ran against (and easily beat) two Republican candidates.[63]

Unlike many state party leaders, Cuney was not particularly open to financial deals with presidential hopefuls to guarantee Texas' support at national conventions. For example, in advance of the 1884 convention, the Arthur campaign attempted to buy the support of Texas delegates, but Cuney and a number of other delegates cast their lot with James Blaine instead.[64] Indeed, Cuney's unwillingness to play ball with presidential hopefuls cost him control of the Texas party. In the run-up to the 1896 convention, Mark Hanna – laboring in the South to win support for William McKinley's candidacy – reached out to Cuney to ensure support for his candidate from the Texas delegation, offering to cover any "expenses" Cuney might face in the process.[65] Cuney decided to support Iowa Senator William Allison instead. During the state convention in March 1896, Cuney succeeded in sending a delegation to the national convention supporting Allison despite a physical altercation between McKinley supporters and himself.[66] In reporting on the state convention, the *Dallas Morning News* concluded that Cuney was "on top" of the state party and "for the first time in many moons ... will sleep soundly without having his slumbers haunted by the hob-goblins of nervous unrest. It was a great victory ... It was a fight to the finish, a contest in which the very political existence of The Galveston man was involved."[67]

Yet Cuney's victory at the state convention proved to be only a minor setback for the Lily-Whites. The McKinley supporters in the Texas GOP – who were mostly whites – voted to send their own alternate delegation to the national convention. And at the convention, the Credentials Committee, which was dominated by McKinley supporters, voted to seat only a small number of the regular Texas delegates, with McKinley-supporting Lily-Whites making up the rest of the slate. By betting on the wrong candidate, Cuney lost control of the Texas party: he was replaced as member of the RNC immediately after McKinley's nomination and voted out as chairman of the state party convention in the fall of 1896. By then, Cuney already was facing poor health and, while hoping for a political comeback, he died in March 1898.[68]

After Cuney's fall from grace, the Lily-White wing of the Texas GOP – now under the control of Robert B. Hawley, who had backed McKinley at the

[63] Casdorph, *A History of the Republican Party in Texas*, 63–64.
[64] Hales, *A Southern Family in White and Black*, 65–66.
[65] The full quote from Hanna's letter to Cuney was as follows: "I will say to you frankly that I am very anxious to have you take charge of Gov. McKinley's interest in Texas, which I feel should soon receive some attention. I appreciate that it is something of a task to fully perfect an organization and that there would be expenses, etc., which no one should be asked to bear alone" (ibid., 89).
[66] Casdorph, *A History of the Republican Party in Texas*, 65–66.
[67] "Cuney is on Top," *Dallas Morning News*, March 25, 1896.
[68] Hales, *A Southern Family in White and Black*, 92.

1896 national convention and himself had a won a seat in Congress that year – became ascendant. With Hawley both the top Republican elected official in the state and on good terms with the McKinley administration, the Black-and-Tans in the Texas party – now controlled by E. H. R. Green, a wealthy white man born in the United Kingdom who had moved to Texas in the early 1890s, and W. M. "Gooseneck" McDonald, a black Republican politician – lacked control over patronage. Still, between 1898 and 1902, the Black-and-Tans and Lily-Whites continued to battle over control of the state party. In 1900, two delegations made their way to the national convention, both claiming to represent the "true" Texas Republican Party. While the majority of the Hawley faction was seated by the RNC, several delegates of the Black-and-Tan organization were also included.[69]

This, however, proved to be the last stand for what remained of Cuney's party organization. By 1902, Cecil A. Lyon – the new chairman of the Texas GOP State Executive Committee and a representative of the Lily-White wing – brokered a peace agreement with Green and McDonald, and all three leaders appeared together at the state convention in a show of unity. Yet the agreement in practice represented a surrender for the Black-and-Tans: by 1904 the Texas Republican Party was dominated by the Lily-Whites with the previously dominant black Republicans clearly in the minority. As one observer of the 1904 state convention described it:

The most remarkable feature of the convention as compared with previous Republican conventions was the large excess in numbers of the whites over the Negroes. There were large bunches of Negroes here and there among the seats through the convention, but they looked lonesome. They realized sorrowfully that they were a very small factor in the Proceedings.[70]

The consequences of this were clearest in the number of black delegates Texas sent to national conventions before and after 1904: while blacks previously made up between 24 and 45 percent of the delegation, in 1904 the number dropped to a mere 10 percent. While the Black-and-Tans would make a minor comeback during the 1912 Taft–Roosevelt clash, black representation after 1912 consistently remained below 10 percent.

NORTH CAROLINA: A TALE OF TWO EXTREMES

In North Carolina, black Republicans made up a considerable part of the state's party organization through the middle of the 1890s. For example, as late as the 1896 GOP convention, blacks made up almost 41 percent of the state's delegation. However, after 1896, the Black-and-Tans rapidly lost control over the state party: in 1900 and 1904, black representation at the GOP convention dropped to 13.3 and 11.6 percent, respectively. And in 1908, there were *no*

---

[69] Casdorph, *A History of the Republican Party in Texas*, 73–78.   [70] Ibid., 81.

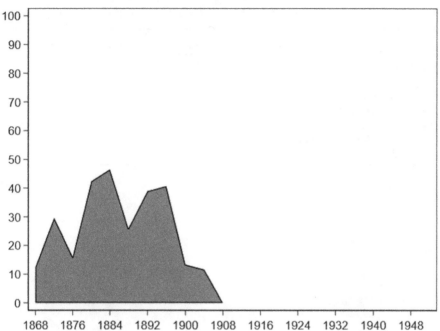

FIGURE 7.5 Percentage of GOP convention delegates from North Carolina that were black, 1868–1952
Source: Data collected by authors.

blacks in North Carolina's convention delegation (see Figure 7.5). The rapid decline in black delegates in such a short period of time is particularly notable since North Carolina was somewhat unique among Southern states, in that it continued to elect Republicans to Congress and the state legislature through the 1880s and 1890s and even managed to win a gubernatorial election in 1896 (see Table 7.3 and Figure 7.6). Thanks to a significant voting base of ex-Union soldiers in the mountains, a substantial number of black voters who had not yet been disenfranchised, and successful fusion arrangements with Populists, the North Carolina GOP remained competitive in North Carolina far longer than nearly anywhere else in the South.[71] Even more unique was the state's ongoing ability to elect *black* Republicans well into the 1890s.[72] How did the

---

[71] Rob Christensen, *The Paradox of Tar Heel Politics: The Personalities, Elections, and Events That Shaped Modern North Carolina*, 2nd edn. (Chapel Hill: University of North Carolina Press, 2010), 9.
[72] Helen G. Edmonds, *The Negro and Fusion Politics in North Carolina* (New York: Russell & Russell, 1951), 97. See also James M. Beeby, *Revolt of the Tar Heels: The North Carolina Populist Movement, 1890–1901* (Oxford: University of Mississippi Press, 2008).

TABLE 7.3 *Descriptive Republican Party success in North Carolina, 1865–1968*

	1865–1877	1878–1896	1897–1932	1933–1968
Presidential candidate won the state?	✓		✓	✓
Senatorial candidate elected?	✓	✓		
Gubernatorial candidate elected?	✓	✓		
At least one House candidate elected?	✓	✓	✓	✓

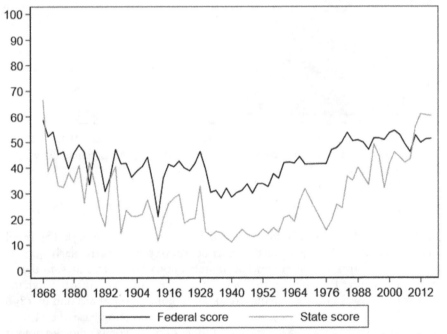

FIGURE 7.6 Republican Party strength at the federal and state levels in North Carolina, 1868–2012

Black-and-Tan coalition come to control the North Carolina Republican Party, and how did it lose control so quickly?

* * * * *

After early attempts at Reconstruction in North Carolina were hijacked by conservatives, Radical Republicans in Congress successfully required the state to make a new attempt at readmission in 1867. This process – which required North Carolina voters to approve a new constitutional convention, elect delegates to it, and subsequently approve the updated constitution it produced – played out in late 1867 and early 1868. Throughout 1867, Republican leaders in the state, including future governor William Woods Holden, began to organize black voters, who could participate in the first election if they were literate and owned at least $100 worth of property. Holden was noticeably different from the standard GOP leaders in the South immediately after Reconstruction. He was white, a North Carolina native, a newspaper publisher, and had a long political career before he joined the Republican Party. Prior to the war, Holden was an active Democrat and had won multiple elections, though he was frequently passed over for higher office by his party. Holden's role during the Civil War was complex: he initially opposed secession but came to support it later on. Yet Holden was also a consistent critic of the Confederate government and, in the 1864 election, ran as a "peace candidate" in the gubernatorial election in North Carolina. After the war, Holden was appointed governor of North Carolina by Andrew Johnson, but lost in the 1865 election. Subsequently, he joined the Republican Party.[73]

In December 1867, North Carolina voters approved the call for a new constitutional convention and elected its delegates. With Democrats largely boycotting the proceedings, Republicans dominated the convention and produced a constitution that officially abolished slavery, introduced universal male suffrage, and mandated free public education regardless of race. During the subsequent ratification process, a majority of registered North Carolinians approved the new constitution and elected an overwhelmingly Republican state legislature.[74] Additionally, Holden was elected governor with 55 percent of the vote.[75]

The Holden era proved to be both tumultuous and short-lived. Within the first few months of taking office, he was confronted with the rise of the Ku Klux Klan (KKK) in North Carolina, resulting in multiple incidents of violence and intimidation against blacks and, in some cases, white Republicans. Holden faced considerable limitations in his ability to counter the Klan. As Horace W. Raper notes:

[in] case after case [Holden] had been unable to bring guilty parties to justice. In many instances, sheriffs themselves were Klan members, and in other cases grand juries refused to return indictments. In Alamance County not only the sheriff but also his deputies were Klan leaders. When bills of indictment were returned and parties arraigned for trial, juries frequently failed to convict ...[76]

---

[73] William C. Harris, *William Woods Holden: Firebrand of North Carolina Politics* (Baton Rouge: Louisiana State University Press, 1987).
[74] Mark L. Bradley, *Bluecoats & Tar Heels: Soldiers and Civilians in Reconstruction North Carolina* (Lexington: University Press of Kentucky, 2009), 181–85.
[75] Michael J. Dubin, *United States Gubernatorial Elections, 1861–1911: The Official Results by State and County* (Jefferson, NC: McFarland & Company, 2010), 4.
[76] Horace W. Raper, *William W. Holden: North Carolina's Political Enigma* (Chapel Hill: University of North Carolina Press, 1985), 159–60.

As Klan abuse increased throughout 1869, Holden successfully persuaded the Republican legislature to pass a new militia law that would allow him to declare counties to be in a state of insurrection and use the state militia to suppress it. After the murders of two Republicans – one black and one white – in Alamance and Caswell counties in February and May 1870, and with the midterm elections approaching, Holden used the new militia law to declare the two counties to be in a state of insurrection. He then appointed Colonel George Kirk as the commanding officer of the militia charged with restoring state rule. In the weeks that followed, Kirk arrested a number of high-profile residents of the counties and engaged in a battle with Klan members in a forest in Chatham County.[77]

The consequences of what came to be known as the Kirk–Holden war for the GOP were largely negative. In elections held in August 1870, Republicans lost four US House seats as well as their majorities in the state legislature. Meanwhile, the notables Kirk had jailed were quickly freed and Holden was impeached by the new Democratically controlled state legislature in March 1871.[78] With Klan violence decreasing by 1872, Tod R. Caldwell, who had been Holden's lieutenant governor and his successor as governor after his impeachment, won a tight race in the 1872 gubernatorial election, beating his Democratic opponent by fewer than 2,000 votes.[79] While Republicans also won some seats in the state legislature, both chambers remained solidly under Democratic control.

Caldwell would prove to be the last Republican governor in the state until 1896. The typical decline of the GOP in the former Confederacy in the 1870s played out in a unique way in North Carolina. First, while the party's electoral fortunes deteriorated from 1876 onwards, Republicans still remained surprisingly competitive. For example, while Republican gubernatorial candidates lost each election between 1876 and 1888, they consistently received more than 46 percent of the vote. Additionally, Republicans regularly won seats in the US House – as many as three out of nine seats (in 1888, 1894, and 1896) and generally at least one. In the state legislature, Republicans never won a majority but maintained a respectable level of representation throughout the 1870s and 1880s. In response, Democrats sought to disenfranchise black voters by adopting new voter registration restrictions in 1889. As a result, starting in 1890, Republicans saw a decline in support and lost 18 of their 35 seats in the Assembly and 6 of their 13 seats in the Senate. In the 1892 gubernatorial election, Republican vote share dropped to just 34 percent.[80] However, the

[77] Bradley, *Bluecoats & Tar Heels*, 217–32.   [78] Raper, *William W. Holden*, 199–219.

[79] Dubin, *United States Gubernatorial Elections, 1861–1911*, 413.

[80] Dubin, *Party Affiliations in the State Legislatures*, 141; Dubin, *United States Gubernatorial Elections, 1861–1911*, 17; Joseph F. Steelman, "Vicissitudes of Republican Party Politics: The Campaign of 1892 in North Carolina," *The North Carolina Historical Review* 43 (October 1966): 430–42.

GOP was thrown a temporary lifeline thanks to the rise of the Populist movement in North Carolina. With the Populist gubernatorial candidate receiving 17 percent of the vote in 1892, neither party came close to beating the Democrats – but combined the Republicans and Populists polled a majority. Thus, immediately after the 1892 election, Republican and Populist leaders began to consider the possibility of a fusion arrangement.[81]

To be sure, not all local Republican leaders supported cooperation with the Populists. Some, like John Baxter Eaves, the chairman of the state party's executive committee, strongly opposed the scheme because they feared it would require the party to share its patronage in the event of a GOP victory in the 1896 presidential election. In this view, maintaining a "pure" but losing Republican Party was more valuable than having to share the spoils of winning with the Populists. Other Republicans, such as (future senator) Jeter C. Pritchard, noted the simple reality that while whites might not be willing to vote Republican in some areas of the state, they would vote Populist. An additional hurdle in any fusion arrangement was that the Populist movement in North Carolina was largely white and not supportive of black civil rights. However, the one crucial issue both sides agreed on was the danger of the 1889 registration law, which Democrats used not just to exclude black voters but also white Populists.[82] A final consideration in favor of a fusion arrangement was that while a successful Republican–Populist coalition would require settling a number of policy disagreements once in office, if the GOP could actually win elections in North Carolina it would increase its influence nationally and thereby generate more patronage for the party.[83]

Despite ongoing opposition from Eaves and many black GOP leaders, negotiations with the Populists began in earnest in early 1894. With the midterm elections ahead, Populist leader Marion Butler showed a willingness to ignore the larger policy issues that divided the two parties – including economic issues like tariffs and the gold standard – and instead focus on what united them: opposition to the local Democratic Party. During the summer of 1894, the two organizations entered into a fusion arrangement whereby each would agree to either run a candidate at the county level or withdraw and endorse the other side.[84] The strategy frustrated many black Republicans (though some supported it), and Democrats used it to appeal to black voters in the 1894 election. Still, in both 1894 and 1896, the strategy was highly successful. Going into the 1894 election, Democrats held 77 percent of seats in the state Assembly and 92 percent of seats in the state Senate; after the election, Republicans and Populists combined to hold 62 percent of seats in the Assembly and 84 percent

---

[81] Joseph F. Steelman, "Republican Party Strategists and the Issue of Fusion with Populists in North Carolina, 1893–1894," *The North Carolina Historical Review* 47 (July 1970): 244–69.
[82] Ibid.   [83] Ibid., 253.   [84] Ibid., 259–64.

in the Senate.[85] In 1896, the coalition repeated its performance and successfully elected a Republican governor: Daniel Lindsay Russell.

While the coalition with the Populists meant a readjustment for black Republicans, they remained influential. Indeed, unlike in other ex-Confederate states, black Republicans won elected office in North Carolina as late as 1896. The most notable example of North Carolina's exceptionalism in this regard was the career of George Henry White. White was the last black Southerner to be elected to Congress before Jim Crow-era legislation disenfranchised blacks across the South. White represented the 2nd district of North Carolina – known as the "black second," a district packed with black Republicans to help elect Democrats in surrounding districts – which elected a series of black Republicans in the 1872–1901 period.[86] White's career in public service provides some insight into the possibilities available to North Carolina's black population in the late nineteenth century: before becoming a two-term US House member, White had been a state legislator, a district attorney (the only black prosecutor in the country at the time), and a delegate to two Republican National Conventions.[87] During his two terms in Congress, Eric Anderson notes that White "had the strong feeling he spoke for all the nation's Negroes" and not merely his own constituents, and opined frequently on the abuse that black Americans received in North Carolina and elsewhere.[88] White also followed suit in his role as legislator, introducing the first anti-lynching bill in Congress.

Although White was perhaps the most prominent of the black Republicans in North Carolina in this period, he was far from alone: the 2nd district elected about fifty black members of the state legislature, as well as "numerous mayors, town commissioners, registers of deeds, sheriffs, and clerks of court."[89] While disenfranchisement and segregation efforts existed, they had not yet been codified in law, and blacks were able to participate in society (including politics) at a level unlike most other Southern states. However, as Rob Christensen notes, "life for African Americans in the last decades of the nineteenth century was better in many ways than it would be for their children."[90] That is, the situation changed dramatically after the 1896 election, as white Democrats increasingly relied on violence to terrorize black voters and their white Republican supporters. While building up over several years, the critical juncture occurred in 1898 when the infamous Wilmington Insurrection resulted in what has been described as the only coup d'état in American

[85] Dubin, *Party Affiliations in the State Legislatures*, 141.
[86] Aside from White, who was elected in 1896 and 1898, three other blacks were elected to he House during this period: John Adams Hyman in 1874, James Edward O'Hara in 1882 and 1884, and Henry Plummer Cheatham in 1888 and 1890. On the black second, see Eric Anderson, *Race and Politics in North Carolina 1872–1901: The Black Second* (Baton Rouge: Louisiana State University, 1981).
[87] Christensen, *The Paradox of Tar Heel Politics*, 12.
[88] Anderson, *Race and Politics in North Carolina 1872–1901*, 280.
[89] Christensen, *The Paradox of Tar Heel Politics*, 14.   [90] Ibid., 12.

history.[91] Despite intimidation attempts by "Red Shirts" – a paramilitary arm of the Democratic Party in North Carolina – the 1898 election produced a victory for the Black-and-Tan fusionist ticket in Wilmington; while the newly elected mayor and two-thirds of the city's aldermen were white, black candidates were successfully elected despite the Democrats' scare tactics and voter disenfranchisement efforts. In response to these election results, a group of 500 armed whites destroyed the offices of the *Wilmington Daily Record*, the only remaining black newspaper in the state. Alfred Moore Waddell, the leader of white supremacists, described the destruction as follows in his memoirs:

A negro printing office was destroyed by a procession of perfectly sober men, but no person was injured until a negro deliberately and without provocation shot a white man, while others, armed and defiant, occupied the streets, and the result was that about twenty of them were killed and the rest of them were scattered ... On the evening of the day of this revolution the Mayor and Board of Alderman, then in charge of the city of Wilmington, one by one resigned and in the same order their successors were nominated and elected.[92]

Prior to the (forced) resignation of the mayor and aldermen, the group of white supremacists – which had now grown to over 2,000 people – had driven opposing white business and political leaders out of town. The subsequent resignation of the elected officials was a non-negotiable demand of the Red Shirts, and Waddell was named the new mayor. In a matter of days, the democratically elected leadership of an American city had been overthrown in a violent coup. Neither the federal nor the state government intervened.[93]

The Wilmington Insurrection had a dramatic effect on North Carolina politics. Democrats were emboldened to push for the full exclusion of blacks from state politics, while at the same time, white Republicans largely embraced the concept of a Lily-White party as an alternative to the Black-and-Tan version, given the increasingly hostile racial relations. As the *Hendersonville Times* noted, "politically we believe the 'elimination' of the negro from politics will be a blessing in disguise for the Republican Party" because with the "negro bug-a-boo eliminated, the whites of the South are sure to split on economic issues."[94] The Democratic majority in the state legislature passed a constitutional amendment in 1899 limiting suffrage, based on a literacy test and poll tax. Importantly, the North Carolina suffrage amendment included a

---

[91] On the Wilmington Insurrection, see David S. Cecelski and Timothy B. Tyson, eds., *Democracy Betrayed: The Wilmington Race Riot of 1898 and Its Legacy* (Chapel Hill: University of North Carolina Press, 1998). The Wilmington Insurrection is sometimes called the Wilmington Race Riot (this was the term used by white Democrats) and the Wilmington Massacre.

[92] Alfred Moore Waddell, *Some Memories of My Life* (Raleigh: Edwards & Broughton Printing Company, 1908), 243–44.

[93] Christensen, *The Paradox of Tar Heel Politics*, 22–27.

[94] Cited in Jeffrey J. Crow and Robert F. Durden, *Maverick Republican in the Old North State: A Political Biography of Daniel L. Russell* (Baton Rouge: Louisiana State University Press, 1977), 138–39.

"grandfather clause," which excluded any citizens or those in direct lineage to them who had held voting rights prior to 1867 from the requirements of the new law. The intended effect of the amendment – which would still need to be ratified at the polls in 1900 – was clear: since slaves did not have voting rights prior to the Civil War, but poor whites often did, the suffrage amendment would almost exclusively affect blacks.[95]

Despite opposition to the amendment by Republican Governor Russell, who called on all non-Democrats in the state to oppose the effort to make black voters the key issue in the 1900 elections, the Populists – who had previously worked amicably with the Republicans but did not support black civil rights – refused to condemn the suffrage amendment.[96] Meanwhile, Republicans actively discouraged black party members from running for public office in the 1900 election, arguing that black candidates would only buttress the Democrats' argument in favor of the suffrage amendment. During the campaign, the Red Shirts once again terrorized black voters and newspaper offices and editors who did not support their white supremacist views. Even Russell did not vote on election day: voting would have required him to travel to Wilmington, which he feared would lead to further riots. In the end, the suffrage amendment was ratified by a landslide vote – 182,217 to 128,285 – and black citizens, from 1900 onwards, would face serious hurdles that would prevent them from participating in elections.[97]

The negative effects of the suffrage amendment on black participation in North Carolina elections were particularly clear in the 2nd district: while George H. White had won reelection in 1898 by a reasonably comfortable margin (49.5 against 42.1 percent of the vote), based largely on support from black voters, he chose not to run for reelection given the disenfranchisement legislation and political violence. In an interview with the *New York Times*, White explained that he could not "live in North Carolina and be treated as a man" and had made up his "mind not to be a candidate for renomination to Congress."[98] The Democratic candidate in the 1900 election (during which blacks were not yet banned from voting but faced the threat of violence from Red Shirt Democrats if they chose to vote) won White's seat with nearly 65 percent of the vote. By 1902, after the implementation of the new voting laws, the Democratic candidate won the seat without a Republican opponent – and received 99 percent of the vote.[99]

[95] Crow and Durden, *Maverick Republican*, 142; James M. Beeby, *Revolt of the Tar Heels: The North Carolina Populist Movement, 1890–1901* (Jackson: University Press of Mississippi, 2008), 191.

[96] Crow and Durden, *Maverick Republican*, 150.

[97] Ibid., 155–56; Beeby, *Revolt of the Tar Heels*, 209–10.

[98] Cited in Benjamin R. Justesen, *George Henry White: An Even Chance in the Race of Life* (Baton Rouge: Louisiana State University Press, 2001), 298. White would be the last black from the South to serve in Congress until the 1970s. For more on White, especially during his last years in Congress, see Dinnella-Borrego, *The Risen Phoenix*, 194–96.

[99] *CQ Press Guide to US Elections* (Washington DC: CQ Press, 2010), 1108, 1113, 1118.

The official takeover of the GOP by the Lily-Whites followed at the state party convention in August 1902. Earlier that month, Pritchard – who had been elected US senator by the state legislature in 1895 – had met with President Theodore Roosevelt at his vacation home in Oyster Bay, New York.[100] While it remains unclear exactly what the two discussed, Pritchard presented the conversation as an endorsement of his plan to create a "respectable" Republican Party in the South, which – in Pritchard's assessment – required the complete expulsion of blacks from the party, so that the GOP could appeal to white voters again.[101] At the state convention a week later, Pritchard succeeded in banning participation of all black Republicans, producing the first true Lily-White Republican state convention.[102] Initially, Roosevelt did not appear bothered by this move against blacks: in September of 1902, the president went on a tour of the South, which included speeches in North Carolina and featured appearances by Pritchard. During his talks, Roosevelt avoided the issue of race and instead focused on "the patriotism of the South in the Revolution ... as well as the valor of both sides in the civil war,"[103] while also reminding the crowds that his mother had been born in Georgia.

However, by October 1902, Roosevelt's tone had changed. During a meeting with representatives of the Afro-American Council, he expressed his opposition to the Lily-White movements.[104] Later that month, black Republicans – with the apparent support of the Roosevelt administration – gathered in North Carolina to discuss possible ways to overcome the Lily-White takeover of the party.[105] By December 1902, Pritchard and Roosevelt were on a collision course, with Pritchard arguing that the Lily-White movement was not about exclusion of blacks, but rather securing a future for the Republican Party and – by essentially deescalating racial conflict – safeguarding black North Carolinians in the process:

There has been no disposition on the part of the Republican Party in North Carolina to prevent the colored man from participating as a delegate in any convention to which he may be elected by those who are duly qualified voters; the Republicans in North Carolina simply refused to adopt any policy which has a tendency to create strife and contention among our people as a whole. Every wise colored man knows that anything approaching negro domination in the South would result in disaster for the Republican Party and lasting injury to the colored race.[106]

In Alabama – where Roosevelt was engaged in a similar conflict with local Lily-Whites – the president would continue to support the Black-and-Tans until at least 1904. But in North Carolina, he capitulated quickly. One possible explanation for

[100] "President Starts Today," *Washington Post*, August 22, 1902.
[101] "To Reform Party," *Washington Post*, August 22, 1902.
[102] "Barred by Whites," *Washington Post*, August 29, 1902.
[103] "Last Day in Dixie," *Washington Post*, September 10, 1902.
[104] "Negroes in Politics," *Washington Post*, October 8, 1902.
[105] "The Administration and Southern Politics," *New York Times*, October 20, 1902.
[106] "'Lily-Whites' Will Fight," *New York Times*, December 3, 1902.

this difference is that in Alabama the official party organization was under the control of Black-and-Tans before the 1902 clash. In contrast, Pritchard – as an incumbent senator – had a legitimate claim to the control of the North Carolina machine and the division of patronage in the state. In late December 1902, Roosevelt agreed to nominate a Lily-White selected by Pritchard for collector of customs at Newberne.[107] By February 1903, Roosevelt abandoned his plans to appoint a black man – Samuel H. Vick – postmaster at Wilson, and instead followed Pritchard's recommendations again.[108] Later that year, Roosevelt nominated Pritchard to be a justice on the DC district court.[109] The Lily-White takeover of the North Carolina Republican Party was thus complete.

The noxious way in which Democrats excluded black North Carolinians from the political sphere can help explain why black Republicans were banned entirely from their state's delegation after the 1900 convention. To some extent, black Republicans were a victim of their own success; by participating not only actively but also successfully in their state's political system prior to the 1898 Wilmington Insurrection, they inspired a level of vitriol in the Democratic white supremacist movement that not only disenfranchised black voters but also jump-started the GOP's Lily-White wing. The situation was not helped by the success of the fusion agreement with the Populists in 1894 and 1896, which elevated the Lily-Whites and introduced a number of Populists into the GOP who opposed black civil rights. In effect, white Republicans in North Carolina chose to "blame the victims," by scapegoating their black party members for the 1898–1900 demise of the state Republican Party: in 1902, Lily-White Republicans began to officially exclude black Republicans from the state party.[110] By 1904, only four delegates to the national convention were black; by 1908 there were none – and there would be none thereafter.

The decline of the Black-and-Tan organization in North Carolina was thus largely – though not exclusively – the product of state-level politics. The most important cause was clearly the terror inflicted on black and (to a lesser extent) white Republicans by Democratic organizations. As Democrats successfully prevented blacks from participating in electoral politics in North Carolina, Lily-White Republicans in the state pushed black political leaders out of the party – at least in part based on the hope that this would make the party electorally competitive again. Still, national politics did play into North

---

[107] "'Lily-Whites' Gain Point," *New York Times*, December 21, 1902.
[108] "Negroes Lose Fight in North Carolina," *New York Times*, February 17, 1903.
[109] Justesen, *George Henry White*, 387.
[110] Glenda Elizabeth Gilmore, "False Friends and Avowed Enemies: Southern African Americans and Party Allegiances in the 1920s," in Jane Elizabeth Dailey and Glenda Elizabeth Gilmore, eds., *Jumpin' Jim Crow: Southern Politics from Civil War to Civil Rights* (Princeton, NJ: Princeton University Press, 2000), 223. See also Richard B. Sherman, *The Republican Party and Black America: From McKinley to Hoover, 1896–1933* (Charlottesville: University Press of Virginia, 1973), 29–36; David C. Roller, "The Republican Party of North Carolina, 1900–1916" (Doctoral dissertation, Duke University, 1965), 100–10.

Carolina's internal development: Theodore Roosevelt – concerned that Southern states would support his rival Mark Hanna at the 1904 convention – challenged some new Lily-White organizations, while accepting others. In this regard, Roosevelt's failure to maintain his challenge to the new Lily-White organization in 1902–03 strengthened this group's hand. Indeed, Roosevelt's unwillingness to give up his opposition to the Alabama Lily-Whites likely kept the Black-and-Tan organization there in control well into the 1920s. In North Carolina, however, the Pritchard machine was quickly acknowledged as the official Republican Party.

In terms of actual political success, the Lily-Whites were not very effective in mobilizing white voters to their side. Indeed, after the exclusion of blacks from the party, the new Lily-Whites focused mostly on competing internally over control of the patronage that continued to come from Republican presidential administrations.[111] In 1908, Republicans managed to win three North Carolina House seats, igniting a temporary hope that a breakthrough in the South would be possible. Two years later, however, Democrats regained all three seats. Thus, while North Carolina remained somewhat more hospitable to the GOP than most other Southern states, Democrats maintained their comfortable majorities in the state legislature and continued to dominate gubernatorial elections. And the North Carolina Republicans remained the clear minority party.

ALABAMA: THE SLOW RISE OF LILY-WHITEISM

The post-Civil War lapse of Alabama's GOP organization into Lily-Whiteism was not the product of a specific set of major events. Instead, for much of the period following the war, the Alabama Republican Party – which enjoyed a short period of domination in state politics (see Table 7.4 and Figure 7.7) – was characterized by intra-partisan infighting, with groups organized around different party leaders. While these groups had some concrete differences of opinion on policy issues, they each generally included white scalawags and carpetbaggers as well as blacks. After Alabama embraced Jim Crow disfranchisement with a new constitution in 1901, attempts were made to turn the party into an all-white organization, but actions by President Theodore Roosevelt prevented such a takeover. Instead, Lily-Whiteism came to Alabama slowly – with white party leaders actively reducing black participation at national conventions starting in 1912. In the twelve years that followed, the party's white leadership slowly but surely phased out black convention representation until 1924, when the Alabama delegation was (and would remain) entirely white (see Figure 7.8).

---

[111] David C. Roller, "Republican Factionalism in North Carolina, 1904–1906," *The North Carolina Historical Review* 41 (January 1964): 62–73.

TABLE 7.4 *Descriptive Republican Party success in Alabama, 1865–1968*

	1865–1877	1878–1896	1897–1932	1933–1968
Presidential candidate won the state?	✓			✓
Senatorial candidate elected?	✓			
Gubernatorial candidate elected?	✓			
At least one House candidate elected?	✓	✓	✓	✓

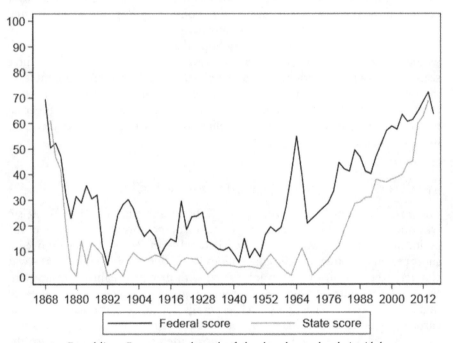

FIGURE 7.7 Republican Party strength at the federal and state levels in Alabama, 1868–2012

* * * * *

In 1867, Republicans dominated the convention that created the new constitution required for Alabama to be readmitted to the Union. Subsequently, Alabama voters had to approve the constitution in an election held in February 1868, which also included votes for governor, state legislative offices, and congressional seats. However, the other election results would only count if voters approved the new constitution. For the gubernatorial race, Republicans

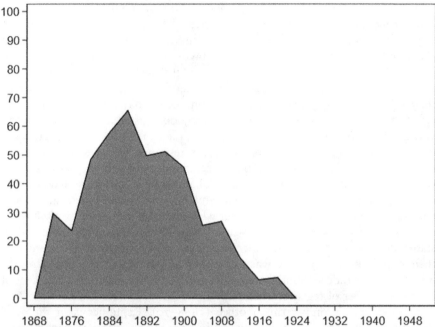

FIGURE 7.8 Percentage of GOP convention delegation from Alabama that was black, 1868–1952
Source: Data collected by authors.

nominated William Hugh Smith – a white plantation owner and former slave-holder. Smith represented one major wing of the new Republican Party in Alabama: white Southerners who had opposed secession but were not the strongest supporters of civil rights for freedmen. Smith's nomination was opposed by black leaders in the party, including James Thomas Rapier, who would go on to serve in Congress and play an important part in GOP politics in Alabama in the 1870s. Notably, while blacks made up 90 percent of the GOP's electoral base (in the estimation of Democratic newspapers at the time), the statewide Republican ticket for 1868, and in nearly all elections after, was entirely white.[112]

---

[112] Note that the Republican Party also had some white support among small farmers in the northern part of the state. Indeed, the major economic cleavage among Alabama whites was between the large plantation owners in the southern part of the state, and the small farmers in the northern part of the state. This cleavage would later fuel the major Populist movement in the state in the 1890s. See Loren Schweninger, *James T. Rapier and Reconstruction* (Chicago: University of Chicago Press, 1978), 63; Michael W. Fitzgerald, "Radical Republicanism and the White Yeomanry during Alabama Reconstruction, 1865–1868," *The Journal of Southern History* 54 (November 1988): 565–96.

The 1868 election proved to be a success for the GOP, but with a major assist from Radical Republicans in Congress. At the time of the election, the requirement for ratification of the constitution was that a majority of all *registered* voters would need to vote in favor of the newly proposed constitution. Democrats – who otherwise boycotted the election and thus did not run any candidates – therefore determined that their best strategy was to encourage their supporters to register but stay home on election day. This proved to be an effective approach: out of approximately 170,000 registered voters only 71,000 voted in favor of the new constitution. Thus, the constitution was rejected and the other election results declared invalid. In response, Congress passed a new Reconstruction Act that declared that only a majority of votes actually cast was required for ratification. As a result, Alabama's new constitution was retroactively ratified, the state readmitted, and Republicans installed and in full control of the state government.[113] But while the GOP came out of 1868 holding all of the state's congressional seats, nearly all state legislative seats, and all statewide offices,[114] the backdoor ratification of the constitution meant that their popularity in the state was not nearly as strong as the election results might indicate. Indeed, Smith received just 68,397 votes – around 40 percent of the total number of registered voters.[115]

During Smith's only term in office (1868–70), Republicans in the state legislature were predominantly white and – over the objection of black Republicans and carpetbaggers – quickly moved to end the suffrage restrictions that the new constitution had placed on white Alabamians implicated in the Confederacy. Many of the scalawags had opposed the Confederacy and had even fought on the Union side during the war, though some were also former slave owners. Regardless, many believed that their fellow white Southerners – in the words of future Republican Governor David P. Lewis – "were forced into rebellion against their votes & their wishes" through the actions of Confederate leaders.[116] Banning them from electoral participation after the war, in this view, was neither fair nor would it help the Republican Party establish itself in the South.

Yet, as the Republican scalawags lifted restrictions on white voting, black voters became the target of violence and threats from the KKK and other white terrorist groups. Rapier, who had become one of the major representatives of black voters in the GOP, fled his home in September 1868 when a group of

---

[113] William Warren Rogers, *Black Belt Scalawag: Charles Hays and the Southern Republicans in the Era of Reconstruction* (Athens: University of Georgia Press 1993), 25.

[114] After the 1868 election, Republicans held 32 of 33 state Senate seats and 97 of 100 Assembly seats. See Dubin, *Party Affiliations in the State Legislatures*, 16; Rogers, *Black Belt Scalawag*, 30.

[115] Dubin, *United States Gubernatorial Elections, 1861–1911*, 4.

[116] Sarah Van V. Woolfolk, "Amnesty and Pardon and Republicanism in Alabama," *The Alabama Historical Quarterly* 26 (1964): 240–48, 242.

whites roamed the countryside looking for blacks to blame for a fire in a local school. Rapier escaped unharmed, but three other black men were captured and lynched.[117] Around the same time, a friend of Rapier's reported that whites were prowling around other parts of the state "intimidating and threatening the Negroes" and that "[a] mood of terrorism and anarchy" reigned in Alabama.[118] In the face of this violence, black Republican leaders refused to back down: as Rapier explained in a speech celebrating the ratification of the Fifteenth Amendment, Alabama was as much his home as it was that of whites.[119] Still, political activity by black Alabamians came at considerable personal risk.

Between 1870 and 1876, the GOP did score occasional successes, largely on the basis of appeals to voters in the state's "black belt" – rural counties known for their dark soil with a large number of cotton plantations and black inhabitants. Because of this, party leaders believed it was important to run black candidates and elect "such of their number as are worthy and competent, to places of honor, profit, and trust."[120] In this regard, Rapier was nominated as the party's candidate for secretary of state in 1870, on the same ticket that renominated Smith. The Republican ticket went down to defeat, and Democrats won a considerable majority in the state assembly.[121] While Rapier won fewer votes than Smith, the difference was relatively minor. Still, after 1870 the GOP ran only all-white statewide tickets. In the 1872 election, the Republican Party saw a momentary resurgence. With Lewis as its candidate, Republicans won a relatively comfortable victory in the gubernatorial election, and while the party was now in the minority in the state legislature, it won back a considerable number of seats.[122] Notably, 1872 also saw Rapier win a seat in Congress, the second consecutive black Republican – Benjamin J. Turner being the first – to hold an Alabama House seat.[123]

---

[117] Schweninger, *James T. Rapier and Reconstruction*, 68–69.   [118] Cited in ibid., 70.

[119] As Rapier noted: "I was born in Alabama and do not know any other place. My mother and father are buried in Alabama on the banks of the beautiful Tennessee river. I have no home in Africa. I expect to stay here." Cited in ibid., 73.

[120] Cited in ibid., 74.

[121] Rapier performed worse than Smith in the statewide vote. Rapier received 72,237 votes while Smith received 76,282. Smith lost his reelection by fewer than 1,500 votes. See ibid., 82; Dubin, *Party Affiliations in the State Legislatures*, 16.

[122] Republicans lost their majority in the state senate which had the first election since 1868. Democrats maintained their majority in the state assembly in 1872, but the differences between the two parties were minor: Republicans won 42 percent of seats in the Senate and 46 percent in the Assembly. See Dubin, *Party Affiliations in the State Legislatures*, 16.

[123] In between his failed run as secretary of state and his election to Congress, Rapier served as assessor of internal revenue, a nomination that received considerable criticism from white conservatives, including Republicans. Additionally, Rapier was also involved in union politics. In Congress, Rapier focused much of his attention on black civil rights. See Loren Schweninger, *James T. Rapier and Reconstruction* (Chicago: University of Chicago Press, 1978), 94–105, 117–32; Loren Schweninger, "James Rapier and the Negro Labor Movement, 1869–1872," *Alabama Review* 28 (July 1975): 185–201; Eugene Feldman, "James T. Rapier, Negro

While these results might have given Republicans hope that they could continue to compete for elected office in Alabama, a major Democratic surge in the 1874 election effectively ended the two-party system. This was largely the product of Democrats "drawing the color line," or framing the election as a battle between blacks and whites in the state. Prior to 1874, Democrats – who largely represented the plantation owners in the southern part of the state – had struggled in their appeals to white voters in the northern part of the state who were largely small farmers. By drawing a strict color line and framing the election in racial terms, Democrats hoped to overcome "the ancient economic, social, and political differences between planters and small farmers."[124] Democrats also stepped up their campaign of terror against blacks. Many black workers who registered to vote were fired by their white employers, GOP campaign meetings were disrupted by armed whites, and several Republicans – mostly blacks, but some whites as well – were murdered.[125] While the terror unleashed on Republicans did not actually result in a major decline in votes for the party (despite massive voting irregularities on election day[126]), framing the 1874 election as a referendum on black versus white rule in the state inspired white Democrats to vote: Democratic candidates received significantly higher vote totals than they had in previous elections. Both Lewis and Rapier lost their battles for reelection.[127]

After the 1874 election, the Republican Party faced considerable decline. While the GOP still won two out of eight seats in Congress (down from six in 1872), the "fortunes of the state Republican party had never been lower."[128]

Congressman from Alabama," *The Phylon Quarterly* 19 (1958): 417–23; Sarah Woolfolk Wiggins, *The Scalawag in Alabama Politics, 1865–1881* (Tuscaloosa: The University of Alabama Press, 2015), 53.

[124] Wiggins, *The Scalawag in Alabama Politics*, 91.

[125] When Charles Hays, by then a member of Congress in his third term, produced an extensive written account of the terror that had gripped Alabama, Republican newspapers presented it as evidence of Democratic criminal behavior, while Democratic newspapers dismissed Hays as a liar. Indeed, Hays's biographer William Warren Rogers notes that some of the claims Hays made in his assessment of Democratic violence against blacks and other Republicans were clearly incorrect while others were at least debatable, and that Hays gave "credence to various rumors and sensationalized alleged incidents in melodramatic prose." Yet, as reporter at the *Hartford Courant* wrote in a private letter at the time: "there has evidently been enough persecution [in Alabama] to establish a good case without alluding to acts of violence not well authenticated." Rogers, *Black Belt Scalawag*, 111–15.

[126] Wiggins, *The Scalawag in Alabama Politics*, 97.

[127] Rapier received 19,169 votes in 1874 versus 19,127 votes in 1872. His opponent in 1874 received 3,980 votes more than the Democratic candidate in 1872. At the gubernatorial level, Lewis received 93,928 votes in 1874 versus 89,868 votes in 1872. However, his Democratic opponent in 1872 received only 81,371 votes while the winner of the 1874 election, George S. Houston, received 107,118 votes. Meanwhile, Hays won reelection but in his district there was "an appreciably increased turnout of white voters" as well. See Schweninger, *James T. Rapier and Reconstruction*, 147; Dubin, *United States Gubernatorial Elections*, 6–7; Rogers, *Black Belt Scalawag*, 119.

[128] Rogers, *Black Belt Scalawag*, 125.

Indeed, the GOP would not elect another Alabama governor until 1986, and Democrats would maintain their majorities in the state legislature well into the 2000s. Thus, from 1875 onwards the GOP became increasingly focused on controlling federal patronage and determining which wing of the party would get to send delegates to the national convention.[129] In 1876, former governor Smith successfully took control of the state party after ending a previously existing coalition with Senator George E. Spencer. The Smith group succeeded in claiming control over that year's national convention delegation, sending among others Smith and Jeremiah Haralson, a black Republican elected to Congress in 1874.[130] The Spencer wing of the party subsequently nominated their own delegation – including Spencer, Hays, and Rapier – but failed to get seated.[131] While both wings had planned to run competing Republican tickets in the 1876 gubernatorial election, pressure from RNC Chairman Zachary Chandler resulted in a unified Republican ticket, which (unsurprisingly) went down to defeat in the general election.[132]

Chandler's peacekeeping attempts could not prevent partisan self-sabotage, which undermined the GOP's electoral goals in the congressional elections. With Rapier out of office since 1874, Haralson was now the top black elected official in Alabama.[133] Yet Haralson's association with Smith meant that he was not as supportive of civil rights as Rapier wanted. Thus, in 1876, Rapier and Haralson both sought the Republican nomination in the 4th district. Rapier received the nomination and, in response, Haralson ran as an independent. The two candidates split the (black) Republican vote, and Democrat Charles Shelley won the election.[134] That same year, Republicans also lost their other remaining congressional seat, the gubernatorial election, and more seats in the state legislature.[135]

---

[129] Of course, patronage had always been an important goal of intra-party politics and had been the basis of many of the feuds that divided the Alabama GOP. See Michael W. Fitzgerald, "Republican Factionalism and Black Empowerment: The Spencer–Warner Controversy and Alabama Reconstruction, 1868–1880," *The Journal of Southern History* 64 (August 1998): 473–94.

[130] Wiggins, *The Scalawag in Alabama Politics*, 111–12.

[131] Schweninger, *James T. Rapier and Reconstruction*, 152.

[132] Wiggins, *The Scalawag in Alabama Politics*, 114.

[133] Between 1870 and 1876 there was consistently one black Republican representing Alabama in Congress: Benjamin S. Turner represented Alabama's 1st district in the 42nd Congress but lost reelection in 1872 when he was challenged by another black candidate running as an independent. The two candidates split the vote, resulting in a white Democrat winning the seat. Rapier represented Alabama's 2nd district in the 43rd Congress. Haralson represented Alabama's 1st district in the 44th Congress.

[134] Schweninger, *James T. Rapier and Reconstruction*, 153–57.

[135] Democratic gubernatorial candidate Houston received 61.4 percent of the vote in the 1876 election. Republicans were left with zero seats in the state Senate and lost half their seats in the state Assembly (leaving just 20 out of 100 seats). See Dubin, *United States Gubernatorial Elections*, 8; Dubin, *Party Affiliations in the State Legislatures*, 16.

After the 1876 clash, the Smith and Spencer wings remained in opposition. Under President Hayes, representatives of both wings received federal appointments. These appointments included former Governor Lewis, and a number of other representatives of the Smith wing.[136] Still, the Smith wing did not fully dominate in this regard either: Rapier was appointed collector of internal revenue for the 2nd district of Alabama in 1878, guaranteeing him some level of influence in the local GOP in the years that followed.[137]

In focusing exclusively on control of federal patronage, the GOP factions essentially ceased competing in state elections. With the exception of those congressional districts that included most of the black belt, the Republicans after 1876 rarely ran candidates and occasionally supported independents instead. Such attempts at cooperation were complicated by the GOP's ongoing image as the "black" party, despite the dominance of white scalawags. In northern Alabama, local Republicans occasionally supported third parties with the promise that they would receive support in other races in exchange. Such support rarely appeared. As historian Samuel L. Webb concludes, independents and Republicans lacked the voting power to win on their own, but if the independents "openly aligned with the GOP, they risked losing many of their supporters."[138]

Still, independents and Republicans managed to cooperate enough to keep Democrats on their toes. In the 1890s in particular, Democrats faced multiple independent gubernatorial runs by Reuben F. Kolb, the former state commissioner of agriculture, with the backing of northern white farmers. Democratic leaders had blocked Kolb from winning their party's gubernatorial nomination in 1890, causing a major schism in the Democratic alliance. In response, Kolb and his supporters organized a Populist party, which came close to defeating the Democrats in the gubernatorial election and won a number of seats in the state legislature.[139] Populists never won the governorship in Alabama, and their strength in the state legislature did not increase much in the years that followed, largely because of extensive voter fraud by the Democrats as well as the disenfranchisement of poor whites. In 1894, a subset of the Kolb-affiliated Democrats proposed an all-white primary as a solution, arguing that by excluding blacks from the political process, the regular Democratic leadership would allow fair competition with the Populists.[140]

---

[136] Wiggins, *The Scalawag in Alabama Politics*, 119–23.

[137] Schweninger, *James T. Rapier and Reconstruction*, 170–71.

[138] Samuel L. Webb, *Two-Party Politics in the One-Party South: Alabama's Hill Country, 1874–1920* (Tuscaloosa: The University of Alabama Press, 2018), 94.

[139] Kolb received 47.7 percent of the vote, and the Populists won 7 seats (out of 33) in the state Senate and 38 (out of 100) in the Assembly. See Dubin, *Party Affiliations in the State Legislatures*, 16; Dubin, *United States Gubernatorial Elections*, 17.

[140] Webb, *Two-Party Politics in the One-Party South*, 133.

As the Populist boom declined in the second half of the 1890s, the white northern voters in Alabama that had constituted this challenge to regular Democratic rule in the state did not return to their traditional party. Instead, for the first time in decades, Republican candidates began to receive some level of support among white voters. In 1900, in particular, Republican vote totals were considerably higher than usual – even despite the fraud and disfranchisement perpetrated by the Democrats. For example, in several counties, William Jennings Bryan received less than 50 percent of the vote, and even lost to William McKinley in twelve of them. In the wake of this election, Democrats were once again concerned that a coalition of blacks and poor whites could end their domination of state politics. And they determined that the solution was the permanent exclusion of blacks from electoral participation. In 1901, a new constitution was ratified that effectively banned black participation in Alabama elections.[141]

The ratification of the new constitution instigated the first attempt by white Republicans to expel blacks entirely from the party. In doing so, the Alabama Lily-Whites locked horns with President Theodore Roosevelt. As noted in Chapter 5, Roosevelt's positions on race and GOP organizations were largely influenced by his own political calculations. Facing the possibility of a convention challenge for the presidential nomination in 1904 from Mark Hanna, Roosevelt supported or opposed different versions of Southern GOP organizations based on whether they were loyal to Hanna or not. In the case of Alabama, the 1901 constitution set in motion attempts at reconfiguring the Alabama GOP as an electorally competitive party, this time along racial lines. As the *New York Times* reported, this new batch of Alabama Lily-Whites, led by attorney J. A. W. Smith, included a number of Democrats who "voted the Democratic ticket only on the race issue, and are really sympathetic with most of the Republican principles"[142] and who sought to "establish the new white party in public confidence."[143]

Initially, the Alabama Lily-Whites assumed that they were working with Roosevelt's support. However, in the fall of 1902, Roosevelt twice chose to appoint Democrats recommended by Booker T. Washington to federal offices rather than go through the Lily-White Republicans.[144] In November 1902, Roosevelt raised the stakes by not only removing Julian H. Bingham, collector of internal revenue and member of the RNC, from his federal office, but also explicitly linking the removal to the Lily-White movement. In a statement, Postmaster General Henry Clay Payne warned the South that "[neither] the Administration nor the Republican Party of the North will stand for the

[141] Ibid., 155–72.
[142] "White Republican Party in the South," *New York Times*, October 21, 1902.
[143] "The Administration and Southern Politics," *New York Times*, October 20, 1902.
[144] "The President Snubs 'White' Republicans," *New York Times*, October 8, 1902; "President's Attitude in Southern Politics," *New York Times*, October 25, 1902.

exclusion of any section of our people by reason of their race or color."[145] As discussed previously, Roosevelt quickly abandoned this anti-Lily-White pos-ition in North Carolina, but not in Alabama where he created a new organiza-tion – known as the President's Board of Referees – to distribute federal patronage. The membership of the board included both white and black Republicans,[146] and the board remained active throughout 1903, with the goal of replacing the leftover office-holders from the McKinley era with Black-and-Tan-approved Roosevelt appointees.[147]

In December 1903, an attempt at uniting the two factions at a White House meeting failed when the Lily-Whites rejected all offers to share power with the Black-and-Tans. Instead, they threatened to throw their support to Hanna at the 1904 convention.[148] Hanna's death in February 1904 removed the power of this threat and left Roosevelt the only real choice for the GOP nomination. At the 1904 convention, the Black-and-Tans controlled the Alabama delega-tion, while the Lily-White leaders were not present.

Roosevelt's intervention in Alabama between 1901 and 1904 saved Black-and-Tan control of the party, if only temporarily. In both 1904 and 1908, blacks made up about 25 percent of delegates to the national convention. But the Lily-White takeover came eventually in Alabama, albeit through a much slower process. In 1912, during the Taft–Roosevelt clash, the Alabama GOP (like most other Southern states) backed Taft with a biracial delegation led by Oscar D. Street, a white man and US Attorney who had taken charge of the party.[149] In the years that followed, the new local party leaders (led by Street) began to shrink the level of black participation in the party. In 1916, Alabama's delegation size was reduced due to the new convention rules and black repre-sentation was down to just two delegates. By 1924, black representation was zero and would remain so through the rest of the Jim Crow era.

Alabama's Republican Party was thus unique in crucial ways. First, unlike many other states, the party did not develop clear-cut Lily-White and Black-and-Tan organizations until relatively late. Indeed, while race was undeniably a core issue facing and dividing the party from Reconstruction onwards, the wings that battled for control between 1868 and 1901 were mixed to some degree. The 1901 adoption of the Jim Crow constitution in Alabama did produce a pure Lily-White movement, but national politics thwarted its attempts to fully exclude blacks from the party. Notably, Roosevelt's interven-tion in this regard was largely based on his own political considerations. With an eye toward winning the 1904 nomination, Roosevelt backed the

[145] "President Deals 'Lily-Whites' Another Blow," *New York Times*, November 11, 1902.
[146] "Roosevelt Boom in Alabama," *New York Times*, May 7, 1903.
[147] "Party Axe in Alabama," *New York Times*, November 15, 1903.
[148] "Alabama Factions Split," *New York Times*, December 16, 1903.
[149] Paul D. Casdorph, *Republicans, Negroes, and Progressives in the South, 1912–1916* (Tusca-loosa: The University of Alabama Press, 1981), 70, 94–95.

Black-and-Tans – since the Lily-Whites in the state favored Mark Hanna. Still, total Lily-Whiteism eventually emerged in Alabama. By 1912, those Republicans loyal to Taft gained control of the party organization and began to slowly exclude blacks. Twelve years later black representation at the national convention had disappeared entirely. Beginning in 1924, the Alabama GOP – like the North Carolina GOP sixteen years earlier – was an exclusively Lily-White party.

CONCLUSION

The Lily-White factions in the state Republican parties in Virginia, Texas, North Carolina, and Alabama all took control of the local party organization at some point in the late nineteenth and early twentieth centuries, and used this control to severely limit black participation within the party. In each of these four states, the result was not just that whites held positions of power in the party, or that they represented a majority of delegates at state and national conventions, but that blacks were entirely (or nearly so) banned from any leadership role in the party.

While the outcomes were similar, the paths toward them were not. In two states – Virginia and North Carolina – the development of "strong" Lily-Whiteism was the product of choices made by local white party leaders with the hope of improving the party's electoral competitiveness. In Virginia, Lily-Whiteism was largely the consequence of decisions made by white party leaders like William Mahone and the Slemp family in response to the anti-black politics of the Democrats. In North Carolina, it was mostly the result of actions by Senator Jeter C. Pritchard, who after the dramatic events of the 1898 and 1900 elections used the 1902 state convention to expel blacks. In both Virginia and North Carolina, this form of Lily-Whiteism did not actually produce a competitive Republican Party, but it did result in the (near) full exclusion of blacks.

In Texas, Lily-Whiteism developed as a response to internal state party politics – in particular, the leadership of Norris Wright Cuney, the black leader of the party in the 1880s and 1890s. However, unlike in Virginia and North Carolina, the context of the Lily-White takeover was rooted in national party politics: the end of the Cuney machine followed his failure to get his delegates seated at the 1896 convention. By supporting Allison instead of McKinley, Cuney bet on the wrong candidate – and the McKinley forces at the national convention seated the Lily-White delegation instead. In the years that followed, the Texas Lily-Whites secured their control over the state party, and expelled the black Texans that had previously dominated the state party and national delegations. Finally, in Alabama, national politics *prevented* an early Lily-White takeover. While Theodore Roosevelt did not stop the Pritchard Lily-White takeover in North Carolina, he refused to accept such an outcome in Alabama. As a result, the local Black-and-Tan faction succeeded in maintaining control through 1912. Still, this faction fell too – once again because of national politics. The Lily-Whites produced a pro-Taft set of delegates at the 1912 convention and were seated. As a result, they gained control of the party organization and began a slow but consistent process of reducing the number of black delegates at conventions in 1916 and 1920, until by 1924 the delegation was (and would remain) entirely white.

8

Arkansas, Louisiana, Florida, and Tennessee

In contrast to the "strong" Lily-White organizations discussed in Chapter 7, Lily-White groups that took control of the Republican state organizations in Arkansas, Louisiana, Florida, and Tennessee never entirely excluded blacks from political participation within the party. To be sure, black GOP representation was minimized by these Lily-White leaders. But they did not engage in the type of exclusion that occurred in Virginia, Texas, North Carolina, and Alabama. Why did Lily-Whiteism play out so differently in these four states?

As the cases presented in this chapter show, the "soft" version of Lily-Whiteism was mostly the product of state-specific political contexts in which white party leaders sought to win control of the party but did not believe the complete exclusion of blacks was worth pursuing. In Arkansas and Louisiana, this was because – unlike in Virginia and North Carolina – there was no real expectation that electoral success was possible even as a white-dominated party. Thus, the goal was more to control federal patronage than to expel all blacks from the party. In Florida, which Herbert Hoover carried in the 1928 presidential election, white party leaders thought that a GOP resurgence might be possible, and they saw an opportunity to take control of the party. While blacks were kept from serving as delegates at the 1932 and 1936 national conventions, strict Lily-Whiteism would not last: after Florida repealed the poll tax in 1937, black Republicans began to organize politically again. And white Republicans in the state determined that it would be easier to provide these black Republicans with a small but consistent level of representation rather than to fight them on it. Finally, in Tennessee, the Republican party organization was long split between an eastern wing and a western wing. While the locus of state GOP power lay in the east and was led by whites, a Black-and-Tan organization was in power in the west. These Black-and-Tans cooperated with local *Democratic* leaders and remained in place until the 1952 convention – producing a small but consistent minority of black GOP delegates.

ARKANSAS: THE CLAYTON–REMMEL MACHINE

In Arkansas, Republicans won control of the state government in 1868 and
maintained their majorities through 1874. By then, the party was deeply
divided in a clash between two competing intra-party factions, which helped
Democrats regain control. In the decades that followed, the Arkansas GOP was
mostly ineffective in competing in elections – resulting in an electoral drought
that would last until the party's victory in the 1966 gubernatorial election (see
Table 8.1 and Figure 8.1). Throughout most of this period, the Arkansas

TABLE 8.1 *Descriptive Republican Party success in Arkansas, 1865–1968*

	1865–1877	1878–1896	1897–1932	1933–1968
Presidential candidate won the state?	✓			
Senatorial candidate elected?	✓			
Gubernatorial candidate elected?	✓			✓
At least one House candidate elected?	✓			✓

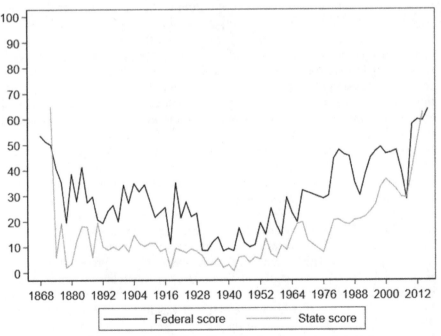

FIGURE 8.1 Republican Party strength at the federal and state levels in Arkansas,
1868–2012

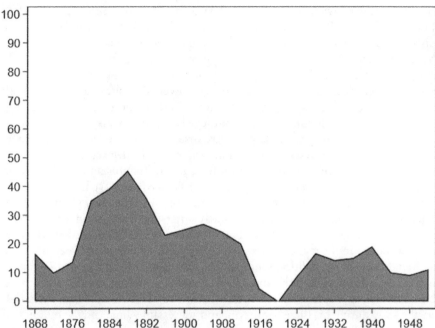

FIGURE 8.2 Percentage of GOP convention delegates from Arkansas that were black, 1868–1952
Source: Data collected by authors.

Republican Party was controlled by a Black-and-Tan coalition. In the early twentieth century, black influence in the party began to decline – though it remained higher than in many other Southern states at the time (see Figure 8.2). Starting in 1916, however, black representation dropped dramatically, and even reached zero in 1920 due to the (temporary) takeover of the party by more extreme Lily-Whites. However, the regular party organization regained control by 1924 and restored a party organization in which whites dominated, but blacks maintained some (small) level of influence.

* * * * *

The early development of the Republican Party in Arkansas followed that of most of the other ex-Confederate states. In March 1867, the first Reconstruction Act placed Arkansas and Mississippi in one military zone, for purposes of preparing the state for readmittance to the Union. A month later, the Republicans (composed of local Unionists, or scalawags; newcomers to the state, or carpetbaggers; and freedmen) convened their first convention in the state, and in November, Arkansas voters (including black men) voted to hold a constitutional convention and elect delegates. The convention convened in January 1868 in Little Rock, and thanks to black voting strength and the disfranchisement of Confederate leaders, the Republicans – including eight black delegates – dominated the convention.[1] A constitution was eventually adopted that provided voting rights for blacks (as well as the rights to hold office and serve on juries and in the militia), universal public education for both races, and sweeping powers to the governor, including the ability to appoint top state officials (including judges) without legislative approval.

In June 1868, Congress welcomed Arkansas back in the Union after voters narrowly ratified the new constitution and the state legislature ratified the Fourteenth Amendment in April. On July 2, 1868, Republican Powell Clayton was inaugurated as governor. Clayton was a Pennsylvania Quaker and former brigadier general in the Union army who purchased a Pine Bluff plantation and relocated his family to Arkansas shortly after the conclusion of the war. Clayton recognized very quickly that Unionists in the state needed to assert their authority in the face of aggressive behavior by ex-rebels and became active in Republican Party politics. Once in the governor's office, Clayton – characterized as a Radical Republican by his enemies – actively sought to foster a biracial GOP in the state. In terms of issue focus, Clayton sought to industrialize the state during his three-year term, and successfully financed the building of railroads and levees via a state bond issue.[2]

But even as he worked to modernize the Arkansas economy, Clayton's focus was continually drawn to domestic disturbances, chief among them the emergence and violence of the Ku Klux Klan.[3] In the spring of 1868, Klan chapters sprang up in various counties, as militant white Arkansans sought to disrupt the new Republican government. By fall, the Klan was focused on preventing the presidential election of Ulysses S. Grant and went on a reign of terror that left over 200 dead.[4] These included mostly black residents, as well as some whites – the most famous being James Hinds, US House member from the 2nd congressional district.[5] Clayton was determined to meet the Klan's violence head on, and he pushed the state legislature to pass a law to create a militia (which would include blacks). He also declared martial law in fourteen counties while nullifying or disallowing voter registration. In the end, Grant won a

[1] William A. Russ, Jr., "The Attempt to Create a Republican Party in Arkansas during Reconstruction," *Arkansas Historical Quarterly* 1 (1942): 206–22; Grif Stockley, *Ruled by Race: Black/White Relations in Arkansas from Slavery to the Present* (Fayetteville: University of Arkansas Press, 2009), 74–77.

[2] Orval Truman Diggs, Jr., "The Issues of the Powell Clayton Regime, 1868–1871," *Arkansas Historical Review* 8 (1949): 1–75.

[3] See Allen W. Trelease, *White Terror: The Ku Klux Klan Conspiracy and Southern Reconstruction* (Baton Rouge: Louisiana State University Press, 1971), 149–74.

[4] Ibid., 154.

[5] William B. Darrow, "The Killing of Congressman James Hinds," *Arkansas Historical Quarterly* 74 (2015): 18–55.

majority in Arkansas in November – tallying 53.7 percent of the vote – and by March 1869, Clayton's active use of the militia brought the Klan to heel.

The Republicans would control Arkansas state government through 1874. In this period, Clayton's goal to create a biracial Republican coalition was achieved, as thirty-two blacks served in the Arkansas General Assembly during these years – with a high of twenty black legislators (sixteen in the House and four in the Senate) in 1873.[6] And while Clayton used his patronage power to build a party committed to his ideals, factionalism quickly developed. Clayton represented the "Minstrel" faction of the party, which was dominated by carpetbaggers. A rival faction, the "Brindletails," comprised mostly of scalawags, formed around Lieutenant Governor James Johnson. The Brindletails blanched at Clayton's use of patronage to disproportionately benefit his faction and criticized the rising debt and questionable dealings associated with the Clayton regime's infrastructure expansion. Factional squabbling became so bad that the Brindletails in the state legislature sought to impeach Clayton on charges of corruption – and nearly succeeded in removing him from office. Eventually, they rid themselves of Clayton by electing him to the US Senate, but not before he was able to replace Johnson with a solid Minstrel (Ozra Hadley).[7]

The Minstrel–Brindletail squabble culminated in the Brooks–Baxter War.[8] The gubernatorial election of 1872 pitted Joseph Brooks, the Brindletail candidate, against Elisha Baxter, the Minstrel candidate. Brooks was a carpetbagger and former Radical, who was a supporter of the national Liberal Republican movement and thus became the candidate of conservative Republicans and Democrats (who ran no candidate of their own). Baxter was a scalawag and a loyal Claytonite, having received appointments as judge of the Third Circuit Court and registrar of bankruptcy for the 1st congressional district.[9] Clayton supported him for governor to leverage his local Unionist background in the hopes of peeling away Brindletail votes.[10] Baxter won a narrow election over Brooks in November 1872,[11] but Brooks claimed that he had actually won and been counted out, as a significant number of votes cast for him had been disqualified by Claytonite election officials. Baxter's election was certified by

---

[6] Blake J. Wintory, "African-American Legislators in the Arkansas General Assembly, 1868– 1893," *Arkansas Historical Quarterly* 65 (2006): 385–434; Chris W. Branam, "'The Africans Have Taken Arkansas': Political Activities of African Americans in the Reconstruction Legislature," *Arkansas Historical Quarterly* 73 (2014): 233–67.

[7] Diggs, Jr., "The Issues of the Powell Clayton Regime."

[8] Earl Woodward, "The Brooks and Baxter War in Arkansas, 1872–1874," *Arkansas Historical Quarterly* 30 (1971): 315–36.

[9] The Brooks–Baxter contest was notable for, among other things, the swapping of backgrounds, with the carpetbagger Brooks serving as the Brindletail candidate and the scalawag Baxter serving as the Minstrel candidate.

[10] Diggs, Jr., "The Issues of the Powell Clayton Regime," 73–74.

[11] The official count was 41,681 to 38,415. See Woodward, "The Brooks and Baxter War in Arkansas," 319.

the state legislature and he was installed as governor, but he maintained a shaky hold on power. More troubling to Clayton was that Baxter became an unreliable Minstrel, as he began to reach out to Democrats for support. For example, Baxter actively supported a constitutional amendment to restore voting rights to ex-Confederates, which was adopted by referendum in March 1873. Baxter also broke with Clayton on his railroad program, which seemed to be the straw that broke the camel's back.

In April 1874, as Clayton sought to entice Baxter to leave office with the promise of a federal job, the Arkansas Circuit Court ruled on a suit that Brooks had brought ten months earlier to dispute the election. The Court ruled in favor of Brooks – without Baxter having any legal counsel present – and issued a writ that made Brooks the legal governor of Arkansas and ordered Baxter to pay back his governor's salary (with interest) to Brooks. Brooks then led a small band of armed followers to the state House, to accompany the sheriff who served the writ. Baxter surrendered the building, but not his right to the governorship. The next month, Arkansas politics descended into chaos, as militias formed around Baxter and Brooks, and sporadic fighting broke out that produced more than 200 casualties. Eventually, on March 15, 1874, President Grant intervened and determined (based on advice from his attorney general) that Baxter was the rightfully elected governor of Arkansas. Grant's intervention brought an end to the Brooks–Baxter War and settled Arkansas's political situation for the moment.[12]

But the Minstrel–Brindletail squabbling had done its damage. In June, the citizenry passed a referendum – by an almost ten-to-one margin – to call for a new constitutional convention (which Baxter had supported). And thanks to the newly enfranchised ex-Confederates, a majority of Democrats were elected. The convention delegates met in July and proceeded to write a new constitution that, among other things, significantly reduced the governor's powers. In October, the citizenry adopted the new constitution by a three-to-one margin. And the following month, the Democrats swept the state elections, installing a new governor – Augustus H. Garland, a former member of the Confederate Congress – and majorities in both legislative chambers.[13] While Arkansas would continue to be represented by Republicans in the US Senate for a time (Clayton through March 1877 and Stephen W. Dorsey through March 1879), the Democrats in the fall 1874 elections had effectively "redeemed" the state.

But the GOP continued to provide a semblance of opposition in the short term. And Democrats, led by a series of Democratic governors, honored black voting rights (as long as they were secure in Democratic dominance). As a result, the small number of Republican election victories (mostly to the state House) were led by black-majority districts in the eastern part of the state.

[12] Diggs, Jr., "The Issues of the Powell Clayton Regime"; Woodward, "The Brooks and Baxter War in Arkansas."
[13] See Stockley, *Ruled by Race*, 84–87; Woodward, "The Brooks and Baxter War in Arkansas."

Moreover, many of these victories were achieved by black candidates. Throughout the 1880s, there were typically more than a half-dozen black legislators in the General Assembly; the post-Reconstruction high-water mark was eleven House members and one senator in 1891.[14] Black delegates at the Republican National Convention also increased post-Reconstruction, with black delegates comprising 39 and 45.5 percent of the Arkansas delegation in 1884 and 1888.

In the post-Reconstruction era, the GOP continued to be guided by Powell Clayton, who remained the Arkansas Republican boss through the early 1910s. Backed by his chief lieutenant, Harmon Remmel, Clayton maintained firm control of federal patronage during this time (and thus benefited from many Republican administrations). Clayton also remained firm that the party stay true to its biracial roots. But the Clayton–Remmel faction constantly faced partisan insurgents, some of which were artifacts of the old Minstrel–Brindletail battles of years past. Often these battles involved the distribution of patronage, but they increasingly took on a racial caste. The first Lily-White organization formed in July 1888, in Pluaski County. And while Lily-Whiteism was nascent at that point, as Todd Lewis notes, "it would grow and remain a point of controversy in Arkansas's Republican Party for the next forty years."[15]

By the mid1880s, the Democrats' dominant position in the state looked less certain. White farmers had been unhappy with the Democrats since the early part of the decade, and in 1882 they organized themselves into the Agricultural Wheel, a group that sought regulation of railroad rates and the repeal of crop lien laws.[16] Within a few years, the "Wheelers" – who did not discriminate against blacks or segregate their meetings – began coordinating with Republicans in the state. By the late 1880s, the fusion arrangement led to an increased number of Republican and Independent (Union Labor) victories in local elections. Small non-Democratic gains had also been made in the state legislature, and the Union Labor candidate for governor (C. M. Norwood) gave the Democratic candidate (James P. Eagle) a scare in 1888, the first real challenge the Democrats had for the governorship in more than a dozen years.[17]

Democrats responded to this political challenge as they had in the past: with violence, intimidation, and election chicanery.[18] White militias formed in some areas of the state, and the Klan reemerged in Conway County. Democratic

[14] See Carl H. Moneyhon, "Black Politics in Arkansas during the Gilded Age, 1876–1900," *Arkansas Historical Quarterly* 44 (1985): 222–45; Wintory, "African-Americans Legislators in the Arkansas General Assembly."
[15] Todd E. Lewis, "'Caesars Are Too Many': Harmon Liveright Remmel and the Republican Party of Arkansas," *Arkansas Historical Quarterly* 56 (1997): 5.
[16] Theodore Saloutos, "The Agricultural Wheel in Arkansas," *Arkansas Historical Quarterly* 2 (1943): 127–40; Stockley, *Ruled by Race*, 109–11.
[17] Clifton Paisley, "The Political Wheelers and Arkansas' Election of 1888," *Arkansas History Review* 25 (1966): 3–21. Norwood received 84,213 votes to 99,214 for Eagle.
[18] Stockley, *Ruled by Race*, 111–13.

sheriffs and their deputies dismissed Republican election judges and supervisors and frightened black voters away from the polls. Masked men stole poll books and ballot boxes. And violence erupted, the notable case being the murder of John Clayton, Powell Clayton's younger brother, who was contesting a narrow defeat in an 1888 US House election. John Clayton was conducting an informal investigation in Plumerville when he was shot through a hotel window by an unknown assassin.[19]

As the Populist threat grew (and a national Populist Party formed) and momentum for a new federal election law (what would become the Lodge Bill) gathered, Democratic leaders recognized the need to find a legal way to achieve what they desired. After the Union Labor–Republican candidate for governor did nearly as well in 1890 as in 1888, the Democrats made their move. In the state legislative session of 1891, two measures were adopted that would undercut any future anti-Democratic efforts.[20] First, a secret ballot law was adopted, which would make it difficult for illiterates to vote. Second, a bill authorizing a referendum for a poll tax amendment to the state constitution was adopted. The amendment came to a vote in September 1892 – with the secret ballot law of 1891 already in place – and passed by a sizable majority.[21] The result of these measures was what Democratic leaders had expected. As Chris Branam contends: "The secret ballot and the poll tax all but eliminated African Americans as a meaningful force in Arkansas politics and crippled challenges to Democratic rule at the state or local level."[22] In the 1894 governor's race, for example, the total number of votes was almost one-third less than in 1890, and the Democrats made a relative gain overall – with the biggest Democratic gains occurring in the six counties with the largest black–white ratios.[23] And in the state legislature, the number of blacks dropped from twelve in 1891, to five in 1893, to zero in 1895.[24] Another eighty years would pass before a black member once again served in the Arkansas General Assembly.

The disenfranchisement provisions also had an effect on the Republican Party internally. Now that the GOP, as constituted, could no longer viably

---

[19] See Kenneth C. Barnes, *Who Killed John Clayton? Political Violence and the Emergence of the New South, 1861–1893* (Durham, NC: Duke University Press, 1998). Clayton lost the election by 846 votes. His election contest in the House – after his death – was decided in his favor, and the seat was vacated.

[20] See John William Graves, "Negro Disfranchisement in Arkansas," *Arkansas Historical Quarterly* 26 (1967): 199–225; J. Morgan Kousser, *The Shaping of Southern Politics: Suffrage Restrictions and the Establishment of the One-Party South, 1880–1910* (New Haven, CT: Yale University Press, 1974), 123–26; Michael Perman, *Struggle for Mastery: Disfranchisement in the South, 1888-1908* (Chapel Hill: University of North Carolina Press, 2001), 59–67.

[21] The vote was 75,847 for and 56,589 against. See Perman, *Struggle for Mastery*, 65.

[22] Chris W. Branam, "Another Look at Disfranchisement in Arkansas, 1888–1894," *Arkansas Historical Quarterly* 69 (2010): 249.

[23] Graves, "Negro Disfranchisement in Arkansas," 220; see also Branam, "Another Look at Disfranchisement in Arkansas."

[24] Wintory, "African-American Legislators in the Arkansas General Assembly," 388.

contest for elective office in Arkansas, some Republican leaders made the case that a change was needed. Specifically, the Lily-White movement that only had a minor following in the late 1880s began to grow. As Tom Dillard notes: "When blacks stopped voting, many white Republicans adopted the idea that the black man was just a costly burden on the struggling party."[25] For the Republican Party to become viable again, this line of argument went, it had to appeal to the updated version of the voting-eligible population – and that was essentially a white population. And to recruit new whites into the party, the Republican organization had to look white, especially in key leadership positions. This argument made sense to many Republicans in post-1892 Arkansas, and Lily-Whiteism spread out from Pulaski County.

Powell Clayton continued to hold fast to his previous beliefs, however, and he maintained control over his Black-and-Tan organization. But the 1890s and 1900s would see a fierce war between the two GOP factions; political battles would be won and lost, but the Clayton–Remmel organization remained in charge and continued to control federal patronage.[26] In 1913, Clayton, in poor health, ceded control of the Black-and-Tan organization to Remmel, before dying the follow year. Now the Arkansas GOP boss, Remmel continued Clayton's policy of a biracial Republican Party. But Lily-Whiteism had grown stronger, and rival conventions were held in 1912 (amid the fracturing in the national GOP between Taft and Roosevelt). And while Remmel used his influence to see that the Black-and-Tans – supporters of Taft – won out and were seated at the national convention, power was beginning to shift within the Arkansas GOP.

The challenge that would eventually topple Harmon Remmel as GOP boss was staged by his nephew, Gus Remmel. Through 1912, Gus Remmel had been loyal to his uncle and had played a key role in the Black-and-Tan organization. But in 1912, his allegiance shifted; in that year, he ran for a seat in Congress and was defeated soundly. Black voters did not turn out in great numbers for him, and the Democrats used white supremacist rhetoric to appeal to racist white voters. As a result, as Todd Lewis recounts: "[Gus] Remmel concluded that black voters were an unreliable source of support ... [and] decided that the only viable way to increase the appeal of the Republican Party was to eliminate blacks from the party."[27] Gus Remmel had become a Lily-White.

In 1914, Gus Remmel took charge of the Pulaski County convention and arranged for it to be held in the Hotel Marion in Little Rock, a whites-only establishment. This effectively excluded blacks from attendance. Over the next

[25] Tom Dillard, "The Back of the Elephant: Racial Conflict in the Arkansas Republican Party," *Arkansas Historical Quarterly* 33 (1974): 3–15.
[26] See Marvin F. Russell, "The Rise of a Republican Leader: Harmon L. Remmel," *Arkansas Historical Quarterly* 36 (1977): 234–57; Dillard, "To the Back of the Elephant"; Lewis, "'Caesars Are Too Many.'"
[27] Lewis, "'Caesars Are Too Many,'" 8.

two years, Harmon and Gus Remmel would vie for control of the party. At the 1916 state convention, Gus Remmel and the Lily-Whites emerged victorious and selected the four at-large delegates to the Republican National Convention. It had been standard practice up until that time to reserve one of the four spots for a black Republican. Gus Remmel opposed that practice, and the Lily-Whites won out. As a result, for the first time in the Arkansas GOP's history, no blacks would be regular national convention delegates in 1916 – and only one would attend as an alternate.[28]

In 1920, the Lily-Whites consolidated their power; multiple counties selected all-white delegations and Gus Remmel firmly controlled the state organization and convention. The Black-and-Tans selected their own slates, but they were shut out – and eventually walked out of the state convention. They contested the all-white slate to the Republican National Convention but were rejected, as the Lily-White delegation was seated instead.[29] Thus, in 1920, no blacks were part of the Arkansas delegation – regular or alternate. Nevertheless, black Republicans continued to push for inclusion in the party. And the Black-and-Tans ran their own nominee for governor in 1920 – black educator J. H. Blount – to face the Lily-White (Wallace Townsend) and Democratic (Thomas McRae) candidates. McRae won easily, and Townsend secured almost four times as many votes as Blount.[30]

While the outlook for black participation in Arkansas GOP politics looked dim at this point, an unexpected event occurred: Gus Remmel died shortly after the 1920 elections. This left the state chairmanship vacant, and Harmon Remmel stepped in to reclaim control of the state party. Back in power, Harmon Remmel worked to mend fences and reestablish the Arkansas Republican Party as a biracial organization. While Lily-Whiteism was still strong, losing Gus Remmel left the faction without a clear leader, and Harmon Remmel used his political and organizational skills to ensure that blacks would be represented again in the 1924 Arkansas delegation to the GOP national convention (via an alternate). And over the next few years, he also made sure that counties that had gone Lily-White during his nephew's reign nominated slates to the state convention that included black delegates.[31]

In 1927, Harmon Remmel died. But his work to convince Republicans in Arkansas to work together and not fracture by race paid off – as white and black leaders reached a compromise in 1928 that would send Scipio Jones (a

---

[28] Lewis, "'Caesars Are Too Many.'"
[29] While the convention seated the Lily-White delegation, they also forbade the practice of selecting delegates at whites-only facilities. See ibid., 16.
[30] McRae would tally 12,604 votes, Townsend 64,339, and Blount 15,627. See Dillard, "To the Back of the Elephant," 12.
[31] Lewis, "'Caesars Are Too Many.'"

TABLE 8.2 *Descriptive Republican Party success in Louisiana, 1865–1968*

	1865–1877	1878–1896	1897–1932	1933–1968
Presidential candidate won the state?	✓			✓
Senatorial candidate elected?	✓			
Gubernatorial candidate elected?	✓			
At least one House candidate elected?	✓	✓		

well-known black attorney and Black-and-Tan leader in Pulaski County) to the Republican National Convention as a regular delegate, along with a black alternate.[32] This cooperation between white and black Republicans continued through the 1930s and into the 1940s, even as blacks in Arkansas began to move wholesale into the Democratic Party. By the early 1950s, the Republican Party in Arkansas, while Lily-White in name, remained a biracial coalition.

LOUISIANA: GOP SUPPORT FOR BLACK DISENFRANCHISEMENT AND BLACK-AND-TAN RULE

In Louisiana, the decline of black participation followed the 1896 election, after the state passed strict disfranchisement laws that banned black voting almost entirely. The drop in black voters also affected the Republican Party's electoral performance: as in all Southern states, the GOP was already on the ropes, but after 1896 support for the party dropped even further (see Table 8.2 and Figure 8.3). At first glance, the connection between the two seems to suggest an ordinary tale of Southern Democrats undermining the Louisiana GOP. However, Louisiana's party system was decidedly more complex than many of the other ex-Confederate states. First, the Republican Party saw major internal divisions, but these were not across color lines.[33] Additionally, black voters did not exclusively vote Republican – sometimes due to Democratic

---

[32] Ibid.; Tom Dillard, "Scipio A. Jones," *Arkansas Historical Quarterly* 31 (1972): 201–19.

[33] That is not to say that race was not relevant. As Lawrence Powell argues, concern about the influence of black Republicans played a major role in the actions taken by Henry Clay Warmoth, Louisiana's first Republican governor after the Civil War. However, unlike in other states where the Black-and-Tans and Lily-Whites came to form clearly separate wings of the same party based on race and segregation, in Louisiana the main fracture lines within the state GOP appear to have been based on considerations other than race alone. See Lawrence Powell, "Centralization and Its Discontents in Reconstruction Louisiana," *Studies in American Political Development* 20 (Fall 2006): 105–31.

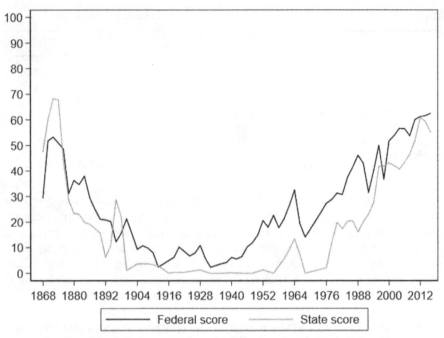

FIGURE 8.3 Republican Party strength at the federal and state levels in Louisiana, 1868–2012

fraud or pressure, but seemingly in some cases also out of free will. In the 1896 election, it was the GOP that charged the Democrats with fraudulently adding black votes to *their* totals. As a result, white conservative Republicans in Louisiana were the ones who pushed for new disfranchisement legislation, and a new constitutional amendment that largely banned blacks from voting. Despite this, the Black-and-Tans succeeded in controlling the Louisiana GOP for much of the late nineteenth and early twentieth centuries, until a Lily-White takeover occurred in the late 1920s (see Figure 8.4).

* * * * *

Louisiana held its first gubernatorial election under Unionist military control in 1864, using the same suffrage qualifications that had existed prior to the Civil War. Michael Hahn, a white German-born attorney from New Orleans, won the election by appealing to racist whites. However, Hahn quickly attempted to trade in his governorship for a Senate seat. But his attempt failed when Radical Republicans in Congress refused to seat him. By then, Hahn had already resigned his governorship and had been succeeded by J. Madison Wells. Wells also opposed black suffrage, and opponents of the Hahn–Wells government began to organize politically. During a convention in September 1865, these

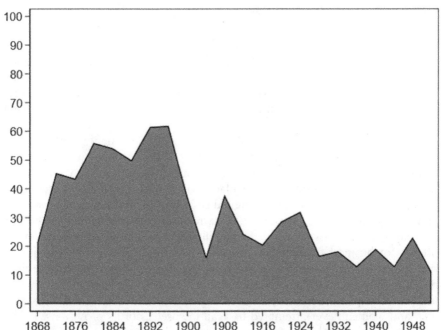

FIGURE 8.4 Percentage of GOP convention delegates from Louisiana that were black, 1868–1952
Source: Data collected by authors.

opponents formed a political organization and claimed the name of the "Republican Party in Louisiana."[34]

In 1866, a Republican attempt at organizing a new constitutional convention in New Orleans to expand black voting rights resulted in a violent clash between white supremacists (including a number of police officers) and blacks protesting in favor of suffrage – which left fifty people killed and many wounded. The massacre created momentum for Radical Republicanism nationwide and helped the Radicals achieve major victories in the 1866 midterms.[35] After the Reconstruction Acts of 1867 required former Confederate states to allow universal suffrage in their constitutional conventions, Louisiana's new Republican Party began to organize for the upcoming elections. By then the party's main leader was Henry C. Warmoth, a young white Civil War veteran

[34] Philip D. Uzee, "The Beginnings of the Louisiana Republican Party," *Louisiana History: The Journal of the Louisiana Historical Association* 12 (Summer 1971): 197–211.
[35] Althea D. Pitre, "The Collapse of the Warmoth Regime, 1870–72," *Louisiana History: The Journal of the Louisiana Historical Association* 6 (Spring 1965): 161–87.

originally from Illinois and nicknamed the "Prince of the Carpetbaggers."[36] Under Warmoth, the Republican Party organized GOP clubs in parishes throughout Louisiana and registered (black) voters.[37] In the 1868 election – the first under the new Louisiana constitution that expanded suffrage – Warmoth was the Republican gubernatorial candidate and, with Democrats refusing to field a ticket, was easily elected with 63.1 percent of the vote. Republicans also won majorities in the state Senate (55.6 percent of seats) and Assembly (55.4 percent).[38]

As governor and party leader, Warmoth proved to be highly controversial, and Republicans spent much of the next four years battling each other over control of the party and the state government. While Warmoth's success in 1868 was due in large part to black votes, once in office he attempted to appeal to white voters as well. He did so in part by appointing conservative and segregationist whites to state offices, which frustrated other GOP leaders.[39] Warmoth also controversially vetoed a bill that would have made it a criminal offense for business owners to refuse service to black patrons. He previously had signed a weaker version of the same type of legislation to impose fines on such business owners. However, as he noted in his autobiography, this law was rarely enforced and, in practical terms, was "a dead letter; colored men and women never attempted to avail themselves of its provisions. Public sentiment was strongly opposed to it, and the colored people were too wise to undertake to force themselves upon white people who did not want them."[40] Regardless, Warmoth's veto amplified the major internal conflict within the party.[41]

---

[36] Ibid., 162.   [37] Uzee, "The Beginnings of the Louisiana Republican Party," 209–11.

[38] See Michael J. Dubin, *United States Gubernatorial Elections, 1861–1911: The Official Results by State and County* (Jefferson, NC: McFarland & Company, 2010), 4; Michael J. Dubin, *Party Affiliations in the State Legislatures: A Year by Year Summary, 1796–2006* (Jefferson, NC: McFarland & Company, 2007), 76. See also F. Wayne Binning, "The Carpetbagger's Triumph: The Louisiana State Election of 1868," *Louisiana History: The Journal of the Louisiana Historical Association* 14 (Winter 1973): 21–39.

[39] In his autobiography, Warmoth noted that "I had antagonized the colored Lieutenant-Governor, the radical *New Orleans Tribune*, and many of their supporters, by making a number of appointments of conservative white men to office, all of whom they declared to be Democrats." See Henry Clay Warmoth, *War, Politics and Reconstruction: Stormy Days in Louisiana* (New York: Negro Universities Press, 1930), 89.

[40] See ibid., 92. Warmoth also argued he had conversations with President Grant on this topic in which both men agreed that "we should protect the colored people in all of their political and civil rights, provide them with schools, give them appointments to offices whose duties they were capable of discharging, and encouraging them in every way possible; but [Grant] did not purpose to make the white people of the South feel that they were not a part of this Republic" (ibid., 102).

[41] It should be noted that Warmoth's appointments of Democrats and his veto of the Civil Rights Bill was hardly the only reason for his controversial role in the Louisiana Republican Party. As Althea D. Pitre notes, Warmoth also clashed with Ulysses S. Grant over the appointment of a customhouse collector, and attempted to greatly expand the power of his office to a point that it became a "virtual dictatorship." Pitre, "The Collapse of the Warmoth Regime," 163.

In response, Radical Republicans began to organize to take over the state party. Warmoth recalled how in 1870 at the GOP's state convention he found to his surprise that

over four-fifths of the Convention was composed of negroes ... All of the officers of the Convention were negroes, and so were a large majority of the members of all of the committees appointed by the President. It was certainly a negro convention. The "Pure Radicals" had been on the job.[42]

By 1872, Warmoth – who was constitutionally banned from running for reelection – had lost control of the party, and supported a fusionist-Democratic ticket rather than Republican gubernatorial candidate William Pitt Kellogg. Warmoth also opposed Grant's reelection due to conflicts that he had with the president over federal appointments in the state. In the 1872 election, Kellogg received the most votes, but his opponent, John McEnery, claimed victory as well. With support from Grant and Republican majorities in the state legislature, Kellogg was declared the victor, and Warmoth was impeached with just thirty-five days left in office.[43] Notably, Warmoth's replacement for the rest of his term was P. B. S Pinchback, a black leader in the GOP, who previously had been an ally of Warmoth but by then had become a supporter of Kellogg.[44]

Kellogg's inauguration, however, did not end the conflict over the 1872 election. McEnery held his own rival inauguration and Democrats organized a separate legislature that passed its own legislation. Unsurprisingly, this conflict over control of the state government turned violent. In 1874, Democrats sent 5,000 armed men into New Orleans and temporarily took over the legislature before fleeing as federal troops approached the city.[45] As a result of this ongoing unrest, Louisiana politics remained highly volatile in the years that followed. The Kellogg administration also proved incapable of achieving basic policy goals. For one, with the government's very legitimacy in dispute, the state had a tough time collecting taxes and, as Kellogg told "his" legislature

---

[42] Warmoth, *War, Politics, and Reconstruction*, 94. In 1871, Warmoth's opponents in the Louisiana Republican Party attempted to block him and his supporters from attending a state convention hastily organized to reorganize the party against its governor. The core of the anti-Warmoth group was formed by Lieutenant Governor Oscar J. Dunn (a black man) and James F. Casey (the customhouse collector in New Orleans and Ulysses S. Grant's brother-in-law). Warmoth's supporters gathered elsewhere in the city to hold a rival state convention. Notably, both groups were biracial. See Pitre, "The Collapse of the Warmoth Regime."

[43] Pitre, "The Collapse of the Warmoth Regime." For more on Warmoth's governorship and his impeachment, see Charles L. Dufour, "The Age of Warmoth," *Louisiana History: The Journal of the Louisiana Historical Association* 6 (Autumn 1965): 335–64; Francis Byers Harris, "Henry Clay Warmoth, Reconstruction Governor of Louisiana," *Louisiana Historical Quarterly* 30 (April 1947): 523–652.

[44] Pitre, "The Collapse of the Warmoth Regime," 176.

[45] Ella Lonn, *Reconstruction in Louisiana after 1868* (Gloucester, MA: Peter Smith, 1967), 206–29; 256–75.

in 1874, "[the] treasury was empty."[46] In addition, the 1873 economic down-turn hit Louisiana, and particularly New Orleans, hard. Kellogg also proved to be more supportive of civil rights than Warmoth had been, further inflaming racist white opposition.[47]

In 1876, the Louisiana GOP faced a perfect storm of discontent and electoral sabotage. In part, the Democrats' victory in the 1876 election – which saw the party win the governorship and majorities in the state legislature – was pro-duced through the same kind of violence toward black voters that was common in other ex-Confederate states. However, in Louisiana black voters did not vote Republican as consistently as elsewhere. Plantation owners in Louisiana still had considerable control over their black workers since many of them still lived and labored on their plantations. Planters used this control for political pur-poses by registering their workers and forcing them to vote Democratic.

Indeed, after the 1876 election, Republicans claimed that Democratic intimi-dation and violence resulted in considerable decline in black support for the GOP. To be sure, congressional investigations confirmed that such violence and intimi-dation did occur and resulted in black voters either sitting out the election or voting for candidates they otherwise would not have supported. However, another House investigation suggested that the Louisiana Republican Party was deeply unpopular with its voting base. Notably, many white supporters of the Warmoth wing of the party did not participate in protest. Meanwhile, a number of black voters seem to have voted for the Democratic Party out of frustration with the GOP's inability to improve their quality of life. Indeed, a number of black voters interviewed for a congressional investigation into voting irregularities com-plained about the lack of education provided for their children. One black voter in East Baton Rouge explained that "[Republicans] would always tell us that the money had run out; and the children never got any schooling, except may be [*sic*] a month or so in a year."[48] Another black voter in the same parish explained his Democratic vote by noting that "I wanted my children educated. We have to pay taxes and I wanted my children to have their rights."[49] As T. B. Tunnell, Jr. explained, while black voters may not have focused on the rampant government corruption under the Warmoth and Kellogg administrations, "they were not so naïve as not to see the obvious relationship between the type of people who held office and the fact that their children had no schools."[50]

With Democrats in control of the state government and federal troops pulled out of the state, the Louisiana GOP faced the same decline that Republicans

[46] Cited in ibid., 247.
[47] James T. Otten, "The Wheeler Adjustment in Louisiana: National Republicans Begin to Reappraise Their Reconstruction Policy," *Louisiana History: The Journal of the Louisiana Historical Association* 13 (Autumn 1972): 349–67.
[48] T. B. Tunnell, Jr., "The Negro, the Republican Party, and the Election of 1876 in Louisiana," *Louisiana History: The Journal of the Louisiana Historical Association* 7 (Spring 1966): 109.
[49] Ibid., 109.   [50] Ibid., 111.

encountered in other Southern states. Still, the party remained capable of electing officials, at the state level as well as the federal level – with four Republicans winning seats in the US House between 1877 and 1890.[51] Yet, the party's influence clearly had declined after the Warmoth–Kellogg era: in the gubernatorial elections of 1879, 1884, and 1888, Republican candidates received on average less than one-third of the vote.[52] In the state legislature, Republican representation dropped from 44.4 percent in the state Senate and 38.2 percent in the Assembly after the 1876 election to zero seats in the Senate and just 2 percent of seats in the Assembly by 1892.[53]

After 1876, both former GOP governors remained active players, and opponents, in intra-party Louisiana politics. Kellogg was elected US senator in 1876 and remained in office for one term. In 1882 he successfully ran for the US House but served only one term after losing his reelection bid in 1884. After his loss, Kellogg retained a residence in Louisiana but reportedly spent most of his time in Washington, DC.[54] After his impeachment, Warmoth initially focused his attention on his sugar plantation and lobbying for his industry's interests. In 1888, he was the Republican gubernatorial candidate but lost in a landslide. In 1890, President Benjamin Harrison appointed him US collector of customs in New Orleans, a position that provided him with direct control over federal patronage appointments in Louisiana – a power he used to appoint a number of black officeholders.[55] Thus, while no one group consistently controlled the party, neither the Kellogg nor the Warmoth wing reflected a Lily-White organization.

In the 1890s, the Democratic Party split over tariffs. Sugar plantation owners in Louisiana – who by and large were Democrats – strongly opposed the Tariff of 1894, which imposed considerable new duties on raw sugar. With the national Democratic Party betraying their economic interests, and the national Republican Party opposing the tariffs, the plantation owners and traders decided to bolt from the local Louisiana Democratic Party. However, with the local GOP being the clear "black party," the sugar planters refused to join the existing party structure. Instead, in September 1894, they determined to

---

[51] Uzee, "The Beginnings of the Louisiana Republican Party," 198.

[52] After the Louisiana state constitution was adjusted to add new limits to voting rights, new elections were held in 1879 for governor and state legislature. In 1879, Republican candidate Beattle received 36.48 percent of the vote. Four years later, Republican gubernatorial candidate Stevenson received 32.88 percent of the vote. In 1888, Warmoth received just 27.55 percent of the vote. See Dubin, *United States Gubernatorial Elections*, 10, 12, 15.

[53] Dubin, *Party Affiliations in the State Legislatures*, 77.

[54] "William Pitt Kellogg, 1831–1918," *Journal of the Illinois State Historical Society* 11 (October 1918): 460.

[55] Justin A. Nystrom, *New Orleans after the Civil War: Race, Politics, and a New Birth of Freedom* (Baltimore: Johns Hopkins University Press, 2010), 308; Harris, "Henry Clay Warmoth," 648–49.

form their own version of the local Republican Party, identified as the "National Republican Party of Louisiana" – to signal their support for the national GOP's economic policies, but also their opposition to the local GOP's race policies.[56] As a result, after 1894, the Louisiana Republican Party came in three versions: the two original competing factions that, combined, comprised the "true" Republican Party of Louisiana and the new segregationist National Republican Party. In 1894, the Nationals invited William McKinley – who as a member of Congress had been the chief architect of the Tariff Act of 1890, which the new tariff undermined – to speak in Louisiana. Republicans of all persuasions used the McKinley visit to "put on a big demonstration, including bonfires and fireworks ... Eight thousand people heard [McKinley's] speech on the benefits of protection."[57]

While the new National Republicans were segregationist, their presence in Louisiana politics also reflected the first real opportunity for the GOP since 1876 to potentially win a gubernatorial election. Thus, in 1896, the Nationals combined with local Populist parties to produce a fusion ticket for the state legislative elections, which was led by gubernatorial candidate John Newton Pharr. At the convention of the regular Republican Party, Warmoth supporters endorsed this ticket. The Pharr campaign would, in the end, be a collection of strange bedfellows: as the *Thibodaux Sentinel* noted, the Populist section of the coalition supported free silver ("paternalism of the most pronounced type"), the National Republicans were white supremacists, the regular Republicans wanted to end racial segregation laws, and Pharr himself strongly supported Prohibition.[58] Yet while each element of the coalition had little in common with the other, they all opposed the Democrats. Thus, while fusion hardly produced consensus on policy, it did create an energetic campaign on behalf of Pharr. Notably, however, the three groups – regular Republicans, National Republicans, and Populists – each ran independent campaigns to support the same candidate.

Facing the first genuine threat to their rule in Louisiana since the 1876 election, Democrats realized they had to replace the white votes they were going to lose to the National Republicans and Populists. They did so by adding additional black votes. As Philip D. Uzee notes, the way they achieved this was through bribery and voter fraud:

To ensure the election of [Democratic gubernatorial candidate] Murphy J. Foster and his ticket, they had to make sure every election commissioner and poll official in the parishes with Negro majorities was a trusted Democrat because the Negro vote would have to

---

[56] Philip D. Uzee, "The Republican Party in the Louisiana Election of 1896," *Louisiana History: The Journal of the Louisiana Historical Association* 2 (Summer 1961): 332–44.
[57] Ibid., 335.   [58] Ibid., 337.

replace the lost white votes. The party was also prepared to buy votes [and Democrats] opened up a special office in New Orleans to purchase Negro votes at $12.50 per vote.[59]

The 1896 Republican fusion coalition and Democratic attempts to stuff ballot boxes and bribe black voters produced a highly peculiar political situation for a Southern state. Unlike in other ex-Confederate states where Democrats pushed for new laws to disenfranchise the base of the Republican Party there, Democrats in Louisiana in the 1890s mostly supported black suffrage because it provided them with the opportunity to commit electoral fraud.

Pharr went on to lose to Democratic candidate Murphy J. Foster, who won a number of parishes in which blacks made up a majority of the electorate and in previous elections had gone Republican. This suggested that Democrats had committed considerable electoral fraud, and some alternative counts suggested that Pharr could have won the election in lieu of such shenanigans. Rather than challenge the election results, however, the National Republicans agreed to acknowledge Foster's victory if, in exchange, a new constitutional convention would be organized to pass a new suffrage amendment. This deal was consummated, and in 1898, the constitution was updated accordingly: black voters were effectively banned from electoral participation in Louisiana moving forward. For the regular Republican Party, the results were predictable: while the GOP in 1896 had won a number of seats in the state legislature, after 1898 the Republicans failed to win any seats in either the Assembly or the state Senate for multiple decades.[60]

Between 1900 and 1916, two competing party organizations – one Lily-White and one Black-and-Tan – consistently sent rival delegations to the GOP national convention. To prevent having to make a choice between the two, the RNC each election year seated half of each delegation, which allowed two Republican parties to coexist in Louisiana. A unification of both factions occurred in 1916 under the leadership of Armand Romaine, a white lawyer from New Orleans who had represented blacks fighting Louisiana's grandfather clause in 1901.[61] However, with Romaine's death in 1918, unity disappeared just as quickly. An RNC assessment of the situation in June 1918 concluded that "there are as many factions [in Louisiana] as Republicans."[62] In 1919, Emil Kuntz – a white businessman, a lifelong Republican, and the head of Louisiana's Black-and-Tan faction – was elected as the state's representative to the RNC by the national committee's other members. From that point forward, Kuntz was recognized as the official leader of the

[59] Ibid., 339.
[60] In 1896, Republicans won 18.4 percent of seats in the state Senate and 24.5 percent in the Assembly. The party would not win another seat in the Assembly until 1964 and in the Senate until 1972. See Dubin, *Party Affiliations in the State Legislatures*, 77.
[61] *The Outlook: A Weekly Newspaper*, vol. LXVIII (Outlook Publishing Company, May–August 1901), 747.
[62] Robert Ellwood Hauser, "Warren G. Harding and His Attempts to Reorganize the Republican Party in the South, 1920–23" (Dissertation, Pennsylvania State University, 1973), 199.

Republican Party in Louisiana. Unlike previous party leaders, Kuntz invested considerably in building the GOP as a genuine party in the state.

Kuntz's control of the party would be challenged directly but unsuccessfully during the Harding administration.[63] In the 1920 presidential election, Harding performed better than expected in Louisiana: while the GOP only received 30 percent of the vote, this was a considerable improvement from previous campaigns and the best Republican performance in the state since the end of Reconstruction.[64] Directly after the 1920 election, Kuntz gathered leaders of the different GOP factions in the state together to produce a list of proposed patronage recipients that all factions could live with. However, in April 1921, when Harding announced his desire to reorganize Southern party organizations to be in line with the voting public in their respective states, the compromise coalition began to fall apart. Former governor Warmoth reemerged to advise the Harding administration against working with the Kuntz organization. In particular, Warmoth warned Harding against Walter L. Cohen, a black ally of Kuntz, who Warmoth believed was the true power in the Black-and-Tan organization:

I have come to tell you that the recognition of these two men as the advisors of the President in Louisiana would be fatal to the Republican party and a most severe shock to the decent men and women of New Orleans. Cohen is the whole thing. Kuntz is merely his puppet and a subservient tool, having some money and a few personal friends outside of the Cohen negroes and his abject followers. The Cohen organization is composed of 49 negroes and 19 irresponsible white men ... Their assumption of being the Republican party is preposterous and impudent beyond measure.[65]

While Kuntz and Cohen quickly informed RNC Chairman Will Hays of their distrust of Warmoth – who had not been involved in GOP politics in the state for many years – their appeal backfired, as Harding began to question whether the Kuntz organization was worth investing in. Over the next several months, both the Kuntz organization and a new rival Lily-White faction led by white businessman Warren Kearney worked to court Harding and the RNC. Both groups suggested candidates for open offices to Harding, who initially was excited about the prospect of a Kearney-dominated party. In correspondence with Kearney, Harding explained that he preferred a merger between the existing party system and Kearney's group of white businessmen:

I am exceedingly grateful for your expression of interest and I want to assure you of my willingness and readiness to cooperate, though I cannot utterly ignore those who have served to the best of their ability in the past. My own thought is that their services ought to be retained, but that we ought to reinforce and encourage them with such support as

---

[63] *Men of the South: A Work for the Newspaper Reference Library* (New Orleans, LA: Southern Biographical Association, 1922), 508.
[64] Hauser, "Warren G. Harding," 205–06.   [65] Ibid., 210–11.

I believe to be possible from the expressions so cordially signed by you and your associates.[66]

It was this desire for compromise that would preserve Kuntz's control over the Louisiana GOP. Throughout 1921 and 1922, Kuntz consistently showed himself willing to negotiate with his Lily-White counterparts and provided the RNC and Harding ample evidence of this.[67] In contrast, the Lily-Whites remained hesitant about working with Kuntz. When they did agree to compromise, they often failed to deliver on their promises. For example, when the two sides finally agreed to form a Committee of Nine with representation from both the Kuntz and the Kearney factions, in order to provide Harding with suggestions for patronage, most of the Kearney representatives failed to attend meetings and those who did lacked a list of candidates to nominate.[68] As a result, Harding lost his faith in Kearney, and Kuntz's organization regained total control. By fall 1922 – though it took considerable effort to move Harding from his previous promise not to appoint blacks to important federal positions in the South – Kuntz even succeeded in pushing the president to appoint Cohen as Controller of Customs with headquarters at New Orleans, which was "one of the most lucrative Federal offices in the South."[69]

In 1924, Kuntz, Cohen, and other representatives of the Black-and-Tan faction were seated at the national convention, while Kearney was not a delegate. However, in the years that followed, Kuntz and Cohen had a falling out, and Kuntz began working with the white businessmen who had entered the party during the Harding era.[70] Thus, once again, Louisiana saw two competing Republican Parties – one controlled by Kuntz and one by Cohen. Kuntz by then had concluded that "bitter experience has taught the fallacy of attempting to oust negro patronage elements except by legal means."[71] Thus, in 1928, the

[66] Ibid., 215–16.

[67] For example, the Kuntz faction quickly agreed to an RNC compromise proposal in 1921 that would see a dramatic decline in black representation in the party organization and a semi-forced retirement of Walter Cohen in exchange for the inclusion of the Kearney faction. Kearney delayed accepting the proposal for months. See ibid., 234–39.

[68] Ibid., 243–45.   [69] "Negro Gets $5,000 Office," *New York Times*, November 5, 1922.

[70] The exact circumstances of the break between Cohen and Kuntz are unclear. However, according to reports in black newspapers after Kuntz's death, he "ousted [Internal Revenue Collector D.A.] Lines and later, yielding to pressure of the 'white leadership' element in the party, turned on Cohen, who, while defeated as secretary of the state committee has successfully retained his post as comptroller of customs." See "Committeeman Who Rose by Cohen's Aid Dies at 65," *The Chicago Defender*, April 5, 1930; Donald J. Lisio, *Hoover, Blacks, and Lily-Whites: A Study of Southern Strategies* (Chapel Hill: University of North Carolina Press, 1985), 39.

[71] Cited in Barbara C. Wingo, "The 1928 Presidential Election in Louisiana," *Louisiana History: The Journal of the Louisiana Historical Association* 18 (Autumn, 1977): 405–35, 407.

Kuntz faction sought to ban Cohen and his followers from attending state party meetings.[72] Later in the spring, the Kuntz faction organized a state convention and nominated delegates who endorsed Herbert Hoover. Cohen and his followers gathered at their own convention and nominated their own slate of delegates.[73] At the convention, the Kuntz group comprised the majority of the delegates, though Cohen and one other delegate from the alternative group were also seated.[74]

After Hoover's election, Kuntz attempted to get rid of Cohen entirely by suggesting to Hoover that he be appointed ambassador to Liberia – a position Cohen showed some interest in, but which came without pay. In the end, Cohen declined the offer and remained in New Orleans and in Louisiana politics.[75] Hoover also refused to remove Cohen from his federal customs position – partly because of the genuine respect Cohen had earned among national Republicans in his long political career, and partly because Hoover feared a backlash among black voters in the North.[76] Thus, Cohen and Kuntz continued to spar during the first part of the Hoover administration.[77] In March 1930, Kuntz died.[78] Assistant Secretary of the Navy Ernest Lee Jahncke – who had entered the party in 1921 as an ally of Kearney – then became the new party leader in Louisiana.[79] In December 1930, Cohen also died. This left the Lily-Whites in de facto control of the Louisiana Republican Party, though some small level of black representation at national conventions would remain.[80]

FLORIDA: A SLOW TREND TO LILY-WHITEISM

The Florida Republican Party faced many of the same problems that other GOP party organizations in the South encountered. Florida Republicans had a brief moment of control of the state government, followed by Democratic violence

---

[72] "LA Whites Still After Walter Cohen," *Afro-American*, January 14, 1928; "Louisiana GOP Goes to Court," *The Pittsburgh Courier*, February 25, 1928; "Lily-White Republicans of New Orleans Take Steps to Halt Walter Cohen," *The Chicago Defender*, March 3, 1928.

[73] "G.O.P. in Louisiana May Take Its Split to the Convention," *Washington Post*, March 29, 1928.

[74] "Walter Cohen and Bean Lose to Lily-Whites," *Philadelphia Tribune*, June 7, 1928; Wingo, "The 1928 Presidential Election in Louisiana," 407; Lisio, *Hoover, Blacks, and Lily-Whites*, 59–60.

[75] Lisio, *Hoover, Blacks, and Lily-Whites*, 168.   [76] Ibid., 168–70.

[77] "Walter Cohen Reopens War on Lily-Whites in Louisiana," *The Chicago Defender*, November 23, 1929.

[78] "Emil Kuntz Dead," *New York Times*, March 24, 1930; "Committeeman Who Rose by Cohen's Aid Dies at 65," *The Chicago Defender*.

[79] "Lily-White Directs Louisiana Patronage," *The Chicago Defender*, July 12, 1930.

[80] "Death of Cohen Leaves Entire South Without Single Federal Office Holder," *Afro-American*, January 3, 1931.

TABLE 8.3 *Descriptive Republican Party success in Florida, 1865–1968*

	1865–1877	1878–1896	1897–1932	1933–1968
Presidential candidate won the state?	✓		✓	✓
Senatorial candidate elected?	✓			✓
Gubernatorial candidate elected?	✓			✓
At least one House candidate elected?	✓	✓		✓

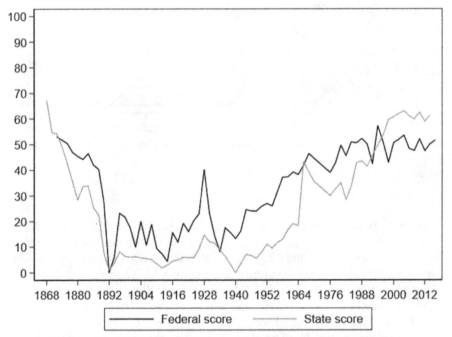

FIGURE 8.5 Republican Party strength at the federal and state levels in Florida, 1868–2012

and the eventual introduction of disfranchisement laws that excluded most of their voting base from political participation. But in Florida the process moved fast: Florida Democrats successfully changed the state constitution in 1885, resulting in a major decline in Republican strength from the 1888 election forward, until the party began to rebound in the middle of the twentieth century (see Table 8.3 and Figure 8.5). In its decline, the GOP faced considerable infighting in the subsequent decades, mostly over control of federal

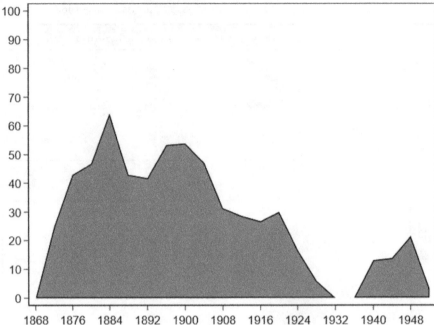

FIGURE 8.6 Percentage of GOP convention delegates from Florida that were black, 1868–1952
Source: Data collected by authors.

patronage. While some of these conflicts have been described as Lily-White versus Black-and-Tan, in practice most groups in the Florida GOP were integrated, and Florida continued to send biracial delegations to national conventions well into the twentieth century (see Figure 8.6). The eventual demise of black participation in the Florida GOP followed a decline in the 1920s, after the death of Joseph Lee, a black party leader and office-holder. It was also accelerated by the temporary resurgence of the party during the 1928 election. With new party leaders and Herbert Hoover winning the state, local Republicans hoped to rebuild their party as a competitive political organization. And to help achieve this, they moved further toward a white-dominated party. However, Florida's repeal of the poll tax in 1937 inspired new activism among black Republicans and the resurgence of a small but consistent level of black representation in Florida's national convention delegation.

*   *   *   *   *

Attempts at organizing black voters in Florida began in 1867 through the Freedman's Bureau and, later, the Union League, with support from the

Republican National Committee.[81] At the same time, local white business leaders united in the Jacksonville Republican Club. The Freedman's Bureau wing of the black Republicans subsequently joined with the white business leaders into a moderate, biracial group. At the Florida constitutional convention in 1868, moderate and Radical Republicans squared off. Initially, the Radicals held a small majority of convention delegates. In response, moderates and the small number of Democratic delegates present bolted the convention, and both groups adopted their own constitutions: one Radical and one moderate.[82] Both constitutions were sent to the Congressional Committee on Reconstruction, which (at the recommendation of Union General George G. Meade) accepted the moderate version.[83]

As a result, the radical and moderate Republicans ran competing tickets in the 1868 election to ratify the constitution. The eventual result represented a victory for the moderates: the constitution was adopted, and their gubernatorial candidate – Harrison Reed, a white man originally from Wisconsin – beat both his Democratic and his Radical Republican opponent.[84] The victory of the moderates put in power, as Jerrell H. Shofner described them, a group of

> business-oriented men who recognized that the state needed to be developed if the problems created by the Civil War were to be permanently solved. These men were interested in Negro rights because the vast majority of their voting supporters were Negroes and because solving the problems created by emancipation was a necessary preliminary to stable political and social conditions. Without this stability, development of the state's economic resources could not succeed.[85]

Thus, moderate Republican leaders sought to please their black voting base but also tried to incorporate white Southerners into the party. For example, Reed appointed a number of Democrats who had served in the Confederate army to state and county offices.[86] Yet Reed also appointed Jonathan C. Gibbs – a black African Methodist Episcopal (AME) minister born in Philadelphia, educated at

---

[81] Jerrell H. Shofner, "Political Reconstruction in Florida," *The Florida Historical Quarterly* 45 (October 1966): 145–70.

[82] The two constitutions were different in terms of the number of elective positions in the state and exclusion of Floridians who had supported the Confederacy. Most importantly, the moderate constitution limited representation in relation to population, thus decreasing the influence of majority black counties in the North in the state legislature. See ibid., 150.

[83] Ibid., 148–50.

[84] Reed received 14,170 votes, the Democratic candidate received 7,852 votes, and the Radical candidate received 2,262 votes. The moderate constitution was ratified by 14,520 to 9,491 votes. See ibid., 152.

[85] Ibid., 146.

[86] Ibid., 153; William H. Gleason and Edward C. Wilaumson, "Florida's First Reconstruction Legislature," *The Florida Historical Quarterly* 32 (July 1953): 41–43.

Dartmouth, and the founder of several schools in Florida – as secretary of state.[87]

While Republicans controlled the Florida state government, the aftermath of the war and hostility of many whites to the new regime meant that Reed had little money or ability to control the state. This resulted in a lack of security for black Floridians. Indeed, in the days after Reed's inauguration and the official end of military rule in Florida, there were multiple white attacks against blacks. Throughout 1868 and 1869, the state government struggled to keep the peace and enforce the law as state troops were scarce and lacked proper weapons. Harry Franklin, a black Republican, was shot and killed by an unknown assailant in Gainesville in March 1869, and the murder was never solved. Another black Republican was kidnapped and his body never retrieved.[88] Thus, Florida – particularly from the perspective of black political leaders – remained in a state of near anarchy throughout the Reed administration. Indeed, in 1871, Reed acknowledged that the state could not protect Republicans – black or white – living in West Florida and Jackson County. Black Methodist ministers recommended that blacks should move out of Jackson County altogether.[89]

During the 1870 midterm elections, which saw an open race for lieutenant governor, Democrats used violence to try to reduce black turnout. On election day in Jackson County, blacks who attempted to vote "were subjected to violence and threats" and several "were stabbed, others were fired upon, and some were clubbed while attempting to get up to the ballot box."[90] The approach worked to some extent: while Democrat William Bloxham appears to have won the lieutenant governor race, Republicans blocked his inauguration and declared Republican Samuel T. Day the winner. Although the Florida Supreme Court would eventually rule Bloxham to be the victor, he would not be inaugurated until June 1872.[91] By then, Reed's own position as governor and leader of the GOP had come under attack after he appointed several legislators to various offices. While these office-holders intended to continue

---

[87] Gibbs served as a delegate to the 1868 constitutional convention on the Radical side of the party. Gibbs remained active in state government throughout the two Republican gubernatorial terms, despite facing considerable hostility and threats from white Floridians. See Joe M. Richardson, "Jonathan C. Gibbs: Florida's Only Negro Cabinet Member," *The Florida Historical Quarterly* 42 (April 1964): 363–68.

[88] While a number of federal troops remained in Florida, many were withdrawn. As a result, there were a number of violent clashes in the state – many involved whites against blacks but there were also some black-on-black and white-on-white. See Ralph L. Peek, "Aftermath of Military Reconstruction, 1868–1869," *The Florida Historical Quarterly* 43 (October 1964): 123–41.

[89] Ralph L. Peek, "Curbing of Voter Intimidation in Florida, 1871," *The Florida Historical Quarterly* 43 (April 1965): 333–48.

[90] Ralph L. Peek, "Election of 1870 and the End of Reconstruction in Florida," *The Florida Historical Quarterly* 45 (April 1967): 352–68, 358.

[91] Peek, "Election of 1870."

serving in the legislature as well, Reed declared their seats vacant. This conflict – combined with a number of gubernatorial vetoes – fostered distrust between Reed and Republican Senator Thomas Osborn, and led to the first of four (failed) attempts by the state legislature to impeach Reed during his single term in office. While Reed managed to serve out his term, he was not re-nominated as the GOP gubernatorial candidate in 1872.[92]

At the same time, the Osborn "ring" in the party suffered losses at county conventions, reducing their influence at the party's state convention where the national delegates to the 1872 Republican National Convention were elected. Black party leaders – including Charles H. Pearce, a state senator and AME bishop – used the state convention to attack carpetbagger control of the Florida GOP, criticizing both Reed and Osborn for the party's internal dysfunction. Later that summer, at a second state convention, Florida Republicans nominated Ossian Bingley Hart, a white justice on the Florida Supreme Court and a failed congressional candidate in 1870, as their gubernatorial candidate. Hart received the nomination in part due to his alliance with black Republicans like Pearce.[93] The 1872 election proved to be less violent than 1870, thanks largely to the deployment of federal troops to ensure a fair election.[94] As a result, black turnout was high and Republicans won the gubernatorial election, both congressional seats, and majorities in both chambers of the state legislature.

Hart was already in poor health when he was nominated, and after the election traveled out of state for medical treatment. He died in office in 1874, and his death elevated Lieutenant Governor Marcellus Stearns – a representative of the carpetbagger faction of the party – to the governorship. Stearns was born in Maine and had served in the Union army during the war, losing one of his arms in battle. As governor, Stearns attempted to move away from issues involving race and the war, stating in his first gubernatorial message to the legislature in 1875 that "slavery and secession are things of the past ... all the States are restored to their Constitutional relations with the General government, and a true and lasting peace has come."[95] However, as Jerrell Shofner notes, during the Hart–Stearns administration, a number of white Republicans began to reassess their partisan allegiances. These Republicans were "interested

---

[92] Cortez A. M. Ewing, "Florida Reconstruction Impeachments: 1. Impeachment of Governor Harrison Reed," *The Florida Historical Quarterly* 36 (April 1958): 299–318.

[93] During the convention the Osborn ring claimed Marcellus Stearns, a carpetbagger from Maine, had won the nomination, but the majority of delegates who supported Hart protested and threatened a riot. In response, Stearns ended his candidacy and instead was nominated as the party's candidate for lieutenant governor. See Canter Brown, Jr., "Carpetbagger Intrigues, Black Leadership, and a Southern Loyalist Triumph: Florida's Gubernatorial Election of 1872," *The Florida Historical Quarterly* 72 (January 1994): 275–301.

[94] Peek, "Curbing of Voter Intimidation in Florida," 347.

[95] Claude R. Flory, "Marcellus L. Stearns, Florida's Last Reconstruction Governor," *The Florida Historical Quarterly* 44 (January 1966): 181–92, 189.

primarily in orderly, economical state government" and began to be swayed by
the possibility of split-ticket voting by supporting "the national Republican
ticket and the Democratic state ticket because of the corruption in the Florida
Republican party."[96]

With the economic depression becoming more serious in the mid-1870s,
maintaining the Republican coalition in Florida proved impossible. In the
1874 midterm elections, the Florida GOP lost one of its congressional seats
and its state Senate majority. At the 1876 state convention, Republican delegates nominated Stearns for a second term, but supporters of Senator Simon
B. Conover bolted the convention and nominated Conover. Under pressure
from other GOP leaders, Conover withdrew from the race before the general
election, but refused to endorse Stearns.[97] Meanwhile, Democrats relied on a
"reform" campaign, calling for a more reliable state government and charging
Republicans with corruption. With the presidential election of 1876 hanging on
results from three Southern states – including Florida – national GOP leaders
urged their Floridian co-partisans to declare Hayes the victor. The Florida
canvassing board responsible for reporting the official election results comprised a majority of Republicans, and they followed the national party's
orders – dismissing 2,000 Democratic ballots and declaring both Hayes and
Stearns the winner in their respective races. In subsequent legal challenges, the
canvassing board eventually declared Democratic candidate George F. Drew
the victor in the gubernatorial election and Hayes the winner in the presidential
race. Thus, while a Republican won the White House thanks to Florida's
electoral votes, the Democrats won the gubernatorial election, majorities in
the state legislature, and both House seats.[98] By then, all federal troops had
been withdrawn from Florida as well – fully ending the Reconstruction era.[99]

The GOP did not fade away immediately after 1876, as the party regained
one of its US House seats following the 1878 election (following an election
contest).[100] Also, while Democratic candidate and longtime party boss William
D. Bloxham won the 1880 gubernatorial election comfortably (now former
Senator) Conover still received 45 percent of the vote. However, by 1884 the
Florida GOP had fallen under the control of the "Bisbee, Eagan, Martin
ring"[101] – referring to House member Horatio Bisbee, collector of internal

---

[96] Shofner, "Political Reconstruction in Florida," 162.   [97] Ibid., 166.

[98] In the Second Congressional District, Republican Horatio Bisbee, Jr. was initially seated. But
the House eventually ruled that Democrat Robert H. M. Davidson was entitled to the seat,
which he claimed on February 20, 1879.

[99] Jerrell H. Shofner, "Florida Courts and the Disputed Election of 1876," *The Florida Historical
Quarterly* 48 (July 1969): 26–46; Karen Guenther, "Potter Committee Investigation of the
Disputed Election of 1876," *The Florida Historical Quarterly* 61 (January 1983): 281–95.

[100] Democrat Noble A. Hull was initially seated. However, the House eventually ruled that Republican
Horatio Bisbee, Jr. was entitled to the seat, which he claimed on January 22, 1881.

[101] Edward C. Williamson, "Independentism a Challenge to the Florida Democracy of 1884," *The
Florida Historical Quarterly* 27 (October 1948): 131–56, 135.

revenue at Jacksonville, Dennis Eagan, and Malachi Martin, surveyor general of the Land Office at Greenville – a group of Republican leaders focused almost exclusively on managing the distribution of federal patronage.

At the same time, the Florida Democratic Party faced an internal split over issues related to the use of land for new railroads in the state. As a result, in 1884 an independent challenge to Democratic rule was attempted through the gubernatorial campaign of Frank Pope, a former Democrat. The independent ticket also included a Republican candidate for lieutenant governor and was endorsed (but not nominated) by the Republican state convention. In accepting his nomination, Pope promised that after the 1876 election had repudiated Republican radicalism, the 1884 election would tear "the mask of Democracy from the equally hideous face of its twin brother Bourbonism."[102] At the Republican state convention, Pope made an appearance and promised that "we shall rout the plundering Democrats from yonder Capital in next November!"[103] Pope appealed to the traditional Republican voting base (including blacks) with a platform that called for better public education and voting rights.

Republican leaders, however, did not fully support Pope. In an interview published in July 1884, Eagan accused Pope of having been involved in Democratic attacks at polling stations, and inciting violence against blacks. Meanwhile, a major black newspaper in Jacksonville called on black voters to support Democratic candidate Perry – dismissing Pope as a "pitiful negro-killing Democrat."[104] Other Republican leaders argued that a defeat in 1884 would be better for the party, in that it would provide them with the possibility of regaining the support they had lost with Pope – the logic being that "[if] the party did not win in 1884, it would in 1888."[105] Pope also faced the dilemma that while he needed GOP votes to win, appearing *too* Republican could cost him votes among white Democrats who were unhappy with their own party but unwilling to vote Republican.

The result was a relatively comfortable victory for the Democrats and the collapse of the Independent movement in Florida politics. Yet Democratic leaders were concerned by the 1884 election, believing their party's coalition was not strong enough to confidently secure future victories. One solution to this problem was to radically restructure the electoral process. After 1876, Democrats had passed legislation that required all voters to re-register. While black Republican legislators such as Robert Meacham protested the bill, it easily carried.[106] In 1885, a new constitutional convention was called that was intended to limit Bourbon power within the Democratic Party; in the

---

[102] Ibid., 138.   [103] Ibid., 146.   [104] Ibid., 149.   [105] Ibid., 144.
[106] Edward C. Williamson, "George F. Drew, Florida's Redemption Governor," *The Florida Historical Quarterly* 38 (January 1960): 206–15, 210.

end, it also included the first major attempt at disenfranchising blacks by introducing a conditional poll tax.[107]

After the new constitution was ratified in November 1886, Republican electoral performance declined. While Conover and Pope both received around 45 percent of the vote in 1880 and 1884, the Republican vote in 1888 dropped below 40 percent. The new constitution did not end black voting or black political participation, however, as black Republicans remained active in counties with black majorities and were regularly elected to city councils. In response, Democrats in the state legislature added new legal restrictions to further limit black suffrage – chief among them a new poll tax law and an eight-box law (which targeted illiterates) in 1889.[108] As a result, from 1890 onwards, the Florida Republican Party often won zero seats in one or both chambers of the legislature[109] and ceased to actively compete in statewide and congressional elections.

In lieu of active electoral competition, Florida Republicans focused their attention on using the party organization as a basis for controlling federal patronage appointments. During much of the 1890s, different groups within the Florida GOP battled for control of this patronage, and in 1896 even ran competing tickets in state elections. While some scholars have described this conflict as part of the broader Lily-White and Black-and-Tan clash that played out elsewhere, in Florida both sides were racially integrated. For example, when "Lily-White" Republicans held their own state convention in 1896, blacks made up a considerable part of the delegation, a black Republican was elected permanent chairman of the convention, and another black Republican was nominated as the faction's candidate for attorney general.[110] While this version of the Lily-Whites may have been more conservative on race issues, it also did not favor the full exclusion of blacks from the Florida GOP. Indeed, Florida's delegation to the Republican National Convention retained considerable black membership through the 1920s.[111]

After 1896, the Florida GOP continued to be in disarray organizationally. As Peter Klingman notes, the Republican Party had "broken apart completely by 1912" and the "factions were too numerous to count, and none rested on solid political ground except for the so-called post office group led by Joseph Lee," a

---

[107] Edward C. Williamson, "The Constitutional Convention of 1885," *The Florida Historical Quarterly* 41 (October 1962): 116–26. The poll tax was conditional in that it was only operative when the legislature authorized it. See J. Morgan Kousser, *The Shaping of Southern Politics: Suffrage Restrictions and the Establishment of the One-Party South, 1880–1910* (New Haven, CT: Yale University Press, 1974), 98.

[108] Kousser, *The Shaping of Southern Politics*, 100–01.

[109] Dubin, *Party Affiliations in the State Legislatures*, 44.

[110] Peter D. Klingman, *Neither Dies Nor Surrenders: A History of the Republican Party in Florida, 1867–1970* (Gainesville: University of Florida Press, 1984), 109.

[111] In 1896, the Black-and-Tan ticket eventually dropped out before the election. Unsurprisingly, Republicans failed to win any statewide offices regardless. See ibid., 110–11.

black office-holder and the secretary of the party's state central committee.[112] In 1912, a more virulent Lily-White group that actively demanded that blacks be excluded from the party emerged. However, because Lee's faction supported Taft and the Lily-Whites backed Roosevelt in the GOP presidential nomination fight, the Lily-Whites failed to win control of the state party and Lee remained in charge for the remainder of the 1910s.[113] The Black-and-Tans continued to control what was left of the Florida GOP after Lee's death in 1920, when George W. Bean – the white postmaster in Tampa – took over as the party's main leader. A legal challenge by Lily-Whites backfired when the Florida Supreme Court ruled in 1921 that, due to the party's failure to perform electorally, the Florida GOP was legally no longer a political party. Justice Jefferson B. Browne wrote:

Having gone out of existence as a political party in the eyes of the law, its officers, as such in the eyes of the law went out of existence with the party. The law does not know such a political party as the Republican Party; it does not know its officers; it has no control over it or its internal affairs.[114]

As a result of Browne's ruling, the GOP essentially became a private organization under Bean's control. This alienated a number of Florida Republicans, who attempted a coup against Bean at the 1928 state convention. The end result was that the party fell under the control of two white millionaires – steel magnate J. Leonard Replogle and Palm Beach mayor Barclay Warbritton. With the influence of black Republicans already in decline after Lee's death, black representation at national conventions declined further under the new party leaders. This may have been an attempt in part to make the Florida GOP attractive again for white voters: while Republicans still lost the other state-level races, Republican candidate Herbert Hoover (in no small part due to religious opposition to Democrat Al Smith) won Florida in the 1928 presidential election. This raised the hope that, with proper management, the Florida GOP might once again become a genuinely competitive political party. This hope was quickly extinguished: in the 1930 election, the Florida GOP was back to its usual anemic performance and in 1932 FDR beat Hoover by nearly 50 percentage points in the state. Still, the temporary resurgence of the GOP in 1928 pushed the party further toward Lily-Whiteism: black representation dropped to zero at the national convention in the immediate aftermath of the 1928 election.

But this Lily-White takeover did not result in the complete banishment of blacks from the party. While the Florida delegation that was seated at the Republican National Convention in 1932 and 1936 was entirely white, delegations from 1940 onward would contain a small percentage of blacks. This was because Florida repealed the poll tax in 1937, which opened the door to a small

---

[112] Ibid., 114.   [113] Ibid., 114–15.   [114] Cited in ibid., 118.

increase in black political participation in the state.[115] To be sure, such participation came at considerable risk, since the Ku Klux Klan was very active in
Florida in the 1930s.[116] Still, in Miami in particular, civil rights leaders began
to mobilize black citizens to vote in elections. One of the leaders of this effort
was Sam B. Solomon – the president of the Negro Citizens' League in Miami
and nicknamed the "Moses of Miami" in black newspapers.[117] In 1940,
Solomon led a rival delegation to the national convention to vie with the regular
Lily-White controlled group – led by J. Leonard Lewis.[118] Solomon and a
number of other black delegates were seated at the 1940 convention together
with the majority Lily-White delegation.[119] This compromise – white leadership of the party and a small minority of black delegates – continued in the
years that followed. For white GOP leaders, this approach proved satisfactory:
as one local Republican leader recounted to V. O. Key, Jr., "we have resolved
the racial difficulty by 'taking in' the right kind of Negroes. By giving them
representation the issue has been kept down."[120]

TENNESSEE: THE CURIOUS CASE OF A
BLACK-AND-TANS–DEMOCRATIC COALITION

Tennessee was perhaps the Southern state with the most Republican Party
success from the Civil War through the late 1960s. While the Republicans did
not control the state for very long during Reconstruction, a vibrant GOP
existed throughout this entire period in the hill country of eastern Tennessee.
This provided the Republican Party with a regular, minority of seats in the US
House and state legislature. Moreover, recurring divisions within the Democratic Party allowed the Republicans to elect three governors and carry the state
for two GOP presidential nominees in the years between the end of Reconstruction and the rise of Franklin Delano Roosevelt and the New Dealers (see
Table 8.4 and Figure 8.7). While the Tennessee Republican Party was white-
controlled during this time, an active Black-and-Tan wing was in operation in
the western part of the state. Moreover, blacks could vote at higher rates in
urban areas than in other parts of the Confederacy. This was due to an alliance
between Black-and-Tan Republicans and the ruling Democratic machine, as

[115] Charles D. Farris, "The Re-Enfranchisement of Negroes in Florida," *The Journal of Negro History* 3 (October 1954): 259–83.
[116] Raymond A. Mohl, "Race Relations in Miami since the 1920s," in David R. Colburn and Jane L. Landers, eds., *The African American Heritage of Florida* (Gainesville: University Press of Florida, 1995), 346.
[117] "Negroes Are Determined to Vote in Miami," *New York Amsterdam News*, January 6, 1940; "'Miami Moses' Here for GOP Meet," *New York Amsterdam News*, June 22, 1940.
[118] "White Primary Law Passed by Senate," *The Pittsburgh Courier*, May 20, 1939.
[119] "Republicans Make Bid to Negro Voters," *Philadelphia Tribune*, June 27, 1940.
[120] V. O. Key, Jr., *Southern Politics in State and Nation* (Knoxville: University of Tennessee Press, 1949), 289.

TABLE 8.4 *Descriptive Republican Party success in Tennessee, 1865–1968*

	1865–1877	1878–1896	1897–1932	1933–1968
Presidential candidate won the state?	✓		✓	✓
Senatorial candidate elected?	✓		*	✓
Gubernatorial candidate elected?	✓	✓	✓	
At least one House candidate elected?	✓	✓	✓	✓

* When Senator Robert Love Taylor (D) died in office, Republican Governor Ben Hooper appointed Republican Newell Sanders to the vacancy. Sanders served until January 1913, when the Tennessee General Assembly elected Democrat William R. Webb to succeed him.

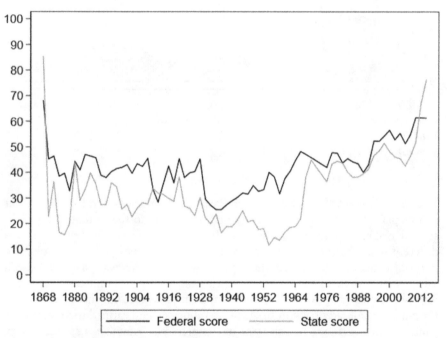

FIGURE 8.7 Republican Party strength at the federal and state levels in Tennessee, 1868–2012

blacks were often used by machine Democratic leaders as key swing votes to hold off insurgent party challengers. This alliance would allow the Black-and-Tans in west Tennessee to remain a critical force through the late 1940s (see Figure 8.8).

* * * * *

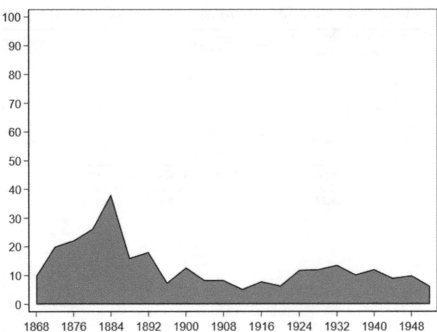

FIGURE 8.8 Percentage of GOP convention delegates from Tennessee that were black, 1868–1952

Source: Data collected by authors.

The development of the Republican Party in Tennessee – and the role that blacks played in it – was shaped by factors unique to the setting. That is, in several respects, politics during and after Reconstruction in Tennessee was different from that of other Southern states. First, Tennessee was not formally part of Reconstruction. When the first Reconstruction Act was passed in March 1867, which divided the ex-Confederate states into five military zones and imposed a military governor upon them, Tennessee was not included because the state was already back in the Union. Tennessee had ratified the Fourteenth Amendment, which the Republicans in Congress had established as a necessary condition for readmittance, in July 1866, while the other Southern states had balked. As a result, Tennessee did not experience the active societal presence by the US military over the next decade that the other Southern states did. This reduced racial tensions and scapegoating considerably, and aside from a brief period of Ku Klux Klan violence in the late 1860s limited the development of a violent white insurgency.

Second, Republican control of the state after the Civil War was short-lived. A Radical government, led by Governor William G. Brownlow, controlled the state through the late 1860s. Brownlow accomplished this in part by advocating for black voting rights, which the Radical-led legislature granted in February 1867, and by disenfranchising a large group of ex-Confederates.[121] Brownlow left the governorship in February 1869 – having been elected to serve in the US Senate – and Republicans became bitterly divided in his absence. The Republican Speaker of the Senate, Dewitt Clinton Senter, became interim governor, broke with the Radicals, and advocated for restoring the voting rights of ex-Confederates. More importantly, Senter replaced most of Brownlow's election commissioners in advance of the regular governor election; this allowed ex-Confederates to vote (as the new commissioners ignored their legal disability) and Senter won election over the Radical Republican candidate, William B. Stokes. In 1870, a new state constitutional convention was held, which formally eliminated the proscription on ex-Confederate voting rights.[122] As a result, the Democrats would quickly return to power and control the state throughout the decade of the 1870s.

Third, despite a quick return to minority status in 1869, the Republicans would remain a meaningful part of the partisan landscape in Tennessee. The GOP consistently dominated the eastern part of the state – the Appalachian hill country – which had been a haven of Union sentiment during the Civil War. And unlike much of the South, blacks continued to vote in Tennessee during the Jim Crow years. That is, while the Democrats adopted disenfranchising laws in 1889, in advance of the wave that occurred across the South over the next two decades, they were not as extreme as they could have been. The two main provisions to limit black (and poor white) suffrage were the Australian ballot – or secret ballot – that targeted illiterates, and a poll tax.[123] As Elizabeth Gritter notes: "Tennessee did not enact common measures of disenfranchisement such as the literacy test or a grandfather clause."[124] Nor was a statewide white primary adopted. Thus, while black voting declined beginning in the 1890s, the reductions were concentrated in the rural areas of the state. Blacks continued to

---

[121] E. Merton Coulter, *William G. Brownlow: Fighting Parson of the Southern Highlands* (Knoxville: University of Tennessee Press, 1999).

[122] Thomas B. Alexander, "Political Reconstruction in Tennessee, 1865–1870," in Richard O. Curry, ed., *Radicalism, Racism, and Party Realignment: The Border States during Reconstruction* (Baltimore: Johns Hopkins University Press, 1969), 37–79; F. Wayne Binning, "The Tennessee Republicans in Decline, 1869–1876: Part I," *Tennessee Historical Review* 39 (1980): 471–84.

[123] See Kousser, *The Shaping of Southern Politics*, 104–23; Michael Perman, *Struggle for Mastery: Disfranchisement in the South, 1888–1908* (Chapel Hill: University of North Carolina Press, 2001), 50–59; Joseph H. Cartwright, *The Triumph of Jim Crow: Tennessee Race Relations in the 1880s* (Knoxville: University of Tennessee Press, 1976). Two other laws were passed along with the secret-ballot and poll tax measures: a law to require voters to register twenty days in advance of an election (in areas with 500 or more votes were cast in the past) and a law that provided for separate ballot boxes for federal and state elections.

[124] Elizabeth Gritter, *River of Hope: Black Politics and the Memphis Freedom Movement, 1865–1954* (Lexington: University Press of Kentucky, 2014), 21.

vote – and support the GOP in statewide and national races – in urban areas such as Memphis.

As a result, thanks to their strength in the eastern part of the state, the GOP would control at least a fifth of Tennessee's seats in the US House and the state House through the early 1960s. Moreover, Democratic divisions in the state occurred frequently, which allowed Republicans – thanks often to urban black voters – to occasionally make other political inroads. For example, prior to the 1950s, the Tennessee GOP won the governorship four times: in 1880, 1910, 1912, and 1920. In 1880, Republican Alvin Hawkins was elected governor in a four-candidate race, after the Democrats split on a state debt issue (more on this below). In 1910, Republican Ben W. Hooper was elected governor when the Democrats divided on prohibition; Hooper defeated incumbent Democratic Governor Robert L. Taylor by over 10,000 votes in 1910 after receiving the endorsement of the prohibition wing of the Democratic Party.[125] He was reelected in 1912, defeating another former Democratic governor, Benton McMillin. And in 1920, Alfred A. Taylor was elected governor when the Democrats split on taxation and the basic urban/rural tax structure. Taylor received considerable support from farmers and women (soon after the Nineteenth Amendment was adopted) to defeat Democratic Governor Albert H. Roberts by more than 40,000 votes.[126] (Hooper and Taylor would be the only Republicans to be elected to statewide office in the ex-Confederacy over a nearly seventy-year period.[127]) In addition, the GOP did better in presidential elections than anywhere else in the South during this time. Republican presidential nominees Warren Harding in 1920 and Herbert Hoover in 1928 both carried Tennessee.

The composition of the Republican Party in Tennessee during and after Reconstruction was split between the eastern mountain wing and the western lowland wing. The eastern GOP was a mostly white group of ex-Unionists; they were not Lily-Whites per se, as few blacks lived in the region, so the party emerged without race being a central issue. And while the eastern Republicans were not racial progressives and often used race-baiting and white supremacist language in election campaigns – in response to Democratic race-baiting and white supremacist language, and thus as a way to take race as an issue off the

---

[125] See Paul E. Isaac, "The Problems of a Republican Governor in a Southern State: Ben Hooper of Tennessee, 1910–1914," *Tennessee Historical Quarterly* 27 (Fall 1968): 229–48. In 1914, after the Democrats ended their split by accepting a prohibition plank in the party platform, Democratic nominee Thomas Rye would defeat Hooper by over 20,000 votes.

[126] See Gary W. Reichard, "The Defeat of Governor Roberts," *Tennessee Historical Quarterly* 30 (Spring 1971): 94–109. In 1922, the Democrats were once again unified, and Democratic nominee Austin Peay would defeat Taylor by nearly 40,000 votes.

[127] Before Hooper and Taylor, the last Republican to be elected in a statewide race in the South was Daniel L. Russell, who was elected governor of North Carolina in 1896. After Hooper and Taylor, the next Republican to be elected in a statewide race in the South was John Tower, who was elected senator in Texas in 1961 (in a special election).

table – they understood the importance of working with the more diverse GOP in the western region. For example, they were willing to share federal patronage and they resisted any attempts by the Democrats to adopt laws that would explicitly disenfranchise blacks.[128]

In the western part of the state, the Republican Party looked more like the GOP in other parts of the South during and after Reconstruction – with both white and black elements. Whites, for the most part, controlled the local GOP organizations, with blacks rarely rising to meaningful leadership positions. That said, blacks held positions on the Nashville and Knoxville City Councils through the 1880s, and fourteen blacks were elected to the Tennessee General Assembly through the early 1890s.[129] And black delegates made up as much as 38 percent of the state's delegation to the Republican National Convention through the mid1880s. Democrats were often divided through the 1870s and 1880s but managed to take control of the state government in 1888 and (as mentioned) passed a set of disenfranchisement laws in 1889. This eroded black voting power (and representation) in the rural areas of the state. But blacks continued to participate politically in urban areas.

Why wasn't the disenfranchisement of blacks more complete? Divisions in the Democratic Party were mostly to blame. During the 1870s and 1880s, the Democrats were divided on a number of economic issues, mostly having to do with how to handle the state's debt (stemming from antebellum railroad construction) in the aftermath of the Civil War. With pro- and anti-repudiation factions emerging, Republicans were often the swing coalition – which led to Republican Alvin Hawkins winning the governorship in a four-candidate race in 1880.[130] More importantly, however, these Democratic divisions led to Democratic candidates in urban areas actively reaching out to black voters, as a way to win elections. Thus, mobilizing black voters became a staple of electoral politics, not just among Republicans in the state. This limited the scope of disenfranchising laws; state Democratic leaders recognized the need to limit Republican electoral power generally (so that the GOP could not easily win statewide offices or take control of the legislature) but also sought to keep blacks in cities (who could be cheaply mobilized) on the voting roll. The Australian ballot and poll tax threaded that needle.

This bipartisan mobilization of black voters helps explain how the GOP in the western part of the state developed in the aftermath of Jim Crow. From the 1890s through the mid-1910s, a Lily-White faction controlled the party in the region, and black voting continued to be used strategically by Democratic

---

[128] Gordon B. McKinney, "Southern Mountain Republicans and the Negro, 1865–1900," *The Journal of Southern History* 41 (1975): 493–516.

[129] Bobby Lovett, *The Civil Rights Movement in Tennessee: A Narrative History* (Knoxville: University of Tennessee Press, 2005), 232.

[130] Robert B. Jones, "Tennessee Gubernatorial Elections, II: 1880 – The Collapse of the Democratic Party," *Tennessee Historical Quarterly* 33 (1974): 49–61.

factions in state politics. In the 1910s, however, Robert R. Church, Jr. of Memphis – a prominent black banker and businessman – began organizing a Black-and-Tan faction to vie with the Lily-Whites for party control. At the core of Church's organizing efforts was the establishment of the Lincoln League, a series of clubs comprising black businessmen and professionals that were built to promote racial solidarity. In 1916, the two Republican factions ran separate slates, and Church's Black-and-Tans outpaced the Lily-Whites by four to one. This established the Black-and-Tans as the regular GOP organization in west Tennessee, with Church as its leader.[131] He was a perennial delegate to the Republican National Convention between 1912 and 1940, an important party spokesman for the South, and a key leader in the distribution of federal patronage not just in Tennessee but throughout the region.

Church built his political influence by coordinating with the political machine of Democrat Edward H. Crump, who was Mayor of Memphis from 1910 to 1915 and the effective Democratic boss of Tennessee for the first half of the twentieth century.[132] Crump would often be in need of votes in the turbulent politics of the state, and he would turn to Church for aid in mobilizing black voters. As Roger Biles notes: "To the dismay of reporters and civic-minded bystanders alike, Crump 'herded' truck-loads of blacks to polling places throughout Shelby County, provided them with poll tax receipts, and told them how to vote – frequently repeating this practice at several locations in the area."[133] From Church's perspective, he and his Black-and-Tan organization benefited from the vote trading: in exchange for their votes in support of Crump's candidates in the Democratic primaries, they received the ability to vote any way they liked in state and national elections. Moreover, Church could extract important municipal services (parks, schools, and so on) for black constituents from the Crump machine.

As GOP leader in west Tennessee, Church forged a good working relationship with Rep. J. Will Taylor (2nd congressional district), the leader of the eastern GOP, to maintain the Black-and-Tan organization in the state through the 1920s and 1930s.[134] Taylor controlled federal patronage in Tennessee and shared the largesse with Church in a fair manner. Church understood the importance of optics, however, and recognized that he was limited in selecting blacks for higher-level positions. He thus used his influence to place whites who he felt would not racially discriminate in positions of authority. Church also made sure to select white candidates for federal judgeships and district attorney who would not threaten the Crump machine, which he used as an additional

[131] Gritter, *River of Hope*, 48.
[132] See William D. Miller, *Mr. Crump of Memphis* (Baton Rouge: Louisiana State University Press, 1964); Key, *Southern Politics in State and Nation*, chapter 4.
[133] Roger Biles, "Robert R. Church, Jr. of Memphis: Black Republican Leader in the Age of Democratic Ascendancy, 1928–1940," *Tennessee Historical Quarterly* 42, 4 (1983): 376.
[134] Gritter, *River of Hope*, 57–58, 68–69.

chit to negotiate with the Tennessee boss. But he also did not ignore his black constituents. Church, in fact, used his influence to help blacks in west Tennessee considerably, distributing a range of lower-level patronage positions – like US mail carriers – to them.[135]

Throughout his tenure as west Tennessee Republican leader, Church had to fend off repeated attempts by Lily-Whites to overturn his Black-and-Tan organization. In 1928, for example, the Lily-Whites charged Church with graft in the distribution of post office appointments. But the charges – thanks to the backing of Taylor and others – did not stick.[136] Church also faced multiple attempts over time to have his Black-and-Tan delegates rejected at the GOP national convention, but his sizable influence always allowed him to win out over the Lily-Whites in the end. Additionally, Taylor, a member of the RNC's Executive Committee from 1929 to 1939, was always an important source of support.

By the late 1930s, however, Church's influence was waning. As the Democrats began a long string of presidential victories in 1932, federal patronage for Republicans dried up. Church's ability to mobilize black voters for the Crump machine in local primaries also ceased to matter. As Roger Biles recounts:

In the thirties Crump became less dependent upon black electoral support as his machine came to maturity. The margins of victory in local elections for machine candidates grew so dramatically – indeed in 1935 and 1939 no candidates even bothered to run for mayor against the Crump-anointed choices – that the black vote no longer loomed as pivotal. Consequently, the Democratic machine ceased to cater so assiduously to black concerns, especially after the 1938 election in which, for the first time in memory, blatant manipulation of the black vote did not occur and the results still constituted a sound victory for the Democrats. Ominously, by the late thirties, such practices as "negro-baiting" and the widespread violation of civil liberties, for years not tolerated by Crump, burst forth in epidemic proportions.[137]

Crump did not stop there, however. No longer needing Church, Crump viewed him as a potential obstacle to his machine and set out to ruin him. He established a campaign of legal harassment against Church, charging him with a variety of code violations on his rental properties and threatening to confiscate his real estate holdings for unpaid taxes. Eventually, Church was forced to flee the state and set up shop in Illinois. While Church tried to continue to exert influence in Tennessee from his new home, his power declined dramatically as any remaining black leaders in the state were under Crump's thumb.[138] Meanwhile, black voters themselves began moving en masse to the Democratic Party, thanks to the success of Franklin Delano Roosevelt and his New Deal policies.

The Black-and-Tans, under George Washington Lee, one of Church's lieutenants, would continue to constitute the Republican organization in west

---

[135] Biles, "Robert R. Church, Jr. of Memphis," 377.   [136] Gritter, *River of Hope*, 101–06.
[137] Biles, "Robert R. Church, Jr. of Memphis," 378.   [138] Ibid., 378–82.

Tennessee in the 1940s. In the early 1950s, a new challenge would emerge. A New Guard Republican movement was organized by white businessmen and white middle-class housewives, to support the candidacy of Dwight D. Eisenhower. The New Guard GOP – different from the old Lily-Whites, who had largely become extinct – was economically conservative, anti-union, and opposed to the Democrats' New Deal policies. Many also did not support the civil rights policies that had begun to emerge. Lee's Black-and-Tan group (now called the "Old Guard") would vie for state party control throughout the 1950s. While the two groups often found a way to share control – and the federal patronage that would come from the Eisenhower administration – the New Guard Republicans had the momentum. They came out strongly for Eisenhower in 1952, while Lee's Old Guard initially supported Robert Taft.[139] Moreover, the conservative nature of the New Guard meshed well with the rightward movement of the national Republican Party, and by 1964 – and Barry Goldwater's nomination – the New Guard was clearly in ascendancy in Tennessee. Republican Howard Baker took advantage of this new conservative movement to win election to the US Senate in 1966, besting former Democratic governor Frank G. Clement. Baker was only the second popularly elected Republican senator in the twentieth-century South.[140]

CONCLUSION

In the four cases presented here, the Lily-Whites, at some point in time, became dominant in the state Republican party organizations. Yet unlike in the states discussed in Chapter 7, Lily-White control did not result in the (near) complete exclusion of blacks from the party. Rather, in each state, a small group of black Republicans remained active in the party at state and national conventions. This outcome was largely the product of state-specific developments. For example, the Tennessee GOP was effectively divided into two geographical wings for much of the first half of the twentieth century. While the party was controlled by whites in the east, black leaders in the west formed a surprising coalition with white Democrats – resulting in a small but consistent percentage of blacks in Tennessee's delegation to the Republican National Convention throughout this period.

Meanwhile, in Louisiana the ruling Black-and-Tan machine came under attack from the Harding administration in the early 1920s. While Harding's attack did not result in the machine's demise, it did introduce new white leaders into the party who began to cooperate with Emil Kuntz, the white leader of the Black-and-Tan group. As a result, by the late 1920s, black leaders were pushed out of the party. After Kuntz's death, a former Lily-White took over control of

[139] Gritter, *River of Hope*, 198–200, 205–08.

[140] John Tower was the first, in the 1961 special election in Texas, to fill Lyndon Johnson's Senate seat. Strom Thurmond was also elected in 1966, after his party switch in 1964.

the party. While Louisiana would continue to have biracial delegations from 1932 onwards, this change in leadership produced a notable decline in black influence in the state party. In Arkansas, leadership changes also affected the standing of black leaders in the party. Under the Clayton–Remmel machine, the GOP was biracial. But the Lily-Whites briefly took control of the state party in the 1910s and sent an all-white delegation to the 1920 national convention. However, deposed chief Harmon Remmel regained control in 1924, after the death of his nephew and Lily-White leader Gus Remmel, and restored some level of black representation.

Finally, in Florida a white-led Black-and-Tan coalition controlled the party up to the 1928 convention but was replaced by a Lily-White group loyal to Hoover. In 1932 and 1936, this group sent all-white delegations to the national convention. By 1940, however, Florida once again had a biracial delegation thanks to the resurgence of (Republican) black activism in the state in the wake of the 1937 repeal of the poll tax. By then, white party leaders believed that allowing blacks a degree of representation was easier than having to fight them at the national level every four years.

9

South Carolina, Georgia, and Mississippi

Of the eleven ex-Confederate states, the large majority saw Lily-Whites take control of the state party sometime in the late nineteenth or early twentieth century. There were, however, three exceptions to this rule: South Carolina, Georgia, and Mississippi. While each of these states eventually saw some form of Lily-Whiteism gain control, the Black-and-Tan organizations managed to hang onto power longer than elsewhere in the South. South Carolina's Black-and-Tan machine finally fell apart at the 1940 national convention. Georgia began to see a clear decline in black delegates in 1952. And, finally, the Mississippi GOP remained under Black-and-Tan control up to the 1960 national convention. Why did these three state organizations buck the trend?

The histories presented in this chapter show that the party organization's survival in each state relied on the ability of individual party leaders to withstand a series of major challenges to their control in the 1920s. Each of the leaders in these state parties – "Tieless Joe" Tolbert in South Carolina, Walter H. Johnson and Ben Davis in Georgia, and Perry Howard in Mississippi – faced considerable opposition, both locally and from national leaders like Harding and Hoover. Yet each leader managed to survive these challenges – at least for a while – through strategic choices, some element of luck, and (in the cases of Johnson, Davis, and Howard) support from black Republicans outside of the South.

SOUTH CAROLINA: "TIELESS JOE" AND THE BLACK-AND-TANS

In South Carolina, Republicans controlled the state government between 1868 and 1876, before experiencing a major decline and full Democratic takeover of the state. In the years that followed, Republican leaders focused their attention on patronage and abandoned any ambition for electoral

TABLE 9.1 *Descriptive Republican Party success in South Carolina, 1865–1968*

	1865–1877	1878–1896	1897–1932	1933–1968
Presidential candidate won the state?	✓			✓
Senatorial candidate elected?	✓			✓
Gubernatorial candidate elected?	✓			
At least one House candidate elected?	✓	✓		✓

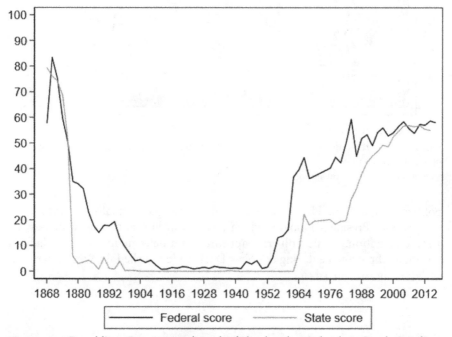

FIGURE 9.1 Republican Party strength at the federal and state levels in South Carolina, 1868–2012

competition (see Table 9.1 and Figure 9.1). Throughout most of this period, and particularly in the first decades of the twentieth century, a Black-and-Tan coalition controlled the South Carolina GOP (see Figure 9.2). The party boss was "Tieless Joe" Tolbert – a white man – who worked with black party members to control the state's delegation to the Republican National Convention and trade its support for federal patronage. Tolbert dominated South Carolina GOP politics for decades despite having a national reputation for

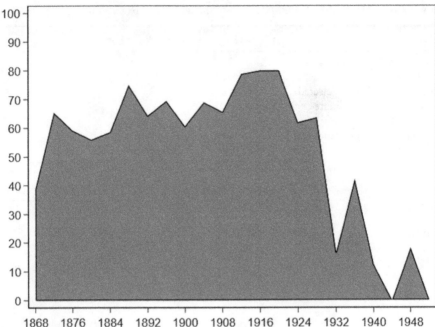

FIGURE 9.2 Percentage of GOP convention delegates from South Carolina that were black, 1868–1952
Source: Data collected by authors.

political corruption. His control over the state party finally declined after clashes with President Hoover, which resulted in him not being seated at the 1932 convention. While Tolbert reappeared as a delegate in 1936, the lack of presidential patronage during the New Deal era led to the Lily-Whites permanently taking over in 1940.

*   *   *   *   *

During the initial period of Reconstruction under Andrew Johnson, South Carolina's political leaders – mostly former Confederates – refused to fully meet Johnson's (mild) terms for re-admittance. While the South Carolina constitutional convention in 1865 begrudgingly agreed to prohibit slavery and repudiate secession, it refused to abolish the state's war debt. Additionally, the new South Carolina legislature passed legislation barring "persons of color" (those deemed to be less than seven-eighths white) from holding any profession other than farmer or servant. This legislation was criticized harshly throughout the North, and the law was quickly invalidated. Still, blacks were banned from voting. Under Radical Reconstruction, a very different approach was taken. A new Republican Party was organized in July 1867, and was dominated by black delegates.[1] And at the constitutional convention in January 1868, there were 124 delegates, a majority (73) of whom were black. The convention decided against setting voting restrictions on former Confederates but opened the franchise to all men regardless of race. The convention also supported the proposal of black delegates like Francis L. Cardozo to create integrated schools. With white voters largely apathetic, and the Union army guaranteeing the safety of the black population, the constitution was ratified by voters in April 1868.[2]

In the same election, Republican Robert Kingston Scott – a carpetbagger originally from Ohio who had worked for the Freedmen's Bureau after the war – was elected governor, and Republicans won substantial majorities (88.7 percent of seats in the Assembly and 80.6 percent in the state Senate) in the state legislature. The GOP would retain control of the state for eight years, winning each biennial gubernatorial election and majorities in the state legislature through 1876. Once in office, however, black and white Republicans found themselves deeply divided on issues related to civil rights and discrimination – with white Republicans often voting with Democrats in the state legislature. After 1870, black Republicans increasingly flexed their muscles – successfully winning elected posts (including multiple congressional seats) and gaining appointed positions – which further alienated some white Republicans.[3]

To try to take back control of government, Democrats relied on a mixed strategy in election campaigns. First, they accused Scott, and his successors Franklin J. Moses (1873–74) and Daniel Henry Chamberlain (1875–76), of corruption and mismanagement of the state government.[4] Second, Democratic-sponsored terror groups increased their violence against black voters. As a result, Republicans began to see a meaningful decline in their vote totals: while Scott and Moses received more than 60 percent of the vote in 1870 and 1872, Chamberlain won the 1874 gubernatorial election with just 54 percent. In 1876, with Chamberlain up for reelection, more violence erupted, including a

---

[1] One Northern observer in a letter to Republicans in Massachusetts stressed the intelligence of the black delegates, noting that he "was astonished at the amount of intelligence and ability shown by the colored men of the Convention. Of all the speeches that were made by the colored portion of the Delegates, and there were a great many for they did their full share of the talking running through three days ... not one speech was made by any of them, that would not have done honor to Faneuil Hall and a Boston audience." Richard H. Abbott, "A Yankee Views the Organization of the Republican Party in South Carolina, July 1867," *The South Carolina Historical Magazine* 85 (July 1984): 247.

[2] Hyman Rubin III, *South Carolina Scalawags* (Columbia: University of South Carolina Press, 2006), 18–36.

[3] Ibid., 61.

[4] At least some of those accusations appear to have been accurate. However, Republicans in the state legislature also accused Republican governors of such behavior and – in 1871 – an attempt was made to impeach Scott for exactly these reasons.

massacre in Hamburg where white supremacists murdered multiple black militiamen. In response, Democrats criticized Chamberlain for trying to involve the federal government.[5]

During the 1876 campaign, Democrats sought to prevent blacks from voting in any way possible. Democratic terror groups murdered multiple black men – with one clash between Red Shirts and a black militia group in Aiken County resulting in the death of thirty blacks. And on election day itself, Democrats engaged in extensive fraud and had armed men appear at the polls to intimidate would-be black voters. In the end, the Democrats managed to win a slim majority in the Assembly and narrowly elect Wade Hampton III – a former Confederate general – governor. While Chamberlain rejected the results for months, President Hayes's decision in April 1877 to withdraw all federal troops from South Carolina settled the issue; Chamberlain had no ability to withstand a Democratic takeover, and he fled the state. Facing threats on their life, many black legislators resigned their seats and others were expelled, setting up new elections for these seats later in the year, which Republicans failed to contest. As a result, Democrats took control of the state Senate and increased their majority in the Assembly.[6]

While in office, Hampton largely refrained from limiting the rights of blacks and even appointed a number of them to minor state offices. To be sure, Hampton and other Democrats had the strong conviction that the white minority in South Carolina should always rule the black majority. Democrats also abolished a number of voting precincts in heavily Republican areas. The loss of power – and internal disagreements between white and black Republicans – left the GOP deeply divided. White Republican leaders urged the party not to nominate any statewide candidates in the 1878 election, with the hope of reducing Democratic activities in the campaign and potentially allowing some Republicans to win in state legislative elections. Black leaders mostly opposed this move, but at the GOP state convention no party ticket was nominated.[7] The results were disastrous: not only did Democrats win the gubernatorial election with 99 percent of the vote, but Republicans lost nearly all of their seats in both the Assembly and the state Senate.[8]

Despite this, party chairman Robert B. Elliott made essentially the same argument at the next GOP state convention two years later: Republicans should not contest any statewide offices in 1880 because Democrats were too

[5] Rubin, *South Carolina Scalawags*, 105–06.
[6] William J. Cooper, Jr., *The Conservative Regime: South Carolina, 1877–1890* (Baltimore: Johns Hopkins University Press, 1968), 24–26; Thomas Holt, *Black Over White: Negro Political Leadership in South Carolina during Reconstruction* (Chicago: University of Illinois Press, 1977), 209.
[7] Holt, *Black Over White*, 213–14.
[8] Michael J. Dubin, *Party Affiliations in the State Legislatures: A Year by Year Summary, 1796–2006* (Jefferson, NC: McFarland & Company, 2007), 172.

powerful, they would refuse to give up office if they were to lose, and Republicans should instead bide their time.[9] Starting in the 1880s, Democrats began to enact new electoral rules intended to limit black participation. For example, in 1882 the legislature passed the "eight-box" election law, which required voters to cast separate ballots for each race and to deposit them in the appropriate ballot box – essentially establishing a literacy requirement. By 1895, the state had gone even further: in a revised version of the state constitution, voters now had to prove they were intelligent enough to vote by passing a literacy test and answering questions about any constitutional provision (an "understanding clause"). These changes almost entirely banned blacks from electoral participation. As a result, Democrats began a long period of electoral domination, with Republicans generally failing to run gubernatorial candidates and seeing their representation in the state legislature remain in the single digits.[10]

As the state party all but disappeared in terms of contesting office, GOP leaders focused their attention instead on patronage and national convention politics. Throughout the 1880s and 1890s, a Black-and-Tan coalition controlled the state party. As Willard B. Gatewood noted, prominent black Republicans were convinced that their only chance at political influence was "to accept the existing repressive order and attract white men into the party who were willing to cooperate with Negroes in return for occupying the most conspicuous offices."[11] Thus, black Republicans like former congressmen Thomas E. Miller and Robert Smalls shared power with white office-holders like Eugene Alonzo Webster, a postmaster in Orangeburgh, SC.[12]

During the McKinley administration, this reigning Black-and-Tan coalition faced a major challenge from the White House and the Republican National Committee. Working with Senator John L. McLaurin (D-SC) – who had become an important ally of the McKinley administration – Mark Hanna attempted to create a new Lily-White party organization in South Carolina by replacing Webster on the RNC with a candidate selected by McLaurin. After both McKinley and Webster died within days of one another, Theodore Roosevelt waded into the complicated political waters by mixing recommendations from McLaurin, Booker T. Washington, and the official Black-and-Tan party organization in determining his federal appointments in South Carolina. Initially, Roosevelt's attempts at working with Democrats and Lily-White Republicans troubled black Republicans, and raised the possibility of an

[9] Holt, *Black Over White*, 216–17.

[10] See Dubin, *Party Affiliations in the State Legislatures*, 171; Michael J. Dubin, *United States Gubernatorial Elections, 1861–1911: The Official Results by State and County* (Jefferson, NC: McFarland & Company, 2010).

[11] Willard B. Gatewood, "Theodore Roosevelt and Southern Republicans: The Case of South Carolina, 1901–1904," *The South Carolina Historical Magazine* 70 (October 1969): 251–66, 252.

[12] *Alumni Record of Wesleyan University* (Hartford, CT: Press of the Case, Lockwood & Brainard Company, 1883), 251.

anti-Roosevelt movement in 1904 in the state. However, Roosevelt's appointment of William D. Crum (a black physician) as collector of the Port of Charleston in 1902 resulted in a major outcry by Lily-Whites and Democrats. Ironically, Crum was not part of the Black-and-Tan coalition, nor its preferred candidate for the position. Yet the opposition to Crum's appointment united the existing party behind Roosevelt in 1904.[13]

In the years that followed, the Black-and-Tans continued their control of the South Carolina GOP. The source of this domination was the strength of a local party machine built around one man – Joseph W. Tolbert – in the first decades of the twentieth century. Based on a lucrative system in which his Black-and-Tan machine sold federal offices to local Republicans and in return provided a consistent state voting bloc at the GOP convention, Tolbert managed to maintain a position of power that made him a reliable – if unattractive – negotiating partner for national leaders seeking South Carolina's convention votes. The son of a two-time failed congressional candidate, Tolbert – commonly known as "Tieless Joe"[14] – was himself white but had managed to build up a party machine consisting of "himself, a few other whites, and handpicked Negroes over the state" with the aim of choosing delegates to the national convention and distributing patronage.[15]

Building this machine did not make Tolbert a popular political figure, either at the national level or at home. *Time* noted that Tolbert's leadership of a largely black party organization meant that "to most decent whites he is guilty of South Carolina's supreme sin."[16] The Tolbert family had direct experience with what the consequences of engaging in this "supreme sin" could be: in 1898, during an attempt at collecting evidence of voter disenfranchisement, Robert Redd Tolbert – Tieless Joe's brother and himself a frequent delegate to Republican National Conventions – was shot and wounded outside a polling station after a conflict with local white Democrats that left one of them dead.[17] In the days that followed, white Democrats went on a rampage, killing several black men in revenge. Tolbert's father was arrested, and the local press blasted the Tolberts for inciting a race riot by encouraging black citizens to vote.[18]

---

[13] Gatewood, "Theodore Roosevelt and Southern Republicans."

[14] Tolbert's view on ties was as follows: "Ain't never worn one. Don't bother with nothing I can do without." See "Joseph W. Tolbert of South Carolina," *New York Times*, October 19, 1946.

[15] V. O. Key, Jr., *Southern Politics in State and Nation* (New York: Knopf, 1949), 288.

[16] "Palmettto Stump, Thirties Style," *Time*, August 24, 1936, 17.

[17] T. P. Tolbert had "set up a box outside the regular polling place in the community of Phoenix. Negroes who were refused the right to vote were asked to fill out a form affidavit and drop it into a box which was in the possession of Tolbert." After a white Democrat challenged Tolbert's right to collect this information, an altercation followed which ended in the death of the Democrat and the wounding of Tolbert. George Brown Tindall, *South Carolina Negroes* (Columbia: University of South Carolina Press, 1952), 256–57.

[18] Ibid., 256–58.

Despite the danger of running a Black-and-Tan organization in the post-Reconstruction South, Tolbert's machine became one of the most successful at fighting off Lily-White challenges. The basis of Tolbert's success lay in his ability to deliver patronage and charge considerable sums for it. The economics of this system became public thanks to a series of accusations against Tolbert in the first half of the 1920s, after President Harding nominated him to be US marshal for the Western district of South Carolina. Harding's decision was surprising, as he represented one of the few Republican presidents in this period that had not relied on a Southern pre-convention strategy to win the nomination. Additionally, the Harding administration in its first months in office postponed all federal appointments (the lifeline of the party machine) in South Carolina, in order to search for an alternative to Tolbert. By 1922, however, Harding had concluded that both the Tolbert machine and any alternative Lily-White organization shared a single-minded focus on controlling access to federal offices, while displaying little passion for Republican policies.[19] As a result, Harding decided to stick with the devil he knew, resulting in Tolbert being nominated for a high-profile federal office.

Tolbert's nomination, however, set off a firestorm that damaged the reputation of the Republican Party in the South and revealed the Tolbert organization for the patronage machine that it was. While the scandal did not threaten Tolbert's control over the South Carolina GOP in the short term, it provided insight into the way the Tolbert machine managed to remain in control of the party for so long. In addition, Harding's unwillingness to drop Tolbert after the scandal broke indicates the value he placed on building a relationship with South Carolina's GOP boss and the important role local Southern Republican leaders played in the party, regardless of the region's inability to provide any electoral votes.

In July 1922, several months after Harding had nominated Tolbert, Senator Nathaniel B. Dial (D-SC) criticized the nomination and accused Tolbert of dividing "the State into districts, in each of which he had stationed a henchman who sold the Federal plums for one-half the first year's salary."[20] Dial claimed that Tolbert stood to gain $100,000 from the sales of federal offices:

I am told of many instances where the offices were sold – one bringing $750, another $1,200, another $600, another $2,000, and different sums all around the State where there was competition. A recent case was reported where $1,200 was paid and the party failed to get the office, and, after considerable wrangling, the funds were returned. It is alleged that appointees to small offices often have to contribute.[21]

[19] Richard B. Sherman, *The Republican Party and Black America: From McKinley to Hoover, 1896–1933* (Charlottesville: University Press of Virginia, 1973), 155–56.
[20] "Dial Charges Sale of Federal Offices in South Carolina," *New York Times*, July 31, 1922.
[21] Ibid.

While Tolbert denied the allegations, the scandal did him in, as the Senate refused to confirm his nomination – despite the Republicans controlling the chamber.[22] Instead of dropping his now toxic candidate, however, Harding chose to use a recess appointment to give Tolbert the position. Once the Senate reconvened, it again refused to confirm Tolbert, which resulted in a second recess appointment.[23] Finally, in late 1923, after Harding's death, Tolbert resigned his position.[24] His resignation, however, did not end the public scrutiny of the Tolbert party machine. In 1924, when a Senate committee on campaign funding heard testimony from J. T. Doyle, secretary of the United States civil service committee, Tolbert was further implicated in the sale of offices:

> Doyle said that Howard A. Littlejohn, postmaster at Belton, S.C., had been told by Joseph W. Tolbert, Republican national committeeman in South Carolina, that he would get him reappointed postmaster "if your heart and pocketbook will get right." He also testified that Maj. James W. Bradford, at Sumter, S.C., had paid $500 to get promoted from assistant postmaster to postmaster.[25]

Despite these charges, Tolbert and his delegation were seated again at the 1924 and 1928 Republican National Conventions. The negative national attention around Tolbert, however, eventually led a rival Lily-White coalition under the leadership of Joe Hambright to emerge. Throughout most of the 1920s, however, the Hambright organization failed to undermine the Tolbert machine.[26] But this would change after the 1928 GOP convention. Unlike most previous Republican presidential candidates, Herbert Hoover was quite popular in the South, thanks in part to his involvement in the Red Cross relief efforts in the wake of the Great Mississippi Flood of 1927, as well as the anti-Catholic bigotry directed against Al Smith, his likely Democratic opponent. During the campaign, Hoover and his allies attempted to convince white Southerners – most of whom were Protestants – to desert the Democratic Party. To achieve this, Hoover invested heavily in Lily-White organizations in the South, a move that Tolbert opposed during the 1928 convention.[27]

---

[22] "Tolbert Denies Sale of Offices," *New York Times*, August 1, 1922.

[23] "Tolbert Reappointment Seen Unconstitutional," *Washington Post*, March 10, 1923.

[24] In resigning his position, Tolbert struck a deal with the new president, Calvin Coolidge, in which his nephew, Joseph A. Tolbert, would be appointed and confirmed as district attorney for the Western District of South Carolina. See Louis Fagan, "'The Principles of Republicanism': Black and Tan Republicans in South Carolina, 1895–1950" (Doctoral dissertation, Emory University, 2018): 322–23.

[25] "Sale of Patronage in South Carolina Charged at Hearing," *Washington Post*, October 31, 1924.

[26] Indeed, while Tolbert himself was seated in every convention between 1900 and 1928, Hambright was not once a delegate in that period. Hanes Walton, Jr., et al., *The African American Electorate*, Vol. I (Washington, DC: CQ Press, 2012), 454.

[27] Donald J. Lisio, *Hoover, Blacks, and Lily-Whites: A Study of Southern Strategies* (Chapel Hill: University of North Carolina Press, 1985), 59–60.

After the general election, Hoover – now president – sought to continue the process of building a more viable Republican Party in the South, by removing the existing leadership of the corrupt Black-and-Tan coalitions. In terms of South Carolina, Hoover attempted to name Hambright the chair of the state Republican Party, hoping to replace the Tolbert machine with one loyal to his administration. The move was largely a failure, but it did initiate the end of the Black-and-Tan domination of the South Carolina GOP. Tolbert, working with Democratic Senator Cole Blease (D-SC), succeeded in delaying or blocking the confirmation of US marshals and postmasters that Hambright recommended for appointment. This subterfuge meant that Hambright did not have the necessary building blocks to create a viable alternative organization: without the jobs, Hambright "lacked security and the proof of leadership needed to build a new state party."[28]

Tolbert, meanwhile, also organized his own state convention, arguing that as an RNC member he represented the true Republican Party in South Carolina; in so doing, he elected party office-holders of his own and declared the rival Hambright party to be illegal. The clash between the two competing party organizations reached its zenith at the 1932 convention, during which Tolbert successfully convinced his fellow RNC members to recognize his organization alone – arguing that it was not in the interests of local party leaders to allow the president to choose his own state party leaders.[29] Hoover, however, was not to be denied. During the convention, he personally interfered: when the Credentials Committee approved the seating of Tolbert's Black-and-Tan delegation, Hoover voiced his disapproval and the committee reversed itself and seated the Hambright delegates instead. As a result, black representation dropped dramatically: in 1928, over 63 percent of the state's delegation was black, while in 1932 the seated (Hambright) delegation was less than 17 percent black.[30]

The Hambright organization's victory proved to be a temporary one. After Hoover's landslide defeat in the 1932 general election, the South Carolina Lily-White organization lost its most prominent national defender, and Tolbert succeeded in getting seated at the 1936 convention. However, during the New Deal, the Black-and-Tan machine no longer had access to the executive patronage that had been the foundation of its existence. By 1940, Tolbert was no longer capable of getting himself or members of his organization seated at the national convention. And by the time of his death in 1946 – due to injuries sustained from a mysterious accident, as he was struck by a truck while walking along a highway in his hometown[31] – Tolbert's machine had been replaced by one led by J. Bates Gerald, who built an organization combining white leadership with a small minority of black representatives from among "Negro college

[28] Ibid., 181.   [29] Ibid., 261–66.
[30] Richard Oulahan, *The Man Who...: The Story of the 1932 Democratic National Convention* (New York: The Dial Press, 1971), 62.
[31] "Joseph W. Tolbert of South Carolina," *New York Times*, October 19, 1946.

TABLE 9.2 *Descriptive Republican Party success in Georgia, 1865–1968*

	1865–1877	1878–1896	1897–1932	1933–1968
Presidential candidate won the state?				✓
Senatorial candidate elected?				
Gubernatorial candidate elected?	✓			
At least one House candidate elected?	✓			✓

presidents, lawyers, doctors, and ... businessmen."[32] Black representation in the South Carolina delegation thus remained below 20 percent for conventions after 1936 – even hitting zero in 1944 and 1952.

South Carolina's uncommon history helps reveal the elements that defined both the Black-and-Tan vs. Lily-White conflict as well as the GOP organizations in general across the South. First, it shows how important control of patronage appointments was to these organizations. Once Tolbert's access to federal jobs was closed off – first by Hoover's opposition to his organization, then by the Democrats' control of the federal government during the New Deal years – his organization collapsed. Importantly, however, the South Carolina case also shows that the Lily-White movement in the early twentieth century did not possess the moral high ground. The Hambright organization's main opposition to the Tolbert machine was that *they* wanted control over patronage distribution, not that South Carolina's existing Republican Party was corrupt.

GEORGIA: PATRONAGE POLITICS AND THE DECLINE OF THE BLACK-AND-TANS UNDER HOOVER

The GOP's electoral decline during Reconstruction proved particularly rapid in Georgia. While Republicans performed reasonably well in the 1868 election, they would control the state government for just two years. By 1870, Democrats began a period of domination that would be unchallenged well into the second half of the twentieth century. Not only did the GOP fail to win statewide offices, Republican victories in the state legislature were rare as well (see Table 9.2 and Figure 9.3). Often the GOP failed to even nominate candidates for statewide races, leaving Democrats running uncontested, as Republicans in the state focused exclusively on managing patronage and fighting over control of the national convention delegation. Notably, Georgia also remained under Black-and-Tan control longer than nearly any other Southern state (see

[32] Key, *Southern Politics*, 288.

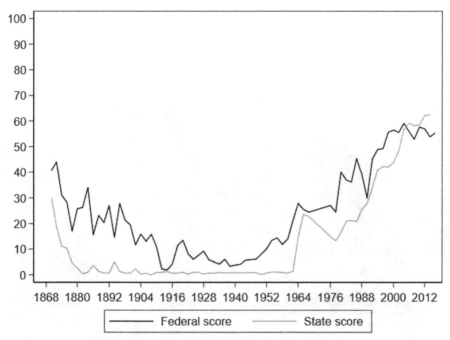

FIGURE 9.3 Republican Party strength at the federal and state level in Georgia, 1868-2012

Figure 9.4). Throughout the period 1872–1928 – and even after the Black-and-Tan domination of the state party ended – Georgia's GOP remained biracial and frequently saw black party leaders in control of the organization. At the same time, this organization came under frequent attack, both from Lily-White alternative groups within the state and presidents – specifically Harding and Hoover – hoping to replace the party machine with a new (white) organization.

* * * * *

After the end of the Civil War, under the rules and restrictions set by President Andrew Johnson, Georgia was readmitted to the Union in 1865, and held a gubernatorial election that was won by Charles J. Jenkins – a former Whig and justice on Georgia's Supreme Court. However, after Republicans in Congress took control of the Reconstruction process, Georgia's re-admittance was undone, and it had to write a new constitution. Like in other states, the Union League in Georgia began to organize freed slaves, and registered them as voters. The first election in which freedmen could vote was a dual ballot to determine whether a constitutional convention should be called and, if so, who the delegates should be. Of the 169 delegates elected, 37 were black, 9 were white carpetbaggers, and the remaining majority of delegates were Southern whites.

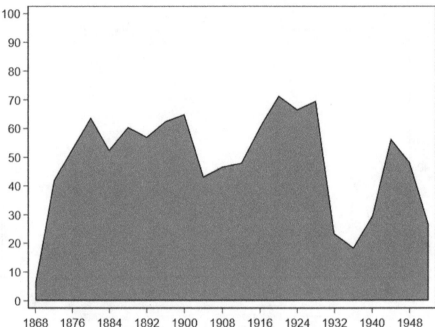

FIGURE 9.4 Percentage of GOP convention delegates from Georgia that were black, 1868-1952.
Source: Data collected by authors.

The GOP in Georgia was founded to help organize the constitutional convention itself, and the overlap between the convention delegates and the founders of the new party was substantial. Indeed, Rufus Brown Bullock, the first Republican gubernatorial candidate after work on the new constitution was completed, was nominated unanimously by the convention delegates.[33]

Bullock was a somewhat surprising choice as the Georgia GOP's first leader. He had been born in New York but had moved to Georgia before the start of the Civil War. Prior to Reconstruction, Bullock had shown little interest in politics but achieved considerable success as a businessman. He won the 1868 gubernatorial election, defeating his Democratic opponent by just five percentage points. And while Republicans won a comfortable majority in the state Senate, Democrats (appeared to have) won a majority in the Assembly.[34]

---

[33] Olive Hall Shadgett, *The Republican Party in Georgia: From Reconstruction through 1900* (Athens: University of Georgia Press, 2010), 1–9.

[34] It is unclear whether Republicans also had a majority in the state Assembly. Michael J. Dubin, whose *Party Affiliations in the State Legislatures* is the best source on the partisan divide in state legislatures in the nineteenth and early twentieth centuries, was unable to identify the partisan

The GOP's limited success was exacerbated by an intra-party split between Radical Republicans (who largely supported Bullock) and moderates, who made up the majority in the party's caucus in both chambers of the state legislature and were more interested in working with Democrats.[35] This split complicated Bullock's time in office almost from the beginning, as the legislature refused to elect his preferred candidate for one of Georgia's US Senate seats. More importantly, the "moderate" Republicans and Democrats also united to expel twenty-five of twenty-nine black representatives in the Assembly. The expulsion was based on the theory that while the Fourteenth Amendment guaranteed black voting rights, it did not guarantee blacks the right to *hold* political office.[36]

In response to violence toward black voters in the 1868 presidential election and the Georgia legislature's vote to reject the Fifteenth Amendment, Bullock began to organize support among Republicans in Congress to force another Reconstruction effort. In December 1869, Congress voted to place Georgia back under military control.[37] During the subsequent brief period of military control, the Georgia legislature was reorganized and a number of white Republicans were expelled. The new legislature re-ratified the Fourteenth Amendment and ratified the Fifteenth.[38] Crucially, Republicans in the state legislature also sought to postpone the state legislative elections of 1870 to 1872. While this plan failed, they did successfully push the election as late as possible (December 20, 1870) and postponed the date in which the new legislature would gather (November 1871). These actions were based on the GOP's belief that Democrats were likely to do very well in the next set of elections. Indeed, in the 1870 state legislative elections, Democrats easily won majorities in both the Assembly and the state Senate.[39]

While Bullock had been successful in postponing the inevitable by delaying the first meeting of the new legislature, his unpopularity in the state generally, and even within his own party, continued to grow. As a result, Bullock's impeachment seemed unavoidable and, rather than waiting out the inevitable,

makeup of the Assembly. However, an alternative source – C. Mildred Thompson's *Reconstruction in Georgia* (New York: Columbia University Press, 1915) – estimated Republicans had 84 seats while Democrats had 88 seats.

[35] Shadgett, *The Republican Party in Georgia*, 9.

[36] Edmund L. Drago, *Black Politicians and Reconstruction in Georgia: A Splendid Failure* (Athens: University of Georgia Press, 1992), 47–49.

[37] W. Calvin Smith, "The Reconstruction 'Triumph' of Rufus B. Bullock," *The Georgia Historical Quarterly* 52 (December 1968): 414–25; Shadgett, *The Republican Party in Georgia*, 12–18.

[38] Smith, "The Reconstruction 'Triumph' of Rufus B. Bullock," 423; Shadgett, *The Republican Party in Georgia*, 18–19.

[39] Republicans did end up controlling three seats in Congress in the 1870 midterms, one of which – the 2nd district seat eventually occupied by Republican Richard Whitely – was a contested election. See William Warren Rogers, Jr., "'Not Reconstructed by a Long Ways Yet': Southwest Georgia's Disputed Congressional Election of 1870," *The Georgia Historical Quarterly* 82 (Summer 1998): 257–82.

he resigned as governor in October 1871 and left the state.[40] Bullock's move officially meant that the current president of the state Senate – Benjamin Conley, a Republican who had held the position in the *previous* legislature – would be appointed governor. However, the Democratic majorities in the state legislature voted (over Conley's veto) to hold a special election in December to elect a new governor to serve out Bullock's term. Republicans strongly opposed this move and did not run a candidate in the election. As Olive Hall Shadgett noted, "[the] bald truth seems to be that the Republicans had neither a candidate nor a platform on which a candidate could run. To base a campaign on the record of the Bullock administration would have been political suicide" and "it is doubtful any man of stature outside of the Bullock camp would have been willing to run under the circumstances."[41] Democrat James Smith ran unopposed and, in the wake of the Democratic victory, a number of politicians who had joined the GOP in 1867 left and joined the Democrats.

Republican rule in Georgia was thus remarkably short-lived: the GOP held the Georgia governorship for less than one term, never held a majority in the state's Assembly, and lost their majority in the state Senate after just two years. From 1872 on, the Republican Party's role as an electoral force in Georgia was almost zero: throughout the rest of the nineteenth century, the party's representation was generally in the single digits in the state Assembly and often zero in the state Senate.[42] Republican gubernatorial candidates in the 1870s and early 1880s received, at most, 34 percent of the vote. After 1884, the GOP did not even run gubernatorial candidates in most elections. Democrats achieved this domination in part by painting the GOP as both the "black party" and highly corrupt. Additionally, as Judson Clements Ward, Jr. notes, they used "threats, fraud, intimidation, trickery, and other devices to prevent the Negroes from effectively employing the franchise against them,"[43] although in some specific parts of the state, Bourbon Democrats did actively compete for black votes. As a result, intra-GOP politics in Georgia almost immediately became focused on who within the party controlled the delegation to the national convention and thus controlled the subsequent patronage delivered by Republican presidents. Indeed, in August 1872, one Republican wrote former Governor Conley to complain about how the Georgia GOP was "entirely grabbed up and controlled by Federal Office Holders … filling every

---

[40] Drago, *Black Politicians and Reconstruction in Georgia*, 57–58, 65; Shadgett, *The Republican Party in Georgia*, 26; Dubin, *Party Affiliations in the State Legislatures*, 49.

[41] Shadgett, *The Republican Party in Georgia*, 29.

[42] Republicans did manage to win three seats in the House of Representatives in 1872 (out of a total of nine seats in Georgia). However, by 1874 Democrats had won these seats as well and would go on to control all congressional seats for decades to come.

[43] Judson Clements Ward, Jr., "The New Departure Democrats of Georgia: An Interpretation," *The Georgia Historical Quarterly* 41 (September 1957): 227–36, 229.

Committee, becoming delegates to every Convention, and shaping every party movement."[44]

Through the first decades of the twentieth century, the Georgia Republican Party remained racially integrated. During the short period of GOP rule between 1867 and 1870, blacks filled a number of important elected offices. For example, James Porter and Henry M. Turner were involved in the constitution-writing process and both served in the state legislature, and Jefferson Franklin Long served as the only black member of Congress from Georgia during Reconstruction.[45] The limited number of Republicans in the state legislature included both blacks and whites. And blacks made up a considerable majority within the party's membership ranks. For example, when Republicans gathered at a state convention in the spring of 1876 to select delegates to the national convention, press reports claimed three-fourths of state delegates were black.[46]

Thanks to this majority, black Republican leaders succeeded in taking control of the party multiple times in the 1880–1928 period. At the 1880 state party convention, John E. Bryant, the white state party chairman, proposed a resolution that would divide federal patronage evenly between white and black Republicans. This resolution was widely dismissed as a meaningless olive branch toward black Republicans, as it concerned an issue outside the control of the state convention. In response, Edwin Belcher, a black GOP leader, proposed an alternative resolution requiring that three-fourths of delegates to the national convention should be black, which the majority of black delegates voted to approve. As a result, black Republicans dominated the national convention delegation and also elected one of their own – William A. Pledger – as state party chairman.[47] In response to the black takeover of the state party organization, a small number of white Republicans held a separate convention in the summer of 1880 in an attempt to create a rival all-white GOP organization. With most white office-holders in the party choosing to remain within the traditional organization, this first attempt at creating a Lily-White movement did not gain any traction.

Two years later, in 1882, white Republicans made another attempt to regain control of the party at that year's state convention. This time around, Lily-Whites and Black-and-Tans held their own conventions at the same time, each claiming to represent the "true" Georgia Republican Party. The

---

[44] Cited in Shadgett, *The Republican Party in Georgia*, 50.

[45] Drago, *Black Politicians and Reconstruction in Georgia*; John M. Matthews, "Negro Republicans in the Reconstruction of Georgia," *The Georgia Historical Quarterly* 60 (Summer 1976): 145–64; E. Morton Coulter, "Henry M. Turner: Georgia Negro Preacher-Politician during the Reconstruction Era," *The Georgia Historical Quarterly* 48 (December 1964): 371–410; Ephraim Samuel Rosenbaum, "Incendiary Negro: The Life and Times of the Honorable Jefferson Franklin Long," *The Georgia Historical Quarterly* 95 (Winter 2011): 498–530.

[46] Shadgett, *The Republican Party in Georgia*, 54.   [47] Ibid., 78–79.

Lily-Whites demanded that the election of state party chairmen should occur at a convention with exclusively white delegates since the state's voting population also had a majority of white voters – a demand the Black-and-Tans rejected outright. While both conventions initially nominated separate tickets for statewide office, factional leaders eventually brokered a compromise ticket – nevertheless, all candidates went down to defeat in November. As part of these negotiations, however, Pledger gave up his position as chairman and was replaced by Alfred Eliab Buck, a white member of the Black-and-Tan faction.[48] Buck was born in Maine and served in the Union army, where he commanded two regiments of colored troops. After the war, he first moved to Alabama and then, in 1873, relocated to Atlanta. Between 1882 and 1897, Buck was the clear boss of the Republican Party in Georgia. During this time, Georgia's GOP was thus under control of the Black-and-Tans, though, as Shadgett notes, the true power was with the white party leaders who "were willing and eager to use the Negroes and to work with them insofar as it was necessary – provided always that the black-and-tan masses should be kept subservient to the white leaders."[49]

Prior to the 1896 GOP national convention, Republican leaders in Georgia were easily incorporated into William McKinley's campaign. Indeed, McKinley's infamous Southern strategy relied on he and Mark Hanna spending time in Thomasville, Georgia, in early 1895 to meet with Southern leaders. On his way to Thomasville, McKinley made a separate trip to visit with Buck, where he met a number of local Georgia Republicans. At the subsequent state convention in 1896, delegates were courted aggressively both by those hoping to send an all-McKinley delegation to the GOP national convention and by McKinley's opponents. The extent to which state delegates were feted was remarkable. At the McKinley campaign headquarters in Atlanta, there was a room open only to state convention delegates "fitted up with tables fairly groaning with eatables and drinkables, sandwiches and cakes, and a hogshead of lemonade."[50] The convention itself was largely disorganized. Buck (who supported McKinley) worked with his predecessor Pledger (who did not) to send a delegation that was mostly, but not exclusively, pro-McKinley. In the end, twenty-two of Georgia's twenty-six delegates voted for McKinley.[51]

After McKinley's victory, Buck was rewarded for his support with an ambassadorship to Japan. His successor, Walter H. Johnson, remained in control of the state party organization from 1898 to 1912.[52] As the *New York*

---

[48] Ibid., 81–86.   [49] Ibid., 87.   [50] Quoted in ibid., 132.   [51] Ibid., 132–34.

[52] Notably, Georgia enacted its disfranchisement legislation in 1908, but this process was almost entirely based on intra-party politics on the Democratic side. Bourbon Democrats relied – at least occasionally – on black votes to continue winning elections. While Democratic candidates for statewide office after the end of the Populist era frequently did not face a challenger, M. Hoke Smith – former secretary of the interior in the Cleveland administration – ran in the 1906 gubernatorial primary on a platform based on disenfranchising blacks, as well as broader Populist

Times reported, during Johnson's time in power "all appointments to Federal offices" in Georgia were made on his recommendation.[53] Still, black Republicans gained control of the Georgia Republican Party in 1912, after Johnson voted with the Roosevelt delegates on a number of decisions prior to the presidential nomination vote. As a result, Taft ordered the removal of Johnson at the Georgia GOP's August state convention. As the *New York Times* described the event:

[Walter H.] Johnson ... vigorously protested at times, and personal violence was feared. Henry Lincoln Johnson, a negro Recorder of Deeds at Washington, was here, it was said, by order of President Taft, and put through the resolution ousting Johnson and Grier. Afterward the committee named Presidential Electors and swore them all to Taft.[54]

Henry Lincoln Johnson, the black man who took control of the party after the ouster of Walter H. Johnson, was a lawyer from Atlanta who previously had worked with Pledger. His leadership of the GOP, however, did not go unchallenged: indeed, in 1916 Walter H. Johnson was part of a rival delegation to the national convention, contesting the legitimacy of the black-controlled party organization.[55] Whites – though usually in a coalition with at least some black Republicans[56] – continued to try to displace the regular GOP organization in Georgia at subsequent conventions. However, at the 1916, 1920, and 1924 conventions, the faction controlled by black Republican leaders was consistently seated.

After Henry Lincoln Johnson's death in 1925, power shifted to Benjamin Jefferson Davis, the black publisher of Atlanta's *Independent* newspaper. Davis' role in intra-Republican politics in Georgia was important from the early twentieth century through 1932. Yet, as historian John M. Matthews has noted, Davis was a complicated man who disdained both white racists and the "Negro aristocracy" of black office-holders in Georgia.[57] As a result, Davis generally relied on aggressive power politics and had a tendency to shift allegiances between the (many) different factions in Georgia GOP politics.

positions. Smith won the primary and was unchallenged in the general election. In 1907, the Georgia state legislature passed a constitutional amendment limiting voting rights in a manner clearly aimed at excluding blacks from political participation. See Dewey W. Grantham, Jr., "Georgia Politics and the Disfranchisement of the Negro," *The Georgia Historical Quarterly* 32 (March 1948): 1–21.

[53] "Read Leader Out of the Party," *New York Times*, August 27, 1912.   [54] Ibid.

[55] "Georgia to Send 2 G.O.P. Delegations to Chicago," *Washington Post*, April 13, 1916.

[56] For example, Henry A. Rucker – the collector of internal revenue in Georgia in the early twentieth century – generally was on the opposite side of Henry Lincoln Johnson and, later, Benjamin Jefferson Davis. For more on the foundation of Rucker's remarkable career, see Gregory Mixon, "The Making of a Black Political Boss: Henry A. Rucker, 1897–1904," *The Georgia Historical Quarterly* 89 (Winter 2005): 485–504.

[57] John M. Matthews, "Black Newspapermen and the Black Community in Georgia, 1890–1930," *The Georgia Historical Quarterly* 68 (Fall 1984): 356–81, 365.

The Johnson–Davis organization faced two crucial challenges to its control over the Georgia Republican Party. After his victory in the 1920 presidential election, Warren G. Harding engaged in a largely unsuccessful attempt at remodeling some of the Southern party organizations he considered to be the most corrupt. Harding's main goal in Georgia appears to have been to unite the competing Black-and-Tan and Lily-White coalitions into one new party organization. Both organizations showed little interest in merging, however, since both wanted to have full control over the new federal jobs that would start coming back to the Georgia GOP after the Wilson years.[58] In response, Harding decided to bypass both rival factions and create an entirely new organization around John Louis Philips, a longtime Republican who was not involved in the Lily-White and Black-and-Tan conflict in the state. With Harding's blessing, Philips traveled across the state to find white businessmen to gather at a state convention and create a new Republican Party. While the majority of these delegates would be white, Harding did expect blacks to have some level of representation in this new party. After this convention, the plan was that Harding would recognize the new party as the "true" Republican organization in the state and begin providing it with access to federal patronage, thereby eliminating both the Black-and-Tan and Lily-White factions entirely.[59]

In practice, nearly all actors on the ground resisted the scheme. The Black-and-Tans strongly opposed the move, warning Harding that replacing blacks in Georgia would cost the GOP black votes in the North. Meanwhile, though the Lily-Whites were excited about the possibility of a local party organization dominated by whites, they were not willing to give up control to Philips. Despite this opposition, Harding, Philips, and the RNC continued to organize the scheduled state convention. Harding offered Walter H. Johnson a federal job in Washington, DC, to convince him to give up his position as member of the RNC and leader of the officially recognized Georgia Republican Party. While Johnson rejected the post, Philips's attempts at replacing the existing party structure with his own did exhibit some success: 250 white businessmen gathered at the long-awaited convention in spring 1922 and elected an all-white executive committee with Philips as its chairman. Additionally, Philips began to travel the state to build enthusiasm and support for the "new" GOP.[60]

However, neither the old Lily-Whites nor the Black-and-Tans were willing to give up easily. While Lily-White leaders attempted a takeover of the new organization by trying to replace Philips with one of their own at an unannounced meeting of the executive committee, the Black-and-Tans organized a rival convention to nominate their own slate of candidates in the upcoming midterm elections. The "Georgia Experiment" was further damaged

---

[58] Robert E. Hauser, "'The Georgia Experiment': President Warren G. Harding's Attempt to Reorganize the Republican Party in Georgia," *The Georgia Historical Quarterly* 62 (Winter 1978): 288–303.

[59] Ibid., 290–91.   [60] Ibid.

when Philips – who owned a lumber factory – was accused of defrauding the government during World War I. By July 1922, Philips was indicted for fraud totaling nearly $1.9 million. Shortly thereafter, Philips was also accused of forcing applicants for federal positions to contribute a set percentage of their salaries to the new party organization – with the implication being that his new party organization existed solely to help sell offices in Georgia. While Philips was not convicted, no real campaign was organized for the 1922 midterms, and Democrats continued their winning streak in the state's elections.[61]

With the Republican Party performing poorly across the country in the 1922 midterms, Harding's willingness to invest time and political capital in reorganizing the Georgia GOP evaporated. While the president did not officially declare the experiment over, his involvement in intra-GOP conflicts in Georgia declined considerably. After Harding's death in August 1923, Calvin Coolidge restored Walter H. Johnson to his previous leadership position – in large part because Coolidge believed that he might need to rely on "solid" Southern support at the 1924 national convention. At the RNC meeting in December 1923, during which the committee began preparations for the convention, Johnson appeared as Georgia's official representative. At the 1924 convention, Johnson and the Black-and-Tans were seated as Georgia's official state delegation and, after Johnson's death in 1925, Ben Davis took control of the organization.[62]

To be sure, the Black-and-Tan organization regularly relied on the same type of activities that Philips was accused of in terms of selling federal offices. One particular case in this regard drew national attention. In April 1928, a postmaster in Douglas, Georgia murdered one of his clerks and then committed suicide. In a note left behind, the postmaster accused the Georgia GOP of forcing him to contribute $2,000 – a considerable amount at the time – to the party's coffers in exchange for his job. In testimony to a subsequent Senate investigation into the murder–suicide, multiple office-holders in Georgia made similar claims regarding the Black-and-Tan party organization. These revelations came in the midst of Herbert Hoover's campaign for the Republican presidential nomination, which had included paying Davis at least $2,000 to "cover" pre-convention expenses.[63] Republican senators postponed the investigation into the sale of federal offices in Georgia and other Southern states until after the 1928 election, but the embarrassment of being linked to the Georgia Republican machine clearly frustrated Hoover.

---

[61] Ibid., 293–98. For more on the Georgia Experiment, see Robert Ellwood Hauser, "Warren G. Harding and His Attempts to Reorganize the Republican Party in the South, 1920–23" (Dissertation, Pennsylvania State University, 1973), 92–162.

[62] Hauser, "The Georgia Experiment," 299–300.

[63] David J. Ginzl, "Patronage, Rape, and Politics: Georgia Republicans during the Hoover Administration," *The Georgia Historical Quarterly* 64 (Fall 1980): 280–93, 280–81.

At the 1928 national convention, Davis' control over the Georgia GOP and seat on the RNC was challenged by a white delegate, Roscoe Pickett. While this attempt failed, it set up a contest that would dominate the state party throughout Hoover's term in office. Indeed, by the end of the year, there were essentially three versions of the Georgia Republican Party competing to be recognized as the "actual" party: the Davis-controlled Black-and-Tan coalition, a group surrounding Pickett, and a Lily-White group controlled by businessman H. G. Hastings.[64] After the 1928 election and further revelations regarding patronage abuses taking place in Georgia, Mississippi, and South Carolina, Hoover announced that he would work to reorganize the Republican Party in a number of Southern states. While he failed to achieve his goal in South Carolina and Mississippi, Hoover would be more successful in Georgia.

Rather than work with one of the existing groups, Hoover followed Harding's playbook and handpicked his own Republican leader: Josiah T. Rose, the (white) internal revenue collector at Atlanta. Rose had been active in the Black-and-Tan organization but was believed to be distant from the Davis machine. While some of Pickett's supporters joined the new Rose organization, the Black-and-Tans refused to accept that they had lost control of the party. To be sure, Rose's control was far from guaranteed. In negotiations with the Hoover administration, for example, he tried to ensure that only office-holders supportive of his new party would be reappointed. But under pressure from other local Georgian Republicans, Hoover reappointed one of Davis' selections.

In March 1930, the reorganization appeared to be finalized when Rose, Davis, and a number of other local party notables met and agreed that Rose would be elected chairman of the party at the April state convention. However, the convention itself ended up in chaos when the delegates could not agree on the election of a temporary chairman. Instead, two competing parties were formed: one surrounding Rose and Pickett and one surrounding Davis, though by then neither leader had complete control over their respective factions. Notably, both groups contained black and white Republicans, though Rose's group had considerably more white than black members.[65]

What followed was nearly two years of conflict between the Rose–Pickett and Davis versions of the Georgia GOP, which was further confused by the addition of occasional other competitors. While Harding's attempt at regime change had failed – in part due to the president's own lack of interest in the process after 1922 – Hoover remained focused on Georgia and continued to back Rose. As a result, by spring 1932 the white-dominated Rose–Pickett group appeared victorious. At the state convention in April, 80 percent of delegates were white. Rose himself reported that there was "no doubt [that]

[64] Ibid., 281–82.
[65] According to Ginzl, the Rose group consisted of "forty-eight whites and sixteen blacks" while the group surrounding Davis consisted of "thirty-eight whites and twenty-six blacks." See ibid., 285.

the state is under complete white leadership, with all the state officers and district officers being white."[66] At the national convention itself, Davis offered his surrender by testifying that the Rose-led delegation had been elected fairly.[67]

But the 1932 convention did not represent the final chapter in Georgia's Black-and-Tan versus Lily-White conflict. Four years later – with Rose already having lost control of the Lily-White GOP in Georgia after Republican federal patronage disappeared – Davis once again led a Black-and-Tan rival delegation to the 1936 GOP national convention.[68] The RNC's initial decisions suggested a near complete victory for Lily-White forces across a number of Southern states – including South Carolina, which saw its longtime political leader "Tieless Joe" Tolbert denied a seat. Georgia's RNC member James W. Arnold celebrated the decision, stating that "[the] white people are 100 per cent in control of the Georgia republican [*sic*] party and we want to keep it that way."[69] However, the decision raised considerable anger among blacks in the North. To downplay the controversy, RNC chairman Henry P. Fletcher appointed several black Republicans (including Davis) to the convention's Credentials Committee, which reassessed some of the RNC's decisions. The committee reinstalled Tolbert, while Davis successfully managed to get himself and a number of other Black-and-Tan delegates seated.[70] Four years later – after the different intra-party factions deadlocked at the Georgia Republican state convention – another mixed, but mostly white, delegation was seated "with little friction."[71]

By 1944, this temporary peace between the two groups would end. In the spring, as Georgia Republicans gathered to elect delegates to the national convention, whites refused to meet with black party members. At the state convention, Lily-White leader Clint Hager led a white walkout once it became clear blacks represented the majority present. With Hager unable to nominate his white delegates through regular procedure, Lily-White and Black-and-Tan Republicans each nominated their own delegations to the national convention.[72] Crucially, the 1944 clash between Black-and-Tans (still under Davis' leadership) and Lily-Whites played out in the immediate aftermath of the Supreme Court's decision in *Smith* v. *Allwright*, which determined that the all-white primary – which both the Texas and Georgia Democratic parties relied

[66] Ibid., 289.   [67] Ibid., 290.
[68] "Political Fight in South among Lilywhites and Black-and-Tans Hot," *Atlanta Daily World*, May 8, 1936.
[69] Olive Hall Shadgett, "A History of the Republican Party in Georgia," *The Georgia Review* 7 (Winter 1953): 438.
[70] "Negroes Threaten Racial Party Split," *New York Times*, June 10, 1936; "Lily-White Issue Stirs G.O.P. Delegates," *Cleveland Call and Post*, June 11, 1936.
[71] "Color Bar Absent as Negro Delegates Register at Philadelphia's Finest Hotels," *Cleveland Call and Post*, June 29, 1940; Shadgett, "A History of the Republican Party in Georgia."
[72] "GOP in 2-Way Split at State Convention Here," *Atlanta Daily World*, May 24, 1944; "Racial Clash in Georgia," *New York Times*, May 24, 1944.

on to exclude blacks from political participation – was unconstitutional. In Georgia, the court decision raised the question as to whether the Democratic Party would be able to continue to exclude blacks from voting in their primary through other means. While the demise of the all-white primary had been a long-term project of the NAACP, Davis proved to be a surprising opponent of racial integration in Georgia, arguing that

Supreme court or no Supreme court, I hope the white folks won't let a single Negro cast a vote in the Democratic primary on July 4 ... It won't mean a thing to Negroes to vote with a party that doesn't want them. I think we ought to let the white folks keep their party.[73]

That is, for Davis the goal was to retain the Republican Party in Georgia as the sole venue for black political participation, and for the local Democratic Party to remain fully segregated.

At the Republican National Convention that year, the Black-and-Tans emerged victorious when the RNC voted to seat a biracial delegation that was led by RNC member Wilson Williams (a white man) but otherwise was majority black.[74] The RNC's determination that the "true" Georgia Republican Party was the organization led by Williams, however, did not end the struggle over control of the state party in 1944. In August, Hagar pulled a surprise move by proposing an all-white group of Republican presidential electors to the state, and succeeded in getting the slate certified.[75] Hagar cooperated with Eugene Talmadge, a former three-term Democratic governor of Georgia, segregationist, and opponent of FDR, and together they produced what the black newspaper *The Chicago Defender* described as "an unholy alliance of 'lily-white' Republicans and independent 'hate Roosevelt' Democrats."[76] In response, the RNC challenged Georgia's decision to certify the Hagar–Talmadge slate of electors, but with little success. After failing to overturn the decision in the Georgia Supreme Court, the party abandoned its opposition and the Lily-White slate remained on the ballot.[77] Despite this victory, the Hagar–Talmadge partnership proved to be very

[73] "Negro GOP Favors Lily-White Vote in Demo Primary," *The Chicago Defender*, June 3, 1944.
[74] "Mixed GOP Delegates Win Chicago Convention Seats," *Atlanta Daily World*, June 24, 1944; "'Negro Issue' Sparks GOP Meeting," *The Pittsburgh Courier*, July 1, 1944.
[75] "Lily-Whites Get Ga. GOP Control," *The Chicago Defender*, August 19, 1944; "Georgia Favors Lily-White GOPs," *The Pittsburgh Courier*, August 19, 1944; "Talmadge to Support Dewey," *The Chicago Defender*, August 26, 1944.
[76] "Expose Talmadge Plot for Ga. 'Hate Ticket'," *The Chicago Defender*, September 2, 1944.
[77] "GOP Backs Mixed Group in Georgia," *The Pittsburgh Courier*, August 26, 1944; "GOP Fight in Fulton Court; Interest High," *Atlanta Daily World*, August 29, 1944; "GOP to Carry Fight in Ga. For 'Black And Tan' Group," *Philadelphia Tribune*, September 2, 1944; "Gov. Arnall Denies GOP Case Authority," *Atlanta Daily World*, September 5, 1944; "Georgia Supreme Court Asked to Reverse Fulton GOP Ruling," *Atlanta Daily World*, September 13, 1944; "Supreme Court Takes Republican Contest," *Atlanta Daily World*, October 3, 1944; "Lily-White GOP Wins in Ballot Row in Georgia," *Atlanta Daily World*, October 7, 1944; "Bars Georgia GOP Split," *New York Times*, October 7, 1944; "Supreme Court Gets Republican

short lived. In December 1944, Hagar died.[78] Two years later, Talmadge returned to the Democratic Party and won a fourth gubernatorial term, but died before he could take office.[79]

While lacking the excitement of the presidential-elector contest, the 1948 and 1952 national conventions followed essentially the same format as the 1944 battle over seating had. In 1948 the two factions again sent competing delegations to the national conventions. The Lily-White faction this time did include three black delegates.[80] Like in 1944, however, the RNC and the convention's Credentials Committee voted to seat the Black-and-Tan faction.[81] In 1952, the RNC and the Credentials Committee did an about-face, as both voted to seat the Lily-Whites – who were supporting Robert Taft – over the Black-and-Tans who favored Eisenhower. That decision was challenged in the full convention, which overturned the decision and seated the pro-Eisenhower faction.[82] While a full Lily-White takeover did not occur, the party's Black-and-Tan coalition became increasingly white: in 1944, a majority of Georgia delegates were black, but this proportion dropped considerably in the years that followed. By 1952, blacks made up just 27 percent of the delegation. By 1960, only four of twenty-four delegates were black.[83] Thus, the influence of black Republicans in Georgia ended not in a clear Lily-White takeover, but through a slower process of exclusion.

MISSISSIPPI: THE LONG REIGN OF THE BLACK-AND-TANS

The Republican Party in Mississippi proved to be the last-standing Black-and-Tan organization. While most other Southern states saw the Lily-Whites take

---

Contest," *The Pittsburgh Courier*, October 14, 1944; "New Motion in GOP Case Today," *Atlanta Daily World*, October 17, 1944; "Ga. GOP Loses Rehearing Motion," *Atlanta Daily World*, October 18, 1944; "GOP Drops Ga. Fight on Talmadge Slate," *The Chicago Defender*, October 21, 1944.

[78] "Lily-White GOP Chieftain Hagar Dies in Georgia," *The Chicago Defender*, December 23, 1944; "Georgia Lily-White Republican Dies," *The Pittsburgh Courier*, December 23, 1944.

[79] "Talmadge Dies as 4th Term Nears," *Washington Post*, December 22, 1946.

[80] "Both Georgia GOP Factions Have Negroes as Delegates," *Atlanta Daily World*, May 5, 1948.

[81] "Georgia GOP Racists War for Convention Seats," *The Chicago Defender*, June 12, 1948; "Republicans Contest Seats in Philadelphia," *Atlanta Daily World*, June 18, 1948; "Tucker Georgia Republican Delegates Win First Round," *Atlanta Daily World*, June 19, 1948; "Georgians Backing Dewey Are Seated," *New York Times*, June 22, 1948.

[82] "Delegate Seating Fight on Horizon," *Los Angeles Times*, June 8, 1952; "Taft Machine Denounced by GOP Leaders Here," *Atlanta Daily World*, July 3, 1952; "Lily-White Georgia Group for Taft; Wins Seating Fight," *Philadelphia Tribune*, July 8, 1952; "GOP Convention Seats 29 Delegates, 34 Alternates," *Afro-American*, July 12, 1952; "Senator Bags Mixed Georgia Unit," *New Journal and Guide*, July 12, 1952; Michael Bowen, *The Roots of Modern Conservatism: Dewey, Taft, and the Battle for the Soul of the Republican Party* (Chapel Hill: University of North Carolina Press, 2011), 148.

[83] "Says GOP Being Bleached Lily-White," *Cleveland Call and Post*, July 30, 1960.

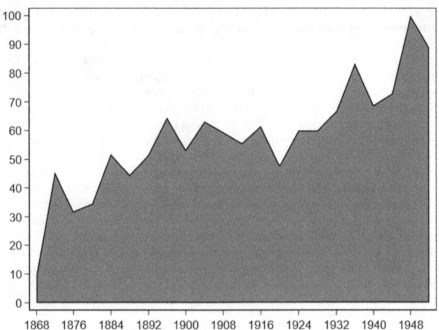

FIGURE 9.5 Percentage of GOP convention delegates from Mississippi that were black, 1868–1952
Source: Data collected by authors.

control in the early twentieth century, and even the outliers of South Carolina and Georgia saw their biracial party organizations fall in the 1930s and 1950s, the Black-and-Tans in Mississippi remained in control until the 1960 Republican National Convention (see Figure 9.5). Much of this success was the product of the political management of one man: Perry W. Howard, a black attorney who took control of the Mississippi GOP in 1924 and remained the state's representative at the RNC until 1960. But the party Howard controlled was little more than a mechanism to sell patronage. Indeed, the Republican Party's period of electoral success in Mississippi was limited – extending from 1869 to 1875 – and once Democrats regained control of the state government, the GOP all but dropped the pretense of participating in electoral competition (see Table 9.3 and Figure 9.6).

* * * * *

Under President Johnson's Reconstruction plan, Mississippi elected Benjamin G. Humphreys – a former Confederate general – governor in 1865. Humphreys actively opposed the rights of former slaves, stating that while slavery had been

TABLE 9.3 *Descriptive Republican Party success in Mississippi, 1865–1968*

	1865–1877	1878–1896	1897–1932	1933–1968
Presidential candidate won the state?	✓			✓
Senatorial candidate elected?	✓			
Gubernatorial candidate elected?	✓			
At least one House candidate elected?	✓	✓		✓

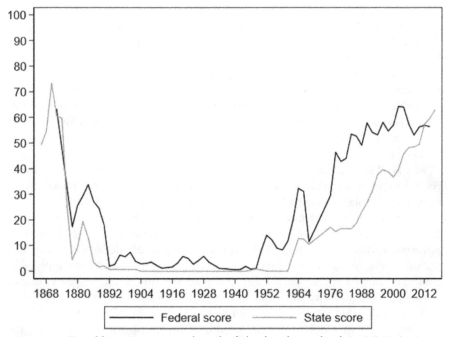

FIGURE 9.6 Republican Party strength at the federal and state levels in Mississippi, 1868–2012

abolished, this did not entitle blacks in Mississippi to citizenship or to political or social equality with whites.[84] After Congress took over the Reconstruction process, Humphreys was deposed and Mississippi was placed under the military

---

[84] James Wilford Garner, *Reconstruction in Mississippi* (Gloucester, MA: The Macmillan Company, 1964), 111.

governorship of Adelbert Ames in 1867.[85] In 1868, a new constitution was drafted and put up for a vote. While the members of the newly formed Republican Party in Mississippi were confident of success, the constitution was rejected by a majority of voters – in no small part due to threats of retaliation made by whites against black voters.[86] In the wake of this defeat, Republicans in Congress debated whether the irregularities in the 1868 election warranted considering the constitution passed – but in the end determined a second vote in 1869 would be required, while placing the responsibility for protecting political rights on the federal government.[87]

Early attempts at organizing a GOP in Mississippi saw the new party divided between conservatives, who were mostly white and in some cases former Democrats, and Radicals, the wing with the biggest level of support from the freedmen. In the spring and summer of 1869, both factions met in separate conventions. Many Democrats in the state supported the conservative Republican platform, and its gubernatorial candidate Louis Dent – a judge and brother-in-law to President Ulysses S. Grant. While the conservatives hoped the family relation would ensure that Grant would back Dent, the president opposed his candidacy in a publicly published letter that rejected the "Conservative Republican party."[88] Meanwhile, the Radical Republican faction nominated James Alcorn, who had been active in Mississippi politics before the war, fought on the Confederate side, and was elected to the Senate during the early years of Reconstruction.[89]

In the 1869 election, the new constitution was overwhelmingly approved, Alcorn easily defeated Dent, and Radical Republicans won large majorities in both state legislative chambers. Alcorn remained in office only through 1871, however, when he was elected to the Senate, where he joined his rival and former military governor, Ames. Alcorn's successor, former lieutenant governor Ridley C. Powers, filled out the remainder of Alcorn's term. In this period – like in the other states in the Deep South – the Mississippi GOP combined carpetbaggers, scalawags, and blacks within the same party. Blacks constituted the majority of the party's membership and voter base, but whites initially dominated leadership positions.[90] In 1873, both Ames and Alcorn competed to win the Republican gubernatorial nomination in a battle for

[85] William C. Harris, *The Day of the Carpetbagger: Republican Reconstruction in Mississippi* (Baton Rouge: Louisiana State University Press, 1979), 180–81.

[86] As Harris notes, although "violence was rare because of the fear of military arrest and trial, rebellious whites devised a variety of ingenious tactics to carry the election for the Democratic party. In numerous cases, blacks en route to the polls were met by whites who reminded them that they would lose their jobs if they voted Republican; some were threatened with violence if they insisted on voting for the constitution." Harris, *The Day of the Carpetbagger*, 193.

[87] Ibid., 199–217.   [88] Garner, *Reconstruction in Mississippi*, 241.

[89] Harris, *The Day of the Carpetbagger*, 244–45.

[90] The election of 1871 saw a first wave of black Republican leaders – including Blanche K. Bruce, who soon after was elected US senator. See ibid., 427.

control of the state party. At the state convention, Ames won a large majority of the delegate support and ran on a statewide ticket with three black candidates, including future party leader James Hill.[91] While Republicans saw a decline in their support in comparison to 1869 and the 1871 state midterms, the GOP maintained unified control of the state government following the 1873 elections.

Mississippi was largely undeveloped at the time of the start of the Civil War, with an economy that relied almost entirely on slavery. By the end of the war, the state thus faced both the economic burden of the war itself and a radically altered economic system. Both would constrain Republican success during Reconstruction and help fuel the Democratic resurgence in the middle of the 1870s. During the Alcorn administration, the state government passed a variety of civil rights bills. Most importantly, the state invested in the creation of a public school system. Ensuring public education for children of all races was crucial in the eyes of GOP leaders because it represented "the energizing agent of modern civilization" and "the corrective for the myopic sectionalism and moral degeneracy that they found in Mississippi society."[92] As a result, under Republican rule, the state significantly increased its spending, more than tripling its 1868 budget by 1871. It also increased taxes, despite an ongoing economic crisis.[93] Additionally, with the Republican Party split between Ames and Alcorn, "acceptable" Republican talent was running thin by 1874, and gubernatorial appointees frequently held multiple offices simultaneously, with some office-holders – including the powerful state superintendent of education Thomas W. Cardozo – accused of corruption.[94]

By 1874, Democrats in Mississippi began to ratchet up their terror tactics to prevent blacks in the state from voting or otherwise participating in politics. The Mississippi state government from the moment of its restoration had been weak in providing security, particularly as William C. Harris notes, in "marginally Republican counties and in communities that were overwhelmingly white and anti-Republican"[95] but ruled by (black) Republican office-holders, resulting in rampant crime and violence. By 1874, however, racial violence was increasing.[96] Despite requests from Ames, President Grant refused to increase the federal military presence in the state, which – in practice – meant that the state government could not guarantee the safety of its (black) citizens or public servants. For example, in Vicksburg a black man was elected sheriff in the

---

[91] Alcorn bolted from the Republican Party and ran as an independent conservative candidate. Ames easily won the election. See ibid., 479.

[92] Ibid., 311.

[93] Ibid., 608–09; Eric Foner, *Reconstruction: America's Unfinished Revolution, 1863–1877* (New York: Harper & Row, 1988), 383–84.

[94] Harry, *The Day of the Carpetbagger*, 617–19. [95] Ibid., 371.

[96] For a recent account of this violence, see Nicholas Lemann, *Redemption: The Last Battle of the Civil War* (New York: Farrar, Straus and Giroux, 2006).

summer of 1874. In the months that followed, whites in the area began to stockpile weapons, and in December groups of armed whites attacked black Republicans gathered at a meeting in town. In that attack, and similar ones in the days that followed, a large number of blacks living in Vicksburg and surrounding areas were killed – with estimates ranging between 29 and 300 deaths.[97]

Combined, the 1875 state midterm elections saw Democrats attacking Republicans on the economic record of the Ames administration, as well as relying on terror and violence to decrease black turnout.[98] Meanwhile, the GOP was in disarray: with most whites having abandoned the party, and with considerable discontent with Ames's performance as governor, the party lacked cohesion. Indeed, through much of 1875, rather than preparing for the upcoming crucial elections, Ames and other party leaders spent most of their time attacking one another. During the fall campaign, political events were disrupted by violence – sometimes the apparent product of individual actions, sometimes structured attacks. In response, Ames organized two black militias, which (perhaps unsurprisingly) further increased the hostility on the Democratic side. The result was a major Democratic victory: the party won four of six congressional seats, a statewide victory in the race for state treasurer, and sizable majorities in both chambers of the state legislature. To some extent, violence and coercion help explain these results, though black turnout was not down much in comparison to 1873. Rather, Democratic success appears to have been achieved mostly through a considerable increase in white turnout.[99]

The Democrats quickly used their supermajorities in the state legislature to oust both Governor Ames and his lieutenant governor and elevate John M. Stone, the Democratic president pro tempore of the Senate, to the governorship. Ames fled the state and would never return. Democrats also used their new unified control of state government to redraw congressional district lines and to pass complex new voter registration rules.[100] With Ames's exit and the altering of the voting rules, Republican rule in Mississippi had ended.

In the meantime, the Republican Party was left deeply divided. By the early 1880s, the Mississippi GOP comprised two factions: one mostly organized around black leaders such as John R. Lynch (a former member of Congress), James Hill (by then the collector of internal revenue), and Blanche K. Bruce (a former senator), while the other was made up mostly of white Republicans surrounding George C. McKee (a former member of Congress and, by then, postmaster in Jackson). While black Republicans had been dominant in the party in recent years, whites now sought to gain control. This attempt was helped along by an internal split within the Democratic Party – allowing

[97] See Emilye Crosby, *A Little Taste of Freedom: The Black Freedom Struggle in Claiborne County, Mississippi* (Chapel Hill: The University of North Carolina Press, 2015), 3.
[98] See Lemann, *Redemption.*   [99] Harris, *The Day of the Carpetbagger*, 685–87.
[100] Ibid., 697.

disgruntled Democrats, former Greenbackers, and white Republicans to work together against the Democrats in at least one congressional district. The white Republicans tried to convince national leaders – most notably William E. Chandler, Arthur's secretary of the Navy and the man who would go on to manage his Southern delegates in 1884 – to kick out the black leaders. The McKee group argued that the black Republicans had offered black votes to Democratic candidates in exchange for Democratic support for the appointment of black federal office-holders. In one letter to Chandler, Harvey R. Ware – a former Confederate soldier, Republican, and chancellor of a Mississippi judicial district – argued that "we cannot destroy Bourbonism here until we first *effectually* and *completely* break the 'Color Line' in politicks [*sic*]."[101]

Specifically, Ware accused Hill of sabotaging the Republicans' chance of retaining a congressional seat by plotting to run for the nomination and, thereby,

thwarted and stifled every effort in the State to broaden the guage [*sic*], and gather effective white recruits for the fight against Bourbonism. Not Content with the evil he has done and is doing, he now proposes to give this District to his Allies the Bourbons, by having himself *intrigued* by his various Deputies into a nomination for Congress. Of course he well knows that although a Republican District he would be overwhelmingly defeated – for even with the rank & file of his own Race he is extremely unpopular.[102]

In a second letter, two weeks later, Ware again asked Chandler to intervene and to either undo Hill's appointment as collector of revenue or, if "the Administration has determined to retain Hill as Collector can it not Suppress him in his purpose to give the District to the Bourbons."[103] McKee himself wrote Chandler to warn that Bruce and Democratic Senator L. Q. C. Lamar "humbug the different administrations, and keep up negro rule in the Rep party in order that fear of negro rule in the State may keep white men in the Dem. party."[104] The letter campaign was not limited to Chandler: Congressman David B. Henderson (R-IA), the secretary of the RCCC, wrote Chandler to complain about similar correspondence he had received and asking Chandler to

drop a line to Each Correspondent urging them to put up with almost anything until the Campaign is over. Hill has bitter foes & the three writers with Genl. McKee are the worst of them. But Hill is the brains of the negroes. Has the political machinery in his hands & it will not do to remove him while both armies are in motion. We must, however, *make* him obey orders where we make them. & he promises to obey squarly [*sic*].[105]

---

[101] Cited in Willie D. Halsell, "Republican Factionalism in Mississippi, 1882–1884," *The Journal of Southern History* 7 (February 1941): 84–101, 87 (emphasis in original).
[102] Ibid., 88. [103] Ibid., 89. [104] Ibid., 93. [105] Ibid., 92.

While Hill did go on to lose his congressional race, and McKee and his allies again tried to get national Republican leaders to intervene and excommunicate the black Mississippi party leaders, Lynch, Hill, and Bruce would continue to dominate the Mississippi GOP through the beginning of the twentieth century. Crucially, these black leaders were comparatively wealthy – both Lynch and Bruce were among the largest plantation owners in the state – or federal office-holders living in Washington, DC, most of the time.[106] This period of black control of the GOP did not mean there was no internal conflict. Starting in the 1890s, both Hill and Lynch led competing delegations to the Republican National Convention. In 1896, both groups supported McKinley, but it was Hill's biracial delegation that was seated – and Hill became the official party leader in the eyes of the RNC.[107]

By 1904, with both Bruce and Hill dead and Lynch having left the state entirely, control of the Mississippi GOP returned to a white man: Lonzo B. Moseley, who became the state's representative on the RNC. Under Moseley, the Mississippi Republican Party was a Black-and-Tan coalition under white leadership. Unsurprisingly, Moseley – like most other Southern party leaders at the time, whether Black-and-Tan or Lily-White – used his position mostly to control patronage and to influence the outcome of GOP national conventions. In particular, Moseley played an interesting role in the 1912 pre-convention campaign between Taft and Roosevelt. Moseley was loyal to Taft – who controlled federal patronage – but believed that Roosevelt's campaign had been trying to bribe some of the black delegates who were pledged to Taft. Moseley and his second-in-command Michael Joseph Mulvihill (who had been appointed postmaster of Vicksburg in 1902[108]) wrote a memo to Taft's personal secretary, Charles D. Hilles, warning him that a black delegate had reported that "the Roosevelt people have offered to pay the expense of his campaign for election as a delegate and his expenses at the State Convention, an amount that he estimates at slightly under four hundred dollars."[109] Moseley and Mulvihill proposed a simple solution to this threat to Taft's control over Southern delegates: have local party leaders recommend that individual delegates take the money but vote with the Taft forces at the convention. This, Moseley and Mulvihill argued, was a creative update of the already common process of convention vote selling, as

[106] Stephen Cresswell, *Rednecks, Redeemers, and Race: Mississippi after Reconstruction, 1877–1917* (Jackson: University Press of Mississippi, 2006), 70.

[107] Stephen Cresswell, *Multiparty Politics in Mississippi, 1877–1912* (Jackson: University Press of Mississippi, 1995), 185.

[108] "Michael J. Mulvihill," *The Postal Record: A Monthly Journal of the National Association of Letter Carriers* 23 (1910): 16.

[109] Cited in Geoffrey Cowan, *Let the People Rule: Theodore Roosevelt and the Birth of the Presidential Primary* (New York: Norton, 2016), 164.

[heretofore] it has been an ordinary occurrence for the Negro to sell his vote; but usually when he has sold it he has delivered the goods. The novelty of the present suggestion is that it opens a channel of confidence between the delegate and the head of the delegation which will result in keeping you posted as to what attempts are being made to seal the delegates by corruption, and it will check the delegate from delivering the vote he has sold.[110]

At the 1912 convention, only four of Mississippi's twenty delegates voted with Roosevelt on two crucial ballots: selecting the convention chairman and allowing the challenged Taft delegates to vote on issues unrelated to their own seating.[111]

After Moseley's death in 1918, Mulvihill took over control of the Mississippi GOP. However, Mulvihill's refusal to appoint black Republicans to important patronage positions ended up undermining his control and allowed for the rise of Perry W. Howard. Born in Ebenezer, Mississippi in 1877 to two former slaves, Howard – like his six brothers – earned a college degree. He then went on to acquire a law degree, and after stints as a small college president and professor of mathematics, he became a practicing attorney for fifteen years in Jackson, Mississippi. Howard then moved to Washington, DC, where he achieved partner in the capital's leading black law firm, Howard, Hayes, and Davis. Politics, though, was Howard's passion. He served as a delegate to every Republican National Convention from 1912 to 1960 (with the exception of 1920), and in 1912 he was identified by Theodore Roosevelt as one "particularly fit" to second his nomination.[112]

In 1920, Howard sought a seat on the RNC from Mississippi but was defeated by Mulvihill. Despite this setback, Howard was still seen as a rising "Negro star" in the party, and in 1921 President Harding appointed him special assistant to the attorney general; in that capacity, he represented the Department of Justice in the United States Court of Claims. This position's work, however, was "largely public relations." As Neil McMillen notes: "An intelligent, congenial, articulate man of 'gentlemanly bearing and unfailing courtesy,' Howard was a conspicuous and useful token. In an administration not otherwise sensitive to Afro-American aspirations, he was a symbol to

---

[110] Cited in ibid.

[111] *CQ Press Guide to U.S. Elections*, 6th edn. (Washington, DC: CQ Press, 2010), 706.

[112] Neil R. McMillen, "Perry W. Howard, Boss of Black-and-Tan Republicanism in Mississippi, 1924–1960," *The Journal of Southern History* 48 (May 1982): 205–06. Howard would not have a chance to offer a seconding speech, however, as Roosevelt withdrew from consideration for the GOP nomination prior to the presentation of candidates. Roosevelt believed that the Republican National Committee awarded fraudulent delegates to William Howard Taft, and asked his delegates to decline to vote on any matter before the convention. He would subsequently run an independent Progressive Party (commonly referred to as "Bull Moose") campaign. See Doris Kearns Goodwin, *The Bully Pulpit: Theodore Roosevelt, William Howard Taft, and the Golden Age of Journalism* (New York: Simon & Schuster, 2013), 710–12.

northern Negroes of the party's concern for blacks."[113] From his federal position, Howard once again sought a national committee seat in 1924, and this time defeated Mulvihill. With his election, Howard was the first black to serve on the RNC in a quarter century[114] and quickly used his authority – as federal special assistant and RNC member – to elevate himself to the top of the Republican Party machine in Mississippi.

While Howard would spend most of the rest of his life living in Washington, DC,[115] as state party boss, he now was in a position to distribute federal patronage positions in Mississippi and deliver delegate slates at Republican National Conventions. Howard was able to control the party without being present much in Mississippi because by then the organization was "fundamentally a paper organization":[116] with the Republicans rarely running candidates, let alone winning elections, in the state, control of patronage through relations with the national party leadership was more important in the 1920s than being physically present to manage any party-building activities. As one county chairman explained:

During the presidential campaigns, our committee performs its only cause for being. We proselytize these few score Negroes to vote ... and, after pocketing the handouts from the party slush fund – and this is the only real purpose of our organization – we put our committee back in moth balls to await another presidential election.[117]

Once entrenched as party boss, Howard pursued a course to safeguard and enhance his personal well-being. He understood the conditions that existed in Jim Crow Mississippi: trying to build a viable Republican Party and running serious GOP candidates in elections would amount to nothing, except perhaps to enrage the governing white Democrats in the state. Instead, Howard operated in a purely instrumental way, seeking to convert what authority he possessed into personal gain. For example, he acquired a reputation for selling patronage appointments to the highest bidder – getting $500 to $1,500 for lower-level postal positions, and as much as $2,500 for postmaster, revenue collector, US marshal, and US attorney positions. During a Senate investigation into the sale of postmasterships, one man recalled how in 1926 – in an attempt to help a friend be appointed postmaster of Okolona – he engaged in a number of financial transactions with the Howard machine:

I saw Clem Bascom (colored), of Buena Vista, Miss., who is the Republican chairman for Chikasaw County. I saw Bascom several times and on almost every occasion he asked me for money for incidental expenses relative to securing the appointment and also for money for campaign funds ... Bascom stated that the appointment would cost $500,

---

[113] McMillen, "Perry W. Howard," 208.
[114] Howard would be joined on the RNC by Mary Booze, daughter of Isaiah Montgomery, a prominent black politician and businessman in Mississippi. Neil R. McMillen, *Dark Journey: Black Mississippians in the Age of Jim Crow* (Urbana: University of Illinois Press, 1989), 64.
[115] McMillen, "Perry W. Howard," 205.   [116] Ibid. 207.   [117] Cited in ibid., 209–10.

$200 of which was to be in cash and the rest to be paid at the rate of $50 a month after the appointment was received. Bascom told me that one-half of this money was to go to Perry M. Howard and that he, Bascom, was to retain the other half.[118]

During a meeting with Howard in Washington, the man expressed concern that he could not afford the cost, but Howard replied that "Bascom's figure was about as reasonable as one could ask."[119] Howard also received cash payments to deliver convention votes. In advance of the 1928 GOP convention, for example, Herbert Hoover's handlers paid him $200 a week, and over $4,000 in total, to ostensibly cover "campaign expenses."[120]

Federal agents – from the Post Office Department and the Federal Bureau of Investigation – had been collecting evidence on Howard's activities since 1925, but no charges were brought initially. Republican leaders still saw Howard as an asset and had little stomach for another party scandal – with Teapot Dome and other Harding-era scandals not long in the past. The allegations swirling around Howard and his Black-and-Tan organization, however, made them vulnerable, and a Lily-White organization emerged in 1927 to vie for recognition by the national Republican Party. Led by former Nebraska governor George L. Sheldon and former Chicago postmaster Charles U. Gordon, the Lily-Whites reached out to business-friendly white Democrats in Mississippi to develop their organization, and they selected an uninstructed (and predominantly white) delegation to contest for the state's representation at the 1928 Republican National Convention. Hoover's supporters dominated the RNC, however, and despite Howard's baggage, they voted to seat his Black-and-Tan delegation over the Lily-White alternative. Howard had previously come out in support of Hoover, and Hoover's people felt he could be counted on (especially after establishing a payment schedule with him) to deliver Mississippi's delegates at the convention.[121] That said, Hoover found the state of the Republican Party in the South unsettling, and upon election hoped to clean house and build a more reputable (and largely white) Southern organization that could realistically and consistently provide electoral votes to the GOP in the future.

A month after the convention, in July 1928, Howard's would-be legal troubles finally became real, as the Justice Department obtained grand jury indictments against him and seven of his associates (four of whom had been

---

[118] Subcommittee of the Committee on Post Offices and Post Roads, *Influencing Appointments to Postmasterships – Part 2* (Washington, DC: United States Government Printing Office, 1929), 351.

[119] Ibid., 352.

[120] David J. Ginzl, "Lily-Whites versus Black-and-Tans: Mississippi Republicans during the Hoover Administration," *Journal of Mississippi History* 42 (September 1980): 195–96; McMillen, "Perry W. Howard," 210–11. The progressive news magazine the *Independent* wrote extensively on alleged corruption within the Southern Republican Party in the 1920s as well as within the Mississippi GOP specifically. See Lisio, *Hoover, Blacks, and Lily-Whites*, 43–46.

[121] Ginzl, "Lily-Whites versus Black-and-Tans," 196–98; Lisio, *Hoover, Blacks, and Lily-Whites*, 59.

convention delegates) – the charge being the sale of federal patronage appointments.[122] In December, Howard and four of his indicted associates stood trial
in Jackson, Mississippi. Coming to Howard's aid was an unlikely group of
important Democrats, including prominent politicians (like Governor
Theodore Bilbo), newspaper editors (like Colonel Frederick Sullens of the
Jackson Daily News), lawyers, and even the Grand Dragon of the Mississippi
Ku Klux Klan.[123] As McMillen notes:

> Many Democrats ... saw a link between Howard's fate and the future partisan align-
> ment of the state ... As long as the Republican party functioned primarily as the
> instrument of the state's miniscule black electorate it threatened neither the Democracy
> nor white supremacy. The conviction of Howard and his principal associates, however,
> portended undesirable change. As nearly every observer agreed, the discredited regulars
> would be supplanted by the lily-whites, an altogether more formidable organization ...
> [a] new and all-white Republican organization might cast off the burdens of Reconstruc-
> tion. It might compete with the Democracy in state and local contests. Worst of all, it
> might divide the white vote, giving blacks once again the balance of power.[124]

With the effective power of the state behind him, Howard began his trial in a
strong position. His two (Democratic) lawyers painted the case against him as a
conspiracy organized by his Lily-White opponents and made clear to the all-
white jury that he and his co-defendants were "white men's negroes [who] have
been good to the Democratic party."[125] To support this claim, they noted that
Howard had distributed 93 percent of his appointments to Democrats.[126]
Whether this estimate was accurate or not, Howard clearly sought to be an
accommodationist in his boss role, never doing anything to upset the governing
white Democratic hierarchy in the state – to the point of upsetting his black
Republican colleagues (in Mississippi and nationally) on numerous occasions.
Nevertheless, influential black leaders like W. E. B. Du Bois and Kelly Miller,
Howard University dean, supported Howard, arguing that he was being singled
out for his race – and that his behavior was no better or worse than that of
white Southern Republicans in similar positions.[127]

The all-white jury voted to acquit Howard and his compatriots. All involved
saw the decision as a defeat for Mississippi's Lily-White movement. The Justice

[122] At nearly the same time, Howard was also a focus of Senate hearings by the Committee on Post
Offices and Post Roads, led by Smith W. Brookhart (R-IL), on patronage irregularities in
the South.
[123] McMillen, "Perry W. Howard," 217–19.
[124] Ibid., 217. McMillen's source for this argument comes from a series of editorials written by Fred
Sullens in the *Jackson Daily News*. One of Sullens's editorials, for example, stated: "A Republican party in Mississippi under the leadership of negroes offers no peril to white supremacy.
A Republican party led by white men backed by almost limitless wealth and greed for power
and prestige, would constitute a decided menace."
[125] Quoted in McMillen, "Perry W. Howard," 219.
[126] Ginzl, "Lily-Whites versus Black-and-Tans," 200.
[127] McMillen, "Perry W. Howard," 214–15.

Department indicted Howard (and two of his colleagues) again shortly thereafter; in April 1929, he stood trial and was again acquitted by an all-white jury. Thus, Howard survived the legal onslaught. But he would quickly face a new challenge. Hoover, now in the White House, sought to reform the Southern wing of the GOP[128] and stripped Howard of his patronage authority and his federal position – and desired his outright removal as leader of the Mississippi Republican Party. But Hoover and his supporters trod carefully, understanding the symbolic value of working against Howard and the cost that it might involve. As David Ginzl states, "[considerations] of the importance of the black vote in key northern industrial states prevented the Hoover administration from taking forceful steps to oust Howard."[129]

As the 1932 Republican National Convention approached, the Lily-Whites sought to replace Howard on the national committee. They appeared before the RNC in June 1932, and offered a legal case that Howard and his Black-and-Tan organization had violated state election laws while in power. The RNC, however, rejected the Lily-Whites' challenge and voted instead to seat Howard's delegation – along with the Black-and-Tan delegation from South Carolina (led by "Tieless Joe" Tolbert). In doing so, the RNC opposed the Hoover administration, which had supported the Lily-White organizations from those two states. In making this choice, the RNC sought to avoid "large black defections in crucial northern states if the convention ignored the southern black-and-tan organizations."[130]

Only one avenue was left for Hoover, if he were to continue his Southern reform agenda: pressure the members of the Republican National Convention's Credentials Committee. This he did, which resulted in a compromise. Working through Postmaster General Walter Brown, Hoover arranged a deal with the committee in which he would accept the seating of Howard's delegation, but only if Tolbert's delegation in South Carolina would be replaced by the rival Lily-White delegation.[131] Howard and his Black-and-Tans had thus survived. Why was Tolbert sacrificed and Howard retained? The answer was largely due to "optics." While Hoover sought to build more reputable organizations in the South, explicit moves toward white supremacy were controversial. The Lily-Whites in South Carolina made rejection of the Black-and-Tan organization there easier by including several blacks in their alternative convention delegation. The Lily-Whites in Mississippi, however, proposed an all-white convention slate to replace Howard's delegation. In addition, replacing Tolbert – a white man – was easier than replacing Howard, a black man who was supported by influential blacks throughout the North. As removing Howard would almost certainly lead to his subsequent removal from the RNC as well, Hoover

---

[128] For details on Hoover's Southern reform plan, see Lisio, *Hoover, Blacks, and Lily-Whites*, 118–27.
[129] Ginzl, "Lily-Whites versus Black-and-Tans," 207.   [130] Ibid., 209.   [131] Ibid.

knew that such a series of decisions could cost him and Republicans critically important votes in the upcoming 1932 elections.

Once the Lily-White challenge was turned back and Hoover lost his reelection bid to Franklin D. Roosevelt in 1932, Howard managed to cement his control over the Mississippi GOP establishment. For much of the remainder of his career, this meant very little – as patronage opportunities dried up considerably (with Democratic control of the White House) until Dwight D. Eisenhower's election in 1952, which resulted in new Lily-White challenges to Howard's authority.[132] By then Howard's luck and influence had run out: in 1956, the RNC's subcommittee on elections split Mississippi's convention delegation evenly between the Black-and-Tans and Lily-Whites.[133] In 1960, the Lily-Whites finally won out: Howard – at age 83 – announced his retirement as RNC member due to ill health, and an all-white Lily-White delegation was seated. Thus, the reign of the last Black-and-Tan party organization in the South had come to an end.[134]

CONCLUSION

Despite challenges to their authority, Black-and-Tan leaders in South Carolina, Georgia, and Mississippi were able to remain in control of Republican Party organizations much longer than their colleagues in other Southern states. In each case, the party organizations were built on the basis of selling federal offices. To be sure, such corruption was not unique to the Black-and-Tans: indeed, the alternative Lily-White groups relied on the exact same approach. As a result, the survival of these party organizations relied on their leaders' ability to get their delegations seated at national conventions. Of the three cases, the South Carolina GOP led by "Tieless Joe" declined the fastest: while Tolbert had been able to negotiate with the Harding administration, he received considerable opposition from Hoover and failed to have his delegation seated in 1932. However, the lack of federal patronage after the 1932 election meant that the Hoover-backed organization failed to consolidate its control over the state party. As a result, Tolbert managed a brief comeback at the 1936 convention – the last time he was a delegate and also the last time his organization would be seated.

The Black-and-Tan organizations in Georgia and Mississippi managed to survive longer, something that is particularly noteworthy given the power of black politicians in these state parties. In Georgia, the black-dominated Black-and-Tan coalition that controlled the state party after the 1912 national

[132] Howard had backed Robert Taft's presidential candidacy in 1952.
[133] Bowen, *The Roots of Modern Conservatism*, 196–97.
[134] "Perry W. Howard, GOP Leader, Retires," *Atlanta Daily World*, May 6, 1960; "Perry Howard is Honored in DC," *Atlanta Daily World*, October 21, 1960; "Perry Howard; Flamboyant Knight of GOP Politics," *Afro-American*, August 13, 1960.

convention remained in place up to the 1932 convention, when a Lily-White group supported by Hoover was seated instead. However, as in South Carolina, the end of federal patronage in the state during the New Deal undermined the strength of the Lily-Whites. Additionally, black Republicans outside of the South strongly supported the few remaining black leaders – Ben Davis in Georgia and Perry Howard in Mississippi – and ensured (part of) their delegations were seated in 1936 and 1940. In Mississippi, Howard also survived a series of legal challenges regarding his selling of federal offices, thanks to the assistance of an unlikely set of allies: white segregationist Democrats in his home state. Believing that a Republican state party under black control was the best possible outcome for the continuation of their own political domination, white Democrats ensured Howard was not convicted and remained leader of the Mississippi GOP.

Conclusion: The Relevance of the South in the Republican Party

The relationship between the GOP and the South between the end of Reconstruction and the rise of the party's modern "Southern Strategy" has received relatively little scholarly attention. At first glance, this lack of coverage might appear logical: with very few exceptions, the Republican Party was unable to compete effectively in Southern elections during this period. Indeed, the South was largely a single-party (Democratic) system and – per the assessment of Robert Mickey – in certain states an "authoritarian enclave."[1] With the local GOP organizations in the South rarely winning elections, and often failing to even run candidates, it is not surprising that scholars have largely ignored the South's role in Republican Party politics during this period.

Despite this, our analysis in the preceding chapters shows that the South remained consistently relevant within the Republican Party throughout this period of one-party Democratic rule. It did so in two ways: first, national Republican leaders – in particular, presidents – often came up with new schemes intended to revitalize the party in the South. These attempts were usually not very successful, but those leaders nonetheless invested considerable time and political capital in them. Second, the presence of Southern delegates at Republican National Conventions meant that state party leaders from the region continued to have considerable influence on important intra-party decisions – including the selection of presidential and vice-presidential candidates. And, particularly prior to the 1916 convention, Southern representation was significant, as around 25 percent of Republican delegates were from the South.

As we have shown, the combination of Southern state parties being uncompetitive in elections at home but maintaining their influence at the national level

---

[1] Robert Mickey, *Paths Out of Dixie: The Democratization of Authoritarian Enclaves in America's Deep South, 1944–1972* (Princeton, NJ: Princeton University Press, 2015).

set these organizations up to be used by both national and local political actors. On the national level, party leaders – most notably presidents and presidential candidates – began to invest significant resources in courting local Southern party leaders to buy their convention support. William McKinley's 1896 strategy was notable in this regard. McKinley and Mark Hanna, his main political advisor, spent considerable time in the South meeting with local party leaders and lining up their delegations for the convention. But McKinley was hardly the only presidential hopeful who engaged in this version of a Southern strategy: indeed, as we have shown, it was a common approach in this period.

At the local level, the GOP's lack of electoral success meant that state party leaders began to focus their attention on the element of party politics that they could still control and benefit from: federal patronage. That is, with the Southern GOP prevented from competing electorally in a serious way – thanks to Jim Crow-era disenfranchisement laws – it could no longer achieve the main goal of a political party organization: winning elections. But, with Republicans dominant in presidential elections between 1880 and 1928, and with the party in the White House able to provide federal appointments, the Southern state party organizations had relatively consistent access to patronage. The combination of national Republican leaders using (the promise of) patronage to buy Southern national convention delegates and Southern party leaders distributing or selling those federal jobs to maintain their control of the state organizations, meant that the GOP in most Southern states by the early twentieth century had turned into a set of "rotten boroughs."

That these state party organizations were not actively competing for votes and largely subsisting off the sale of government jobs made them an easy target for national Republican leaders who did not receive those states' delegate support at national conventions. Indeed, after 1896, a number of attempts were made to limit the influence of the South by reducing their share of convention delegates. The most important of these attempts – the decision to link the size of delegations to electoral performance after the 1912 election – shrunk the size of Southern delegations considerably from 1916 onwards. To be sure, though, not all attempts in the Republican National Committee or at the convention to diminish the South were made in earnest. Indeed, as we have shown, the corruption of most Southern state party organizations allowed other national Republican leaders to coerce them into supporting their goals, whether it be the selection of a convention city (in 1899) or the nomination of a vice-presidential candidate (Theodore Roosevelt in 1900).

Despite these attempts at reducing delegation size or the occasional presidential efforts at altering existing party organizations, Southern Republican leaders were able to benefit considerably from their control over an otherwise ineffective electoral organization. As a result, *who* controlled the state party continued to be relevant: those who were in charge could select national convention delegates and, therefore, receive patronage and other benefits from national leaders. As a result, throughout the late nineteenth and early twentieth centuries, control over Republican state party organizations in the South was often contested.

Initially, these contests between different state-level factions were organized around different (former) elected officials and office-holders. While race was always salient, and some of these groups were dominated by whites, they generally were biracial. However, by the late 1880s white Republicans across the South began to challenge those biracial (or Black-and-Tan) factions in control of state party organizations. Starting in Texas, where Norris Wright Cuney was the black leader of the state party, these Lily-White groups sought to take over the state party and radically limit the level of black participation. In all Southern states, this white takeover of the GOP occurred eventually. But, as we have documented, there was considerable variation in the timing of these Lily-White victories and the extent to which black Republicans were subsequently excluded.

In states like Virginia and North Carolina, where the GOP's electoral performance was stronger, white Republicans excluded blacks at least in part because they believed an all-white party would allow it to compete electorally again. In an electoral world where the effective electorate was almost wholly white, Lily-White Republicans argued that Southern white voters would only vote for the GOP if it was "respectable" – which, in the vernacular of the time, meant "white." In Texas and Alabama, blacks were also excluded entirely from the party, for similar reasons. In contrast, in Arkansas, Florida, Louisiana, and Tennessee, the Lily-White takeover resulted in whites controlling the party organization but with ongoing minority black representation at national conventions. Finally, in three states – South Carolina, Georgia, and Mississippi – Black-and-Tan organizations managed to stay in power much longer, in large part because they survived the "purge" of the Hoover years.

While the Virginia and North Carolina Lily-Whites did not fully achieve their electoral goals right away, we find some evidence for their argument. That is, we show (in Chapter 2) that the Republican Party made electoral gains in the South after the introduction of disfranchisement laws more quickly in those states that went Lily-White more fully. Thus, we find that arguments and evidence for "whiteness" mattering in contemporary Republican Party politics have clear historical antecedents. Stated simply, whiteness was both a critical factor in the electoral development of the Republican Party in the South in the first half of the twentieth century (especially in the Outer South) and a necessary condition for making the Southern GOP a powerful – and, ultimately, dominant – electoral force in the second half of the century.

After the Democratic victories of the New Deal era, GOP leaders initially lost interest in the South. While Republican Senator Robert Taft still relied on attempts at building Southern convention support for his (failed) presidential campaigns, without patronage the state organizations could not as easily be bought – and delegations consolidated – as before. Additionally, with the GOP fighting for electoral survival across the country, regaining ground in the South was not its first priority. By the late 1940s, however, with black voters now part of the Democratic coalition and white conservatives in the South (or Dixiecrats) increasingly an uncomfortable minority in the party they used to dominate, national Republican leaders once again began reaching out to Southern white voters. With Dwight Eisenhower as the presidential nominee in 1952 and 1956, the GOP succeeded in winning a number of Southern states, but Democrats remained dominant in all other office contests. After Richard Nixon's close defeat in 1960, conservatives in the party doubled down on the South as the only path for the GOP to regain majorities in the Electoral College *and* Congress. However, Barry Goldwater's dramatic loss in the 1964 presidential election raised considerable concerns within the party that appealing to white segregationists in the South would alienate voters elsewhere in the country.

By 1968, the Republican Party had found a solution to this problem in the form of Richard Nixon's Southern Strategy: while rejecting segregation, Nixon appealed to (white) Southern Republican leaders and Dixiecrats by promising to slow down the integration process. Additionally, by running on a law-and-order message, Nixon was able to appeal to white voters in both the South and the rest of the country. To be sure, this modern version of the Republican Southern Strategy did not result in the immediate takeover of the South. At the presidential level, success came earliest and most consistently: with the exception of 1976 – when Georgian Jimmy Carter was the Democratic nominee – Republican presidential candidates from 1972 onwards won a majority of Southern states. In Congress, the GOP has controlled a majority of Southern seats since the 1994 midterms. Meanwhile, Republicans have held a majority of seats in Southern state legislatures since 2010. The Republican Party has thus come full circle: after nearly a century and a half, the party now dominates in the region that had been its bugaboo for so long.

By laying out this history, we have added an important element to Southern politics in the nineteenth and twentieth centuries and to the broader history of American political development. In doing so, we have also added to the considerable recent literature on the South in American politics.[2] Additionally, we believe this book contributes to our understanding in three other areas: the role of presidents as party leaders, the historical development of race in the Republican Party, and the study of political parties as organizations in the United States.

---

[2] See, among others, Mickey, *Paths Out of Dixie*; David A. Bateman, Ira Katznelson, and John S. Lapinski, *Southern Nation: Congress and White Supremacy after Reconstruction* (Princeton, NJ: Princeton University Press, 2018); Devin Caughey, *The Unsolid South: Mass Politics and National Representation in a One-Party Enclave* (Princeton, NJ: Princeton University Press, 2018); John H. Aldrich and John D. Griffin, *Why Parties Matter: Political Competition and Democracy in the American South* (Chicago: University of Chicago Press, 2018); Avidit Acharya, Matthew Blackwell, and Maya Sen, *Deep Roots: How Slavery Still Shapes Southern Politics* (Princeton, NJ: Princeton University Press, 2018).

TABLE 10.1 *Republican presidents' Southern strategies, 1868–1968*

President	Southern party-building strategy	Southern convention delegate strategy
Ulysses S. Grant	✓	
Rutherford B. Hayes	✓	
James A. Garfield	✓	
Chester A. Arthur	✓	✓
Benjamin Harrison	✓	✓
William McKinley		✓
Theodore Roosevelt		✓
William Howard Taft		✓
Warren G. Harding	✓	
Calvin Coolidge		✓
Herbert Hoover	✓	✓
Dwight D. Eisenhower	✓	✓
Richard Nixon	✓	✓

PRESIDENTIAL POLITICS AND THE SOUTH IN THE GOP

Our assessment of GOP politics in the South in this period reveals a consistent theme regarding the role that Republican presidents played in this process. In practice, Republican presidents engaged in two types of Southern strategies: they attempted to control the Southern state party organizations with the goal of winning (re-)nomination at the national convention, and they attempted to radically alter existing Southern party organizations with the goal of revitalizing the party's electoral performance in the ex-Confederacy. As Table 10.1 illustrates, every Republican president between Grant and Nixon engaged in one or both of these Southern strategies.

Both of these activities are noteworthy in their own right. That Republican presidents – with the exception of McKinley, Roosevelt, Taft, and Coolidge – sought to revitalize the party in the South suggests that chief executives even prior to the New Deal were active participants in trying to manage their party's electoral coalition.[3] At the same time, the general failure of these attempts illustrates the limitations of presidential action in this regard. Even when presidents did well in the South – such as Harding in 1920, Hoover in 1928, and Eisenhower in 1952 and 1956 – creating coattails for the party in congressional or state-level elections proved difficult. Yet, despite this long history of failure, if Republican presidents had an inkling that a resurgence in the South

---

[3] This is consistent with the argument made recently by Daniel Klinghard, *The Nationalization of American Political Parties, 1880–1896* (Cambridge: Cambridge University Press, 2010).

might be possible, they responded by investing heavily in trying to achieve this goal.

Starting with Arthur, every Republican president (with the sole exception of Harding) sought to ensure support from Southern delegates at Republican National Conventions. In some cases, these relationships with Southern party leaders were built before the candidate made it to the White House. For example, McKinley began "buying" Southern support months before the 1896 convention. In other cases, the need to invest in the South arose later. For example, both vice presidents who ascended to the presidency after the death of their running mate – Theodore Roosevelt and Calvin Coolidge – made deals with Southern party leaders to ensure support at the upcoming national convention (that would nominate them in their own right).

These findings suggest a number of things about the relationship between presidents and parties. First, most studies on presidential leadership of political parties have focused on the post-New Deal era.[4] We show that presidents have been focused on managing their party – in this case by trying to influence the actions and leadership of state party organizations – much earlier than that. As noted, these attempts were based partly on ensuring their re-nomination (or, in the case of Roosevelt in 1908, the nomination of their chosen successor) at the national convention. Sometimes – most notably the Republican presidents who served in the 1870s and 1880s – the goal may have been ensuring their own reelection in the extremely close presidential elections that were common then. But in other cases, presidents were attempting true leadership: Harding and Hoover in particular believed that their above-average performance in the South suggested the possibility of a breakthrough in the region for the GOP and invested considerable time and energy in trying to change the party organizations in multiple states.

RACE AND REPUBLICAN STATE-LEVEL POLITICS

For a long time, the standard view of Southern Republicans during and after Reconstruction was determined by the "Dunning school" – based on studies produced by Columbia historian William Dunning and his students around the turn of the twentieth century.[5] In this view, Republicans who took control of state governments proved corrupt and incapable of running a functioning government, in no small part because the Dunningites believed that the

[4] See, for example, Sidney M. Milkis, *The President and the Parties: The Transformation of the American Party System since the New Deal* (Oxford: Oxford University Press, 1993); Daniel J. Galvin, *Presidential Party Building: Dwight D. Eisenhower to George W. Bush* (Princeton, NJ: Princeton University Press, 2009).

[5] For a recent, in-depth examination of the Dunning School, see John David Smith and J. Vincent Lowery, eds., *The Dunning School: Historians, Race, and the Meaning of Reconstruction* (Lexington: University Press of Kentucky, 2013).

freedmen were incapable of basic self-governance. Thus, the failure of Reconstruction represented the welcome end of a failed experiment in allowing black
Southerners to govern themselves. A similar perspective emerged with regard to
black leaders in the Republican Party after Reconstruction: the Southern party
organizations under Black-and-Tan control were often dismissed as corrupt
organizations, while black delegates were dismissed as "so many chattels to be
purchased by the highest bidder."[6]

To be sure, our case studies show that Republican Party organizations in the
South suffered from corruption. After the end of Reconstruction, the GOP was
effectively incapable of competing in any real sense for elected office in most
parts of the South. After the introduction of disfranchisement laws, the situation worsened and left the Republican state parties with nothing but patronage and national convention politics. In nearly all cases, the result was a system
that relied on party leaders selling offices in their states for financial gain. As
some of our case studies show, these offices went for substantial amounts and
brought local party leaders considerable personal wealth. To some extent, the
choices by these individual actors were understandable: given their forced
exclusion from "regular" politics, party leaders like Mississippi's Perry
Howard took advantage of the one remaining position of political power left
open to them.

But black Republicans were in no way alone in using state party organizations for these purposes: whenever Black-and-Tan organizations were replaced
by Lily-White ones, the new leadership relied on the same approach as the
previous one did. Indeed, some of the attempts at changing state party leadership during the Harding and Hoover years failed in large part because the new
white leaders these presidents selected showed little interest in party-building
activities and instead engaged in the same office-selling practices their competitors relied on. While some Lily-Whites may have believed their official argument – that in turning the state party into a (nearly) all-white group, the GOP
could reemerge as a competitive party in statewide elections – once in control,
they often forgot those electoral considerations in short order.

At the same time, though, our analysis in Chapter 2 does show that the racial
makeup of the state party did matter in terms of Republican electoral performance. Prior to the enactment of disfranchisement laws – when black voters were
the backbone of the GOP's electoral base in most states – a decline in black
delegates at national conventions is associated with a decline in the party's
electoral performance. This suggests that black voters were aware of a decline
of influence in "their" party and punished it accordingly on election day.
However, following the enactment of disfranchisement laws – after which the
number of black voters dropped to near zero throughout much of the South – a
decline in black convention participation is associated with an *increase* in

[6] "To Reduce Southern Representation," *Charlotte Daily Observer*, November 29, 1899.

Republican vote share. That is, while the Lily-White argument of making their state parties more "respectable" by excluding blacks may have been disingenuous – made to rationalize their power grab – it did reflect a correct assessment of the political reality: after disenfranchisement, the local GOP in a Southern state (especially in the Outer South) performed better electorally when it became a whiter party.

Based on this, we argue that the Lily-White takeover of the Republican state party organizations was a necessary – but by itself insufficient – condition for Republican electoral success in the South. When a GOP organization was under Black-and-Tan control – and thus blacks were to some degree in public leadership positions – white Southern voters during the Jim Crow era were extremely unlikely to support the party. Once the GOP organization had been "whitened," the potential for electoral success was there, though the actual payoff was slow – and real success (in the form of winning elections consistently up and down the ticket) remained decades in the future, after other necessary conditions (the national Democratic Party moving leftward on civil rights and the national Republican Party cementing itself as the party of racial conservatism) had also occurred.

THE STUDY OF PARTY ORGANIZATIONS

Finally, this book raises questions as to what our findings tell us about the study of American parties as political institutions. Traditionally, much of the research on parties has relied on a basic assumption made by a number of rational-choice scholars, including Anthony Downs, Joseph Schlesinger, and John Aldrich: that parties exist to help ambitious office-seekers win elections by winning over the median voter in the electorate.[7] In this perspective, parties are endogenous institutions – created by political actors and used by them to improve their probability of electoral success. This basic assumption has been the foundation underlying most studies of parties in Congress, the activities of national committees, and presidential leadership of political parties. A more recent perspective on parties – known colloquially as the "UCLA School" – has proposed a different take, arguing that parties are best understood as "coalitions of interest groups and activists seeking to capture and use government for their particular goals."[8] In this view, interest groups control parties and select candidates that share their preferences, which are usually more

---

[7] Anthony Downs, *An Economic Theory of Democracy* (New York: Harper, 1957); Joseph A. Schlesinger, *Political Parties and the Winning of Office* (Ann Arbor: University of Michigan Press, 1991); John H. Aldrich, *Why Parties? The Origin and Transformation of Political Parties in America* (Chicago: University of Chicago Press, 1995).

[8] Kathleen Bawn, Martin Cohen, David Karol, Seth Masket, Hans Noel, and John Zaller, "A Theory of Political Parties: Groups, Policy Demands, and Nominations in American Politics," *Perspectives on Politics* 10 (2012): 571.

extreme than the average voter prefers. However, because voters pay only limited attention to politics, the more extreme candidates still get elected and subsequently provide the groups with the policies they prefer.

The story presented in this book does not fit comfortably in either narrative. The Southern party organizations in this period were not engaged in catering to the median voter. While local leaders may have had some preference in helping select winning presidential nominees – if only because White House control was necessary to keep patronage income flowing – their actions otherwise included almost no electoral considerations.[9] At the same time, one would be hard pressed to identify traditional interest groups as underlying the state party organizations. And, even if we were to consider the Black-and-Tans and Lily-Whites as groups in this regard, neither group after Reconstruction had particularly strong issue preferences or a major interest in candidate nominations – the core element of the UCLA perspective. To be sure, in most cases in American politics the goal of a political party is to win elections – and in that regard, the Republican Party in the South may simply have been too extreme an outlier to explain with conventional political science theories. But neither the desire to control patronage nor the maintenance of party organizations in geographical areas in which the party is highly unlikely to succeed are entirely unique to the GOP in the South – and it is debatable to what extent the two dominant theories of political party activity explain these versions of political parties.

More relevant in this regard is that the history presented here reveals the limitations of one of the main goals of both the traditional and the UCLA perspectives on studying parties as institutions: identifying those political actors or groups who *control* the party. As we have shown, there were essentially no actors with complete control over the Southern GOP. Presidents tried to change state party organizations – in some cases, in cooperation with the RNC – but generally failed in their efforts.[10] State party leaders, however, were hardly

---

[9] Indeed, in a recent book, John Aldrich, perhaps the leading scholar of the traditional (rational-choice) approach, spends little time examining the Republican Party during the Jim Crow era. He and his co-author John Griffin state: "Outside of the limited mountain areas, a Republican Party existed almost solely as a basis for receiving whatever modest pork the national Republican Party would send its way when it was in power (which all but ended in 1932)." Aldrich and Griffin only begin to examine the Republican Party in the South as a "real party" beginning in 1965. See Aldrich and Griffin, *Why Parties Matter*, 109–10, 126–30.

[10] On this point, there may be some utility to applying a principal–agent perspective to the study of party organizations. Just as scholars of the presidency will often use a principal–agent model to study the executive branch, and identify when and to what degree a president will suffer "agency loss" in having his wishes fulfilled by administrative aides and bureaucrats, scholars of political parties might benefit from analyzing the party-as-organization in a similar way. The president is at the top of the party system and has a variety of tools and resources to help (or hurt) actors in his party at the national, state, and local levels. During our era of examination here, presidents relied heavily on executive patronage to establish and maintain some control over the local GOP organizations in the South. Their success in doing so varied, as we have shown. Much of this

secure in their own positions: at every national convention they ran the risk of failing to be seated and, thereby, losing their positions of power within their states. Other national leaders tried to restrict the influence of the South, but these attempts were usually blocked – even if they had majority support at national conventions or within the national committee. Thus, the image of intra-party politics that emerges is not one of a unified structure built to provide for a specific set of actors (congressional leaders, presidents, interest groups), but rather groups of actors in different intra-party coalitions who battle one another over temporary control but never achieve the consistent power to determine what happens within the party.

FINAL THOUGHTS

Vital to the study of American Political Development (APD) is the notion that important aspects of American politics have "deep historical roots."[11] That is, contemporary political processes and institutions are fundamentally and continually shaped by decisions and events that occurred in the (often-distant) past. As we argue in this book, political parties are no exception. In recent years, political scientists, pundits, and journalists have spent considerable time studying the rise of racial identity – especially white identity and white nationalism – in contemporary American politics, and its importance to the Republican Party generally and the rise of Donald Trump specifically.[12] While some have noted that race has been fundamental to GOP politics for decades – going back to the presidential campaigns of Barry Goldwater, Richard Nixon, and Patrick

---

could be attributed to the time and resources that particular presidents devoted to monitoring and oversight. These musings aside, we believe this to be a course of study – if done well – that could provide valuable and unique insights in the future.

[11] We attribute this phrase to our friend and colleague, Sidney M. Milkis. See, for example, Sidney M. Milkis, *Political Parties and Constitutional Government: Remaking American Democracy* (Baltimore: Johns Hopkins University Press, 1999), x; Sidney M. Milkis, *Theodore Roosevelt, the Progressive Party, and the Transformation of American Democracy* (Lawrence: University Press of Kansas, 2009), back inside cover; Sidney M. Milkis and Michael C. Nelson, *The American Presidency: Origins and Development, 1776–2011*, 6th edn. (Washington, DC: CQ Press, 2011), xii. For another example, more in the modern social science vein, see Acharya, Blackwell, and Sen, *Deep Roots*.

[12] Examples include David Neiwart, *Alt-America: The Rise of the Radical Right in the Age of Trump* (New York: Verso, 2017); John Sides, Michael Tesler, and Lynn Vavreck, *Identity Crisis: The 2016 Presidential Campaign and the Battle for the Meaning of America* (Princeton, NJ: Princeton University Press, 2018); Lilliana Mason, *Uncivil Agreement: How Politics Became Our Identity* (Chicago: University of Chicago Press, 2018); Ashley Jardina, *White Identity Politics* (Cambridge: Cambridge University Press, 2019); Adam Serwer, "White Nationalism's Deep American Roots," *The Atlantic*, April 2019. www.theatlantic.com/magazine/archive/2019/04/adam-serwer-madison-grant-white-nationalism/583258/ (accessed June 1, 2019).

Buchanan, for example[13] – our work suggests the connections between "whiteness" and Republicanism go back much deeper in the past.

From the Republican Party's very beginnings in the post-Civil War South, race was a pivotal factor. By building a political coalition of pro-Union whites (scalawags and carpetbaggers) and blacks, while temporarily preventing many white ex-Confederates from participating, the GOP was able to control nearly all Southern state governments by the late 1860s. In time, however, the Democratic Party took advantage of the lifting of voting restrictions on most ex-Confederates, an economic depression, and terror campaigns against black voters to regain power. And, during this time, much of the GOP's white support in the South (which was never large) was eroded by the Democrats' successful efforts to brand the Republicans as the "black party." After the demise of Reconstruction, a succession of Republican presidents – Rutherford Hayes, James Garfield, and Benjamin Harrison – tried to rebuild the Southern GOP by persuading whites that it was in their economic interests to become Republicans. These efforts failed. Whites in the South – even if they found the GOP's economic arguments convincing – could not cross the color line; the "black party brand" (and the social backlash they would face) was too strong.

Once laws to disenfranchise blacks were passed throughout the South, race once again defined Republican politics. This time, the division occurred *within* the party. A new group of Republicans – the Lily-Whites – emerged, and argued that in the new Jim Crow world of Southern politics, where the electorate was almost exclusively white, the Republican Party would need to become all white in order to viably compete in elections. While the Lily-Whites may have had other motives in mind – like taking control of federal patronage from the Black-and-Tans – they were able to commandeer most Southern state parties by the early 1900s. And, indeed, as we find, the "whitening" of the GOP in the aftermath of Jim Crow did in fact lead to a significant increase in the Republican Party's vote totals in the South. This whitening of the party, we argue, was a necessary condition for the GOP to become competitive – and then ultimately dominant – in Southern elections in the second half of the twentieth century.

Thus, to understand the nature of the Republican Party's brand in the early twenty-first century, we must understand the electoral bedrock of its success. That bedrock is the South, which has gone Republican in every presidential election since 1980. The composition of that electoral support has been white voters, many of whom are both economically and racially conservative. Thus, the Party of Lincoln, which was built on tenets of free-soil and emancipation and emerged in the post-Civil War South thanks largely to the votes of former slaves, became over time the party of white, conservative America. Our book shows that this process began far earlier than most studies acknowledge. The GOP's early electoral success in the post-World War II South – during the

---

[13] See, for example, Jardina, *White Identity Politics*.

1950s and 1960s – was possible *only* because it had shed its label as the "black party" in most Southern states decades earlier. Thus, as the national Democratic Party moved to the left on civil rights while the national Republican Party moved to the right, white Southern voters realized more and more that they had a real choice on election day.

The GOP's Southern dominance in contemporary America, therefore, has deep roots that extend back more than a century. Simply stated, the success of the contemporary Republican Party is linked directly to its Southern wing going Lily-White in the early part of the twentieth century. By becoming a Lily-White party, the GOP in the Jim Crow South helped create the Republican brand that we observe today.

Index

CPSIA information can be obtained
at www.ICGtesting.com
Printed in the USA
LVHW092218210321
682035LV00001B/10